# Civilizations and World Systems

## Studying World-Historical Change

# Civilizations and World Systems

## Studying World-Historical Change

■

## Stephen K. Sanderson
### *Editor*

**ALTAMIRA**
P R E S S
*A Division of Sage Publications, Inc.*
Walnut Creek ■ London ■ New Delhi

*For information address:*

AltaMira Press
1630 North Main Street
Suite 367
Walnut Creek, California 94596

SAGE Publications Ltd.
6 Bonhill Street
London EC2A 4PU
United Kingdom

SAGE Publications India Pvt. Ltd.
M-32 Market
Greater Kailash I
New Delhi 110 048 India

Printed in the United States of America

**Library of Congress Cataloging-in-Publication Data**

Civilizations and world systems : studying world-historical change /
    Stephen K. Sanderson, editor.
        p.   cm.
    Includes bibliographical references and index.
    ISBN 0-7619-9104-2. -- ISBN 0-7619-9105-0 (pbk.)
    1. Civilization--Study and teaching.   2. Civilization--Philosophy.
I.  Sanderson, Stephen K.
CB20.C49   1995
901--dc20                                                    95-41739
                                                                CIP


96  97  98  10  9  8  7  6  5  4  3  2

Production Services: Sue Oppenheim
Book and Cover Design: Kathleen Szawiola
Cover Design: Prow of a Roman galley, provided by the Bettmann Archive

# Contents

# PART III: CIVILIZATIONS AND WORLD SYSTEMS: DIALOGUE AND INTERPLAY

# PART IV: EPILOGUE

# Preface

At the annual meetings of the International Society for the Comparative Study of Civilizations (ISCSC) held in Scranton, Pennsylvania in June 1993, Wayne Bledsoe, the editor of the *Comparative Civilizations Review*, the ISCSC's official journal, suggested to me the idea of devoting a special issue of the journal to a dialogue between civilizationists and world-system theorists. The proximate source of the idea was a session of the 1993 ISCSC meetings that included a paper by Thomas Hall, a world-system theorist, suggesting certain possible and desirable lines of convergence between civilizationists and world-system theorists, and a reply to Hall's paper by Matthew Melko, a civilizationist. The ultimate source of the idea was probably the fact that in the late 1980s some world-system theorists had become members of the ISCSC and began promoting their approach as another way of studying long-term historical change. In any event, I passed along Bledsoe's idea to Hall and to Christopher Chase-Dunn, another world-system theorist and ISCSC member, and they were as enthusiastic as I about having such an issue. After considerable discussion, it was decided that I would serve as a guest editor for this special issue. I asked for contributions from Matthew Melko and Roger Wescott (both civilizationists); from Andre Gunder Frank, Thomas Hall, Christopher Chase-Dunn, Albert Bergesen, and Immanuel Wallerstein (all world-system theorists); and from David Wilkinson (a civilizationist originally, but a scholar extensively familiar with the world-system literature and comfortable in both camps). I also had an idea for an article that I myself would write. All nine invited contributors submitted articles, and the special issue was published as No. 30, Spring 1994.

Once the issue was completed Immanuel Wallerstein suggested to me that the issue might be reprinted as a book, and this seemed like a good idea inasmuch as the special issue was attracting a good deal of interest. However, to make a suitable book I felt that the special issue needed to be revised and expanded. Ultimately it was decided to reprint three articles from the special issue and two articles from earlier issues of *Comparative Civilizations Review*, and to join these articles with two other previously published works and six brand new essays. Mitchell Allen of AltaMira Press agreed to publish the resulting volume. In fact, inasmuch as he is an archaeologist as well as a publisher, and inasmuch as he is highly knowledgeable of the world-systems literature, he played a role in helping to design it. We think that the book is not only interesting but provocative, and we hope that it will generate considerable interest.

What the book tries to do is to present civilizational analysis and world-systems theory as the two most promising general approaches to the study of long-term historical change, and by long-term is meant basically the last 5,000 years. Part I contains essays by Matthew Melko and David Wilkinson that lay out some of the leading ideas of civilizational analysis, although they have somewhat different ways of doing this kind of analysis. The final essay in Part I, by William Eckhardt, uses civilizational ideas to explore the evolution of empires and wars throughout world history.

Part II is devoted to world-systems analysis. Essays by Christopher Chase-Dunn and Thomas Hall, by Barry Gills, and by Andre Gunder Frank present different world-system approaches to long-term history. These are followed by an essay by Albert Bergesen that comments on Frank's world-system approach and teases out its implications, as well as an essay by Andrew Bosworth that empirically evaluates a claim made by Gills and Frank for the existence of long cycles of economic growth and decline over more than three millennia.

Part III is devoted largely to attempts at dialogue between civilizationists and world-system theorists. The opening essay in this section, by Immanuel Wallerstein, critiques the concept of civilization and suggests reasons for skepticism concerning the attempts to apply his original world-system concepts and principles to the time period before AD 1500. An essay by David Wilkinson takes a completely different tack, embracing both civilizational analysis and world-system theory and suggesting that these approaches are basically studying the same thing and that their ideas can be merged. My own essay tries to show that the notion of expanding world commercialization—the idea that there has been a steady growth of production for exchange and trade at a world level since 3000 BC—is one that unites the concerns of the two camps. The final essay of this section, by Victor Roudometof and Roland Robertson, critiques both civilizational analysis and world-system theory from a perspective different from that of nearly all of the other contributors to this volume. In particular, Roudometof and Robertson seek to make the concept of culture vital to historical sociological analysis.

Part IV, an epilogue, contains a single essay by William H. McNeill. One of the Western world's leading historical thinkers, McNeill devotes his essay to an autocritique of his famous 1963 book *The Rise of the West*. His main message is that his analysis of world civilizations in that book did not devote enough attention to the links between those civilizations, and, indeed, to their unification into larger economic, political-military, cultural, and information networks. This essay highlights the common ground between the two camps very nicely.

In 1966, at the tender age of 20 and while still an undergraduate student, I took a seminar in social change in which I gave a long oral presentation on the work of Arnold J. Toynbee. Based on discussion in that class, and on the basis of things I heard since, I had long been under the impression that the works of Toynbee (and similar civilizationists) had been largely discredited, or at least had become passé. When Christopher Chase-Dunn asked me to give a paper in 1989 at the annual meetings of the ISCSC in Berkeley (an organization I had never heard of), I was surprised to discover that many of the members of this professional body held fast to civilizationist thinking. So these ideas are still very much alive. And from my point of view it is a good thing, too, for the civilizationists are devoting themselves to exactly the intellectual problem that interests me and the contributors to this volume the most (and that no doubt must have interested me greatly 30 years ago): the patterns that are revealed by the rise and fall, modification and transformation, of large-scale sociocultural systems over very long expanses of time. Civilizationists and world-system theorists are united in their contention that human history is not just "one damned thing after another," that it has long-term and large-scale patterns, and that it is important, both intellectually and politically, to comprehend these patterns. I hope that scholars who share these concerns will find this volume of use.

## Acknowledgments

We gratefully acknowledge the following for permission to reprint previously published materials:

Matthew Melko for permission to reprint material from pages 1–37 of *The Nature of Civilizations*, by Matthew Melko, Boston: Porter Sargent, 1969.

David Wilkinson for permission to reprint "Central Civilization," by David Wilkinson, which appeared in *Comparative Civilizations Review*, no. 17, pp. 31–59, 1987; and for "Civilizations *are* World-Systems!," by David Wilkinson, which appeared in *Comparative Civilizations Review*, no. 30, pp. 59–71, 1994.

Mrs. William Eckhardt for permission to reprint "A Dialectical Evolutionary Theory of Civilizations, Empires, and Wars," by William Eckhardt, which appeared in *Comparative Civilizations Review*, no. 25, pp. 54–78, 1992.

Immanuel Wallerstein for permission to reprint "Hold the Tiller Firm: On Method and the Unit of Analysis," by Immanuel Wallerstein, which appeared in *Comparative Civilizations Review*, no. 30, pp. 72–80, 1994.

Stephen K. Sanderson for permission to reprint "Expanding World Commercialization: The Link Between World-Systems and Civilizations," by Stephen K. Sanderson, which appeared in *Comparative Civilizations Review*, no. 30, pp. 91–103, 1994.

University of Hawaii Press for permission to reprint "*The Rise of the West* after Twenty-Five Years," by William H. McNeill, which appeared in *Journal of World History*, vol. 1, pp. 1–21, 1990.

Stephen K. Sanderson
Indiana, Pennsylvania
June 2, 1995

# About the Authors

**Albert Bergesen** is Professor of Sociology at the University of Arizona. He is the author of numerous articles and the author or editor of several books, including *Studies of the Modern World-System* (Academic Press, 1980) and *America's Changing Role in the World-System* (coedited with Terry Boswell; Praeger, 1987). His article "Regime Change in the Semiperiphery: Democratization in Latin America and the Socialist Bloc," published in *Sociological Perspectives* in 1992, won the Distinguished Article Award of the Pacific Sociological Association.

**Andrew Bosworth** recently finished his Ph.D. in political science at the University of Washington. His dissertation focused on the world city system and its evolution over the last several thousand years.

**Christopher Chase-Dunn** is Professor of Sociology at Johns Hopkins University. A leading specialist in the study of world-systems, he has published many articles and several books on the subject, including *Socialist States in the World-System* (Sage, 1982), *Global Formation: Structures of the World-Economy* (Blackwell, 1989), and *Core/Periphery Relations in Precapitalist Worlds* (coedited with Thomas D. Hall; Westview, 1991). He founded and serves as editor of *The Journal of World-Systems Research*, a new electronic journal.

The late **William Eckhardt** worked at the Lentz Peace Research Laboratory in St. Louis, Missouri. He was a prominent member of the ISCSC and authored several books, among them *Governments Under Fire: Civil Conflict and Imperialism* (with Christopher Young; Human Relations Area Files Press, 1977), and *Civilizations, Empires, and Wars* (McFarland, 1992).

**Andre Gunder Frank** is Professor Emeritus of Development Economics and Social Sciences at the University of Amsterdam. His publications in 25 languages include 30 books, chapters in over 130 edited readers or anthologies, and articles in over 500 issues of periodicals. His books include *Capitalism and Underdevelopment in Latin America* (Monthly Review Press, 1967), *World Accumulation 1492–1789* (Monthly Review Press, 1978), *Crisis: In the World Economy* (Holmes & Meier, 1980), *Transforming the Revolution: Social Movements and the World-System* (with Samir Amin, Giovanni Arrighi, and Immanuel Wallerstein; Monthly Review Press, 1990), and *The World System: Five Hundred Years or Five Thousand?* (coedited with Barry K. Gills; Routledge, 1993).

**Barry K. Gills** is Lecturer in International Politics at the University of Newcastle upon Tyne, UK. He is the author of many articles and has edited or coedited several books, including *The World System: Five Hundred Years or Five Thousand?* (coedited with Andre Gunder Frank; Routledge, 1993), *Transcending the State-Global Divide* (coedited with R. Palan; Lynne Rienner, 1994), and *Regimes in Crisis* (coedited with S. Qadir; Zed Books, 1995). He is a founding editor of *Review of International Political Economy*, was a founding member of the World Historical Systems Group of the International Studies Association, and was also a founding member of the Standing Group on Third World Politics in the European Consortium for Political Research.

**Thomas D. Hall** is Professor of Sociology at DePauw University in Greencastle, Indiana. A specialist in the study of long-term social evolution and comparative world-systems, his writings include, in addition to many articles, *Social Change in the Southwest, 1350–1880* (University Press of Kansas, 1989) and *Core/Periphery Relations in Precapitalist Worlds* (coedited with Christopher Chase-Dunn; Westview, 1991).

**William H. McNeill** is Professor Emeritus of History at the University of Chicago and currently lives in Colebrook, Connecticut. One of the leading historians of his generation, McNeill is the author of numerous celebrated books, including *The Rise of the West* (University of Chicago Press, 1963), *Venice: The Hinge of Europe, 1081–1797* (University of Chicago Press, 1974), *Plagues and Peoples* (Anchor, 1976), *The Human Condition: An Ecological and Historical View* (Princeton University Press, 1980), and *The Pursuit of Power: Technology, Armed Force, and Society* (University of Chicago Press, 1982).

**Matthew Melko** is Professor of Sociology at Wright State University in Dayton, Ohio. His books include *The Nature of Civilizations* (Porter Sargent, 1969), *The Boundaries of Civilizations in Space and Time* (coedited with

Leighton R. Scott; University Press of America, 1987), and *Peace in Our Time* (Paragon, 1990).

**Victor Roudometof** is a doctoral candidate in sociology and cultural studies at the University of Pittsburgh. His dissertation examines the emergence of nationalism in southeastern Europe in the course of the 19th century. He has published articles on globalization, nationalism, and the problem of national minorities in the Balkans.

**Roland Robertson** is Professor of Sociology at the University of Pittsburgh. He is the coauthor (with J.P. Nettl) of *International Systems and the Modernization of Societies* (Basic Books, 1968), the author of *Globalization* (Sage, 1992), and a coeditor (with Mike Featherstone and Scott Lash) of *Global Modernities* (Sage, 1995). He has written other books and numerous articles on social theory, the sociology of religion, and globality.

**Stephen K. Sanderson** is Professor of Sociology at Indiana University of Pennsylvania. A specialist in long-term social evolution, comparative societies, and social theory, his books include *Macrosociology: An Introduction to Human Societies* (3rd ed. HarperCollins, 1995), *Social Evolutionism: A Critical History* (Blackwell, 1990), *Sociological Worlds: Comparative and Historical Readings on Society* (Roxbury, 1995), and *Social Transformations: A General Theory of Historical Development* (Blackwell, 1995).

**Immanuel Wallerstein** is Distinguished Professor of Sociology and directs the Fernand Braudel Center for the Study of Economies, Historical Systems, and Civilizations at Binghamton University of the State University of New York. He splits his time between Binghamton and the Maison des Sciences de l'Homme in Paris. He founded the Braudel Center and its official journal, *Review*. The father of world-system theory, he has published countless articles and his most important books are *The Modern World-System* (Academic Press, 3 volumes, 1974, 1980, 1989), *The Capitalist World-Economy* (Cambridge University Press, 1979), *Historical Capitalism* (Verso, 1983), *The Politics of the World-Economy* (Cambridge University Press, 1984), *Geopolitics and Geoculture* (Cambridge University Press, 1991), and *Unthinking Social Science* (Polity Press, 1991). He is still in the process of completing his multivolumed history of the capitalist world-system.

**David Wilkinson** is Professor of Political Science at UCLA. He is the author of many articles on civilizational analysis. His books include *Malraux: An Essay in Political Criticism* (Harvard University Press, 1967), *Revolutionary Civil War: The Elements of Victory and Defeat* (Page-Ficklin, 1975), and *Deadly Quarrels: Lewis F. Richardson and the Statistical Study of War* (University of California Press, 1980) .

PART I

# Civilizational Approaches to World-Historical Change

Civilizationists are distinctive and unique among historians not only in seeing patterns in historical change, but also in conceptualizing these patterns as largely cyclical in nature. Among the most important of these comparative historians are Oswald Spengler, Arnold Toynbee, Pitirim Sorokin, Alfred Kroeber, Philip Bagby, Rushton Coulborn, and Carroll Quigley (Melko 1969). In this introduction the works of Toynbee, Sorokin, and Quigley will be briefly considered.

Arnold Toynbee developed perhaps the most famous of the cyclical theories of historical change in his monumental 12-volume work, *A Study of History* (1934–61). Toynbee offered no systematic definition of civilizations, but he implicitly seemed to conceive them as large-scale social groups that were larger (often much larger) than individual states and that shared common cultural characteristics, such as artistic, religious, philosophical, and linguistic styles or traits. Civilizations differed from primitive societies in that they were dynamic rather than static. Toynbee's initial roster of civilizations demarcated 23 such groups: Egyptiac, Andean, Sumeric, Minoan, Indus, Shang, Mayan, Babylonic, Hittite, Hellenic, Syriac, Indic, Sinic, Yucatec, Mexic, Orthodox Christian (main body), Orthodox Christian (Russian off-shoot), Western, Arabic, Iranic Muslim, Hindu, Far Eastern (main body), and Far Eastern (Japanese offshoot). In his *Reconsiderations* (Volume 12 of *A Study of History*) he offered a revised list. These were Middle American, Andean, Sumero-Akkadian, Egyptiac, Aegean, Indus, Sinic, Syriac, Hellenic, Indic, Orthodox Christian, Western, Islamic, Mississippian, South-Western, North Andean, South Andean,

Elamite, Hittite, Urartian, Iranian, Korean, Japanese, Vietnamian, Italic, South-East Asian, Tibetan, and Russian.

Toynbee likened civilizations to organisms; just as organisms displayed life cycles, so did civilizations. All civilizations, said Toynbee, passed through four stages: genesis, growth, breakdown, and disintegration. The mechanism for the emergence of civilizations from primitive societies Toynbee termed "challenge-and-response." Societies are confronted throughout their existence with various challenges or pressures to which they must respond if they are to become civilizations and grow and expand. It is the leaders of a society, what Toynbee termed a "creative minority," who are in a position to put forth favorable responses to challenges. Toynbee identified five basic types of challenges: (1) the stimulus of hard countries, as represented by such environmental phenomena as barren and rough terrain, vast wildernesses, or tropical forests; (2) the stimulus of new ground, as represented by virgin territory, especially when the territory must be reached by an ocean voyage; (3) the stimulus of blows, as represented by sudden crushing defeats through war or revolution; (4) the stimulus of pressures, as represented by a geopolitical situation in which a society is constantly being marched upon and attacked by surrounding societies; and (5) the stimulus of penalizations, as represented by various disadvantages placed upon conquered peoples, such as slavery, racial or religious discrimination, and class inferiority. Toynbee thought that there was an optimal level of challenge that would lead to a creative response and the formation of a civilization. Challenges should be harsh, but they should not be too harsh.

Once civilizations are formed their growth is not automatically ensured, for growth is a matter of further responses to continuing challenges. Genuine growth involves a process that Toynbee terms "etherialization," which he defines as "an overcoming of material obstacles in a society in order that the energies of the society can be released and the society can thus respond to challenges." The challenges involved in growth are internal rather than external to the civilization, and responses to them take the form of self-determination and self-direction. The creativity necessary to civilizational growth can be enhanced by a technique Toynbee calls "withdrawal-and-return." In this process, a leader withdraws from his society for a period of time in order to receive enlightenment; he then returns to his society in order to implement his new wisdom. Jesus's withdrawal into the wilderness for 40 days is a prime example given by Toynbee.

All civilizations that grow eventually reach a peak, from which they begin to decline. They enter the third stage of the civilizational life cycle, that of breakdown. Breakdown results primarily from a failure of the process of self-determination to continue. The creative minority begins to lose its creative capacity, the masses recognize this and withdraw their imitation of these leaders, and the society begins to lose its social unity. The loss of self-direction is displayed in one or more of several ways: leadership becomes mechanical or habitual, or leaders become so self-satisfied that they "rest on their oars;" old institutions are reorganized to meet new challenges when what is really needed are new institutions; the society uses up so much energy in its successful response to a challenge that it has no energy left for further challenges; or a civilization's leaders become "intoxicated with victory" and use power unwisely and recklessly in pursuing further aims.

After breakdown reaches a certain point—after an accumulation of unsuccessful responses to challenges—the civilization begins to disintegrate. A "schism in the body social" ensues, with the society splitting into three basic factions: a "dominant minority," or an old creative minority that has lost the capacity to lead; an "internal proletariat," or a group of individuals who have become alienated from the dominant minority but that continue to live among it; and an "external proletariat," or a group of alienated individuals that is geographically separated from the dominant minority. These groups promote the disintegration of the civilization by each creating an additional faction. The dominant minority creates a Universal State, which tries to maintain control by imposing order. The internal proletariat creates a Universal Church, through which missionary religions try to convert mankind. And the external proletariat creates Barbarian War-Bands, which attack the civilization militarily. These war-bands ultimately defeat the state, and at this point the complete disintegration of the civilization has taken place, for the war-bands are themselves unfit for rule.

Pitirim Sorokin, professionally a sociologist rather than a comparative historian, was severely critical of Toynbee's classification of civilizations, arguing that his civilizations were not logically or meaningfully integrated wholes, but "congeries," or unintegrated and incoherent mixtures (Wilkinson 1995). Sorokin charged that Toynbee inconsistently used a variety of criteria in classifying civilizations, and that this made rather a mess of things. Nevertheless, as David Wilkinson (1995) has pointed out, Sorokin did admire many aspects of Toynbee's general conception of historical change: its focus on very large-scale structures that change over long periods of time, its replacement of the notion of linear change with the idea that change was cyclical or rhythmical, and its recognition "that each of the vast cultural systems and supersystems is based upon some major premise or ultimate value" (Sorokin 1966, p. 380).

In the formulation of his own theory of cultural change in his 4-volume work *Social and Cultural Dynamics* (1937–41), Sorokin developed this last point in great depth. Civilizations, or "cultural supersystems" as he often called them, were identifiable primarily in terms of some central organizing principle that was essentially a mode of human thought and feeling. There were three such organizing principles, and civilizations passed, over extremely long periods of time, through all three in a cyclical fashion. First there was the *Ideational* type of cultural mentality. This type of mentality views reality as essentially nonmaterial and emphasizes spiritual needs and goals. These goals are reached primarily by minimizing or eliminating most of the individual's physical needs, that is, by an attitude of self-renunciation or asceticism. Opposite the Ideational cultural mentality is the *Sensate*. Here reality is seen as fundamentally material or physical, and the most important human needs are those relating to the body. The good consists of the maximum satisfaction of these material needs. Mottos such as "Eat, drink, and be merry," "Life is short," and "Wine, women, and song" are the leading mottos of this type of cultural mentality. Sensate culture is also notable for its attempts to interpret, actively control, and master both the world of nature and that of human society. Finally there is a third cultural mentality that is something of a mixture of the first two, or a form intermediate between them. This mentality Sorokin calls *Idealistic*. It represents a balance of needs and ends, conceiving reality as both material and spiritual, and seeking the satisfaction of both physical and spiritual needs.

Sorokin argued that human history reveals a definite rhythmical relationship between these types of cultural mentality. Each type runs its course and always gives way to another, which eventually runs its course, and so forth. And the order is always the same. The Ideational mentality is succeeded by the dominance of the Sensate mentality, and when this runs its course it is followed by the Idealistic. This, in turn, eventually gives way to another phase of Ideational culture. This new Ideational culture, though, is not just a repetition of the old Ideational culture, for it has its own uniqueness.

The three cultural mentalities identified by Sorokin are all expressed in a society's art and architecture, in its music and literature, in its systems of truth and knowledge, in its systems of ethics, and in its social and political relationships. What causes the shift from one cultural mentality to another in such a regular fashion? Sorokin's answer is contained in his notion of *immanent change*. Each cultural mentality bears within itself the seeds of its own change and of its own destruction. All of the logical possibilities of a mentality are carried as far as they can go; the mentality eventually exhausts itself and paves the way for its successor. As Sorokin puts it (1957, p. 681):

[T]he *super-rhythm studied seems to be possible only under the condition that each of the three main systems of truth and reality—and the corresponding form of culture—is partly true and partly false, partly adequate and partly inadequate.* Only because each of them contains a vital part does it give to its human bearers the possibility of an adaptation to their milieu—cosmic, organic, and social. . . . But because each of the three systems has also an invalid part—error and fallacy side by side with truth—each of these systems leads its human bearers away from the reality, gives them pseudo knowledge instead of real knowledge, and hinders their adaptation and the satisfaction of their physiological, social, and cultural needs. . . . The net result of such a trend is that as the domination of the system increases, it becomes more and more inadequate. . . . The society and culture built on such a premise become more and more empty, false, inexperienced, ignorant. . . .

The moment comes when the false part of the system begins to overweigh its valid part. Under such conditions, the society of its bearers is doomed either to perish, or it has to change its major premise. . . .

In this way the dominant system prepares its own downfall and paves the way for the ascendance and domination of one of the rival systems of truth and reality, which is, under the circumstances, more true and valid than the outworn and degenerated dominant system. The new dominant system undergoes again the same tragedy, and sooner or later is replaced by its rival; and so these *corsi* and *recorsi* must go on, and have been going on.

Sorokin argued that contemporary Western civilization embodied a Sensate mentality that had been expanding for at least 500 years and was now reaching its limit. This mentality would soon die out, he argued, and be replaced with its Idealistic successor, which he wholeheartedly welcomed.

Carroll Quigley, in his *The Evolution of Civilizations* (1961), gives us a cyclical theory that closely resembles Toynbee's, but with some significant differences. He tells us that "civilizations come into existence, rise and flourish, and go out of existence by a slow process which covers decades or even centuries" (p. 66). Quigley identifies two fundamentally different types of societies, parasitic societies and producing societies. Parasitic societies do not create or expand wealth, but simply subsist. Producing societies increase the amount of wealth in the world. Civilizations represent a special type of producing society. They generally have, says Quigley, writing and city life. Quigley identifies sixteen major civilizations throughout world history: Mesopotamian, Egyptian, Indic, Cretan, Sinic, Hittite, Canaanite, Classical, Mesoamerican, Andean, Hindu, Islamic, Chinese, Japanese, Orthodox, and Western.

But it turns out that there is more to a civilization than just writing and city life. A civilization is also a producing society that has an *instrument of expansion*. Any society that has an instrument of expansion is organized so as to carry out three activities: (1) it has an incentive to invent new things or new ways of doing old things; (2) it is able to produce and accumulate an economic surplus, or wealth that does not need to be consumed immediately; and (3) it is able to use its economic surplus to pay for or make use of those things it invents. However, different civilizations employ different instruments of expansion. For ancient Mesopotamia, Quigley says, it was the Sumerian priesthood. In the Egyptian and Andean civilizations it was a state that created surplus through taxation. In Classical civilization it was an economy that rested on large-scale slavery. In early Western civilization it was the type of military organization known as feudalism. In later Western civilization it was capitalism.

Quigley points out that every civilization's instrument of expansion always slows down, and this slowing of the rate of expansion leads to a crisis. The development and eventual outcome of this crisis are characterized by Quigley in the form of seven stages of civilizational change: Mixture, Gestation, Expansion, Age of Conflict, Universal Empire, Decay, and Invasion. Civilizations are generally created on the peripheries of earlier civilizations through the mixture of societies and cultures. Societies that are formed in such a way have an instrument of expansion. Expansion involves four fundamental processes: increased production of goods, population growth, geographical spread, and increased knowledge. As a result of geographical expansion, a civilization "comes to be divided into two areas: the core area, which the civilization occupied at the end of Stage 2, and the peripheral area into which it expanded during Stage 3. The core area of Mesopotamian Civilization [for example] was the lower valley of the Tigris and Euphrates rivers; the peripheral area was the highlands surrounding this valley and more remote areas like Iran, Syria, and Anatolia" (p. 81).[1]

Once the instrument of expansion has become an institution, the rate of expansion slows, often markedly, and the Age of Conflict ensues. Like the stage of expansion, this stage is also marked by four characteristics: in addition to a declining rate of expansion, these include increasing class conflicts, increasingly frequent and violent imperialist wars, and growing irrationality, pessimism, superstitiousness, and otherworldliness. The Age of Conflict gives way to the stage of Universal Empire as a result of the outcomes of imperialist wars. One state emerges triumphant from these wars. Quigley holds that this stage is associated with a Golden Age, or a period of relative peace and prosperity. However, this prosperity is deceiving, for "little real economic expansion is possible because no real instrument of expansion exists. New inventions are rare, and real economic investment is lacking. The vested interests have triumphed and are living off their capital, building unproductive and blatant monuments like the Pyramids, the 'Hanging Gardens of Babylon,' the Colosseum, or (as premature examples) Hitler's Chancellery and the Victor Emmanuel Memorial. The masses of the people in such an empire live from the waste of these nonproductive expenditures. The Golden Age is really the glow of overripeness, and soon decline begins" (p. 88).

When decline becomes evident, the stage of Decay has been reached. It is a period marked by "acute economic depression, declining standards of living, civil wars between the various vested interests, and growing illiteracy" (p. 88). Eventually, the religious, intellectual, and political elites lose the allegiance of the large mass of the population. There is an increasing reluctance on the part of the masses to act to defend or support the society, and a point is reached at which the civilization is incapable of defending itself. At this point it is vulnerable to the military actions of barbarian invaders. As the invaders overrun the civilization, it ceases to exist.

\*    \*    \*

The preceding discussion should serve to give readers unfamiliar with civilizational approaches to history some feel for their basic nature. The essays in this section extend or apply some of these basic lines of argument. Matthew Melko's selection is drawn from his book *The Nature of Civilizations* (1969). Melko lays out some elements of a basic model of civilizations. Civilizations, he tells us, are large and complex cultures that are more dynamic than primitive cultures and that have greater control over their environments. They are complex wholes that usually contain a multiplicity of cultures and languages. Some are highly integrated, others more loosely integrated, but they do have basic patterns that allow them to be distinguished from each other. Every civilization is unique and seems to have, as Spengler thought, some basic "essence" that characterizes it. Melko goes on to discuss the boundaries of civilizations, and the delineations of civilizations in the works of Toynbee, Spengler, Sorokin, Quigley, Kroeber, and Bagby. He also takes up questions regarding the origins, changes in, and collapses and recoveries of civilizations.

David Wilkinson is a major contemporary civilizationist, but he takes a unique approach. For Wilkinson, civilizations are not cultural groups but rather sociopolitical groups. They are social units that are larger than states, and their constituent states are locked into either political conflict or political alliance with one another. Civilizations for Wilkinson are not only not cultural groups, but are *polycultures*, or social units within which there is considerable cultural variety. In his article in this section Wilkinson sets forth a roster of fourteen civilizations, of which today only one survives. This Wilkinson calls Central Civilization, which originally formed through the merger of two earlier civilizations, Egyptian and Mesopotamian, in approximately 1500 BC. Much of Wilkinson's article is taken up with a detailed exploration of the characteristics and historical development of Central Civilization.

William Eckhardt's article is of special interest because it applies a civilizational perspective to the study of empires and wars, and as such nicely illustrates many of the key underlying assumptions of the perspective. Eckhardt presents empirical data showing that, historically, civilizations and empires have been extremely closely related. As humans became more civilized they created larger empires that controlled more of the earth's surface and people. Moreover, both civilizations and empires are highly correlated with wars. The more advanced the civilizations and the larger the empires, the greater the scale and scope of war. Eckhardt concludes that civilizations, empires, and wars form a positive feedback loop in which changes in the scale of each factor contributes to changes in the scale of the other factors. The three variables are inextricably intertwined.

## NOTES

I am grateful to David Wilkinson for his comments on this introduction.

1.   The use of the terms "core" and "periphery" is an interesting anticipation of Immanuel Wallerstein's later use of these terms. However, it should be noted that, despite the parallel terminology, what Quigley meant by core and periphery is not quite the same as what Wallerstein means.

## References

Melko, Matthew. 1969. *The Nature of Civilizations*. Boston: Porter Sargent.
Quigley, Carroll. 1961. *The Evolution of Civilizations*. New York: Macmillan.
Sorokin, Pitirim. 1937–41. *Social and Cultural Dynamics*. 4 vols. New York: American Book Co. (Revised and abridged by the author in one volume, Boston: Porter Sargent, 1957.)

————. 1966. *Sociological Theories of Today*. New York: Harper & Row.

Toynbee, Arnold J. 1934–61. *A Study of History*. 12 vols. Oxford and New York: Oxford University Press.

Wilkinson, David. 1995. "Sorokin vs. Toynbee on Congeries and Civilizations: A Critical Reconstruction." In *Sorokin: A Centennial Assessment*, edited by Joseph Ford, Palmer Talbutt, and Michel Richard. New Brunswick, NJ: Transaction Books.

*Chapter One*

# The Nature of Civilizations

## The Need for a Model

Valiant attempts to define and describe giant cultures have become familiar in the 20th century. Spengler, Toynbee, Sorokin, and Kroeber have each offered impressive systems involving the conception of a number of exclusive, durable, mortal macrocultures that have come to be called "civilizations." That these attempts have aroused considerable interest derives, no doubt, from a feeling that our own civilization might be facing the possibility of coming to an end, of "dying" if you will, as others apparently have in the past.

But most scholars, while praising the authors for their learning and audacity, have raised central questions about the validity of the whole approach. Do these civilizations, ranging over thousands of miles and years, really have meaningful internal relationships? Should anyone attempt to characterize them as if they were historical personalities? Is it possible to unravel the maze of history and compartmentalize it in this fashion? And if a Spengler or Toynbee does all this, has he discovered anything real or has he only found a way of simplifying history that happens to be convenient for him?

The answers given to these questions, at the time they were raised, were overwhelmingly negative. The civilizations of Spengler and Toynbee behaved themselves so beautifully because they were fictitious creations. Since they were not real, they could not live or die and they certainly could not have personalities.

But time has given a different answer. Many historians write today with a sharpened awareness of cultural integration and characterization. They seek relationships between politics, economics, and aesthetics, and they dismiss cause-and-effect political history as out of date, something that belongs to the 19th century. What they have rejected in the system builders is their dogmatic periodization. The basic concepts have stood. Civilizations do have meaningful inner relationships, they can be characterized, they can be distinguished from one another.

In the last year of his life, Rushton Coulborn wrote that a task "of pressing importance for the comparative study of civilized societies . . . is the establishment of an outline body of doctrine for the whole field secure enough for all scholars working within it to accept." In the essay that follows I hope to make a beginning on the task this thoughtful scholar believed to be so important. I have tried to sift out the areas of agreement that exist among the students of comparative history who, together, have studied most of the civilizations of the world. What, from these areas of agreement, seem to be the recurrent, the usual, the normal characteristics of most civilizations? What is a normal civilization?

Coulborn liked to apply Thomas Kuhn's term, paradigm, to a body of doctrine accepted by almost everyone working within a given field. What I am attempting here, of course, might be called a model of civilization. Others may modify this, or propose alternatives. Out of this kind of interaction, a paradigm for the study of civilization could arise.

Let me stress again that most of the generalizations in this essay are drawn from the observations of comparative historians, and not from an exhaustive study of history itself. In fact, because I do not have an adequate general knowledge of many civilizations, I have tried to set aside my own observations of history or at least to relegate them to the notes. It will, however, be necessary to illustrate some points with examples, which I shall draw from my knowledge of Chinese, Russian, Indian, Egyptian, and Western history. . . .

## Comparative Historians

Each civilization has a history of its own. We might, therefore, refer to those who have considered the history of one civilization in relation to the history of others as comparative historians.

There have been quite a few comparative historians through the centuries: Orosius, Ibn Khaldun, Bodin, Le Roy, Vico, Danilevsky, Burckhardt, Brooks, and Henry Adams. But there is no doubt that the 20th-century crisis of the two world wars, coupled with significant developments in the methods of archaeology and anthropology, cleared the way for the emergence of the most knowledgeable and interesting comparative historians who have ever lived. Of these the most influential have been Spengler, Toynbee, Sorokin, and Kroeber.

Oswald Spengler, an obscure German schoolmaster, began his *Der Untergang des Abendlandes* as an effort to comprehend the political events that preceded World War I. Eventually he enlarged his original scope, believing that politics could only be understood in relation to artistic and philosophical developments. His book is primarily a comparison of Western and Greco-Roman civilizations, with side glances at a half-dozen others. He is dogmatically insistent on the independence of civilizations from external influences. He writes with leaping flashes of intuition which may be exciting, inspiring, annoying, or baffling. His book has been translated by C.F. Atkinson as *The Decline of the West* (1932).

The British historian, Arnold Toynbee, began publishing *A Study of History* (1934–61) a few years before the outbreak of World War II. Toynbee draws from a wider knowledge of history than Spengler, documents his material more thoroughly, and has at his command an astonishing amount of information on numerous and disparate subjects. He delineates more than twenty civilizations, though even for him Western and Classical civilizations provide the core of his support. He is less concerned than Spengler with characterizing civilizations, more concerned with the criteria by which they are to be determined. The *Study* is both pleasing and exhausting because of its winding side paths, many carried to footnotes and annexes, where they often lead to observations more significant than the point they are illustrating.

As Toynbee worked steadily on his staggering one-man task, Russian-born Pitirim Sorokin mobilized a small army of Harvard graduate students to help him tackle similar questions from a sociological viewpoint. He concentrates even more than Spengler and Toynbee on the Classical-Western tradition. His *Social and Cultural Dynamics* (1937–41) overflows with statistics on all conceivable components of a culture, from types of art and systems of truth to methods of government and practice of war. Sorokin and his students have not only studied them, they have tried to weigh and measure them. Basing his writing on these data, Sorokin is often difficult to read. Fortunately his books are salted with pugnacious overtones, particularly in the footnotes. Though a harsh critic of his fellow comparative historians, he is also a staunch defender of what they are trying to do.

A.L. Kroeber, born four years before Spengler, did not publish his *Configurations of Culture Growth* (1944) until the latter part of World War II (though it was virtually completed nearly a decade earlier). Kroeber is more temperate and less conclusive than the others. He suggests areas for further investigation without trying to supply final answers to his own questions. He has consistently attempted to reconcile conflicting views of his fellow writers in the field without interpreting them, as Sorokin tends to do, in his own terms. He approaches civilizations from an anthropological viewpoint, seeing them as more complex, but not magically different, from simpler cultures. He is the most comfortable of the four in dealing with non-Western cultures. He writes in a mellow style, sometimes overelaborated by his anxiety to qualify and avoid overstatement.

A number of other 20th-century scholars have made significant contributions to comparative history. The British Egyptologist, Flinders Petrie, anticipated Spengler and Toynbee in his bold, scarcely-supported speculations about the nature and development of civilizations, the relations between them, and the nature of progress. Christopher Dawson, British Catholic historian, approaches the subject as a student of comparative religion, avoids constructions of central theories and, like Kroeber, stresses the importance of intermediate cultures. Quincy Wright, drawing heavily on Toynbee for theoretical support, concentrates on the structures of international societies. Shepard Clough focuses on the relationship between the development of civilizations and their economic system. Philip Bagby, an American anthropologist, outlined methods and suggested studies that ought to be undertaken in comparative history, but his early death prevented him from completing any significant study of his own.

Two other comparative historians, writing more recently, have made important contributions. Rushton Coulborn concentrated on the origin and revival of civilizations. He stressed the tendency of civilizations to endure and recover, the importance of "style" in determining their delineation, and the necessity of remaining receptive to partial comparisons ("uniformities") without imposing a rigid, overall structure. Carroll Quigley has written a concentrated, sophisticated explanation of *The Evolution of Civilizations* (1961). His style is simple, direct, and often humorous; he is particularly concerned about explaining the correlation in the development of psychic, governmental, and economic aspects of a civilization. Coulborn and Quigley represent a new generation: their tools are more refined than those of their predecessors, and they are less dogmatic. Perhaps because they have been in a position to support themselves with more certainty they are less outrageous and have therefore attracted less attention. This is unfortunate, because they have much to say and there is still much to be said. . . .

## How Civilizations are Integrated

The term "culture" is used to describe the way men live in relation to one another. Sometimes the culture may be simple and complete, easy to understand as a whole, as is frequently the case with the island cultures studied by anthropologists.

Civilizations are large and complex cultures, usually distinguished from simpler cultures by a greater control of environment, including the practice of agriculture on a large scale and the domestication of animals. They are technically advanced enough to use metals and to employ the wheel for transportation. These economic advantages give them enough of a surplus of food and necessities to free some of their members, at least in part, from subsistence work. This freedom usually leads to the building of cities, and the development of more complex art forms and some kind of writing to convey ideas and to maintain records. For whereas a simpler culture changes so slowly that it is usually studied in static terms, a civilization changes rapidly enough to be considered chronologically: it has a history (Quigley 1961 pp. 69–76).

Usually civilizations incorporate a multiplicity of cultures and languages. But they have never expanded indefinitely, and it has been possible to distinguish them not only from their component cultures, but also from other civilizations. When Marco Polo traveled to China, he was aware that he was seeing a distinct civilization. The Chinese and Europeans each lived their own lives, and contact between them was rare. There was no society which included Europe and China. They were clearly separate entities. The geographical distinction is not always so clear, but civilizations that form and develop separately tend to remain distinct even after they come into physical contact.

Toynbee sums up the incorporative but distinct characteristics of civilizations when he describes them as institutions that "comprehend without being comprehended by others" (1934–61, Vol. 1, p. 455, n. 1).

These civilizations must have a certain degree of integration. Their parts are defined by their relationship to each other and to the whole. If the civilization is composed of states, these states will have more relation to one another than they do to states outside the civilization. They might fight more, and engage more frequently in diplomatic relations. They will be more interdependent economically. There will be pervading aesthetic and philosophical currents.

The degree of integration that exists will vary from one civilization to another and it will vary within a civilization from time to time. Sometimes the parts will be so closely related that a change in one part will affect all the others, both geographically and in terms of ideas and attitudes. Sometimes the parts will be loosely related, so that a change in one part will have very little effect on the others. These degrees of integration are familiar in other systems. If you pull a man out of a football team, you still have a team that works, less efficiently perhaps, but it does work and is still clearly identifiable as the same team. If you knock a neutron out of an atom you get an isotope with considerably different properties. Similarly, the Polish Partition involved the removal of a state, but still the system worked, less efficiently perhaps, but it did work and was clearly identifiable as the same state system. But the Reformation involved a replacement of qualities so integrated in the system that the change led to a reconstitution of the civilization with considerably different properties.

Civilizations change. Sometimes civilizations are closely integrated, sometimes loosely, and sometimes the integration becomes so faint and the external influences so considerable that we have difficulty determining whether they exist at all. Some civilizations never attain a high degree of integration and some remain at a well-integrated stage for a long time. Perfect integration is approached but never achieved. If it were, change would be impossible—a condition that is apparently attained in some primitive cultures, which are in what physicists call a "steady state," involving a minimum of adjustment, as distinguished from the "stable state" of an artifact.

Civilizations are composed of a multitude of integrated "systems"—regional and provincial systems of government, agricultural and industrial districts—each of which is broken down still further. I am taking this use of the term "system" from Sorokin. Alternatively, using Kroeber's term (1948, p. 311), civilizations can be seen as being composed of "patterns"—systems of art, philosophy, religion that are again broken down into various schools and movements. The patterns are the arrangements that give the parts a relationship to one another and to the civilization as a whole, whereas systems have their own unity, regardless of whether they happen to form a part of a still larger system. The subsystems are like blocks that a child uses to build a castle. The patterns are like strands in a woven rug. Patterns are best studied in relation to the system they compose; we should study Impressionist art with reference to the society in which it existed, although we can study Russian government to see how it functions without concerning ourselves with Russian history. . . .

## The Unique Character of Each Civilization

Marco Polo was struck by the fact that the Chinese ate differently, thought differently, and had different customs from the Europeans. The patterns of their activities and ideas gave distinctive qualities to their respective cultures. Since the patterns relate to one another in a culture, it is usually possible to distinguish the outstanding characteristics of various peoples.

Concentration on the outstanding differences between Englishmen and Americans enables the social historian to characterize each country. Concentration on their similarities enables him to characterize their common culture, and thereby to distinguish the civilization to which they belong from other civilizations. To an American the differences might be important: the Englishmen might seem old-fashioned, remote, charming. To the Chinese, the similarities might be overriding: the Westerners seem technologically-oriented, dynamic, superficial. Individual cultures and whole civilizations thus can be characterized in a few terms or a single word.

Though we may characterize civilizations as a whole, we can best see the characteristics operating by comparing individuals, preferably individuals who are operating under identical conditions. For example, if you give a volleyball to a group of Western soldiers stationed in Korea, they will form two teams and play a competitive game. If you give the same ball in the same area to Korean soldiers, they will form a circle and kick the ball to one another. The Westerners keep score, play aggressively, achieve recognition by blending their abilities with those of teammates and discuss the game after it is played. The Koreans keep no score, yield readily to other participants, achieve recognition by adroit individual manipulation, and talk little about the game after it is over. The way in which the individuals behave, and the form their recreation takes, reflects their society. But at the same time, their culture is what it is because they do these things; the form of their game fits the individuals and the individuals fit the form: each modifies the other. The Westerners say it is "like the Koreans" to play in the manner they do. What they mean is that the Koreans' approach to recreation seems consistent with the approach to other things they do, that they have characteristic ways of behavior.

All the characteristics of a civilization, then, tend to relate to and modify one another. Nations tend to borrow from one another, developments in art and history in one area tend to be modified by those in other areas, and all these interacting and modifying elements tend to give an image to the civilization as a whole. This image, in turn, pervades the civilization and tends to influence and modify the disparate elements. Once these characteristics become established, they tend to persist through this reciprocal reinforcement, even though the civilization is undergoing momentous change. Thus Spengler and Toynbee take it for granted that the civilization of Homer is the civilization of Diocletian.

Spengler sees this image as a "soul" that appears at the beginning of a civilization's existence and pervades and directs it throughout. This view has been modified by Kroeber who sees the "soul" only as a generalization about the relatedness of the patterns to the whole (Spengler 1932, pp. 179–80; Kroeber 1957, pp. 101–102). Though I concur with Kroeber's modifications, Spengler certainly has conveyed the early appearance of the image in saying that the soul exists at the "birth" of the civilization: We cannot be sure a civilization is there until we can discern an image.

Spengler has also been criticized for overdrawing his characterizations and for overstressing their pervasiveness. For him, "pure and limitless space" describes the West, "the sensuously-present individual body" the Greco-Roman, a "wandering way" the Chinese, and so on (1932, pp. 183, 190). But I find these sharply drawn contrasts useful. We all know they are simplifications and that they may have to be modified for different situations, but if civilizations are going to be described at all, we must try to pick out those characteristics that make them unique. A watered-down, excessively elaborated description is difficult to work with. Somerset Maugham has pointed out that if a novelist is too detailed and exact in his characterization, his character appears senseless and inconsistent. We are no longer able to apprehend his image.

Inevitably characterization is a matter of individual judgment and inevitably it will reflect the personality of that individual. But this is also true, of course, of the writing of any narrative history: When data are plentiful, the observer must select; when they are lacking, he must draw inferences. The danger in characterization is that once it has been made it tends to commit the observer in further observations he may make. If he says that Western civilization is Faustian—that its representatives tend to have an indomitable urge to explore, penetrate, or meddle—he may feel he ought to apologize for individuals who do not fit this characterization, or he may seek further evidence to prove that after all, despite appearances, they do fit. But this is a problem inherent in all hypothetical formulations. Characterizers, model builders, and image-makers must expect their creations to be modified or even destroyed by empirical data. . . .

## Boundaries of Civilizations

If civilizations have an internal consistency, if they have discernible, unique characteristics, then they can be distinguished from one another. Not that they do not interact and collide and occasionally destroy one another. But once they have a chance to develop, once they become sufficiently large and complex, they can withstand a considerable amount of buffeting and still retain their identity. One civilization rarely receives material from another without changing the nature of that material to fit its own patterns. Anything that can be transmitted without change is concerned with basic, mechanistic functions—and if such things are not transmitted they may be reinvented anyway when the need arises.

A good measure of agreement has already been reached on the methods for delineating civilizations, and on when and where these civilizations existed. Disagreements exist on whether more stress should be placed on the existence of specific patterns such as language, religion, technological development, and forms of art, or on the existence of historical processes and distinctive phases of development. Disagreements also persist on the margins of time and space, on whether smaller, less developed, or interrupted cultures should be called civilizations at all, and whether long, irregular periods of history should be studied as one or more civilizations. Out of this discussion separate civilizations are generally distinguished in the following areas:

- the Far East between 2000 BC and the present
- India between 2500 BC and the present
- Egypt between 4000 BC and 300 BC
- the Middle East between 4000 BC and the present
- the Mediterranean between 3000 BC and AD 1500
- Western Europe between AD 700 and the present
- Central America between AD 1 and AD 1600
- western South America between AD 1 and AD 1600

Further, there is a pronounced but less frequent tendency to distinguish an Islamic civilization around the southern Mediterranean between 500 and the present, an Orthodox civilization in eastern Europe at roughly the same period, and a civilization in Japan, since possibly 400 BC, that has been sufficiently distinct from China to merit separate classification.

The delineation of civilizations is usually unsatisfactory, often esoteric and sometimes rather quibbly, but it is important because in any attempt to portray the history of a civilization it is necessary to understand the reasons for its limits and divisions; because a measure of agreement on civilizations by the comparative historians will make their own writing more useful for comparison with one another; and because generalizations about recurrence will have more meaning when the structures of the civilizations in which recurrences take place are better understood.

The relationship between historical recurrences and civilizations is particularly important. If we are interested in Napoleon, we might explain his failure to unify Europe in terms of his own shortcomings, or in terms of a peculiar recuperative vitality manifested in Europe. But was it the man or the situation that prevented unification? Or was it a fortuitous combination of both? We begin to look for other examples in history. Alexander also failed to create a long-standing empire. Was this because he and Napoleon faced similar situations? And how was it that these two most famous and gifted men failed to do what an Augustus, a Chandragupta, or an Ivan III did succeed in doing? If we study the careers of these men we can come up with some answers that probably will throw more light on the career of Napoleon. But we shall have a deeper understanding still if we also try to understand the context of the civilization in which the empire builders lived, if we can discern whether they were, to use one of Toynbee's more preposterous phrases, "philosophically contemporaneous."

In discussing the delineation of civilizations, there is a tendency to be apologetic because there are so few examples. Toynbee is sorry because he can find only 30 while the lucky entomologist has all those millions of specimens to work on. He asks us to be patient because in a few hundred thousand years, if all goes well, which (he says) it probably will not, we shall have many more samples. More anthropologically-oriented historians, on the other hand, think we can partly make up for this difficulty by making studies of intermediate and primitive cultures, which will he easier to handle and will throw more light on methods of study in tackling the larger systems (Kroeber 1957, pp. 158–59; Dawson 1957, p. 425).

This is all very well when you are making suggestions for other people to carry out, but when you are thinking of tackling these problems yourself it becomes frightening. Toynbee's maximum of 30 civilizations, or even the assessments of Spengler, Kroeber, Coulborn, and Quigley at between 8 and 15 major civilizations, are already enough to occupy anyone for a lifetime. Anyone now living was born none too soon. As for the minor and derivative and humble cultures, they will be useful in time for criticism and verification. But, understandably, comparative historians have been gravitating toward Spengler's intuitive generalizations rather than Toynbee's perhaps more sophisticated delineations. There are not too few civilizations, there are too many—for any one man. So let the pioneers draw their material from an insufficient sample, as Spengler and Toynbee have done, and let these hypotheses be modified or destroyed by the detailed work of scholars, by reconsideration, and by time. . . .

## Six Delineations of Civilizations

The extent of consensus thus far attained might he gauged by comparing the delineations of six comparative historians who have been most explicit on the subject (see Table 1.1). In Table 1.1, I have taken the liberty of giving a date (preceded by 'c.') where the writer has indicated perhaps no more than a millennium. A question mark following a date indicates that the date is inferred. A question mark without a date indicates that no inference was attempted.

Coulborn's datings in primary civilizations are invariably earlier than those of the others, probably because he is trying to indicate where "civilization" has its origins rather than determine whether "civilizations" could be said to exist. Toynbee, Kroeber, Bagby, and Quigley would agree, I imagine, that high-level cultures existed in these periods, but they would either deny that they had attained the level of civilization, or, more likely, contend that the classification of these periods is still uncertain.

Some comments on the individual areas may be helpful in decoding the chart.

*The Far East.*   Toynbee dates the Sinic civilization from 1500 BC to AD 172 and the Far Eastern civilization from AD 500 to 1853. Quigley makes

TABLE 1.1

Civilizational Delineations of Six Comparative Historians

| Area of Origin | Spengler | Toynbee | Kroeber | Bagby | Coulborn | Quigley |
|---|---|---|---|---|---|---|
| Far East | Chinese 1300 BC–AD 220 | Sinic/Far Eastern 1500 BC–AD 18 3 | Chinese 1200 BC–AD 1400 | Chinese 1500 BC–present | Chinese c. 2800 BC–present | Sinic/Chinese 2000 BC–AD 1930 |
| | — | "Far Eastern Offshoot" AD 500–1853 | Japanese 400 BC–AD 1800 | — | — | Japanese 100 BC–AD 1950 |
| India | Indian 1500–200 (?) BC | Indic 1500 BC–AD 47 5  00 | Indian 600 BC–AD 1200 | Indian 1500 BC–present | Indian c. 2500 BC–present | Hindu 1500 BC–AD 1900 |
| Middle East | Babylonian 3000–200 (?) BC | Sumero-Akkadian c. 3500 BC–AD 00 | | Babylonian c. 300–100 BC | Mesopotamian c. 4500–600 (?) BC | Mesopotamian c. 6000–300 BC |
| | Magian AD 1–present | Islamic AD 1300–present | Islam AD 530–1500 | Near-Eastern AD 1–present | Islamic AD 500 (?)–present | Islamic AD 600–1940 |
| | — | | — | — | — | — |
| Egypt | Egyptian 2900–1205 BC | Egyptaic c. 4000–1175 BC | Egyptian c. 3315–663 BC | Egyptian c. 2700–500 BC | Egyptian c. 4500–600 (?) BC | Egyptian c. 5500–300 BC |

(continues)

TABLE 1.1
(*Continued*)

| Area of Origin | Spengler | Toynbee | Kroeber | Bagby | Coulborn | Quigley |
|---|---|---|---|---|---|---|
| Mediterranean | — | Minoan c. 3000–1400 BC | | | Cretan c. 3000–1100 (?) BC | Cretan 3000–1100 BC |
| | Classical 1100 BC–AD 200 | Hellenic 1100 BC–AD 378 | Mediterranean 1200 BC–AD 1453 | Classical 1200 BC–AD 300 | Graeco-Roman 1200 (?) BC–AD 500 (?) | Classical 1100 BC–AD 500 |
| Eastern Europe | | Orthodox AD 700–1768 | | — | Byzantine AD 600 (?)–present | Orthodox AD 600–present |
| Western Europe | Western AD 900–2200 | Western AD 700–present | Occidental AD 800–present | Western European AD 900–present | Western AD 500 (?)–present | Western AD 500–present |
| Central America | Mexican 160 BC–AD 1521 | Middle American 500 BC–AD 1821 | Meso-American ?–AD 1550 (?) | Middle American AD 1–1550 | Middle American c. 1800 BC–AD 1600 (?) | Meso-American 1000 BC–AD 1550 |
| South America | | Andean 500 (?) BC–AD 1533 | Andean ?–AD 1550 (?) | Peruvian AD 1–1550 | Andean c. 1200 BC–AD 1600 (?) | Andean 1500 BC–AD 1600 |

SOURCES:   Spengler (1932); Toynbee (1946, Vol. I, p. 567, Table V); Kroeber (1944, pp. 663–758); Bagby (1958, pp. 165–70); Coulborn (1959, pp. 3–9); Quigley (1961, pp. 37–93).

a similar division for his two civilizations: the Sinic from 2000 BC to AD 400, and the Chinese from 400 to AD 1930.

Toynbee thinks the separation of modern Chinese civilization is open to question (1934–61, Vol. XII, pp. 173–83). He and probably some of the others would agree with Coulborn that a high level of culture existed in China before 1500 BC, but the question seems to be whether this culture should be classified as a civilization. Spengler rejects the separate classification of Japan (1932, Vol. II, p. 49); Bagby thinks the classification is still open to question; Coulborn apparently includes it with the Chinese.

*India.* Toynbee adds a second civilization, the Hindu (AD 800 to the present), but he also grants this is debatable. The disagreement on whether there was an Indian civilization as far back as the 3rd and 4th millennium is similar to the disagreement on the dating of the Chinese.

*The Middle East.* This seems to be the most difficult area to classify. Kroeber apparently would have included an "Ancient Near Eastern Civilization" in an unfinished "roster" published after his death (1962, p. 21). This would probably have corresponded to the Mesopotamian-Sumerian-Babylonian civilization distinguished by others. Toynbee's Sumero-Akkadian civilization represents a revised view developed in *Reconsiderations*. Toynbee and Quigley distinguish a separate Hittite civilization in the 2nd millennium BC, Kroeber and Coulborn consider the Jews to have had a separate civilization beginning in the 2nd millennium BC, while Quigley includes the Jews, Phoenicians, and Carthaginians in a Canaanite civilization (2200–100 BC). Kroeber and Coulborn distinguish an Iranian civilization beginning in the 1st millennium BC. Toynbee discerns a Syriac civilization that seems to have specialized in hatching religions (1100 BC–AD 969).

*Egypt.* Considerable agreement here. No one seems to have accepted Petrie's view that successive civilizations existed in Egypt.

*Mediterranean.* Recent research on Crete indicates that there were Mycenaean influences both on Crete and on Greece. At present, however, the culture of Crete seems to be considered as distinct from that of Greece. Spengler regards the civilization of Crete as an Egyptian offshoot, a view unsupported by later scholars. Bagby considers it a "secondary" culture, not a civilization. Agreement on Classical civilization is fairly close, though Kroeber includes the Byzantine civilization with the Roman.

*Eastern Europe.* Spengler, Kroeber, and Bagby incorporate Byzantium in their Magian, Mediterranean, and Near Eastern civilizations respectively. Russia gets mixed reviews. It is treated as a separate civilization by Spengler and Toynbee, as part of Byzantine civilization by Coulborn and Quigley, as European by Kroeber, and as uncertain by Bagby. Coulborn's last position was to regard the Byzantine as a separate civilization.

*Western Europe.*   The only disagreement here is on whether to include the Dark Ages or to start Western civilization at some point where recovery has begun.

*America.*   Originally Toynbee distinguished three civilizations in Central America. He reduced them to one in his *Reconsiderations* (1934–61, Vol. XII, pp. 173–83). According to Coulborn, Kroeber apparently concluded, after the publication of *Configurations*, that there was enough evidence to warrant delineation of civilizations in Central and South America. In his revision of *Anthropology* (1948) he still refers to Meso-American and Andean "high cultures" (pp. 777–801). Spengler never elaborates on Peruvian civilization. He couples it once with the Mexican (1932, Vol. II, p. 46), but he never classifies it. . . .

## Change and Continuity

Although civilizations change continuously, they maintain their identity for centuries. The change comes about because the civilization is a going, functioning system. When the actions of men break restraining customs and set off processes of development in part of the system, this in turn sets off related development in other parts of the system.

Despite change, civilizations maintain their identity once well-integrated patterns have been established. If changes are to be induced, they must have some relationship to these patterns, and leaders who fail to take these patterns into consideration are likely to be replaced.

It seems natural in describing these processes to fall back on organic terms: to talk about the growth or unfolding of a civilization on the one hand and about its exhaustion and death on the other. This gives pain to many students of society who feel that after all, Spengler notwithstanding, cultures are not organisms (Spengler 1932, p. 104). These terms arise, however, not only because no better ones are available but also because the analogies are so tempting. Men, like cultures, change constantly yet maintain their identity. Yet many do seem to maintain only a steady state, to go on living without becoming. If they do develop, it is because something inside them drives them to it or because qualities they have are allowed to develop by the culture in which they live. Once a man's patterns become established, it is difficult for him or anyone else to change them. Eventually a man runs down, disintegrates, dies, or is overwhelmed by external circumstances or killed by accident or design.

Civilizations are living systems; men are living systems too. . . .

## Origins and Liberation

Often the characteristics of a civilization become manifest rather rapidly, so that Spengler could speak of the birth of its soul. The appearance of Gothic cathedrals in the 11th century dramatically commemorates the birth of Faustian Man. What really has happened, of course, is that we have identified a civilization through certain characteristics, we trace these characteristics back as far as we can, and the earliest point at which we think they emerge we call the beginning a civilization. When the civilization has begun to develop, it may continue to exist long after the cultures from which it originally sprang have lost their identity through merger, division, disintegration, or destruction. Thus the Jewish civilization survived the Mesopotamian, the Byzantine survived the Classical.

The confluence of patterns that had to do with the origins of the first civilizations may have been related to environmental challenges, but there is still considerable uncertainty about the nature of these challenges, and disagreement about whether civilizations were invented more than once. But there must have been some compelling reason for man to change his way of life, moving from a nomadic existence based primarily on hunting to a sedentary agricultural life in the great river valleys of the world (Coulborn 1959, pp. 67–109, modified in "Structure and Process in the Rise and Fall of Civilized Societies" [1966], p. 410). The challenge involved in this transition must have been immensely difficult, requiring astonishing changes in political and economic concepts, and probably producing many failures before two civilizations—the Sumerian and the Egyptian—emerged nearly at the same time. Toynbee suggests a possible human challenge: the migration of peoples (which might have an environmental origin) often forces another people to move and face the challenge of a new situation, or else produces an intermixture of peoples that sometimes precedes the flowering of a new civilization (1946–57, Vol. 1, pp. 75–79; also Dawson 1957, p. 8).

In view of the importance of understanding the nature of patterns, you might suppose that there would be a great deal of concern about the origins or causes of civilizations. This has not been the case. There has been a tendency to avoid the study of origins that derives, I suspect, from the comparative historians' rejection of the narrative historians' cause-and-effect approach to history. The historians of that period tended to look for the cause of World War I in the sequence of diplomatic events in the years preceding, without giving sufficient consideration to the social atmosphere of the entire civilization. The implication of looking for cause in preceding events was that ultimate cause was to be found in whatever came first—the origin of the situation—rather than in overall relationships. But more recently, as narrative historians have responded more to rational and less to sequential cause, comparative historians like Coulborn and Quigley seem to have been able to pursue the study of origins without apology.

It is clear that the understanding of a particular aspect of a culture is bound up with the understanding of the culture itself. And if we can see it in its formative phase, we can distinguish better the patterns that are inclined to become more elaborated and more obscured in later phases. Moreover, if you are studying parallel developments in different cultures, anomalies may sometimes be explained not in the contemporary events, but in pattern variations that derive from formative periods. Thus the Russian Revolution in many aspects followed paths analogous to earlier European revolutions. We should expect, therefore, to learn a good deal about the Russian Revolution by comparing it, as Crane Brinton has done, with the French and the English. But in many respects the society emerging from the Russian Revolution differed considerably from the France of the 19th century. These differences derive partly from the intervening development of the industrial revolution, but also partly from differences in the patterns of Russian and French history.

Some form of ritualized religion is repeatedly associated with the early stage of cultural development. Comparative historians agree almost unanimously on its dominant role in the formation of cultures. This is as true of those who, like Coulborn and Spengler, regard religion purely as a factor to be considered in the study of societies, as it is of those who, like Toynbee and Dawson, regard religion as "the foundations on which the great civilizations rest." Some kind of theocratic leadership seems to be necessary to inspire the support of the members of a culture that is still too fragile to withstand internal disunity. Often this religious unity seems to be closely related to an economic system that places strong emphasis on the value of the land and on family relationships. Sometimes it is closely connected with government, as in the Iranian and Chinese civilizations; at others distinct, as in the Classical and Western.

And if religion forms the unifying element in most developing or reviving civilizations, the nature of that religion will surely influence the process of secularization that accompanies a civilization's development. Secularization—the gradual freeing of patterns from the dominance of the original ritualized religion—seems to be a recurrent and necessary process. This process, which may last many centuries, involves the freeing of all political, economic, and aesthetic patterns from their close ties with religion. Without secularization, civilization cannot develop. Apparently no religious crystallization or synthesis can be maintained except at the cost of internal ossification, the smothering of all processes of development by an autocratic priesthood.

The study of origins, then, and particularly the study of religion will frequently have tremendous relevance to the understanding of secular problems developing in later phases. And comparisons of secular problems will frequently be clarified by comparisons of origins. . . .

## Collapses and Recoveries

Once a civilization has achieved a measure of coherence, with an established relationship between its components, potentialities for change become increasingly limited. This applies to systems at all levels and to the patterns that compose them. The limits of a particular civilization depend largely but not entirely on the character it assumed in its formative period. Once established, the various patterns of a civilization tend to develop in relation to one another until each has achieved its potential.

For example, the development of geometry was the Greek style of mathematics, a pattern in their culture. It appears to be related to the Greek emphasis on proportion and their preference for visible and tangible bodies—hence the preference for integral numbers and the avoidance of negative numbers and fractions. It is easy to see that once the full possibilities of geometry are reached, creativity in the field must die out, or mathematical activity must shift to some other form, or some way must be found to add new elements to geometry that will give scope for further development. If such additions and changes were made, however, the resulting configurations might bear very little relation to what had been called geometry. They would come to be classified under a new name and to be thought of as components of a different kind of mathematics.

But if geometry develops in an integrated society, if it is one manifestation of a Greco-Roman preference for tangibly present forms, related to the nude statue, the "sensuous cult of the Olympian gods," and the politically individual city-states (Spengler 1932, p. 183), it is likely to change only if the whole culture is likewise in a process of transition. Otherwise, if new elements were added, geometry would lose its relationship to its culture. Such changes do take place, but rarely unless the culture as a whole is on the threshold of disintegration. In the case of the Greeks, the changes did not take place. "What they would do with their geometrical and whole-number manner of style, they achieved. Other mathematical possibilities . . . were simply left to be realized by other peoples and other times" (Kroeber 1948, p. 330).

The geometry pattern, then, is inherently limited. Clearly all patterns tend to reach culminations unless new material is gradually and constantly added. And when the limits of possibilities are sensed, there is likely to be some casting around. After a vein or complex of veins has been developed, miners face a dilemma. They can explore subordinate, low-yield areas further; they can go back and try to find some ore overlooked when the major veins were freely yielding; they can look for new veins; they can close the mine and dig another; they can give up.

Art patterns are somewhat similar to the patterns of a mine. After an idea or major complex of ideas has been developed and explored, the developing artist is faced with a dilemma. Whereas fifty years previously artists were creating freely and prolifically, now they find that the additions they can make to the existing pattern are of a secondary or elaborative nature. Some will content themselves with doing this, some will repeat the patterns of immediate predecessors, some will return to earlier periods hoping that when development came, some possibilities were overlooked. Some will cast about, will feel uncomfortable, will experiment, will challenge the old patterns instead of trying to develop them further. Some will give up.

Individual culminations of patterns, occurring in succession, form a culmination for the civilization as a whole. The culmination tends to come rather early in the life of the pattern, long before the creative phase has completely ended. Manifestations of creativeness appear long after the underlying factors that give rise to them have begun to change. In China, for instance, the Hundred Schools of philosophy (c. 500–300 BC) had given form to the civilization's outlook before the first of a series of great empires was formed. Sculpture had two important periods of development during the Han (200 BC–AD 100) and T'ang (AD 500–600) Empires, poetry reaching a long, high active period (AD 200–800) through the time of the Three Kingdoms and the T'ang, painting reaching a peak during the period of the Sung (AD 950–1100). Though there is development in drama and the novel in post-Sung periods, they seem less dynamic than the earlier periods. By the time of the highly refined Sung period, decline was setting in, but as early as the Three Kingdoms period most of the patterns had been set, and the philosophical patterns, which proved to be central to Chinese style, had been clearly delineated nearly a millennium before general decline had set in.

Once a pattern or series of related patterns have passed a culmination, three possibilities remain open: they may disintegrate and disappear, they may become fixed in a steady state, or they may experience a period of transition in which disintegration takes place while new material is being added, before the onset of further development. Civilizations, like lesser systems, face these alternatives: they either disintegrate, ossify, or reconstitute themselves and develop further.

In all systems, in all patterns, there are forces working both for integration and for disintegration. In earlier periods of development, the former dominate until the culminating point of a given pattern or system. If the subsequent disintegration continues unchecked in a civilization for a long period, the civilization may cease to exist. It dies. Between AD 100 and 700 the Roman Empire virtually disappeared from the western Mediterranean. The culture in this area changed so rapidly that hardly anyone would find in it a unity and continuity of existence. The lesser patterns that compose a civilization of course disintegrate and disappear frequently, even when its total processes may tend toward integration and unity.

It may happen that the process of integration is checked through the ossification of the most significant patterns. A strong central government, by maintaining the system as it is without permitting normal changes, may enable the civilization to hold the line for a very long time. But it will be sterile, its forms endlessly repeated, its creativity dried up, its activities without meaning beyond mere survival. This appears to have happened to the Egyptian civilization and more recently in the Chinese and Islamic civilizations. In a civilization capable of strong centralized control of political and economic functions, it can happen again. Ossification occurs far more commonly within the subsystems of a civilization. These often become so overelaborated that they are no longer able to function, but they may continue to exist in a ceremonial capacity while their functions are taken over by other systems that have relevance to a particular problem. The changes in the relationships between the British monarchy and parliament, or between the Japanese emperor and shogunate, will serve as examples.

The process of disintegration may be resolved by internal effort, or by the impingement from outside of new material and new attitudes, probably resulting in the violent collapse of the old, unadapted framework. But then, because new answers are being sought, or because the internal disruption makes possible the absorption of alien ideas and artifacts, a new period of development may take place. What appeared to be a disastrous disintegration of old patterns turns out to be the creation of a condition from which a new and perhaps greater development can take place. The collapse and recovery of the T'ang empire and the emergence of the Western Renaissance are examples of reconstitutions of this kind. If men had adhered to cherished Confucian or Christian patterns, their respective civilizations might have disappeared. As it was, they were able to make a transition to unfamiliar patterns, the pattern of Chinese empire was given a viable foundation, the Renaissance took place, and the modern phase of Western history became one of fresh development.

This concept of reconstitution raises hob with those of us who are trying to arrange history in an orderly manner. If disintegrating civilizations can recover and go on to further phases of development, it is obviously going to be very difficult to cut them into orderly segments, with this phase lasting 312 years and that phase 435 years. It is going to be difficult to make accurate predictions about the doom of those still in existence. Revelation can do that just about as accurately and far more impressively. To make matters worse, the frequent intrusion of alien civilizations in these periods makes it difficult to decide whether recovery has taken place or whether the disintegrating civilization has simply been replaced by another. Is the Babylonian civilization a separate entity or a second phase of Sumerian civilization? To describe the fall of the Roman Empire must you, as Gibbon did, tell the story of Byzantium as well?

What does emerge from this concept, though, is a striking similarity between formative periods and periods of disintegration. In both, things are in flux, and while men have great opportunities to share their destinies, they also face great risk of failure. And men pay for the glories, achievements, and security of periods of integration with the loss of their capacity to do much more than manage a going concern. They can achieve great things within the system, but they cannot change the system. So you can say that there are periods of high integration and periods of low integration. In the latter there are both disintegrating and formative forces in action, and only in retrospect can you be certain which proved dominant.

After all these modifications, how much is it possible to generalize about the formation and development of civilizations? Perhaps a symphonic analogy would be useful: The theme or themes of a symphony are roughly equivalent to the central idea or the symbols by which we characterize civilizations. The completion of the exposition is equivalent to the culmination of a civilization. The development is equivalent to disintegration, in which the original compact material is exploited, considered, elaborated, but little new is added. The recapitulation may be compared to those aspects of development that have to do with the reexamination of earlier times, the seeking for the restoration of basic foundations. The coda might represent the final collapse, the end, or it might prove to be a codetta leading to new themes, enabling new combinations and development to take place, the equivalent of reconstitution. If you were listening to a familiar symphony you would know what the coda signified, but if you were hearing it for the first time, you would have to wait and see. Should the development be carried too far, without recapitulation or coda, the thematic material becoming more worn out and repetitive, the symphony, like some civilizations, would become ossified, losing its interest. If the terminating coda is followed after a pause by a new movement beginning new themes in a new time and key, this is the equivalent of a heroic age . . . in an affiliated civilization, the formation of a new set of patterns.

Civilizations, like symphonies, retain characteristic patterns notwithstanding fluxes of formation, disintegration, and reconstitution. . . .

## References

Bagby, Philip. 1958. *Culture and History*. London: Longmans, Green.

Coulborn, Rushton. 1959. *The Origin of Civilized Societies*. Princeton, NJ: Princeton University Press.

———. 1966. "Structure and Process in the Rise and Fall of Civilized Societies." *Comparative Studies in Society and History* 8:404–31.

Dawson, Christopher. 1957. *The Dynamics of World History*. London: Sheed and Ward.

Kroeber, A.L. 1944. *Configurations of Culture Growth*. Berkeley: University of California Press.

———. 1948. *Anthropology*. 2nd ed. New York: Harcourt, Brace.

———. 1957. *Style and Civilizations*. Ithaca, NY: Cornell University Press.

———. 1962. *A Roster of Civilizations and Culture*. New York: Viking Fund Publications.

Quigley, Carroll. 1961. *The Evolution of Civilizations*. New York: Macmillan.

Sorokin, Pitirim. 1937–41. *Social and Cultural Dynamics*. 4 vols. New York: American Book Co. (Revised and abridged by the author in one volume, Boston: Porter Sargent, 1957.)

Spengler, Oswald. 1932. *Decline of the West*. Trans. C.F. Atkinson. London: Allen and Unwin.

Toynbee, Arnold J. 1934–61. *A Study of History*. 12 volumes. London: Oxford University Press. (First 10 volumes abridged by D.C. Somervell, Oxford University Press, 1946–57.)

*Chapter Two*

# Central Civilization

Today there exists on Earth only one civilization, a single global civilization. As recently as the 19th century several independent civilizations still existed (i.e., those centered on China, Japan, and the West); now there remains but one.

## Central Civilization

The single global civilization is the lineal descendant of, or rather I should say the current manifestation of, a civilization that emerged about 1500 BC in the Near East when Egyptian and Mesopotamian civilizations collided and fused. This new fusional entity has since then expanded over the entire planet and absorbed, on unequal terms, all other previously independent civilizations.

I label this entity "Central" civilization. The other independent civilizations that have existed are listed in Table 2.1; their absorption is illustrated in Figure 2.1, where the horizontal axis roughly represents Mercator geography and the vertical axis time. Solid lines enclose named civilizations' careers, while five phases in the expansion of Central Civilization are separated by dashed lines.

"Central" is a historical and positional nomenclature which deliberately avoids any specific geographic or cultural references, thereby indicating that this society is not to be characterized by references to a single river basin, and that its development has not been determined by that of a single culture, nation, or people. Central Civilization is of course positionally "central" only in retrospect, by reason of its omnidirectional expansion: this network, originally located where Asia and Africa meet, spread over time in all

TABLE 2.1
*A Roster of Fourteen Civilizations*
*(in approximate order of their incorporation into Central Civilization)*

| Civilization | Duration | Terminus |
|---|---|---|
| 1. Mesopotamian | before 3000 BC–c. 1500 BC | Coupled with Egyptian to form Central |
| 2. Egyptian | before 3100 BC–c. 1500 BC | Coupled with Mesopotamian to form Central |
| 3. Aegean | c. 2700 BC–c. 560 BC | Engulfed by Central |
| 4. Indic | c. 2300 BC–c. AD 1000 | Engulfed by Central |
| 5. Irish | c. AD 450–c. 1050 | Engulfed by Central |
| 6. Mexican | before 1100 BC–c. AD 1520 | Engulfed by Central |
| 7. Peruvian | before c. 200 BC–c. AD 1530 | Engulfed by Central |
| 8. Chibchan | ? –c. AD 1530 | Engulfed by Central |
| 9. Indonesian | before AD 700–c. 1550 | Engulfed by Central |
| 10. West African | c. AD 350–c. 1550 | Engulfed by Central |
| 11. Mississippian | c. AD 700–c. 1590 | Destroyed (Pestilence?) |
| 12. Far Eastern | before 1500 BC–c. AD 1850 | Engulfed by Central |
| 13. Japanese | c. AD 650–c. 1850 | Engulfed by Central |
| 14. Central | c. 1500 BC–present | ? |

directions, encompassing the civilized networks of Europe, West Africa, and the Americas by moving west and those of South and East Asia by moving east, and thereby rendering itself historically "central" as well.

## Defining Central Civilization Into Possibility

One's criterion for defining "a civilization" affects, or more accurately determines, one's roster of civilizations. I defend a transactional definition with a criterion of *connectedness* rather than *uniformity* for locating the spatiotemporal boundaries of an urbanized society. On a connectedness criterion, cities whose people are interacting intensely, significantly, and continuously thereby belong to the same civilization, even if their cultures are very dissimilar and their interactions mostly hostile. Central Civilization becomes historically *visible*—is defined into observability—only when one chooses a criterion for defining and bounding a civilization based on transactions and connectedness rather than cultural similarity. Why make that choice?

The definition of "civilization" which makes Central Civilization visible and obvious is permitted only by a social theoretic in which fighting is bonding. Conflict, hostility, and even warfare, when durable (habitual,

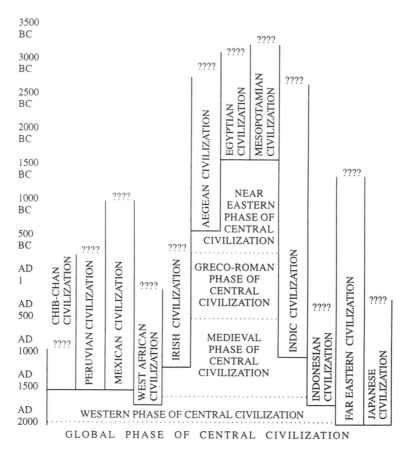

*Figure 2.1.* The incorporation of twelve civilizations into one.

protracted, or inescapable), are *forms of association* that create a social relationship between, and a social system composed of, the contestants, antagonists, and foes.

Many forms of antagonistic bonding are recognized in religions, social life, and social theory as well as in language itself. The very words "dissonance," "contradiction," "argument," "drama," "collision," "war," imply that we recognize that there exist entities created by and consisting of oppositions between sounds, ideas, persons, characters, bodies, and groups. Oppositions unite Taoist genders, Hindu castes, Marxist classes, and Kantian antinomies, thereby creating unities or systems. The Socratic and Hegelian dialectics, Israel and Judah, the Homeric pantheon, Congress, counterraiding tribes, the two-party system, the Seven Against Thebes, a Punch and Judy show, and the Hitler-Stalin pact are all antagonistic couples and collections of separate entities commonly recognized as internally antagonistic unities.

But the theoretical idea that conflict should systematically be treated, when found, as associative and indeed as an association, has not yet been widely accepted. Rather it forms a particular tendency in social theory, represented by, for example, Georg Simmel and Lewis Coser.

Neither Simmel nor Coser (to my knowledge) actually proposed a systematic inventory of social oppositions as social structures, although that would surely be an interesting and worthy undertaking. Simmel's repeated assertion that conflict (*Kampf, Streit*) is sociation (*Vergesellschaftung*) (1955, p. 13) led him into a discussion of the complex balances between opposition and cooperation rather than to a search for conflictual sociations previously unrecognized as genuine social systems.

Coser's (1956) reflections on conflict and integration more fully articulate their intimate relationship.

1.  Conflict links the conflicting entities,[1] and other entities that are drawn in.[2]
2.  Conflict establishes, defines, bounds, maintains, and integrates the internal structure of those entities *between* which it occurs (pp. 38, 87, 95, 110).
3.  Conflict may lead to later, less conflictual linkages between the antagonists.[3]
4.  Conflict may lead to increased social order and structure.[4]

I would accept all these assertions and, in their axiomatic spirit, go a bit beyond. Conflict *always* integrates in a mildly significant way, in that the transaction of conflicting always creates a new social entity, the conflict itself. But durable conflict also integrates more significantly, by creating a new social entity that contains the conflict but is not reducible to it, within which the conflict must be seen as occurring, which is often of a larger scale and longer lived than the conflict that constituted it.

It is therefore legitimate, and it is indeed necessary, to posit the existence of a social system, a single social whole, even where we can find no evidence of that whole existence other than the protracted, recurrent, or habitual fighting of a pair of belligerents. Such a continuing relation, however hostile, between groups however different, necessarily indicates that both are (were or have become) parts of some larger group or system.

*A fortiori* then we must recognize that a unifying social entity or system exists where we have evidence that a pair of groups alternates war with negotiation, or war with trade, or war with coalition, or war with subordination, or war with watchful waiting, or war with threats and preparations for war.

And if we accept that people, peoples, groups, and organizations which are in close touch with each other, and which fight, or hate, or fear, or threaten, or compete with, or dominate, or exploit, or conquer, or rebel against each other, are thereby linked, and constitute an associative entity with a social structure, it becomes appropriate to scan the human ecumene looking for fight, threats, exploitations, rebellions, and so forth. Once we can visualize a single social system as composed of antagonistic elements, it is easy to realize that, conversely, when we find a collection of (more or less) antagonistic but briskly interacting elements, we have located a single social system.

And when we scan the human ecumene and find a collection of (more or less) antagonistic but briskly interacting cities,[5] we have located a single civilization.

## Recognizing Central Civilization as a Reality

When applied to rosters of civilizations, the proposition that a collection of antagonistically interacting cities are to be treated as parts of the same civilization means that some "civilizations" on the commonly used rosters should be stricken from the records because they were at all times parts of a larger (even if oppositional) association.

### *Recognizing a Single Entity in Adjacent "Civilizations"*

The most marked cases are a widely accepted collection of three to five recent Northwest Old World "civilizations." Quigley, for instance, lists as separate entities Western (AD 500–   ), Orthodox (600–   ), and Islamic (600–   ) civilizations (1961, p. 37). Toynbee's original listing similarly included a "Western," one or two "Orthodox Christian" (a main body and a Russian offshoot), and two "Muslim" (Arabic Muslim and Iranic Muslim); Toynbee's revised list pares them back to three, Western, Orthodox Christian, and Islamic (1961, pp. 546–47, 558–61). But no matter whether three or four or five, these cultural entities were coexistent, adjacent, mutually aware, culturally dissimilar, sporadically cooperative, more often hostile, and recurrently involved in wars. Our proposition renders them as inescapably parts of a single social system. There were Western cities, Orthodox cities, Muslim cities; there was no Western civilization, no Orthodox, no Islamic civilization. There were civilized peoples and territories in the Northwest Old World; they were members of a single civilization. One might call it Northwest Old World Civilization; because of its later history I called it "Central Civilization."

It might be mentioned that Toynbee himself recognized a comparable phenomenon in the Middle New World. His original roster showed three civilizations on the territory of contemporary Mexico and Guatemala: "Mayan" and its affiliates "Yucatec" and "Mexic." Toynbee's revised roster combines the three into one "middle American" civilization, like Quigley's "Mesoamerican," Toynbee having decided that "provincial idiosyncrasies" (and local "breaks in continuity") were to be treated as variety within a larger cultural unity (1961, pp. 557–58). I would treat the differences of the Peoples of the Book(s) as "provincial idiosyncracies" constitutive of a larger social unity.

## Recognizing a Single Entity after Civilizations Collide

If two "civilizations" that were *always* adjacent and vigorously interacting are thereby in fact parts of a single civilization, then two historically autonomous civilizations which *become* adjacent (through expansions or shifts) thereby become a single civilization.

Toynbee's Egyptiac and Sumero-Akkadian civilizations, which he graphs as having lasted for about 3,000 years after about 3000 BC (1961, p. 559), and Quigley's parallel Egyptian (5500–300 BC) and Mesopotamian (6000–300 BC) civilizations clearly grew in area and collided. I place the collision in the mid-2nd millennium BC (Wilkinson 1984). As I see neither root civilization having overpowered or engulfed the other, I classify the resultant successor civilization as a new entity. One might call it Middle Eastern Civilization,[6] I call it the same "Central Civilization."

Some historic collisions require us to revise our rosters of past civilizations, others those of the civilizations that exist today. Quigley's roster shows two civilizations as definitely in current existence, Orthodox and Western: European invaders "terminated" the existence of Chinese (1930), Islamic (1940), Hindu (1900), and—perhaps—Japanese (1950), as well as Mesoamerican (1550) and Andean (1600) (Quigley 1961, p. 37). The chart that illustrates Toynbee's revised roster shows as current (as of AD 1961) not only Western and Islamic civilizations, but also a Sinic civilization, along with "satellite" civilizations—Russian, Southeast Asian, Tibetan, Korean, Vietnamian, and "Southwestern" (Pueblo-Hopi). Orthodox Christian, Indic, and a "satellite" Japanese civilization are shown as recently ended. Perhaps all—as a note to the table suggests—will yet even so contribute to a "future oecumenical civilization, starting in a Western framework and on a Western basis, but progressively drawing contributions from the living non-Western civilizations embraced in it" (Toynbee 1961, p. 559).

Termination for Quigley seems to require that a civilization be not merely invaded but fundamentally disrupted by outsiders; for Toynbee, that there be some sort of fusion and assimilation of cultures. If instead we accept that the independent history of a civilization ends whenever it becomes locked with another civilization into a larger social system and process, loses the historical autonomy which the larger process gains, the dates of termination will clearly change. Quigley's dates become somewhat too conservative for "Mesoamerican" and "Andean" (which lose their historical autonomy with the Spanish invasions, not the conquests), more so for "Chinese" and Japanese (which lose their autonomy somewhere between the forced opening to economic penetration and their enrollment in the World War I alliance system and the League of Nations), much too conservative for "Hindu" (for which there is a band width of possible loss of autonomy dates from the Muslim invasions of the 11th century AD to the European invasions of the 18th), and irrelevant for "Russian" and "Islamic" (which never had historical autonomy). Not one of these former (or putative) civilizations exists today outside a larger social system, which is clearly global. In this sense, Toynbee's "future oecumenical civilization" is not future but present, and indeed about a century old. It has been drawing "contributions" from engulfed (enstewed, melanged, but never simply assimilated) areas, formerly autonomous civilizations, long before having become ecumenical. It has drawn in military "contributions" (alliances and attacks), political "contributions" (ideologies, obedience, subversions, revolutions, propaganda), economic "contributions" (surplus, inventions, innovations, labor, markets, supplies, competition), religious, philosophical, artistic, epidemiological, and demographic "contributions." The scope of its reach would surely justify calling the global citified system "Oecumenical Civilization;" but again I call it—Central Civilization.

## Recognizing a Single Entity When "Civilizations" Succeed Each Other

A final and dramatic change is enforced on the traditional rosters by the simple insistence that unless a civilization's urban centers vanish, it does not fall. It may terminate by fission into two separate and more or less equal historically autonomous entities which cease to interact dynamically; it may terminate in fusion with some other civilization. Without fission, fusion, or fall there is no end to the civilization's system and process. If there is no end, there can be no succession.

A variety of civilizational successions has been proposed. For evident reasons, we shall confine our attention to successions of civilizations asserted to have occurred in the Northwest Old World.

Toynbee's original list provides the following Northwest Old World terminations and successions: Egyptiac civilization, terminated with no successor; Sumeric civilization, succeeded by Babylonic and Hittite, these having no further successors; Minoan civilization, succeeded by Hellenic and Syriac; Hellenic civilization, succeeded by Orthodox Christian (main body and Russian offshoot) and Western; Syriac civilization, succeeded by Arabic Muslim and Iranic Muslim (Toynbee 1961, pp. 546–47).

Toynbee's revised list presents a more complex web of successions of independent civilizations: Egyptiac (c. 2800 BC–c. AD 300) and Sumero-Akkadian (c. 3000 BC–c. AD 100) were succeeded by Syriac; Aegean (c. 2500 BC–c. AD 700) and Hellenic (same dates as Syriac) were jointly succeeded by Orthodox Christian (c. AD 400–before AD 1961), Western (c. AD 400–present) and Islamic (c. AD 950–present). (Three to six satellite and six abortive civilizations in the same area complicate the picture further [Toynbee 1961, pp. 558–61; dates estimated from chart on p. 559].) Implicitly, there must have been an epoch of unusual cultural turnover in the Northwest Old World AD 100–950, with four civilizations dying and three new ones born.

Quigley recognizes seven terminations of civilizations as having occurred in the Northwest Old World: Egyptian, terminated by Greeks 300 BC, but being culturally ancestral to, as well as for a time coexisting with, Cretan (origin c. 3000 BC); Mesopotamian, terminated by Greeks 300 BC, with Cretan, Hittite (1900 BC), and Canaanite (2200 BC) descendants; Hittite, terminated by Phrygians 1000 BC, no descendants; Cretan, terminated by Dorian invaders 1100 BC, ancestral to Classical (1100 BC); Canaanite, terminated by Romans 100 BC, descendants Classical, Western (AD 500), Islamic (AD 600); classical, terminated by Germans AD 500, ancestral to Western, Islamic, and Orthodox (AD 600); Islamic, terminated by Europeans AD 1940, no posterity (Quigley 1961, p. 37). This suggests two major turnovers in the Northwest Old World, one around 1100–1000 BC, the other around AD 500–600.

These cultural turnovers may or may not have been successions of civilizations, in the definition we are using. Egyptian and Mesopotamian appear to have terminated by fusing into Central Civilization. Aegean/Cretan may genuinely have fallen back to a preurban stage (due to natural catastrophe and barbarian invasion), but seems more likely to have shifted its urban centers to Greece and Anatolia, there to collide with Phrygian and Lydian marchmen of Central Civilization. What other successions have occurred? And, more particularly. . . .

## Did Central Civilization Ever Fall?

The fall of Rome comes at once to mind as a potential marker. Gibbon (n.d., pp. 860–61) evokes Poggius' view of the desolation of Rome: "The benches of the senators are concealed by a dunghill. The forum of the Roman people . . . is now enclosed for cultivation of pot-herbs, or thrown open for the reception of swine and buffaloes." Yet these evidences of the triumph of country over city date from the middle, not of the 5th, but of the 15th century; and Gibbon himself doubts (n.d., p. 869) that even in the 14th century, the numbers of Romans "could be reduced to a contemptible list of thirty-three thousand inhabitants."

More to our point, Rome is not the sole city of Central Civilization. And no multiurban civilization can properly be said to have fallen until *all* its cities are gone—not merely gone to the depths to which Rome sank, but destroyed like Carthage by Rome, or depopulated like Baghdad by Timur. Has any such epoch of deurbanization ever occurred in the Northwest Old World?

Tables 2.2 and 2.3 provide one approach to an answer. They list the named cities that appear on Colin McEvedy's economic maps in his *Penguin Atlas of Ancient History* (1967) and *Medieval History* (1961). The *Ancient* maps cover terrain from beyond Iceland (NW) to beyond Somalia (SE), and from Mali (SW) to the east end of the Tarim basin (NE). The *Medieval* set covers a smaller area: from beyond Ireland (NW) to the Rub al-Khali (SE), and from southern Algeria (SW) to the Urals (NE). The *Ancient* economic maps provide snapshots of urbanization in the covered territory at 2250, 1300, 825, 375, and 145 BC and AD 230 and 362; the *Medieval* maps at AD 528, 737, 1028, 1212, and 1478. The population estimates are McEvedy's.

McEvedy usually uses threshold population estimates—minima, not ranges. These mask population leaps and collapses between thresholds, and above the highest threshold. While such masking makes threshold estimates unsuitable for answering some questions (e.g., "Did Central Civilization ever decline?"), it leaves them perfectly suited to the question "Did Central Civilization ever *fall?*"

### *Was There an Ancient Fall?*

McEvedy's atlas page for 2250 BC shows three literate areas, one with four towns of 10,000–15,000 (Memphis, Heracleopolis, Abydos, Coptos), one with two (Harappa and Mohenjo-Daro), and one with six (Kish, Umma, Erech, Ur, Lagash, Susa). These are the areas usually assigned to Mesopotamian, Indus, and Egyptian civilization; in later maps, the Indus basin no longer shows cities, and one continuous literate area (i.e., Central

TABLE 2.2
*Ancient City Turnover Table*

| City | Year | | | | | | | |
|---|---|---|---|---|---|---|---|---|
| | −2250 | −1300 | −825 | −375 | −145 | 230 | 362 | 362 |
| Coptos | 10 | | | | | | | |
| Abydos | 10 | | | | | | | |
| Heracleopolis | 10 | 10 | | | | | | |
| Memphis | 10 | 10 | 30 | 30 | 30 | 10 | 10 | |
| Kish | 10 | | | | | | | |
| Umma | 10 | | | | | | | |
| Erech | 10 | | 10 | 10 | 10 | 10 | | |
| Ur | 10 | 10 | 10 | | | | | |
| Lagash | 10 | | | | | | | |
| Susa | 10 | 10 | 10 | 10 | | | | |
| Harappa | 10 | | | | | | | |
| Mohenjo-Daro | 10 | | | | | | | |
| Thebes (Egypt) | | 10 | 10 | 10 | | | | |
| Avaris | | 10 | | | | | | |
| Lachish | | 10 | | | | | | |
| Hazor | | 10 | | | | | | |
| Damascus | | 10 | 10 | 10 | 10 | 10 | 10 | |
| Byblos | | 10 | | | | | | |
| Ugarit | | 10 | | | | | | |
| Aleppo | | 10 | 10 | 10 | 10 | | | |
| Carchemish | | 10 | 10 | | | | | |
| Hattusas | | 10 | 10 | | | | | |
| Assur | | 10 | 10 | | | | | |
| Babylon | | 10 | 30 | 30 | 10 | | | |
| Nippur | | 10 | | | | | | |
| Larsa | | 10 | | | | | | |
| Tanis | | | 10 | 10 | 10 | 10 | | |
| Gaza | | | 10 | | | | | |
| Samaria | | | 10 | | | | | |
| Tyre | | | 30 | 10 | 10 | 10 | 10 | |
| Sidon | | | 10 | 10 | 10 | 10 | | |
| Hama | | | 10 | | | | | |
| Nineveh | | | 30 | | | | | |
| Nimrud | | | 30 | | | | | |
| Sais | | | | 10 | | | | |
| Harran | | | | 10 | | | | |
| Ecbatana/Hamadan | | | | 10 | | | | |
| Rayy | | | | 10 | 10 | 10 | 30 | 25 |
| Persepolis/Istakhr | | | | 10 | 10 | 30 | 30 | 25 |
| Rhodes | | | | 10 | 30 | 10 | | |
| Miletus | | | | 10 | | | | |

*(continues)*

TABLE 2.2
*(Continued)*

| City | \-2250 | \-1300 | \-825 | \-375 | \-145 | 230 | 362 | 362 |
|---|---|---|---|---|---|---|---|---|
| Sardes | | | | 10 | 10 | 10 | 10 | |
| Byzantium/Constantinople | | | | 10 | 10 | 10 | 90 | 75 |
| Athens | | | | 30 | 30 | 30 | 10 | |
| Corinth | | | | 30 | | 10 | | |
| Thebes (Greece) | | | | 10 | | | | |
| Sparta | | | | 10 | | | | |
| Syracuse | | | | 30 | 10 | 10 | 10 | |
| Messene | | | | 10 | | | | |
| Gela | | | | 10 | | | | |
| Carthage | | | | 30 | | 30 | 30 | 25 |
| Utica | | | | 10 | 10 | 10 | 10 | |
| Tarentum | | | | 10 | | | | |
| Naples | | | | 10 | 10 | 10 | 10 | |
| Capua | | | | 10 | 10 | 10 | | |
| Rome | | | | 10 | 90 | 90 | 90 | 75 |
| Ptolemais | | | | | 10 | 10 | 10 | |
| Alexandria | | | | | 90 | 90 | 90 | 75 |
| Cyrene | | | | | 10 | 10 | | |
| Petra | | | | | 10 | 10 | | |
| Apamea (Syria) | | | | | 10 | 10 | 10 | |
| Laodicea (Syria) | | | | | 10 | 10 | 10 | |
| Antioch | | | | | 90 | 90 | 90 | 75 |
| Edessa | | | | | 10 | 10 | 10 | |
| Seleucia | | | | | 30 | 30 | 30 | 25 |
| Charax | | | | | 10 | | | |
| Hecatompylus/Damghan | | | | 10 | 10 | 10 | | |
| Merv | | | | | 10 | 10 | 10 | |
| Balkh | | | | | 10 | 10 | 10 | |
| Ephesus | | | | | 10 | 30 | 10 | |
| Smyrna | | | | | 10 | 30 | 10 | |
| Pergamum | | | | | 10 | 30 | 10 | |
| Nicaea | | | | | 10 | 10 | 10 | |
| Delos | | | | | 10 | | | |
| Puteoli | | | | | 10 | 10 | | |
| Antinoopolis | | | | | | 10 | 10 | |
| Caesarea | | | | | | 10 | 10 | |
| Jerash | | | | | | 10 | | |
| Palmyra | | | | | | 30 | | |
| Cyrrhus | | | | | | 10 | 10 | |
| Hatra | | | | | | 30 | | |
| Isfahan | | | | | | 10 | 10 | |

*(continues)*

TABLE 2.2
*(Continued)*

| City | Year | | | | | | | |
|------|--------|--------|------|------|------|-----|-----|-----|
| | −2250 | −1300 | −825 | −375 | −145 | 230 | 362 | 362 |
| Darabjird | | | | | | 10 | 10 | |
| Tarsus | | | | | | 10 | 10 | |
| Iconium | | | | | | 10 | 10 | |
| Apamea (Anatolia) | | | | | | 10 | 10 | |
| Laodicea (Anatolia) | | | | | | 10 | | |
| Cyzicus | | | | | | 10 | 30 | 25 |
| Salonica | | | | | | 10 | | |
| Ceptis Magna | | | | | | 10 | | |
| Beneventum | | | | | | 10 | 10 | |
| Ostia | | | | | | 10 | | |
| Padua | | | | | | 10 | | |
| Verona | | | | | | 10 | 10 | |
| Milan | | | | | | 10 | 30 | 25 |
| Trier | | | | | | 10 | 30 | 25 |
| London | | | | | | 10 | 10 | |
| Autun | | | | | | 10 | | |
| Lyons | | | | | | 10 | | |
| Nimes | | | | | | 10 | | |
| Narbonne | | | | | | 10 | 10 | |
| New Carthage | | | | | | 10 | 10 | |
| Cadiz | | | | | | 10 | 10 | |
| Pelusium | | | | | | | 10 | |
| Jerusalem | | | | | | | 10 | |
| Scythopolis | | | | | | | 10 | |
| Nisibis | | | | | | | 10 | |
| Ctesiphon | | | | | | | 10 | |
| Jundi Shapur | | | | | | | 10 | |
| Ahwaz | | | | | | | 10 | |
| Jur | | | | | | | 10 | |
| Nishapur | | | | | | | 10 | |
| Nicomedia | | | | | | | 10 | |
| Aquileia | | | | | | | 10 | |
| Mainz | | | | | | | 10 | |
| Metz | | | | | | | 10 | |
| Vienne | | | | | | | 10 | |
| Count | 12 | 18 | 18 | 32 | 39 | 65 | 58 | 11 |
| Minimum Total | 120 | 180 | 280 | 440 | 730 | 1090 | 1040 | 475 |

SOURCE:  McEvedy (1967).

*(continues)*

TABLE 2.2
*(Continued)*

Cities are those which appear in the Northwest Old World Maps in Colin McEvedy's *Penguin Atlas of Ancient History* (1967). Numbers (10, 30, 90) are population thresholds—estimated minimum population per city, in thousands, per McEvedy's three-category symbolism. 'Count' is total number of cites in all 3 classes in the map-year. 'Minimum total' is the sum of all thresholds, therefore a minimum total urban population for the entire Northwest Old World in the map-year.

The second column for AD 362 omits the smallest class of cities, and uses slightly lower estimated minima for the other two groups. Its count and minimum total are more comparable to the following table, for McEvedy's *Penguin Atlas of Medieval History* (1961), which shows only cities above thresholds of 25,000 and 75,000 (vs. the *Ancient* thresholds of 10,000, 30,000 and 90,000).

For 2250 BC, Coptos, Abydos, Heracleopolis, and Memphis are assigned to Egyptian civilization; Harappa and Mohenjo-Daro to Indus civilization; and all other cities to Mesopotamian civilization. From 1300 BC on, all cities mentioned are assigned to Central Civilization. Until AD 1028, all urbanized areas of Central Civilization are probably on McEvedy's maps; after that, Central Civilization's frontier probably passes the map edge in India, and perhaps in Central Asia, so some qualified threshold cities may be omitted from these tables.

TABLE 2.3
*Medieval City Turnover Table*

| City | 528 | 737 | 1028 | 1212 | 1478 |
|---|---|---|---|---|---|
| Alexandria | 75 | 25 | | | |
| Antioch | 75 | 25 | 25 | 25 | |
| Ctesiphon | 25 | | | | |
| Hamadan | 25 | 25 | 25 | 25 | |
| Istakhr | 25 | 25 | | | |
| Rayy | 25 | | | | |
| Constantinople | 75 | 75 | 75 | 75 | 75 |
| Salonika | 25 | 25 | 25 | 25 | 25 |
| Rome | 25 | 25 | | 25 | 25 |
| Carthage | 25 | | | | |
| Milan | 25 | | | 25 | 25 |
| Damascus | | 25 | 25 | 25 | 25 |
| Aleppo | | 25 | 25 | 25 | 25 |
| Kufa | | 25 | | | |
| Wasit | | 25 | 25 | | |
| Basra | | 25 | 25 | 25 | 25 |
| Merv | | 25 | | 25 | |
| Venice | | 25 | 25 | 75 | 75 |
| Kairouan | | 25 | | | |
| Cairo | | | 75 | 75 | 75 |
| Baghdad | | | 75 | 75 | 25 |
| Isfaham | | | 25 | 25 | 25 |
| Shiraz | | | 25 | 25 | 25 |

*(continues)*

TABLE 2.3
*(Continued)*

| City | Year 528 | 737 | 1028 | 1212 | 1478 |
|------|------|------|------|------|------|
| Siraf | | | 25 | 25 | |
| Nishapur | | | 25 | 25 | 25 |
| Herat | | | 25 | 25 | 25 |
| Bukhara | | | 25 | 25 | 25 |
| Palermo | | | 25 | 25 | 25 |
| Mahdia | | | 25 | 25 | |
| Cordova | | | 25 | | |
| Seville | | | 25 | 25 | 25 |
| Fez | | | 25 | 25 | 25 |
| Urganj | | | | 25 | 25 |
| Naples | | | | 25 | 25 |
| Florence | | | | 25 | 25 |
| Genoa | | | | 25 | 25 |
| Paris | | | | 25 | 25 |
| Cologne | | | | 25 | 25 |
| Novgorod | | | | 25 | 25 |
| Tabriz | | | | | 75 |
| Khiva | | | | | 25 |
| Tunis | | | | | 25 |
| Bologna | | | | | 25 |
| Verona | | | | | 25 |
| Barcelona | | | | | 25 |
| Granada | | | | | 25 |
| London | | | | | 25 |
| Ghent | | | | | 25 |
| Bruges | | | | | 25 |
| Antwerp | | | | | 25 |
| Brussels | | | | | 25 |
| Lubeck | | | | | 25 |
| Moscow | | | | | 25 |
| Count | 11 | 15 | 22 | 30 | 38 |
| Minimum Total | 425 | 425 | 700 | 950 | 1250 |

SOURCE:    McEvedy (1967).

Civilization) combines and expands the formerly separate Egyptian and Mesopotamian literate areas.

McEvedy's first map that covers Central Civilization, as I have defined it, is that for 1300 BC. It shows 18 urban centers that meet or exceed the 10,000 population threshold, 14 of them for the first time (8 prior qualifiers having vanished from the map). The same number, 18, appears in 825 BC, though it once more conceals considerable turnover: 8 cities having fallen below the threshold and 8 others (including one returnee, Ur) having risen above it. Furthermore, by 825, 5 cities—Babylon, Nineveh, Nimrud, Tyre, Memphis—have exceeded a second threshold of 30,000 population.

In 375 BC there are 32 centers, 22 of them new, 8 old ones again having fallen out of the lists. Six exceed 30,000 (Memphis, Babylon, Athens, Corinth, Syracuse, Carthage). Another rank-level (90,000–150,000+) is added in 145 BC, when we find 3 first-rankers (Rome, Antioch, Alexandria), 5 second-rankers (30,000+), and 31 third-rankers (10,000–15,000+); 19 cities are newly added to the list, 11 have fallen out, for a total of 39. In AD 230 we see the same 3 first-rankers, 10 second-rankers, and 52 third-rankers, for a total of 65; 28 are new-added, 2 (Corinth and Carthage) reappear, 4 drop out. AD 362 concludes McEvedy's "Ancient" sequence, showing 4 first-rankers (Constantinople is added), 7 second-rankers, and 47 third-rankers, 58 in all; 14 new cities qualify, 21 lose standing.

These data are tabulated below, along with a minimum urban population for the mapped area as a whole, estimated from the thresholds.

|  | –2250 | –1300 | –825 | –375 | –145 | 230 | 362 |
|---|---|---|---|---|---|---|---|
| Rank 1 | 0 | 0 | 0 | 0 | 3 | 3 | 4 |
| Rank 2 | 0 | 0 | 5 | 6 | 5 | 10 | 7 |
| Rank 3 | 12 | 18 | 13 | 26 | 31 | 53 | 47 |
| All ranks | 12 | 18 | 18 | 32 | 39 | 64 | 58 |
| Entries | 12 | 14 | 8 | 22 | 19 | 30 | 14 |
| Exits | 0 | 8 | 8 | 8 | 11 | 4 | 21 |
| Minimum population in thousands | 120 | 180 | 280 | 440 | 730 | 1090 | 1040 |

If the data between these snapshots could be determined by interpolation (they cannot), we would confidently assert that there is no sign of any ancient fall of civilization except in the Indus basin, and in particular no sign of any fall of Central Civilization. There is plenty of evidence of local collapse (shown by the exit data). Granted this, and granted that there is a general setback between AD 230 and 362, still we find *civilization* always present—there is no sign of a cityless epoch.

Still, the snapshots do not reflect smooth trends. Does this fact offer any prospect that researchers will be able to find a collapse? It is incredible that the 43 cities which appear on both the AD 230 and AD 362 lists will be shown by closer research to have been abandoned and refounded in that interval. The longer interval from 1300 to 825 BC offers a bit more hope for the hypothesis of a fall: still one doubts that all 9 cities which appear on both lists—Babylon, Memphis, Ur, Susa, Egyptian Thebes, Damascus, Aleppo, Carchemish, Assur—will be found to have *simultaneously* been reduced below 10,000 (and no substitute centers founded), and then all resurrected and repopulated later in the half-millennium. It seems more likely that Central Civilization will be found to have persisted, even if wounded and reduced, throughout its Iron Age troubles. If so, there was no ancient fall.

### *Was There a Medieval Fall?*

Perhaps the Dark Ages offer more hope for the civilizational pessimist. The data are reclassified: McEvedy's *Medieval* atlas eliminates the third-rank cities, and changes the thresholds for the first and second ranks to 75,000 and 25,000 respectively. (By dropping the third-rankers from the AD 362 *Ancient* list, we can establish an approximate connection, but not an exact parallelism, between the two data sets.) In the medieval collection, we see 3 first-rankers (Constantinople, Antioch, Alexandria) and 8 second-rankers in AD 528; 1 (Constantinople alone) and 14 in 737; 3 (adding Baghdad and Cairo) and 19 in 1028; 4 (adding Venice) and 26 in 1212; 6 (dropping Baghdad, adding Milan, Paris, and Tabriz) and 31 in 1478. A fuller tabulation follows:

| | 362 | 528 | 737 | 1028 | 1212 | 1478 |
|---|---|---|---|---|---|---|
| Rank 1 | 4 | 3 | 1 | 3 | 4 | 6 |
| Rank 2 | 7 | 8 | 14 | 19 | 26 | 31 |
| Both ranks | 11 | 11 | 15 | 22 | 30 | 38 |
| Entries | n/a | 2 | 8 | 13 | 10 | 14 |
| Exits | n/a | 2 | 4 | 6 | 2 | 6 |
| Minimum population in thousands | 475 | 425 | 425 | 700 | 950 | 1250 |

Once again, there is plenty of evidence of local setbacks to civilization in the exit data. There is evidence of a general setback to urban population between 362 and 528, and of a setback to the larger cities between 362 and 737. Civilization continues in the Northwest Old World; Central Civilization therefore remains continuously in existence. There is a medieval decline; but there is no medieval fall.

## Rome's Fall Versus Civilization's Fall

Thus, however far Rome fell, its fall was not that of the civilization in which it had a place; not even remotely. Indeed, Rome remains on McEvedy's atlas pages as a second-rank demographic and economic center through AD 737, by which time it is really on the far western fringe of Central Civilization's city-collection (which includes Venice, Salonika, Constantinople, Antioch, Aleppo, Hamadan, Merv, Istakhr, Basra, Wasit, Kufa, Damascus, Alexandria, and Kairouan). The disappearance of Rome from McEvedy's next economic page, AD 1028, is no more momentous than the departure of Merv, Istakhr, Kufa, Alexandria, and Kairouan, and is more than compensated by the addition of Baghdad and Cairo, not to mention Bukhara, Nishapur, Herat, Shiraz, Isfahan, Siraf, Mahdia, Palermo, Seville, Cordova, and Fez. Westerners may not concur; but after all, Rome does return to the following map! Melancholy indeed its epoch of desolation and eclipse (the possible but unsolicited opinions of Roman gardeners, swineherds, even dung beetles to the contrary notwithstanding), but when it fell as it fell no *civilization* fell; one city alone fell.

## Continuity of Northwest Old World Civilization

What is true of Rome's fall is true of the fall of other cities. Each fall (from one rank to another, or out of the list entirely) could have been horrifying and tragic. Some surely were, those of Hazor, Nineveh, Nimrud, Tyre, Babylon, Corinth, Syracuse, Carthage, and Baghdad being notorious among them.

But these seem to have been *local* catastrophes, balanced or more than balanced elsewhere within or at the edge of the urbanized area. Other Egyptian, Mesopotamian, and Syrian cities remained or rose when their neighbors fell 2250–825 BC; semiperipheral Mediterranean cities rose while Middle East core cities fell 825–375 BC; Rome, Rhodes, Rayy, Seleucia, Antioch, Alexandria rose while Carthage, Syracuse, Corinth, Babylon declined 375–145 BC; Constantinople rose as Rome fell, Tabriz rose—and semiperipheral Paris, Milan, and Venice rose—as Baghdad fell. This is a picture of turnover, *not* of collapse and rebirth, at a civilizational level.

In these pictures, then, one need find no general fall in the Northwest Old World. There are local falls, and general setbacks; but these underlie a general pattern of growth. There is no empirically persuasive evidence that civilization in the Northwest Old World *ever* fell, and plenty of reason to suspect that it *never* fell.

So if we apply consistently the rule that no multiurban society has ended its history as a civilization until all its cities are destroyed or depopulated, then we have no tolerable warrant for accepting the epochs of succession, nor indeed most of the successions, in the lists of Toynbee and Quigley.

Given our definition of civilizations, there appears to be no greater persuasiveness to Quigley's than to Toynbee's original, or to Toynbee's original than to his revised list of Northwest Old World civilizations. I suggest an Alexandrine solution to the Gordian problem, namely the . . .

## Recognition of Central Civilization as a Whole

From the growing together of the Egyptian and Mesopotamian urbanized areas—civilizations—in the mid-second millennium BC there has been one and only one civilization in the Northwest Old World.

It would be parochial and mistaken to label that civilization by the nomenclatures of any of the nations that have successively populated, of the states that have successively dominated, or of the regions that have successively centered it.

At this moment, in this place, and in this culture, it seems not mistaken, and not too parochial, to call it Central Civilization.

## The World Economy of Central Civilization

A world system will certainly have a world economy associated with it, and it is worthwhile trying to describe such an economy, and seek theoretical assimilation of the description. Terminology adequate to describe holistically the economic structure of a civilization does not yet exist. It cannot be produced simply by adapting and generalizing "macroeconomic" terminology suited to describe the economy of a state or the economic institutions of a culture, since a civilization is neither a state nor a culture. World economies do not appear to be characterized by sufficiently homogeneous class systems, property systems, production relations, divisions of labor, or instruments of expansion, to make holistic Marxian, Wallersteinian, or Quigleyan characterizations very revealing. There are coexisting and contradictory property types rather than a prevailing property type, coexisting and inconsistent class structures rather than a prevailing class structure, heterogeneous divisions of labor, and several competing instruments of expansion.

At this moment it is probably more useful to characterize the sorts of empirical data which a satisfactory theory of world economy must assimilate. The city tables (Tables 2.2 and 2.3) describe one very salient feature of the world economy of Central Civilization, for those years during which it was confined to the Northwest Old World, that is, about 1500 BC to about

TABLE 2.4

*Traded Goods in the Northwest Old World*

| Commodity | -2250 | -1300 | -825 | -375 | -145 | 230 | 362 | 528 | 737 | 1028 | 1212 | 1478 |
|---|---|---|---|---|---|---|---|---|---|---|---|---|
| Gold | ■ | ■ | ■ | ■ | ■ | ■ | ■ | ■ | ■ | ■ | ■ | ■ |
| Silver | ■ | ■ | ■ | ■ | ■ | ■ | ■ | ■ | ■ | ■ | ■ | ■ |
| Copper | ■ | ■ | ■ | ■ | ■ | ■ | ■ | ■ | ■ | ■ | ■ | ■ |
| Ivory | ■ | ■ | ■ | ■ | ■ | ■ | ■ | ■ | ■ | ■ | ■ | ■ |
| Timber | ■ | ■ | ■ | ■ | ■ | ■ | ■ | ■ | ■ | ■ | ■ | ■ |
| Granite | ■ | ■ | | | | | | | | | | |
| Dates | ■ | ■ | | | | | | | | | | |
| Tin | ■ | ■ | ■ | ■ | ■ | ■ | ■ | ■ | ■ | ■ | ■ | ■ |
| Iron | ■ | ■ | ■ | ■ | ■ | ■ | ■ | ■ | ■ | ■ | ■ | ■ |
| Faience | ■ | ■ | ■ | ■ | ■ | ■ | ■ | | | | | |
| Glass | | ■ | ■ | ■ | ■ | ■ | ■ | | | | | |
| Linen | | ■ | ■ | ■ | ■ | ■ | ■ | | | | | |
| Papyrus | | ■ | ■ | ■ | ■ | ■ | ■ | | ■ | | | |
| Resins | | ■ | ■ | ■ | ■ | ■ | ■ | ■ | ■ | | | |
| Amber | | | | | ■ | ■ | ■ | ■ | ■ | ■ | ■ | ■ |
| Spices | | | | | ■ | ■ | ■ | ■ | ■ | ■ | ■ | ■ |
| Textiles | | | | | ■ | ■ | ■ | | | ■ | ■ | ■ |
| Wool | | | | ■ | ■ | ■ | ■ | | | ■ | ■ | ■ |
| Mercury | | | | | | | | | | | | ■ |

Fish
Wheat
Oil
Wine
Pottery
Furs
Metalwork
Silk
Lead
Slaves
Sugar
Beer
Tallow
Honey
Wax
Paper
Salt
Fruit
Coal

Count

27  25  23  13  9  21  21  20  21  17  14  12  6

The data reflect mention of the commodity in question on one or more of the trade maps in Colin McEvedy's *Penguin Atlas of Medieval History* (1961) and *Penguin Atlas of Ancient History* (1967). The Ancient (2250 BC–AD 362) and Medieval (AD 528–1478) series are not fully comparable, so that the significance of the fall-off between 362 and 528 is not self-evident.

AD 1500. McEvedy and Jones (1978) present population data which can also be mapped onto civilizations, and also demand theoretical rendition.

Another sort of civilizational economic data is also to be found in McEvedy's *Ancient* and *Medieval* map series. The economic "snapshots" also contain useful information about trade: sources, sinks, routes, and nodes. And important trade commodities are mentioned for each mapped year: the commodity pattern is summarized in Table 2.4.

We have clearly only just begun the theoretically salient description of Central Civilization's world economy. The following propositions are offered in an impressionistic spirit, as descriptions of the Central world economy inspired by, but not entirely derived from, a contemplation of McEvedy's maps, and of the various (Quigleyan, Marxian, Wallersteinian) macrohistorical-macroeconomic institutional typologies.

1. Extracivilizational as well as intracivilizational trade characterized Central Civilization's Egyptian and Mesopotamian predecessors, and Central Civilization itself from its inception until its incorporation of the globe.
2. The borders and cities of Central Civilization expanded preferentially toward commodity sources, but not always quickly, effectively, or uniformly.
3. World-economic commodities have tended strongly to be elite goods—luxury food, clothing, shelter, and display items—along with the trade tools of elite-supporting soldiers and bureaucrats (weapon-metal, paper for record-keeping).
4. Early trade in precious metals may, and coinage does, imply the development of mobile free persons, merchant classes, and economic versus politico-military elites, characterized by private property in portable wealth.
5. The entry into world economy of fish, wheat, oil and wine, suggests mass consumption driven either by political redistribution to hire the loyalty of armed men, clients, voters, etc.) or by markets, probably varyingly by both. Luxury goods may also have spread more widely through the social structure.
6. The general trend over time is clearly toward a continuing increase in the number and variety of commodities traded in the world economy. Within this trend there are temporary and permanent commodity dropouts, shifts in regional contributions, epochs of faster and slower commodity increase; but the trend remains.
7. There is as yet discernible no clear increase in the per capita wealth or living standards of the median individual over the three (premodern!) millennia covered. It appears that increased production is mostly utilized to increase total population and total urban population. The aggregate wealth of the wealthiest strata (typically politically rather than economically defined) must have increased, but it is not clear that the per capita wealth of those strata also increased. Modernization is another story.
8. It is an interesting fact, and one worth reflecting on, not just a given, that Central Civilization has never yet been completely penetrated by any particu-

lar "instrument of expansion" (in the Quigleyan sense) or "mode of production" (in the Marxian sense).

9.  Whatever may be true for state and local economies, it is not correct at any time to describe the world economy of Central Civilization as fundamentally feudal, or slave, or hydraulic, or free-peasant, or communal, or corporate, or hierocratic; nor is it fundamentally, in the Wallersteinian sense, either a "world-economy" or a "world-empire."

10. The apparent reason why the world economy of Central Civilization has never been fully statist is that the universal states of Central Civilization have been either short-lived, with their extraction capabilities confined to the civilizational core, or tolerant of private property and merchant classes.

11. The apparent reason why the world economy of Central Civilization has never been fully capitalist (private-propertarian, individualist, marketive) is the unbroken prominence of the political state, based on force, and of political-military-religious elites based on ground rents, taxes, and extraction by force.

12. For whatever reason, the Central economy is at all times a mixed political economy, embodying trade and war, coercion and bargaining, the one few-and-many. The balance shifts with time, scale, region, commodity.

13. The balance shifts more toward "capitalism" (without ever coming close) as states are small, weak and numerous, more toward "statism" as they are few, strong and large.

14. Local economies and short-range trade probably account for most economic activity most of the time, with the extraction of food from each city's hinterland and its distribution to the city population of primary importance.

15. The core/semiperiphery distinction is not that of a straightforward division of labor between political coercion and economic supply, or between primary and higher-tech products; but both divisions are notably present.

16. It is the politico-military predominance of the core, not any purely economic differentiation or "unequal exchange" tradition, that mainly accounts for the tendency for the core to drain the semiperiphery: loot, tribute, taxes, price controls, confiscations, trade route closures, and enforced monopolies are primarily political ventures.

17. A significant fraction of primary products come from within the core, from the hinterlands of core cities.

18. Citification, and eventually core status, tends to move toward major semiperipheral supply sources.

19. One useful indicator of the statist/capitalist balance in the civilization might be the balance between cities of the same size that are state capitals (i.e., power-maintained) and those that are commercial centers (i.e., trade-maintained).

20. There is no clear evidence of an endogenously economic general crisis or collapse ever having occurred in the Central world economy, although there have been city-level and state-level disasters, and system-wide periods of setback and stagnation, usually deriving from politico-military events.

21. Wherever it is possible to map the distribution of wealth in Central Civilization, inequality prominently appears: by city, by region, by political power,

by inheritance, in law, by age and family status, and by gender. The several inequalities do not appear to be reducible to any one fundamental root inequality.

22. The basic expansive process in Central Civilization appears to be circularly causal, dependent upon the presence of an unpopulated or underpopulated geoeconomic periphery and a Malthusian pressure: population expands; more and larger and more dispersed cities with more populous hinterlands extend and intensify settlement; there is greater division of labor and specialization; sufficient demand arises to mobilize new products or longer routes to more distant sources; total production rises; increased production mainly serves to support an enlarged population; etc.

There is plenty of room for theory and observation, dialectic and eristic, in the contemplation of the world economies of Central and other civilizations. One may also want to consider the Old World ecumenical macroeconomy, a multicivilizational structure which apparently provided the highest-level, largest-scale economic order until the global reach of Central Civilization, as the evolving context of the world economies of the various Eurasian civilizations linked by the silk, spice, slave, gold, and ivory trade.

TABLE 2.5
*States Systems and Universal Empires in Central Civilization*

| States Systems | Notable States | Duration |
|---|---|---|
| Pre-Assurbanapal c. 1500–663 BC | Egypt, Mitanni, Hittites, Elam, Babylon, Assyria, Urartu, Damascus, Israel, Tyre, Judah, Ethiopia, Media, Nubia | 837 |
| Pre-Darius 652–525 BC | Assyria, Armenia, Elam, Babylonia, Media Anshan, Persia, Lydia, Egypt, Libya, Ionians, Judah, Tyre, Meroe | 127 |
| Pre-Augustan 316–20 BC | Syracuse, Carthage, Macedonia, Rome, Seleucids, Egypt, Pontus, Armenia, Parthia | 296 |
| Post-Roman AD 235–present | Rome, Persia, Byzantium, Arab Caliphate, Frankish Empire, Holy Roman Empire, Mongol Khanate, Ottoman Sultanate, Spain, Austria, France, Britain, Germany, Japan, Russia, America | 1748 |

| Universal Empires | Span | Duration |
|---|---|---|
| Neo-Assyrian | 663–652 BC | 11 |
| Persian-Macedonian | 525–316 BC | 209 |
| Roman | 20 BC–AD 235 | 255 |

TABLE 2.6
*Dominant Powers in Central Civilization*
*(since the fall of the Roman Universal Empire)*

| | Dominant Power | Florescence | Leaders | Opponents[a] | References[b] The Atlas of World History | References[b] Penguin Atlas |
|---|---|---|---|---|---|---|
| 1. | Byzantine Empire | AD 527–565 | Justinian | Goths, Vandals, Lombards, Slavs, Avars | vol. 1 138–139 | Medieval 406–737 |
| 2. | Arab Caliphate | 632–750 | Orthodox and Omayyad caliphs | Franks, Byzantines, Visigoths, Persians | vol. 1 134–137 | Medieval 628–888 |
| 3. | Frankish Empire | 714–814 | Charles Martel ("Hammer"), Charlemagne | Saxons, Lombards, Slavs, Avars, Arabs | vol. 1 120–125 | Medieval 650–888 |
| 4. | Holy Roman Empire (First German Reich) | 919–1254 | Saxon, Salian, and Hohenstaufen dynasties | Roman papacy, German dukes, Lombard Italian cities, Franks, France, Slavs, Magyars, Vikings, Danes, Arabs, Byzantines | vol. 1 142–149 164–165 170–173 | Medieval 923–1278 |
| 5. | Mongol Khanate | 1196–1405 | Genghis Khan, Ogodei, Batu, Subotai, Mongka, Hulagu, Kublai Khan, Tamerlane | Chinese, Japanese, Vietnamese, Persians, Slavs, Turks, Egyptian Mameluks | vol. 1 178–179 210–211 | Medieval 1230–1478 |
| 6. | Ottoman Turkish Sultanate | 1413–1571 | Mohamed I the Restorer, Murad II, Mohamed II the Conqueror, Selim I the Grim, Suleiman II the Magnificant | Papacy, Spain, Venice, Byzantines, Mamelukes, Mongols, Serbs, Bulgars, Crusaders, Albania, Austria, Hungary, Persia | vol. 1 206–209 | Medieval 1360–1478 Modern 1483–1559 |
| 7. | Spanish Empire | 1469–1598 | Ferdinand of Aragon, Isabella of Castille, Emperor Charles V, Philip II, Philip III | Holland, France, England, German Protestant states | vol. 1 186–187 224–225 236–237 242–247 | Medieval 1478 Modern 1483–1600 |

*(continues)*

TABLE 2.6
(Continued)

| | | | | References[b] | |
| Dominant Power | Florescence | Leaders | Opponents[a] | The Atlas of World History | Penguin Atlas |
|---|---|---|---|---|---|
| 8. Austrian Habsburg Empire | 1576–1648 | Rudolf II of Habsburg, Matthias, Ferdinand II, Ferdinand III | *France*, German Protestant states, Denmark, Sweden, Holland, England | vol. 1 250–255 | Modern 1483–1648 |
| 9. French (Bourbon) Monarchy | 1667–1713 | Louis XIV | Holland, *England*, Spain, *Austria*, Brandenburg-*Prussia*, Hanover, Portugal, Savoy | vol. 1 258–259 268–269 | Modern 1634–1715 |
| 10. French Revolutionary and Napoleanic Empire | 1792–1815 | Napoleon Bonaparte | *Britain*, French royalists, *Austria*, *Prussia, Russia*, the Netherlands, Sweden, *Spain*, Naples, Turkey, Portugal | vol. 2 16–39 | Modern 1797–1815 |
| 11. British Empire | 1642–1783 (or as late as 1920?) | Oliver Cromwell, William III of Orange, William Pitt the Elder, Robert Clive, Benjamin Disraeli, Joseph Chamberlain | America, *France*, Spain, Netherlands, *Germany* | vol. 1 266–267, 276–277, 282–283; vol. 2 12–13, 30–31, 96–99, 102–104, 132–133, 170–171, 189–199 | Modern 1715–1783 Recent pp. 2–63 |
| 12. German Empire (Second Reich) | 1861–1918 | Wilhelm I, Otto von Bismarck, Wilhelm II | *France, Britain, Russia, America*, etc. | vol. 2 74–83 108–109 132–133 | Recent pp. 2–63 |

| | | | Opponents[a] | The Atlas of World History[b] | Penguin Atlas[b] |
|---|---|---|---|---|---|
| 13. | German Third Reich | 1933–1945 | Adolf Hitler | *France, Britain, Russia, America, etc.* | Recent pp. 68–86 ... vol. 2 148–151, 154–157, 164–165, 182–183, 192–218 |
| 14. | Japanese Empire | 1895–1945 | Meiji, Taisho, and Showa Emperors; Gens. Tanaka, Tojo | *America, Britain,* China, *Russia,* etc. | vol. 2 114–115, 172–175, 216–217 |
| 15. | American Empire | 1898–1953 (or to 1975? or later?) | Theodore Roosevelt, W. Wilson, Franklin D. Roosevelt, H. S. Truman, Dean Acheson, George C. Marshall | *Spain, Germany, Japan, Russia,* N. Korea, N. Vietnam | vol. 2 92–93 116–117 127–137 176–177 218–219 222–224 234–241 |
| 16. | Soviet Russian Empire | 1917–? | V. I. Lenin, Josef Stalin | *Germany, America, Britain, France, Japan,* China, etc. | Recent pp. 62–90 ... vol. 2 140–143 188–189 198–199 214–215 226–228 230–245 252–257 |

[a]Opponents in italics (e.g., *Franks, Byzantines*) were themselves previously or later dominant powers.
[b]For *The Atlas of World History* see Kinder and Hilgemann (1975, 1978); for *Penguin Atlas* see McEvedy (1961, 1972, 1982).

## The World Political Process of Central Civilization

The fundamental political process in Central Civilization, as in others, appears to be twofold. First, there is an alternation between the states system organization and the universal state (see Table 2.5 and Wilkinson 1983). Second, within the more prevalent state-system form, there is a succession of dominant powers, states which advance toward universal empire, and then fall back to be replaced by others (see Table 2.6 and Wilkinson 1985, 1986) for the succession during the latest states-system of Central Civilization.

I have dealt previously with the nature of the civilizational political process (Wilkinson 1983, 1985, 1986). At present it is enough to say that a single social system ought to display a unitary political process, and that Tables 2.5 and 2.6 display such a process for Central Civilization.

## Conclusion

Conflict is a form of association; internally connected, heterogeneous, divided, conflicted entities may and do exist. If we choose a criterion of connectedness (vs. uniformity) in our definition of civilization, it has a profound effect on our rosters of civilizations. About half of the units customarily analyzed simply disappear.

The effect of applying a criterion of transactional connectedness is particularly drastic for the Northwest Old World. Where a criterion of uniformity would discover a collection of adjacent (e.g., "Western," "Orthodox," "Islamic") or successive (e.g., "Middle Eastern," "Greco-Roman," "Medieval," "Western") Northwest Old World civilizations, the transactional criterion replaces all of them with a single entity, one connected, heterogeneous, divided, conflicted system. This entity is justly labeled Central Civilization.

Central Civilization, born in the Near East about 3,500 years ago, and now grown to global scale, shows a long-term trend of steady geographic and demographic expansion, despite occasional declines and many local setbacks. Rome fell, many cities have fallen; Central Civilization never fell.

Central Civilization is the chief entity to which theories of class society, the social system, world economy, and world systems must apply if they are to apply at all. A suitable theoretical account of its economic process does not yet exist; one for its political process may. The political process of Central Civilization seems to have a closer relation to existing world-political theories than its economic process has to existing world economic theories.

NOTES

1. Conflict "binds antagonists . . . the very act of entering into conflict with an antagonist establishes relations where none may have existed before. Conflict is . . . a binding element between parties that may previously have stood in no relation to each other" (p. 121).

2. Conflict may lead "to the formation of associations and coalitions between previously unrelated parties," producing unifying bonds between the allies that "may lead to increasing cohesiveness and structuring of a social system" (p. 140), should "common values and norms develop in the course of struggling together" (p. 146).

3. War, for instance, "is indeed one of the means of establishing contact between groups" (p. 122). Where neither participant is totally destroyed, warfare "tends to lead to other forms of interaction," even to friendly interaction, and to "cross-fertilization of previously unrelated cultures" (p. 122). War may lead to the acquisition of knowledge about the initially unknown stranger (pp. 122–23), including a revelation of comparative strength which itself serves as the most effective deterrent to future conflict (p. 133).

4. Warfare "serves as a balancing mechanism which helps to maintain and consolidate societies." As between opponents, "in the course of conflict new rules are continuously created," norms and laws and rules established or extended (pp. 123–26). And conflict "helps to structure the larger social environment by assigning positions to the various subgroups within the system and by helping to define the power relations between them" (p. 155). Cf. Park: "Conflict tends to bring about an integration and a superordination and subordination of the conflict groups" (1941, p. 565).

5. And record-keeping/writing/money; evidence of production of surplus; specialists; classes; "hinterlands" belonging to each city, or to collections of cities; and so forth.

6. Philip Bagby (1958, pp. 167–68) recognizes a "Near-Eastern" civilization, but this is a different kettle of fish entirely; since Bagby defines a civilization as the largest distinctive super-culture, his "Near-Eastern" entity, which is Spengler's Magian, comes into existence about AD 1, coexists for a while with Egyptian and Classical cultures, and is now coexisting with still others.

*References*

Bagby, Philip. 1958. *Culture and History*. New York: Longmans Green.
Coser, Lewis A. 1956. *The Functions of Social Conflict*. New York: Free Press.
Gibbon, Edward. n.d. *The Decline and Fall of the Roman Empire*. Vol. III: *1185 AD–1453 AD*. New York: The Modern Library.
Kinder, Herman, and Werner Hilgemann. 1975. *The Atlas of World History, Vol. 1. Garden City*, NY: Doubleday/Anchor.
———. 1978. *The Atlas of World History*, Vol. 2. Garden City, NY: Doubleday/Anchor.
McEvedy, Colin. 1961. *Penguin Atlas of Medieval History*. New York: Penguin.
———. 1967. *Penguin Atlas of Ancient History*. New York: Penguin.

————. 1972. *Penguin Atlas of Modern History.* New York: Penguin.

————. 1982. *Penguin Atlas of Recent History.* New York: Penguin

McEvedy, Colin, and Richard Jones. 1978. *Atlas of World Population History.* New York: Penguin.

Park, Robert E. 1941. "The Social Function of War." *American Journal of Sociology* 46:551–70.

Quigley, Carroll. 1961. *The Evolution of Civilizations.* New York: Macmillan.

Simmel, Georg. 1955. *Conflict*, Trans. Kurt H. Wolff, and *The Web of Group Affiliations*, Trans. Reinhard Bendix. New York: The Free Press of Glencoe.

Toynbee, Arnold J. 1961. *A Study of History.* Vol. XII: *Reconsiderations.* Oxford: Oxford University Press.

Wilkinson, David. 1983. "Civilizations, States Systems and Universal Empires." Unpublished manuscript, University of California at Los Angeles.

————. 1984. "Encounters Between Civilizations: Coexistence, Fusion, Fission, Collision." Unpublished manuscript, University of California at Los Angeles.

————. 1985. "States Systems: Ethos and Pathos." Unpublished manuscript, University of California at Los Angeles.

————. 1986. "States Systems: Pathology and Survival." Unpublished manuscript, University of California at Los Angeles.

WILLIAM ECKHARDT ■

*Chapter Three*

# A Dialectical Evolutionary Theory of Civilizations, Empires, and Wars

A "dialectical evolutionary theory" tries to relate the concepts of civilization, empire, and war to one another in such a way that their interaction results in positive feedback loops leading them ever upward and onward in a spiraling motion, unless and until it leads them in the opposite direction by way of negative feedback loops which reverse the direction of the spiral. The theory is especially interested in what determines which direction these loops take, but this special part of the theory will receive more attention in future research. This article will concentrate on the more general relations between civilizations, empires, and wars.

In order to establish the relations between civilizations, empires, and wars, we have to find ways of measuring these variables. Then it will be simple enough to correlate these measures with one another, and to find out how much they vary together, if at all. We begin with civilizations, and then go on to empires and wars.

## Measuring Civilizations

Both Kroeber (1944) and Sorokin (1937–41) provided a means of measuring civilization. Their methods were similar in that they both counted the number of (mostly) men who had engaged in civilized or cultural activities to such an extent as to get themselves recognized in encyclopedias and textbooks for the quality of their accomplishments. Kroeber was more selective than Sorokin, counting only "geniuses," which he defined as "superior individuals" (pp. 7, 8), whose superiority was established by the consensus of encyclopedia and textbook authors (p. 23). Their activities included philosophy, science, grammar (philology), sculpture, painting, drama, and literature. These activities were pursued from 4000 BC to AD 1900 in five civilizations: Middle East (Egypt, Mesopotamia, and Islam), Far East (China and Japan), South Asia (mainly India), Greece and Rome, and the West (Europe).

Kroeber did not actually count these individuals, but he did identify them, making it possible to get a rough count for various regions at various times. I sorted Kroeber's seven cultural activities over the 49 centuries from 3000 BC to AD 1900, then logged them to correct for skewness, and then correlated them with one another. All of the correlations were significant at the .01 level of confidence, ranging from .43 between grammar and drama to .89 between painting and sculpture. They were all significantly correlated with time (as measured by centuries) from .64 (grammar) to .92 (literature), so that the number of geniuses in the world (as represented by the geographical regions of Europe, Far East, India, and Middle East) were increasing exponentially over these 49 centuries. When this correlation matrix was factor analyzed, a single factor emerged: Literature (.95), Century (.92), Science (.92), Sculpture (.89), Painting (.86), Philosophy (.85), Drama (.80), and Grammar (.75). Factor scores could be generated to provide a measure of world civilization, but the simple sum of the seven activities (as measured by the number of geniuses) will be quite adequate for the time being.

This sum was used to measure the rise and fall of civilizations in the four geographical regions of the world: Europe, Far East (China and Japan), India, and the Middle East (Egypt, Mesopotamia, and Islam). These four (logged) regions were significantly correlated with one another over these 49 centuries, except for Europe with the Middle East. They were all significantly correlated with time, but the Middle Eastern correlation was significant only at the .10 level of confidence. When this correlation matrix was factor analyzed, two factors were generated, the first of which was Far East (.98), Century (.96), India (.88), Europe (.84), and the Middle East (.29). The low loading of the Middle East on this factor shows that its pattern of rising and falling civilized activities (geniuses) was not so correlated with time (centuries) as the other three regions were, as shown in Table 3.1, where the Middle East provided the overwhelming majority of geniuses in the first two millennia from 3000 to 800 BC, when Europe took over for the most part until AD 500 followed by the Far East for a few centuries, then the Middle East prevailed for a few more centuries, until Europe took over again in the 12th century.

When the three non-European regions were added together, the sum of their geniuses was correlated .66 with the European sum, so that both Europe and the rest of the world (Asia) were significantly similar in the historical distribution of their geniuses. When all four regions were added

TABLE 3.1
*Kroeber's Geniuses*

| Century | Europe | Far East | India | Middle East | Non-Europe | Total | Europe (%) |
|---|---|---|---|---|---|---|---|
| −30 | 0 | 0 | 0 | 4 | 4 | 4 | 0 |
| −29 | 0 | 0 | 0 | 0 | 0 | 0 | |
| −28 | 0 | 0 | 0 | 3 | 3 | 3 | 0 |
| −27 | 0 | 0 | 0 | 4 | 4 | 4 | 0 |
| −26 | 0 | 0 | 0 | 2 | 2 | 2 | 0 |
| −25 | 0 | 0 | 0 | 4 | 4 | 4 | 0 |
| −24 | 0 | 0 | 0 | 0 | 0 | 0 | |
| −23 | 0 | 0 | 0 | 0 | 0 | 0 | |
| −22 | 0 | 0 | 0 | 0 | 0 | 0 | |
| −21 | 0 | 0 | 0 | 0 | 0 | 0 | |
| −20 | 0 | 0 | 0 | 9 | 9 | 9 | 0 |
| −19 | 0 | 0 | 0 | 6 | 6 | 6 | 0 |
| −18 | 0 | 0 | 0 | 6 | 6 | 6 | 0 |
| −17 | 1 | 0 | 0 | 2 | 2 | 3 | 33 |
| −16 | 1 | 0 | 0 | 2 | 2 | 3 | 33 |
| −15 | 1 | 0 | 0 | 2 | 2 | 3 | 33 |
| −14 | 1 | 0 | 0 | 2 | 2 | 3 | 33 |
| −13 | 0 | 0 | 0 | 9 | 9 | 9 | 0 |
| −12 | 0 | 0 | 0 | 1 | 1 | 1 | 0 |
| −11 | 0 | 0 | 0 | 0 | 0 | 0 | |
| −10 | 0 | 0 | 0 | 2 | 2 | 2 | 0 |
| −9 | 2 | 0 | 0 | 3 | 3 | 5 | 40 |
| −8 | 7 | 0 | 0 | 2 | 2 | 9 | 78 |
| −7 | 14 | 1 | 0 | 6 | 7 | 21 | 67 |
| −6 | 39 | 3 | 5 | 3 | 11 | 50 | 78 |
| −5 | 108 | 9 | 1 | 2 | 12 | 120 | 90 |
| −4 | 100 | 11 | 3 | 0 | 14 | 114 | 88 |
| −3 | 35 | 10 | 4 | 0 | 14 | 49 | 71 |
| −2 | 45 | 15 | 5 | 0 | 20 | 65 | 69 |
| −1 | 52 | 6 | 3 | 0 | 9 | 61 | 85 |
| 1 | 59 | 9 | 2 | 0 | 11 | 70 | 84 |
| 2 | 49 | 21 | 13 | 0 | 34 | 83 | 59 |
| 3 | 15 | 18 | 5 | 0 | 23 | 38 | 39 |
| 4 | 25 | 15 | 11 | 0 | 26 | 51 | 49 |
| 5 | 15 | 12 | 19 | 0 | 31 | 46 | 33 |
| 6 | 5 | 19 | 10 | 15 | 44 | 49 | 10 |
| 7 | 1 | 48 | 19 | 8 | 75 | 76 | 1 |
| 8 | 2 | 43 | 11 | 32 | 86 | 88 | 2 |
| 9 | 6 | 27 | 14 | 52 | 93 | 99 | 6 |
| 10 | 9 | 24 | 7 | 77 | 108 | 117 | 8 |
| 11 | 21 | 50 | 6 | 61 | 117 | 138 | 15 |
| 12 | 65 | 34 | 12 | 42 | 88 | 153 | 42 |
| 13 | 121 | 33 | 4 | 29 | 66 | 187 | 65 |
| 14 | 80 | 14 | 3 | 12 | 29 | 109 | 73 |
| 15 | 194 | 18 | 8 | 5 | 31 | 125 | 86 |
| 16 | 391 | 23 | 4 | 6 | 33 | 424 | 92 |
| 17 | 360 | 47 | 5 | 0 | 52 | 412 | 87 |
| 18 | 377 | 56 | 1 | 0 | 57 | 434 | 87 |
| 19 | 767 | 27 | 1 | 0 | 28 | 795 | 96 |
| Sum | 2,968 | 593 | 167 | 413 | 1,182 | 4,150 | 72 |

SOURCE: Kroeber (1944).

together (resulting in the same sum as the seven civilized activities), this provided a measure of world civilization, which is shown in the next to the last column of Table 3.1. Although the European and non-European *pattern* of civilized activities was similar, the same cannot be said about the *level* of their activities, where Europe produced more than twice as many geniuses as the rest of the civilized world during these 49 centuries: 72 percent of the total, as shown in the last column of the last row in Table 3.1.

Sorokin (1937–41, Vol. 4, pp. 328–29) also provided a measure of cultural values going back to 4000 BC, but the data were rather sketchy until the 11th century BC, and they were more Eurocentric than Kroeber's geniuses, since Europeans constituted 85 percent of the total. These data represented historical persons who were mentioned in the 9th edition of the *Encyclopedia Britannica*, which was published in 1875–89, as having made a notable contribution to one or more fields of culture, including statesmanship, philosophy, religion, literature, fine arts, miscellaneous, scholarship, science, music, and business. John V. Boldyreff gathered these data for his doctoral dissertation, but Sorokin is the most accessible reference for them. Each person was weighted by the number of lines used to describe his (mostly male) accomplishments. Only one figure was provided for the 4th millennium BC, another one for the 3rd millennium BC, and another one for the 15th century BC. After that, data were available for every 50 years from 1050 BC to AD 1849. Sorokin provided arithmetic averages of the 10 cultural areas previously listed, noting that "almost all 10 series move more or less alike and in a similar direction, parallel" (1937–41, Vol. 4, p. 352). In this respect Sorokin's 10 cultural activities were similar to Kroeber's 7 civilized activities: they all tended to rise and fall together.

However, as already noted, the historical persons in the 9th edition of the *Encyclopedia Britannica* were largely Europeans, so that the use of them to represent *world* civilization may be questionable. To test the validity of this procedure, I correlated the European scores (Sorokin 1937–41, Vol. 3, p. 516) with the non-European scores (total scores minus European scores) over the 49 centuries from 3000 BC to AD 1900. The correlation, when both scores were logged to correct for skewness, was .90, which showed that, regardless of the difference in *level*, the *pattern* of European scores was quite similar to that of non-European scores over these centuries, and consequently that this measure of world civilization was quite adequate for the purpose of measuring the relative civilization of these 49 centuries, although it might be inadequate for comparing European and non-European civilizations within any century or for all centuries taken together. The correlation between centuries and the total (logged) score was .92, showing a significant and exponential increase in the number of these historical persons over these centuries.

When Sorokin's historical persons were logged and correlated with Kroeber's (logged) geniuses, the correlation was .93, suggesting that either Kroeber's geniuses or Sorokin's historical persons could be used as a measure of world civilization. Kroeber's geniuses will be used in this article because they are less Eurocentric, and they provide a further breakdown of non-European civilizations which is not available in Sorokin's data.

Sorokin also provided a count of scientific discoveries and technological inventions (1937–41, Vol. 2, ch. 3), which could be used as a measure of European and world civilization, since they were correlated .89 with Sorokin's world civilization and .91 with Sorokin's European civilization. However, they will not be used in this article, because no breakdown outside of European civilization is possible with these data.

Naroll et al. (1971, p. 182), like Kroeber and Sorokin, "concluded that the counting of creative individuals was the most useful measure of the total creativity of the society to which they belonged at the period of time in which they lived." Naroll et al. used these counts of Kroeber's data to measure a civilization's creativity. I assume that these counts may be used as a measure of civilization itself. This assumption seems to be implied in the work of Kroeber and Sorokin. Kroeber's problem was to study "high cultural developments" (1944, p. 6). Individual geniuses were used as an index of these cultural developments. The curves of "different activities of [Egyptian] culture" (p. 240) were taken as rough indicators of "Egyptian civilization as a whole" (p. 241). Likewise, the Assyrian history of sculpture was "also the outline of the history of higher civilization in accentuated form" (p. 311). Sorokin referred to the weighted number of his historical persons as an indicator of the "total creativeness of cultural values" (1937–41, Vol. 4, p. 323), and again as an indicator of "cultural creativeness" (p. 325), so that Naroll's interpretation of Kroeber's data came closer to that of Sorokin than to that of Kroeber. My interpretation of Kroeber's data will follow that of Kroeber to the effect that the number of individual geniuses provide a measure of the height of civilization itself. It is quite possible that Naroll and Sorokin assumed implicitly that creativeness and civilization were synonymous terms or, at least, indicative of each other.

## Measuring Empires

Taagepera's (1978) imperial sizes will be used in this article as a measure of empires, by which Taagepera meant "any large sovereign political entity whose components are not sovereign" (p. 113). He measured empires in terms of square megameters, each one of which is equivalent to 386,000 square miles. Empires did not amount to much prior to 600 BC, when the Medes and the Persians introduced a degree of hierarchical bureaucracy (satrapy) unknown before in human history. Even from 500 BC to AD 1500, the "progress" in imperial sizes was not spectacular. Then there was another great leap into the modern period of history following AD 1600, which Taagepera attributed to the European industrial-communication revolution. History, however, clearly shows the rise and fall of civilizations and empires, not only once, but several times. Although the global picture is an ever upward spiral, so far, the regional pictures are full of falls and rises, as shown in Table 3.2.

Table 3.2 shows the rises and falls in eight regional empires, whose imperial sizes are summed in the last column, providing a measure of how much of the earth came under imperial control century by century. This sum shows that empires occupied very little of the earth up to and including the

TABLE 3.2
*Taagepera's Imperial Sizes*

| Century | Egypt | Mesopo-tamia | India | China | Turkey | Persia | Central Asia | Europe | World |
|---|---|---|---|---|---|---|---|---|---|
| −30 | 0.15 | 0.00 | | | | | | | 0.15 |
| −29 | 0.20 | 0.00 | | | | | | | 0.20 |
| −28 | 0.25 | 0.01 | | | | | | | 0.26 |
| −27 | 0.30 | 0.02 | | | | | | | 0.32 |
| −26 | 0.35 | 0.02 | | | | | | | 0.37 |
| −25 | 0.40 | 0.03 | | | | | | | 0.43 |
| −24 | 0.40 | 0.05 | 0.05 | | | | | | 0.50 |
| −23 | 0.20 | 0.60 | 0.10 | | | | | | 0.90 |
| −22 | 0.10 | 0.20 | 0.10 | | | | | | 0.40 |
| −21 | 0.10 | 0.03 | 0.15 | | | | | | 0.28 |
| −20 | 0.20 | 0.10 | 0.20 | | | | | | 0.50 |
| −19 | 0.50 | | 0.20 | 0.10 | | | | | 0.80 |
| −18 | 0.50 | | 0.30 | 0.45 | | | | | 1.25 |
| −17 | 0.25 | 0.45 | | 0.40 | | | | | 1.10 |
| −16 | 0.60 | 0.20 | | 0.40 | 0.10 | | | | 1.35 |
| −15 | 1.00 | 0.40 | | 0.50 | 0.15 | | | | 2.05 |
| −14 | 0.90 | 0.40 | | 0.65 | 0.20 | 0.10 | | | 2.25 |
| −13 | 1.00 | 0.25 | | 0.90 | 0.45 | 0.10 | | | 2.70 |
| −12 | 0.75 | 0.20 | | 1.10 | 0.40 | 0.20 | | | 2.65 |
| −11 | 0.60 | 0.35 | | 0.55 | 0.10 | | | | 1.60 |
| −10 | 0.40 | 0.15 | | 0.45 | | | | | 1.00 |
| −9 | 0.20 | 0.60 | | 0.35 | | | | | 1.15 |
| −8 | | 0.70 | | 0.25 | 0.20 | | | | 1.15 |
| −7 | 0.50 | 1.30 | | | 0.15 | | | | 3.10 |
| −6 | 0.65 | 0.60 | 0.50 | 0.10 | 0.50 | 5.50 | | | 7.85 |
| −5 | | 0.15 | 0.30 | 0.30 | | 5.50 | | | 6.25 |

(*continues*)

TABLE 3.2
*(Continued)*

| Century | Egypt | Mesopo-tamia | India | China | Turkey | Persia | Central Asia | Europe | World |
|---|---|---|---|---|---|---|---|---|---|
| -4 | | 0.20 | 1.00 | 0.50 | | 4.00 | | | 5.70 |
| -3 | | 1.20 | 3.50 | 1.30 | | 5.20 | 0.50 | 0.15 | 11.85 |
| -2 | | | 3.00 | 2.50 | | 3.30 | 5.70 | 0.65 | 15.15 |
| -1 | | | 1.50 | 6.20 | | 3.20 | 2.00 | 3.50 | 16.40 |
| 1 | | | 3.50 | 6.50 | | 2.50 | 1.50 | 4.40 | 18.40 |
| 2 | | | 1.20 | 5.70 | | 2.50 | | 4.40 | 13.80 |
| 3 | | | 1.30 | 5.50 | | 3.50 | | 4.40 | 14.70 |
| 4 | | | | 2.80 | | 3.50 | | 7.40 | 13.70 |
| 5 | | | 1.70 | 5.80 | | 3.50 | 1.00 | 5.90 | 17.90 |
| 6 | | | | 6.40 | 1.30 | 3.40 | 7.20 | 2.70 | 21.00 |
| 7 | | 9.00 | | 5.20 | | | 2.80 | 1.00 | 18.00 |
| 8 | | 11.00 | | 5.20 | | | 7.50 | 1.00 | 24.70 |
| 9 | | 4.50 | 1.00 | 3.00 | 1.00 | 2.00 | 4.70 | 2.30 | 18.50 |
| 10 | | 3.10 | | 3.00 | 1.00 | 2.30 | 5.00 | 2.60 | 17.00 |
| 11 | | 2.50 | | 3.00 | 4.00 | | 5.00 | 2.50 | 17.00 |
| 12 | | 3.30 | | 4.30 | | | 2.50 | | 10.10 |
| 13 | | 3.00 | 2.50 | 2.00 | | | 25.00 | | 32.70 |
| 14 | | 2.00 | 2.80 | 15.00 | | 4.00 | 8.00 | | 31.80 |
| 15 | | 3.00 | | 6.50 | 1.00 | 2.30 | 2.50 | 2.80 | 17.10 |
| 16 | | | 2.00 | 3.50 | 4.50 | | | 12.20 | 22.20 |
| 17 | | | 3.00 | 11.30 | 4.00 | | | 25.50 | 43.80 |
| 18 | | | 1.00 | 15.00 | 4.00 | | | 41.00 | 61.00 |
| 19 | | | | 13.50 | 5.00 | | | 83.50 | 102.00 |
| 20 | 1.00 | 0.43 | 4.00 | 9.70 | 1.00 | 1.65 | 1.56 | 101.00 | 120.35 |
| Sum | 11.55 | 49.05 | 34.90 | 149.90 | 29.05 | 59.40 | 82.66 | 308.90 | 725.41 |
| Avg | 0.43 | 1.07 | 1.29 | 3.84 | 1.45 | 2.58 | 4.86 | 15.44 | 14.51 |
| Std | 0.30 | 2.18 | 1.27 | 4.16 | 1.70 | 1.70 | 5.64 | 27.46 | 23.38 |

SOURCE: Taagepera (1978).
The largest size achieved by any empire in any century was entered in this table. For the few centuries (29th, 27th, and 26th BC) not included in Taagepera (1978), his data were interpolated. The imperial regions in this table closely followed Taagepera's "empire cores" (p. 116). Africa and America were omitted from this table because of the rare occurrence of data in these regions: Among the three largest empires, these included only Carthage in 500 BC, Ptolemee in the 3rd century BC, Mali in AD 1300, Inca in AD 1500, and Canada in the 20th century. Carthage and Ptolemee were included in Mesopotamia; Australia, Canada, and the United States were included in Europe; and Mali, Inca, Argentina, and Brazil were omitted entirely.

8th century BC. Imperial areas did not cover one percent of the earth's surface until the 16th century BC. In the 15th to 12th centuries BC, all of the imperial areas together constituted no more than two percent of the earth's surface, most of which was controlled by China and Egypt, after which imperial areas returned to the one percent level until the 7th century BC.

In the 6th century BC, less than 6 percent of the earth's surface was covered with empires. This grew to 95 percent in the 20th century AD. While some 94 percent of the earth was occupied by gatherers and hunters, farmers and herders, in 600 BC, there was only 5 percent of the earth so occupied in the 20th century AD, and virtually zero percent today. Self-sufficient primitive tribes and villages were clearly no match for civilized communities with their civilized ways of conquest, domination, and exploitation. It took more than 2,500 years to wipe them out, but we did it, not to mention wiping one another out from time to time in the process.

## Measuring Wars

The most important measure of war would be the number of deaths caused by it. However, these data are not available much before the modern period. However, I found a significant correlation of .70 between battles per war and deaths per war during the modern period, and I also found a significant correlation of .91 between battles per half-century and war deaths per half-century during the modern period (Eckhardt 1990), suggesting that battles may be used as a measure of war's intensity in the absence of more positive data on war deaths. Since then, I have found significant correlations between several sets of battle and war frequencies, on the one hand, and two sets of war casualties and deaths, on the other, both over the centuries from 1500 BC to AD 2000, and over battles per war and casualties/deaths per war, so that there is hardly any doubt that battle and war frequencies may be used as indicators of war intensities, when casualties or fatalities are not available for this purpose. These correlations are shown in Table 3.3.

Although written records have been kept since 3000 BC, the first recorded battle did not occur until about 1469 BC between Egypt and the Palestinians at Megiddo (Dupuy and Dupuy 1986, p. 6). In that century and the seven centuries to follow there was no more than one recorded battle per century until the 7th century BC, when there were three recorded battles, and the 6th century BC when there were six recorded battles (Dupuy and Dupuy 1986). Other authors (Harbottle 1904 [revised by Bruce 1981]; Eggenberger 1985) found even fewer battles prior to 500 BC, with the earliest one being at Troy in the 12th century BC. Wars, themselves, averaged only five or six per century from 2000 BC to 500 BC (Kohn 1987), and the

TABLE 3.3

*Correlations Between Frequencies and Intensities*

| Battle Frequencies[a] | War Casualties[b] | Dates | N | Correlations[c] |
|---|---|---|---|---|
| *Per Centuries* | | | | |
| Harbottle | Sorokin | 500 BC–AD 500 | 21 Cs. | .79 |
| Eggenberger | " | " | " | .79 |
| Dupuys | " | " | " | .78 |
| Kohn Wars | " | " | " | .71 |
| Sorokin Wars | " | " | " | .67 |
| *Per War* | | | | |
| Eggenberger | " | " | 83 Wars | .63 |
| Wright | " | AD 1500– 1925 | 97 Wars | .79 |
| Wright | Levy | 1500–1940 | 88 Wars | .95 |

SOURCES: Dupuy and Dupuy (1986); Eggenberger (1985); Harbottle (1904; Bruce 1981); Kohn (1987); Levy (1983); Sorokin (1937–41); Wright ([1942] 1965).

[a]Battles were obtained from all authors in Column 1, unless otherwise indicated, such as by "Kohn Wars."

[b]Casualties were obtained from Sorokin in Column 2, but deaths were obtained from Levy.

[c]Correlations were significant at the .01 level of confidence.

war record prior to 2000 BC was rather vague at best, although there is some evidence that wars occurred prior to that time.

Since records were kept since about 3000 BC, and since historians have always been very careful to record such events as battles and wars, I assume that no record of these events in historical times means that they did not occur, or that, if they did occur, they did not amount to very much. In a 1500 page encyclopedia of military history (Dupuy and Dupuy 1986), only 15 pages, or one percent of the total, was devoted to the "dawn of military history" from 3500 to 600 BC. In short, the first half of military history was such as to require very little space, presumably because not very much happened to warrant recording by historians until the emergence of the Medes and the Persians about 600 BC, when war started to become an art. It was much later before it started to become a science as well.

I have analyzed three sets of battles (Bruce 1981; Eggenberger 1985; Dupuy and Dupuy 1986) and three sets of wars (Dupuy and Dupuy 1986; Kohn 1987; Sorokin 1937–41, Vol. 3). Since battles are more like one another in their intensity than wars, they would be preferred as a measure of war's intensity. Since the Dupuys' battles are more numerous and less Eurocentric than Harbottle's and Eggenberger's battles, they will be used as the preferred measure of war's intensity in this article. Their total distribution is shown in the last column of Table 3.4. About half of this total has been sorted according to regions, and this sample is shown in the rest of this table. The sample was quite adequate, since it was correlated .99 with the total number

TABLE 3.4
*Dupuy and Dupuy's Battles*

| Century | Europe | Middle East | Far East | South Asia | Africa | Latin America | North America | Total Sample | Non-Europe | Europe Sample (%) | Grand Total |
|---|---|---|---|---|---|---|---|---|---|---|---|
| -15 | | | | | | | | 0 | 0 | | 1 |
| -14 | | | | | | | | 0 | 0 | | 0 |
| -13 | | 1 | | | | | | 1 | 1 | 0 | 1 |
| -12 | | | | | | | | 0 | 0 | | 1 |
| -11 | | | | | | | | 0 | 0 | | 1 |
| -10 | | | | | | | | 0 | 0 | | 0 |
| -9 | | | | | | | | 0 | 0 | | 1 |
| -8 | | | | | | | | 0 | 0 | | 1 |
| -7 | | 3 | | | | | | 3 | 3 | 0 | 3 |
| -6 | | 2 | | | | | | 2 | 2 | 0 | 6 |
| -5 | 14 | 5 | | | | | | 19 | 5 | 74 | 42 |
| -4 | 19 | 9 | | 1 | | | | 29 | 10 | 66 | 43 |
| -3 | 37 | 6 | | | | | | 43 | 6 | 86 | 75 |
| -2 | 10 | 12 | | | | | | 22 | 12 | 45 | 30 |
| -1 | 23 | 10 | | 1 | | | | 34 | 11 | 68 | 61 |
| 1 | 3 | 2 | | | | | | 5 | 2 | 60 | 9 |
| 2 | 3 | 5 | | | | | | 8 | 5 | 38 | 12 |

|      | C1   | C2   | C3  | C4  | C5 | C6 | C7  | C8   | C9   | C10 | C11  |
|------|------|------|-----|-----|----|----|-----|------|------|-----|------|
| 3    | 10   | 15   |     |     |    |    |     | 25   | 15   | 40  | 44   |
| 4    | 11   | 5    |     |     |    |    |     | 17   | 6    | 65  | 38   |
| 5    | 18   | 3    | 1   |     |    |    |     | 21   | 3    | 86  | 51   |
| 6    | 4    | 12   |     |     |    |    |     | 17   | 13   | 24  | 53   |
| 7    | 14   | 50   | 1   | 4   |    |    |     | 67   | 53   | 21  | 102  |
| 8    | 19   | 13   | 3   | 3   |    |    |     | 38   | 19   | 50  | 66   |
| 9    | 29   | 15   | 5   | 1   |    |    |     | 50   | 21   | 58  | 73   |
| 10   | 22   | 19   |     |     |    |    |     | 41   | 19   | 54  | 70   |
| 11   | 25   | 26   |     | 3   |    |    |     | 54   | 29   | 46  | 91   |
| 12   | 26   | 32   | 2   | 5   |    |    |     | 69   | 43   | 38  | 108  |
| 13   | 45   | 18   | 11  | 5   | 1  |    |     | 80   | 35   | 56  | 125  |
| 14   | 38   | 5    | 4   | 6   |    |    |     | 53   | 15   | 72  | 112  |
| 15   | 68   | 8    | 9   |     |    |    |     | 85   | 17   | 80  | 164  |
| 16   | 99   | 18   | 7   | 20  | 1  | 1  | 2   | 148  | 49   | 67  | 292  |
| 17   | 203  | 18   | 14  | 22  | 9  | 6  | 18  | 290  | 87   | 70  | 500  |
| 18   | 207  | 28   | 5   | 32  | 1  | 13 | 52  | 338  | 131  | 61  | 765  |
| 20   | 213  | 93   | 148 | 13  | 25 | 5  | 2   | 449  | 286  | 43  | 973  |
| Sum  | 1294 | 464  | 230 | 162 | 71 | 67 | 189 | 2477 | 1183 | 52  | 4511 |
| Mean | 51.76 | 16.57 | 16.43 | 11.57 | 11.83 | 13.4 | 37.8 | 70.77 | 33.8 |     | 128.9 |
| Std  | 64.69 | 18.47 | 36.85 | 12.83 | 13.07 | 14.81 | 42.7 | 120.7 | 67.5 |    | 224.6 |

SOURCE: Depuy and Depuy (1986).

of battles over the centuries. The Dupuys' battles were significantly correlated with other lists (Sorokin 1937–41, Vol. 3; Wright [1942] 1965; Bruce 1981; Eggenberger 1985; Kohn 1987), in addition to which it was the most comprehensive and reliable list available.

## Correlations between Civilizations, Empires, and Wars at the Global Level of Analysis

We now have the measures that we need for the purpose of correlational analysis: the number of geniuses as a measure of civilization or creativity, imperial sizes as a measure of empires, and battle frequencies as a measure of the destructiveness or intensity of war. Correlations, of course, measure only similarities of distribution, not causes, which have to be determined by logical argument or empirical evidence outside of the statistical situation.

The dialectical evolutionary theory of civilizations, empires, and wars would suggest that these three should be significantly correlated with one another and, furthermore, that all three should be correlated with time. The correlation between both the raw and the logged scores of world civilization and empire was .90, accounting for 81 percent of the variance. At the world level, the correlation between civilization and empire was very high indeed. The more civilized we became, the larger was the area of the earth that came under imperial control. Civilizations and empires may not be twins, but they were very close relatives indeed. Civilization seemed to precede empire in time, but empire had the effect of spreading civilization over larger territories, which generally included more people. If civilization was the parent of empire, empire returned the favor by increasing the territory over which civilization was extended. According to this description, there was a dialectical evolutionary relationship between civilization and empire, in the sense that they fed back and forth into each other, contributing to each other's growth in the process.

When the sum of the Dupuy battles over these centuries was correlated with the sum of imperial sizes, both variables being logged to correct for skewness, the correlation was .94, which was significant well beyond the .001 level of confidence. When these battles were correlated with the sum of Kroeber's seven civilized activities, both variables being logged, the correlation was .94, which was significant well beyond the .001 level of confidence. The correlations among these three variables were all more than .90, suggesting a very close relationship among them, which is what was required to confirm the dialectical evolutionary theory. It is worth noting

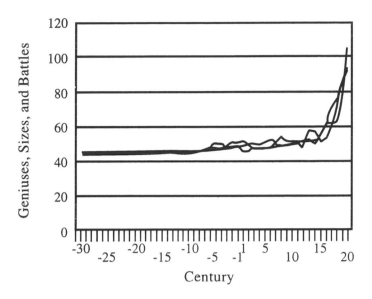

*Figure 3.1.* Civilizations, empires, and wars, 3000 BC–AD 2000.

that these three measures were obtained from three independent sources (Kroeber, Taagepera, and Dupuy and Dupuy), so that their correlations were not contaminated by any bias that might have been generated had they been obtained from a single source.

When all of these measures were logged and correlated with the 50 centuries from 3000 BC to AD 2000 (as a measure of historical time), and when these correlations were factor analyzed, a single factor emerged from this process: number of battles (.98), imperial sizes (.98), centuries (.97), and number of geniuses (.97). The components of this factor are shown in Figure 3.1, where the raw scores in Tables 3.1 to 3.3 have been converted into standard scores with a mean of 50 and a standard deviation of 10, in order to make these 3 sets of scores comparable to one another. Factors, like correlations, establish structural similarities, but not causal direction, which has to be established outside of statistical analysis.

These results clearly show that, not only were civilizations, empires, and wars correlated with one another, but that all of them were correlated with time, that is to say that all of them were increasing significantly and exponentially over these centuries at the global level of analysis.

# Regional Correlations

This confirmation at the global level was further confirmed at the regional levels. All four of these variables were significantly correlated with one another in Europe and non-Europe, and also in the Middle East, India, and the Far East, taken separately. When these correlation matrices were factor analyzed, a single factor emerged in all regions, as shown in Table 3.5. The factor coefficients were all significant, but the loading of Kroeber's geniuses in the Middle East was rather low.

As far as they go, these results confirmed the dialectical evolutionary theory of fairly close relations between civilizations, empires, and wars over the centuries from 3000 BC to AD 2000, supporting this theory at the regional levels of analysis as well as at the global level. It is worth emphasizing (again) that the measures of these three variables were obtained from three independent sources, which presumably had no influence on one another.

These statistical findings were consistent with Kroeber's (1944) findings by inspection: "A definitely successful [Egyptian] dynasty regularly meant military expansion, accumulation and diffusion of wealth, notable building operations, high-grade sculpture, painting, and often literature. . . . So regular, on the whole, is the concordance of the several curves that evidently they are all only functions of one underlying factor or group of related factors" (p. 240). Indeed, only one underlying factor was found by statistical analysis. Furthermore, "It is evident that Assyrian sculpture followed the fortunes of empire, as Egyptian sculpture had done earlier. . . . It is clear that

TABLE 3.5
*Factor Analyses of Civilizations, Empires, and Wars*

| Regions | Century | Geniuses | Empires | Battles | Explained Variance (%) |
|---|---|---|---|---|---|
| World | .97 | .97 | .98 | .98 | 95 |
| Europe | .94 | .93 | .86 | .96 | 85 |
| Non-Europe | .97 | .93 | .96 | .95 | 91 |
| Middle East | .95 | .38 | .94 | .95 | 71 |
| India | .95 | .78 | .69 | .75 | 64 |
| Far East | .97 | .95 | .94 | .80 | 84 |

The figures in the body of the table are factor coefficients, which are a rough measure of the correlation of each variable with the single factor that emerged from the analysis of the correlation matrix in each region. The last column indicates how much of the variance in these variables over the 50 centuries from 3000 BC to AD 2000 was explained by the single general factor. Non-Europe was simply the sum of the Middle East, India, and Far East. Africa and the Americas were left out of these analyses because they became part of the historical world too late for such analyses to be meaningful in their cases. All of the factor coefficients were significant, according to Harman's (1967) table of standard errors of factor coefficients (p. 435), but the loading of Kroeber's geniuses in the Middle East was rather low.

whether the period was one of city-states or of empires, the achievements of sculpture were dependent on military and political successes" (pp. 245, 247). "The books [encyclopedias and textbooks] regularly describe the architecture, sculpture, and painting [in Egypt] as rising and falling in accord with the politico-economic fortunes to a surprising degree" (p. 665). The correlation between national achievement and cultural achievement was only partial in China (p. 670) and low in India (p. 684), but in conclusion: "On the whole, ethnic or national energy and higher cultural energy tend to be related; but . . . the relationship is not complete. . . . To the question whether there may be national florescences without accompanying cultural ones, the answer must be yes, although such happenings are rare in history" (pp. 795, 844). Clearly, the agreement between Kroeber's insights and the results of factor analysis are striking indeed.

More definite conclusions about the relationships between political or military success and artistic creativity can be drawn from Kavolis (1972, p. 40), who notes that "a correlation between periods of warfare and those of artistic creativity has been noted, mostly in Asian civilizations by Mukerjee (1951, pp. 27–28) and, in Europe, by Sorokin (1937–41, Vol. 3, p. 365)." Kavolis (p. 155) also cites a factor analysis of 40 modern nations by Cattell, Breul, and Hartman (1952), who found that creative variables, such as high creativity in science and philosophy, high musical creativity, and many Nobel Prizes in Science, Literature, and Peace, tended to cluster together with aggressive variables, such as a large number of riots and frequent involvement in war. Kavolis's more detailed historical analysis suggested that "artistic creativity tends to increase in periods following those of intensive goal-oriented action (warfare or political consolidations) in the political sphere" (p. 54).

However, Naroll et al. (1971) found no significant relationship between their counts of Kroeber's geniuses and the *number of years* of external warfare of the most "conspicuous state" or great power of the civilization during any century. Since the number of years of war tends to increase as we go back in time, even though the actual fighting time decreases, it may not be as accurate a measure of war's intensity as the *number of battles* used in the present study. They also found no significant relationship between creativity and the size of the civilization's largest city, the growth of the civilization, and the degree of centralization: "On the other hand, we found some tentative support for the hypothesis that the more politically fragmented a civilization [the number of independent states within it], the higher its creativity level" (p. 187). This last correlation was .286, which was significant at the .05 level of confidence, but which accounted for only 8 percent of the total variance. The authors recognized the need to retest this hypothesis on a new sample before it could be credited.

## Some Theories about Regional Rises and Falls

Although civilizations, empires, and wars increased significantly and exponentially at the global level, there were rises and falls at the regional levels,
which is why the regional factor coefficients in Table 3.5 were lower than
the global ones.

Spengler (1926–28) attributed these rises and falls to something like a
biological process of birth, development, maturity, and decay. This process
of growth and decay seemed to be pretty much determined by the nature of
the process itself. There was not much in this theory to prevent the decline
of the West, which Spengler predicted.

Toynbee (1972) was less deterministic, emphasizing the adequacy of
responses to challenges as the determining factor of rises and falls. Adequate
or appropriate responses contributed to rising, while inadequate or inappropriate responses contributed to falling. The emphasis was on moral, religious, or spiritual challenges more than physical or environmental ones, but
he also emphasized that civilizational rising and falling depended very much
upon the rising and falling of the economy: "The inability of a pre-scientific
agricultural economy to bear this economic load [of providing more and
more civilian and military services] is evidently one of the causes of the
unwished-for collapses by which so many universal states have been over-
taken so many times in succession" (Toynbee and Caplan [1934–61] 1972,
p. 63). Just *who* or *what* challenged civilizations was not entirely clear, nor
just *how* civilizations responded. But the concept allowed for some free play
in the rise and fall of civilizations, and it challenges us to find out what it
means operationally if we can, so that it can be studied more scientifically.

More recently, the economic factor has been emphasized by Kennedy
(1987) to account for the rise and fall of the great powers in modern history.
Armed force is what makes or breaks a great power, according to this theory,
and armed forces cost money. Great powers need money in order to become
great in the first place, and more money in order to stay great in the second
place. But there seems to be a strong tendency for great powers to outspend
their greatness. Military expenditures overreach their economic base, exhausting themselves in the process, and losing the next war to an upcoming
power that has not yet bankrupted its economy with its military expenditures: "The historical record suggests that there is a very clear connection *in
the long run* between an individual Great Power's economic rise and fall and
its growth and decline as an important military power (or world empire)"
(p. xxii). The author has emphasized the long run because he is talking about
a process that takes time as well as money, but his study of the last 500 years
convinced him that "there is a very strong correlation between the eventual
outcome of the *major coalition wars* for European or global mastery, and the

amount of productive resources mobilized by each side . . . victory has repeatedly gone to the side with the more flourishing productive base . . . the power position of the leading nations has closely paralleled their relative economic position over the past five centuries" (pp. xxiii–xxiv).

In short, wars cost money. To be sure, they also make money, and therein lies the gamble: Can you make more than it costs to make it? If so, war can be a profitable business, forgetting about the casualties for the moment. At least, somebody can make some money (i.e., surplus wealth) from it. But, if it costs more than it makes, then bankruptcy follows, and down goes the empire. The trick seems to be to make war pay by making somebody else pay for it, and to forget about the casualties on both sides, including civilians as well as soldiers.

## Summary and Conclusions

The dialectical evolutionary theory proposed relations between civilizations, empires, and wars, such that these three were supposed to interact in such a way as to promote one another's growth up to a point where surplus wealth was diminished until it turned into a deficit. At this point, civilizations, empires, and wars could no longer be afforded, so they were lost instead of gained. This loss, however, was somebody else's gain. The loss took the form either of direct conquest by others with more surplus wealth, or of decentralization which made the smaller units prey to future conquest. Consequently, the way up and the way down were virtually the same way of conquest, either directly and immediately, as in the case of Alexander's conquest of the Persian empire, or indirectly and sequentially, as in the case of the many times that Chinese empires were fragmented into feudal states which were later centralized by another conqueror. In either event, civilizations, empires, and wars tended to go and grow together; wars served as both midwives and undertakers in the rise and fall of civilizations in the course of human history.

This dialectical process of evolution (and devolution) presumably began among primitive peoples, although there is little or no trace of it until the beginning of civilization some 5,000 years ago. Even at this time the evidence was rather sparse for battles and wars, which did not clearly emerge until about 1500 BC, and which did not amount to much until about 500 BC. However, something like this process may be responsible for some of the movement from the primitive bands to the larger tribes of the gatherers and hunters to the villages of the farmers and herders who emerged some 10,000 years ago.

The same process was presumably responsible for the movement from the agricultural villages to the civilized cities which emerged some 5,000 years ago. The process was hardly noticeable for several million years. Neither anthropological nor archaeological evidence suggested much growth in population or territory among the gatherers and hunters, and not much more among the farmers and the herders. Even the first 2,500 years of civilization showed no dramatic increases in population, or territory, or in signs of civilization, such as statesmanship, philosophy, religion, literature, fine arts, scholarship, science, music, business, and so forth.

The great leap forward in all of these areas occurred about 600 BC, when the Medes and the Persians developed civilization, empire, and war into arts based on a hierarchical delegation of power such as the world had not known before. The next great leap came with the Muslims in the 7th century AD, another with the Mongols in the 13th century, and finally with the Europeans in the 16th century. The Europeans reached their apex in the 19th and 20th centuries, but they may well be running out of steam and other signs of surplus wealth today. However, they had their ups and downs before, so that even if they may be on their way down now this hardly precludes another rise in the future unless, of course, they happen to blow up the whole world on their way down.

While the whole world tended to spiral upward, as a general rule during the last 5,000 years (judging by Kroeber's geniuses, Taagepera's imperial sizes, and Dupuy and Dupuy's battles) regional areas had their ups and downs, their rises and their falls. Consequently, the general pattern suggested by the analyses in this paper was that of an evolutionary trend in one direction at the global level, which was composed of somewhat cyclical processes at regional levels. At both the global and regional levels, civilizations, empires, and wars were significantly related to one another, tending to rise and fall together. How to explain this basic finding?

It was only after we became civilized, that is, dependent upon land, labor, capital, and trade for making a living, that anything like imperialism and militarism started to make any sense at all. And then they became necessary in order to gain, maintain, and increase the surplus wealth without which there could be no civilization.

At the regional levels, the rises were associated with the establishment of centralized controls by a strong leader whose income exceeded his expenditures in the process. When his or his followers' expenditures exceeded their incomes, then came the falls, which were characterized by decentralization, feudalization, or foreign conquest. In all cases, the way up not only increased the *quantity* of civilization, empire, and war, but also changed the social *structure* to one of greater inequality, indicated by slavery, caste, class, social stratification, and so forth. This inequality characterized the relations *between* civilizations as well as *within* them. It would, of course, be most desirable to develop more precise measures of these inequalities in the process of further research. So far, the evidence on this score is largely qualitative, which needs to be strengthened by making it more quantitative.

The terms "rise" and "fall," "up" and "down," and so forth follow conventional usage. However, so far as they may connote value judgments of "better" and "worse," they may well be questioned. More civilization and more empire meant more war. More civilization would seem to be better, at least for those who get it or who get more of it. More empire may be better for the imperial civilizations, but not for their colonies. More war would definitely seem to be worse, all other things being equal, but those who win the wars might not agree with this. A crucial question for further research might be: Do the pleasures of civilization justify the horrors of war? A more pressing question might be: Can we have civilization without war?

Unless we have an instinct of exploitation (which I doubt very much), that is, a desire to benefit ourselves at the expense of others, it would seem that we have no need for war. Human nature is pretty much determined by human beings and human choices. The dialectical evolutionary theory would suggest that we gradually developed ourselves into a pattern of domination and exploitation which virtually made war inevitable. So far as this is true, it means that we can change the structure of the civilization that we have created by changing our choices, which means changing our values, which hardly means changing human nature, whatever that may be.

What values need to be changed in order to have a civilization without domination and exploitation, and therefore without war? One clue would seem to lie in the basic difference between primitive and civilized societies. Primitive societies seem to be more free and equal in their human relations than the civilized societies that we have created so far (Eckhardt 1975, 1982). If we created more free and equal human relations, we might be able to create a civilization without war. But we have much more to learn before we can achieve that happy ending.

## References

Bruce, George. 1981. *Harbottle's Dictionary of Battles from the Earliest Date to the Present Time*. 3rd ed. New York: Van Nostrand Reinhold.

Cattell, Raymond B., H. Breul, and H. Parker Hartman. 1952. "An Attempt at More Refined Definition of the Cultural Dimensions of Syntality in Modern Nations." *American Sociological Review* 17:408–21.

Dupuy, R. Ernest, and Trevor N. Dupuy. 1986. *The Encyclopedia of Military History from 3500 BC to the Present*. 2nd rev. ed. New York: Harper & Row.

Eckhardt, William. 1975. "Primitive Militarism." *Journal of Peace Research* 12:55–62.

———. 1982. "Atrocities, Civilizations, and Savages." *Bulletin of Peace Proposals* 13:34–49.

———. 1990. "Civilizations, Empires, and Wars." *Journal of Peace Research* 27:9–24.

Eggenberger, David. 1985. *An Encyclopedia of Battles*. New York: Dover.

Harbottle, Thomas B. 1904. *Dictionary of Battles from the Earliest Date to the Present Time*. London: Sonneschein.

Harman, Harry H. 1967. *Modern Factor Analysis*. Chicago: University of Chicago Press.

Kavolis, Vytautas. 1972. *History on Art's Side*. Ithaca, NY: Cornell University Press.

Kennedy, Paul. 1987. *The Rise and Fall of the Great Powers: Economic Change and Military Conflict from 1500 to 2000*. New York: Random House.

Kohn, George C. 1987. *Dictionary of Wars*. Garden City, NY: Anchor/Doubleday.

Kroeber, Alfred L. 1944. *Configurations of Culture Growth*. Berkeley and Los Angeles: University of California Press.

Levy, Jack S. 1983. *War in the Modern Great Power System, 1495–1975*. Lexington: University of Kentucky Press.

McEvedy, Colin, and Richard Jones. 1978. *Atlas of World Population History*. New York: Facts on File.

Mukerjee, Radhakamal. 1951. *The Social Functions of Art*. Bombay: Hind Kittabs.

Naroll, Raoul, E.C. Benjamin, F.K. Fohl, M.J. Fried, R.E. Hildreth, and J.M. Schaefer. 1971. "Creativity: A Cross-Historical Pilot Survey." *Journal of Cross-Cultural Psychology* 2:181–88.

Sorokin, Pitirim A. 1937–41. *Social and Cultural Dynamics*. 4 vols. New York: American Book.

Spengler, Oswald. 1926–28. *The Decline of the West*. 2 vols. New York: Knopf.

Taagepera, Rein. 1978. "Size and Duration of Empires: Systematics of Size." *Social Science Research* 7:108–27.

Toynbee, Arnold J., and Jane Caplan (1934–61) 1972. *A Study of History*. New York: Oxford University Press. (Revised and abridged one-volume edition of the original 12 volumes.)

Wright, Quincy. (1942) 1965. *A Study of War*. 2nd rev. ed. Chicago: University of Chicago Press.

STEPHEN K. SANDERSON ■
THOMAS D. HALL

# PART II

# World System Approaches to World-Historical Change

World-system theory was launched in 1974 with the publication by Immanuel Wallerstein of the first volume of his *The Modern World-System* (1974a) and a major article summarizing the approach (1974b). (To follow the development of Wallerstein's work, see, in addition to the works cited above, Wallerstein [1979, 1980, 1983, 1984, 1989]. This theoretical approach, which would in due time revolutionize the study of many aspects of social life and historical change, was a synthesis of Braudelian historiography, Marxian historical materialism, and dependency theory à la Andre Gunder Frank. The eminent French historian Fernand Braudel's most famous work was, of course, *The Mediterranean and the Mediterranean World in the Age of Philip II*, which appeared in two large volumes (Braudel [1949] 1972–1973). Braudel was the first to formulate the notion of a world-system, doing so in order to understand the large-scale regional economy centered around the Mediterranean Sea in early modern times. Wallerstein generalized this notion of a world-system, both temporally and spatially. World-systems thus became in his hands much more general than anything proposed by Braudel. The world-system centered around Europe became, for Wallerstein, the basic unit of analysis necessary to comprehend the evolution of capitalism over the past 500 years. In his analysis of capitalism Wallerstein took the basic Marxian notion of class struggle within capitalism and extended it to the world as a whole, and within this world-system economically dominant and dependent countries and regions interacted along the lines of Frank's metropoles and satellites.

For Wallerstein, a world-system is any relatively large social system that exhibits three basic characteristics. It is autonomous, which means that, although it interacts with other systems, it can persist on its own. It also has a complex division of labor along both economic and geographical lines. Regions within the system come to be specialized around the performance of certain types of economic production, and these regions interact with each other on the basis of these specializations. Finally, a world-system contains a plurality of societies and cultures. A world-system is rarely—only in the late 20th century has this been the case—coextensive with the world as a whole, but is a large intersocietal and intercultural network that "is a world."

Wallerstein argued that two basic types of world-systems had been found in history. The most common type was the *world-empire*, a world-system that was politically and militarily unified, such as the Roman Empire, or the various empires of China, India, or Persia. *World-economies* had also existed throughout history. These were world-systems that lacked political or military unification. They were held together by loose networks of economic production and exchange and contained numerous sovereign or semisovereign states, which competed fiercely. Wallerstein argued that world-economies had to be integrated around the production and exchange of bulk or necessary goods; prestige or luxury goods—preciosities—were insufficient to establish true systemic ties. Wallerstein also thought that world-economies have always been fragile and vulnerable, and thus tended to split apart or to become transformed into world-empires.

All except one that is. This is the capitalist world-economy, which began to emerge in the "long 16th century" (i.e., after about 1450) and that had become consolidated at the end of this century (i.e., by about 1640). Wallerstein's work has concentrated almost exclusively on this one world-system, clearly the greatest of all world-systems. He has devoted himself to the detailed description of this system, as well as to explaining its basic operative principles, to tracing out its historical evolution, and to assessing its future prospects.

The capitalist world-economy has been compartmentalized into three basic components or "zones." The *core* consists of those societies economically and politically dominant within the system and that engage in the production of the most advanced industrial goods using the most advanced forms of technology. The richest capitalists are found here, and a class struggle between bourgeois and proletarians is carried on here. Core societies have led the way in the introduction of wage labor, which has gradually replaced systems of forced labor. At the opposite extreme from the core is the *periphery*. This component or zone consists of societies or regions that use the most outmoded forms of technology and that are economically specialized to produce raw materials for export. They are the least economically and technologically developed part of the world-economy, and are typified by the use of forced labor systems rather than wage labor. In between these two zones is the *semiperiphery* a component of the system that contains features of both the core and the periphery. It is at an intermediate level of economic development. In Wallerstein's view, its intermediate status has given it a prominent role in stabilizing the world-system because it mediates the polarization of core and periphery. One can also talk about an *external arena*, or a region (or set of regions) outside the world-economy but interacting with it in terms of the exchange of preciosities. As the capitalist world-economy has expanded over time many parts of the external arena have gradually come to be incorporated into it.

The three zones of the system interact in four basic ways. First, the core is engaged in extensive exploitation of both the semiperiphery and, especially, the periphery. It organizes (or helps to organize) economic activities in those regions that produce extremely high rates of profit. The semiperiphery, in its turn, also engages in its own form of exploitation of the periphery. Second, within the core itself there is intense economic rivalry, which is expressed not only directly in economic terms, but also at the political and military levels. This rivalry is accompanied by intracore cooperation inasmuch as political and military alliances help facilitate favorable economic consequences. Third, there is both upward and downward mobility with the system, although most societies do not move very far, and the position of any society within the system tends to have a certain permanence. Finally, as already mentioned, the semiperiphery acts as a mediator or buffer between core and periphery.

As formulated by Wallerstein, the capitalist world-economy has prominently displayed both expansionary and evolutionary dynamics. The expansion of the system (sometimes called *broadening*) involves its geographical spread to incorporate more and more of the external arena. At the end of the long 16th century, for example, it is doubtful that the capitalist world-system included more than 20 percent of the inhabitable globe, but today it has incorporated virtually all of it. The long-term evolutionary dynamics of the system, or what is more often called the *deepening* of capitalist development, involve the continual structural change and reorganization that has accompanied its expansion. In the 19th and 20th centuries, for example, the system was radically restructured along urban and industrial lines.

The evolutionary dynamics of the system can be broken down into five basic processes. First there is *commodification*, which means that an ever greater part of economic and social life comes to be organized around the creation of exchange-values rather than use-values. A major dimension of commodification is *proletarianization*, which is the gradual transformation of the labor force into wage workers. A labor market is created in which workers themselves have exchange-values. Third is the process of *mechanization*, which involves the continual advancement of the technology applied to the production process. A fourth evolutionary trend is *contractualization*, which amounts to the increasing formalization of economic (and other human) relationships by legal means. Finally, there is the process of *polarization*, or the increased widening of the economic gap between core and periphery. This last process represents the extension of Marx's notion of immiseration to a world level.

The capitalist world-economy exhibits cyclical as well as linear evolutionary changes. The two most important of these are *Kondratieff cycles* and *hegemony cycles*. Kondratieff cycles were first noted by the Russian economist Nikolai Kondratieff ([1928] 1984) in the 1920s. These are waves of economic prosperity and decline that last on average about 50 years. An "A" phase, or expanding phase, is a period of economic growth that lasts about 25 years, only to peak and then to be followed by a "B" or declining phase that lasts approximately another 25 years. The process then begins again. Hegemony cycles are periods of economic dominance of the world-economy by one nation-state. To be hegemonic a nation-state must dominate the world-economy simultaneously at the levels of economic production, commerce, and finance. A hegemon has a firm military presence in the world, and can generally get its way in what it wants. According to Wallerstein, there have been three brief periods of hegemony in the history of modern capitalism: Holland in 1625–1673, Great Britain in 1815–1873, and the United States in 1945–1967. Once hegemons stop being hegemons, they never become hegemons again (or at least have not so far in the 500-year history of capitalism).

Closely intertwined with the capitalist world-economy is the political side of the system, or the *interstate system*. This is the system of intensely competing, cooperating, and conflicting nation-states that now number about 180 in the world (although they numbered many more in early periods of capitalism). The question has constantly arisen as to the status of the interstate system vis-à-vis the world-economy. Wallerstein and Christopher Chase-Dunn (1989) have regarded these two as inextricably fused components—two sides of the same coin— although it seems clear that they regard the economic side as dominant and the basic foundation for the interstate system.

What is the driving engine, or what one of us has elsewhere (Sanderson 1995) called the "evolutionary logic," of the capitalist system? It is none other than what Marx identified as ceaseless capital accumulation. It is this that is the driving logic of the expansionary and evolutionary dynamics of the system. Everything hangs on this. Driven by this evolutionary logic, the capitalist world-system has evolved through four major stages. At the end of the long 16th century (c. 1640) Holland, England, and northern France were ensconced in the core, the periphery was composed of Eastern Europe and Iberian America, and the semiperiphery consisted of Mediterranean Europe (Spain, Portugal, southern France, and Italy). In the second stage (c. 1640–1760), the system expanded only modestly. The Caribbean and the U.S. South entered the periphery, and Sweden, Prussia, and the U.S. North moved into the semiperiphery. Most of the globe was still outside the system in 1760, but after this time what Wallerstein calls "the second era of great expansion of the capitalist world-economy" ensued. By the end of this third phase (the late 19th or early 20th centuries), all the core states had begun major industrialization, Latin America had become decolonized, and most of Asia and Africa, formerly in the external arena, had been incorporated into the periphery. In the 20th century, the industrial capitalist system was consolidated and evolved at an even more rapid pace. Wallerstein suggests that we are now starting to enter the early phases of the transition from a capitalist world-economy to some very different system, most likely a socialist world-government, which will be on the scene within another 100 to 150 years.

Wallersteinian world-system theory has been severely criticized over the years by many social scientists and historians, but it has survived nonetheless (see Shannon [1989] for a detailed list and assessment of criticisms, and Sanderson [1995] for a similar list but a more positive assessment). And it has not only survived, but, in fact, has held up rather well and is still a major intellectual force. Despite its problems, many scholars contend that it still has much to contribute. Even if one does not accept all of its premises—and who, indeed, would or even could?—it can be argued that it has established a basic methodological dictum: the world-system itself is the fundamental unit of analysis. All its components, explicitly including so-called "modern" nation-states, are not autonomous actors but part of a larger system. As is well known, a key aspect of this argument was Andre Gunder Frank's (1969, 1978, 1979) concept of the "development of underdevelopment": The development of the core states of this system depended on the exploitation of peripheral components. Furthermore, peripheral dependence was not only vital to core development, but necessarily entailed the simultaneous and consequential underdevelopment of the periphery.

The empirical evidence supporting this general claim for the modern world-system is massive and impressive, as are the many subtheories it has generated. (Christopher Chase-Dunn's *Global Formation* [1989] is the single best summary of the evidence.) A major contribution of world-system theory has been to solve a sociological conundrum: Some social processes seem to have opposite results in core and peripheral countries. Some have read this as evidence of the impossibility of a universal sociology. World-system theorists, however, see it as a consequence of world-systemic processes. Thus, in core countries development promotes class formation and undermines status divisions, especially racial and ethnic ones, improves the status of women, and leads to democracy. However, in peripheral countries, class formation is undercut, racial and ethnic divisions are rife, the status of women declines with development, and authoritarianism prevails over democracy.

This, then, is the "modern" world-system camp. How far can its basic ideas be extended beyond its original boundaries (the past 500 years)? Archaeologists and anthropologists quickly saw a potential in world-system theory to clarify several sets of continuing problems. These included the distortions of development among "indigenous" peoples due to their contact with Europeans, and for archaeologists a way to study seemingly systematic interconnections among prehistoric societies. The former might be glossed, in civilizationist terms, as the confrontation of "barbarians and civilizations," while the latter might be glossed as either civilization building or intercivilizational contacts.

The anthropological camp has met with considerable success, spurred by Eric R. Wolf's *Europe and the People Without History* (1982). For those not familiar with this book, the title is a satirical comment on Eurocentric scholars who have tended to view nonliterate indigenous peoples as having no "history" prior to contact or "discovery" by Europeans. Wolf's point is precisely that they do have histories, and that we cannot understand their societies without understanding how their histories have shaped their social lives. A major enterprise in anthropology, history, and ethnohistory has been writing the histories of "the people without history" (see Krech 1991).

Brian Ferguson and Neil Whitehead's title essay in *War in the Tribal Zone* (1992) extends this critique by examining the interaction of state expansion and "tribal" peoples. They find two consistent effects of war in the "tribal zone." Not unexpectedly, wars between state and non-state peoples increase and intensify when states expand into tribal territories. What is less obvious is that wars among "tribal" peoples increase in frequency and intensity with state expansion. Conflicts often center around access to state-supplied goods.

These effects are not unique to modern contacts, but have occurred in most ancient civilizations or world-systems. Ferguson and Whitehead criticize world-system theory for failing to address these issues adequately. The impact of Central Asian nomads on the course of several civilizations is well known (Bentley 1993; Frank 1992; Hall 1991a, 1991b). But many other important, if less dramatic, state-nonstate interactions have shaped civilizational history. Finally, much evolutionary and historical analysis has been distorted by assumptions that the reports of the violence found among nonstate societies was "natural," when in fact it was a product of interactions with states (civilizations). Analysts of precapitalist world-systems differ in the attention they devote to such interactions.

Archaeologists using world-system theory, however, have met with more frustration. The reaction to extreme diffusionism led many cultural ecologists to become overly focused on circumscribed, local processes to the neglect of intersocietal interactions in generating social and cultural change (Schortman and Urban 1992). Several archaeologists have attempted to use world-system theory to overcome this narrow focus. They have struggled to modify, stretch, or transform world-system theory to make it useful in "precapitalist" settings—that is, settings that predate Wallerstein's long 16th century. Most have experienced frustration in that attempt largely because it is so "modern world-system-centric," that is, because it is almost an ad hoc theory focused only on the last 500 years. While this "camp" has yet to produce its own complete, more generalized world-system theory, it is still struggling with extant theory in an attempt to generate a more useful alternative.

Recently several scholars have entered this fray and are developing "precapitalist" world-system theories. Precapitalist world-system analysis has at least five roots. Probably the oldest root is that associated with Ekholm and Friedman (1980, 1982; Ekholm 1980), who claim that capital accumulation has been a continual process since the formation of the first states in ancient Mesopotamia. Their point is that there were capitalist-like processes in ancient states which did not become dominant until circa AD 1500. They see these accumulation processes as fundamental to the generation of inequality within societies and critical to pushing constant expansion.

A second root is represented by those anthropologists and archaeologists who have sought to explain intersocietal interactions, in particular the seeming connections between pre-Columbian Mesoamerica and what is now the American Southwest (Pailes and

Whitecotton 1979, 1986), or complex developments in Oaxaca, Mexico (Blanton and Feinman 1984), or early state formation in Mesopotamia (Kohl 1978, 1979). These (and others) argue that local development or social change is highly conditioned or shaped by the nature and extent of connections with other societies.

A third root is found in the work of those world-system theorists who see a possibility of a major cyclical change coming sometime in the next century and seek to understand that change by looking at past major changes in world-systems. The major representatives of this root are Christopher Chase-Dunn and Thomas Hall, who have been engaged in a systematic delineation and comparison of world-systems, both ancient and modern (Chase-Dunn and Hall 1991, 1993; Hall and Chase-Dunn 1993). They see their work as contributing to a deep understanding of the various principles along which all types of world-systems are organized, and they also want to understand the transformational logic of different world-systems.

The fourth root is the work of Andre Gunder Frank and Barry K. Gills (Frank 1990a, 1990b, 1992; Frank and Gills 1990, 1992; Gills and Frank 1991). They argue, paralleling Ekholm and Friedman, for a long-term process of capital accumulation since the first appearance of states. They argue that the locus of accumulation oscillates between private families and the state, and that this accumulation process takes place within a single, sporadically growing world-system. Here they readily link up with David Wilkinson's argument for the emergence of "Central Civilization" (1987 [chapter 2, this volume]). It is obvious that there are close parallels between the first and fourth roots.

Political scientists George Modelski and William R. Thompson (1995) are developing a new, fifth, root based on their work on seapower and politics (1988). Like the others, Modelski and Thompson argue that the modern world-system has origins in Afroeurasian-wide trade networks. They contend that a succession of active zones of innovation are what drives world-system evolution. Apropos to their disciplinary background, they discuss the political consequences of these successions more fully than some of the others.

The representatives of these five roots all fall into the category that Albert Bergesen (1994) has called "pre-1500ers," or scholars who believe that traditional world-systems analysis can, when appropriately modified, he extended much farther back in world history. In Bergesen's terms, the pre-1500ers contrast with the "post-1500ers," who are scholars suspicious of attempts to extend world-system concepts and principles to earlier and differently organized societies (Immanuel Wallerstein and Samir Amin are perhaps the best known of these). But among the pre-1500ers themselves there is a further split between the "continuationists," represented by Ekholm, Friedman, Frank, and Gills, and the "transformationists," represented by Chase-Dunn and Hall and, to a lesser extent, Modelski and Thompson. The continuationists argue for one continuous, if episodic, world-system that began with the first states (or civilizations) in Mesopotamia some 5,000 years ago. They see the modern world-system of Immanuel Wallerstein as simply the current manifestation of this longer world-system.

The transformationists, on the other hand, argue that there have been many types of systems, and their transformations have been and continue to be problematic. They also argue that future transformations can only be foreseen, and possibly shaped by human action, by studying the logic of past transformations. They contend that their initial assumption of different systems is scientifically conservative in the sense that if the continuationists are, indeed, correct, then this will become readily apparent in the course of pursuing a transformationist, comparative study of world-systems.

Obviously the entire precapitalist world-system research agenda is still expanding and still sorting itself out into camps and positions. What these camps all hold in common, besides obvious debts to Wallerstein and to Frank's early work on dependency, is a focus on intersocietal interaction systems. It is these systems that are conceived as the basic unit of analysis, and as the basic unit that undergoes historical change.

＊　　　＊　　　Ｘ

All of the articles in this section are either pursuing some type of precapitalist world-system analysis or are favorably impressed by it. The article by Chase-Dunn and Hall nicely exemplifies their comparative approach to world-systems. They develop a typology of world-systems in order to address the issue of similarities and differences among small, medium-size, and large-scale intersocietal interaction networks. They conceptualize world-systems as composed of bulk goods, prestige goods, and political/military interaction networks; in these terms, world-systems have grown over the past 10,000 years from small-scale networks among tiny egalitarian societies to the contemporary global system. The authors consider the similarities and differences among kin-based, state-based, and market-based world-systems. They compare sequences of political centralization and decentralization in terms of the rise and fall of chiefdoms, states, and empires, and also compare political/military networks in terms of settlement sizes, size hierarchies, and the territorial size of empires.

Barry Gills's paper serves as an excellent summary of his work with Andre Gunder Frank on the 5,000-year world system. As Gills notes, the leading themes in this work are that capital, capitalist production, and capital accumulation are not modern inventions, but rather have existed in significant extent for thousands of years, and that there has been a very long-term process of cumulative capitalist development that is the central developmental dynamic of world history. As Gills points out, the more he and Frank have explored the history of capital accumulation the more they have discovered how ancient this process really was. Gills also pinpoints several misunderstandings of what he is calling the "perennial political economy perspective." This perspective does not claim that there has been only one single world system throughout the last 5,000 years, and it does not deny that qualitative historical transformations have occurred. Nor is the perspective a rigid form of economic determinism, as it is often made out to be. The "political" is as important as the "economic," and, indeed, they comprise one inseparable "political economy." Gills concludes his paper with some self-reflective criticisms of his own work. Perhaps the most important of these is the tendency toward an "oversystematizing" or "totalizing" view, that is, one that emphasizes system-level processes at the expense of more local processes. The alternative to this, Gills contends, is a model of "interactive causality," or one that examines the continuing dialectical interplay among local, regional, and global processes.

Andre Gunder Frank's article tries to show that Europe in 1500 did not lead the way into the modern world on its own, but rather was enmeshed in a much larger world-system in which Asia was economically dominant. Frank argues that the works of Braudel and Wallerstein are trapped within a Eurocentric framework, one in which Europe is regarded as having unique qualities that gave it alone the power to create the modern world. One of the most intriguing features of Frank's article is his extensive use of quotations from the works of Braudel and Wallerstein to show that their very own evidence points time and again to the economic dominance of Asia in the centuries around 1500. One of the main lines of evidence used by Frank to support his thesis is the existence of economic cycles of varying lengths common to both Europe and Asia. The economic fortunes of these continents have waxed and waned together, he claims, and for him this is virtual proof of their systemic connections. Frank's argument is stunningly bold, and many scholars will resist it. Yet it deserves very serious consideration by all who are interested in the origins of the modern world.

Albert Bergesen seems prepared to accept it. His article is a commentary on what he regards as the extraordinary implications of Frank's argument. Bergesen notes that throughout most of the history of sociological analysis the "society" has been the basic unit of macrosociological study. Many scholars have clung to this view and denied that different kinds of models are needed, but in recent years the accumulation of new historical data has made it increasingly obvious to others that the traditional society-based sociological model is inadequate. These latter scholars have tried to stretch the old society-based model both temporally and spatially. First Braudel, Wallerstein, and Frank created stretched social science models by arguing that societies were enmeshed in larger systems. Then scholars such as Abu-Lughod and Chase-Dunn and Hall argued that this world-system model did not go far enough and had to be stretched even further back in time and farther out in space. But there is yet another option, Bergesen says, and that has been chosen by Gills and (the "new") Frank: letting go of the old models altogether. Letting go is an even more radical step than tracing world-systems or world-systemness back thousands of years in time, for it means abandoning entirely the concept of society or mode of production, and with them the idea of transitions from one society or mode to another. It means seeing world history as one continual thread in one great world-historical process. Bergesen sees letting go as the appropriate option to choose, but choosing it necessitates the creation of a fundamentally new theoretical model, a type of "post-world-system theory." Bergesen highlights a process in which our social science models have been growing deeper and wider, going further back in time and farther out in space. We now need a model, he says, that can encompass the world as a whole from the beginnings of history. Gills and Frank have come close to it, but it still remains to be realized by future scholars.

Andrew Bosworth's article represents an attempt to test empirically Gills and Frank's argument for very long-term (500-year) economic cycles that were world encompassing between 1700 BC and AD 1700. Bosworth uses data from Tertius Chandler on the growth and decline of world cities over this long period. His assumption is that increase in city size is a good indication of economic boom, whereas a decrease in city size indicates economic decline. Bosworth's results suggest to him fairly good support for Gills and Frank's argument. Breaking Gills and Frank's 8 cycles down into 16 A and B phases, Bosworth concludes that Chandler's city-size data strongly support the existence of 8 phases, moderately support 3 phases, mildly or inconclusively support

4 phases, and contradict only 1 phase. Gills and Frank's argument will obviously need further testing, but Bosworth's analysis is an important start, and if his results ring true then the implications could be enormous. If cyclical economic regularities throughout thousands of years of human history are a fact, it is certainly one that cries out for explanation and that suggests an important continuity between modern and premodern times.

## References

Bentley, Jerry H. 1993. *Old World Encounters: Cross-Cultural Contacts and Exchanges in Pre-Modern Times*. Oxford: Oxford University Press.

Bergesen, Albert. 1994. "Pre- vs. Post-1500ers." *Comparative Civilizations Review* 30:81–90.

Blanton, Richard, and Gary Feinman. 1984. "The Mesoamerican World System." *American Anthropologist* 86:673–82.

Braudel, Fernand. (1949) 1972–73. *The Mediterranean and the Mediterranean World in the Age of Philip II*. 2 vols. Trans. Sian Reynolds. New York: Harper & Row.

Chase-Dunn, Christopher. 1989. *Global Formation: Structures of the World-Economy*. Oxford: Basil Blackwell.

Chase-Dunn, Christopher, and Thomas D. Hall. 1991. "Conceptualizing Core/Periphery Hierarchies for Comparative Study." In *Core/Periphery Relations in Precapitalist Worlds*, edited by Christopher Chase-Dunn and Thomas D. Hall. Boulder, CO: Westview Press.

———. 1993. "Comparing World-Systems: Concepts and Working Hypotheses." *Social Forces* 71:851–86.

Ekholm, Kajsa. 1980. "On the Limitations of Civilization: The Structure and Dynamics of Global Systems." *Dialectical Anthropology* 5:155–66.

Ekholm, Kajsa, and Jonathan Friedman. 1980. "Toward a Global Anthropology." In *History and Underdevelopment*, edited by L. Blusse, H.L. Wesseling, and G.D. Winius. Center for the History of European Expansion, Leiden University.

———. 1982. "'Capital' Imperialism and Exploitation in Ancient World-Systems." *Review* 4:87–109.

Ferguson, R. Brian, and Neil L. Whitehead. 1992. "The Violent Edge of Empire." In *War in the Tribal Zone*, edited by R. Brian Ferguson and Neil L. Whitehead. Santa Fe, NM: School of American Research Press.

Frank, Andre Gunder. 1969. *Capitalism and Underdevelopment in Latin America: Historical Studies of Chile and Brazil*. Rev. ed. New York: Monthly Review Press.

———. 1978. *World Accumulation, 1492–1789*. New York: Monthly Review Press.

———. 1979. *Dependent Accumulation and Underdevelopment*. New York: Monthly Review Press.

———. 1990a. "A Theoretical Introduction to 5,000 Years of World System History." *Review* 13: 155–248.

———. 1990b. "The Thirteenth Century World System: A Review Essay." *Journal of World History* 1(2):249–56.

————. 1992. *The Centrality of Central Asia. Comparative Asian Studies No. 8.* Amsterdam: University Press for Center for Asian Studies Amsterdam (CASA).

Frank, Andre Gunder, and Barry K. Gills. 1990. "The Cumulation of Accumulation: Theses and Research Agenda for 5,000 Years of World System History." *Dialectical Anthropology* 15:19–42.

————. 1992. "The Five Thousand Year World System: An Interdisciplinary Introduction." *Humboldt Journal of Social Relations* 18(1):1–79.

Gills, Barry K., and Andre Gunder Frank. 1991. "5,000 Years of World System History: The Cumulation of Accumulation." In *Core/Periphery Relations in Precapitalist Worlds*, edited by Christopher Chase-Dunn and Thomas D. Hall. Boulder, CO: Westview Press.

Hall, Thomas D. 1991a. "Civilizational Change: The Role of Nomads." *Comparative Civilizations Review* 24:34–57.

————. 1991b. "The Role of Nomads in Core/Periphery Relations." In *Core/Periphery Relations in Precapitalist Worlds*, edited by Christopher Chase-Dunn and Thomas D. Hall. Boulder, CO: Westview Press.

Hall, Thomas D., and Christopher Chase-Dunn. 1993. "The World-Systems Perspective and Archaeology: Forward into the Past." *Journal of Archaeological Research* 1(2): 121–43.

Kohl, Philip L. 1978. "The Balance of Trade in Southwestern Asia in the Mid-Third Millennium BC." *Current Anthropology* 19:463–92.

————. 1979. "The 'World Economy' in West Asia in the Third Millennium BC." In *South Asian Archaeology 1977*, edited by M. Toddei. Naples: Instituto Universitario Orientale.

Kondratieff, Nikolai. (1928) 1984. *The Long Wave Cycle*. New York: Richardson and Snyder.

Krech, Shepard III. 1991. "The State of Ethnohistory." *Annual Review of Anthropology* 20:345–75.

Modelski, George, and William R. Thompson. 1988. *Seapower and Global Politics, 1494–1993*. Seattle: University of Washington Press.

————. 1995. *Leading Sectors and World Powers: The Coevolution of Global Politics and Economics*. Columbia: University of South Carolina Press.

Pailes, Richard A., and Joseph W. Whitecotton. 1979. "The Greater Southwest and the Mesoamerican 'World' System: An Exploratory Model of Frontier Relationships." In *The Frontier: Comparative Studies*, Vol. 2, edited by William W. Savage and Stephen I. Thompson. Norman: University of Oklahoma Press.

————. 1986. "New World Pre-Columbian World Systems." In *Ripples in the Chichimec Sea: Consideration of Southwestern-Mesoamerican Interactions*, edited by Frances Joan Mathien and Randall McGuire. Carbondale, IL: Southern Illinois University Press.

Sanderson, Stephen K. 1995. *Social Transformations: A General Theory of Historical Development*. Oxford: Blackwell.

Schortman, Edward M., and Patricia A. Urban. 1992. "The Place of Interaction Studies in Archaeological Thought." In *Resources, Power, and Interregional Interaction*, edited by Edward M. Schortman and Patricia A. Urban. New York: Plenum Press.

Shannon, Thomas Richard. 1989. *An Introduction to the World-System Perspective*. Boulder, CO: Westview Press.

Wallerstein, Immanuel. 1974a. *The Modern World-System: Capitalist Agriculture and the Origins of the European World-Economy in the Sixteenth Century*. New York: Academic Press.

———. 1974b. "The Rise and Future Demise of the World-Capitalist System: Concepts for Comparative Analysis." *Comparative Studies in Society and History* 16:387–415.

———. 1979. *The Capitalist World-Economy*. New York: Cambridge University Press.

———. 1980. *The Modern World-System II: Mercantilism and the Consolidation of the European World-Economy, 1600–1750*. New York: Academic Press.

———. 1983. *Historical Capitalism*. London: Verso.

———. 1984. *The Politics of the World-Economy*. New York: Cambridge University Press.

———. 1989. *The Modern World-System III: The Second Era of Great Expansion of the Capitalist World-Economy, 1730–1840s*. San Diego, CA: Academic Press.

Wilkinson, David. 1987. "Central Civilization." *Comparative Civilizations Review* 17:31–59. (Reprinted as chapter 2, this volume.)

Wolf, Eric R. 1982. *Europe and the People Without History*. Berkeley: University of California Press.

CHRISTOPHER CHASE-DUNN ∎
THOMAS D. HALL

*Chapter Four*

---

# Cross-World-System Comparisons
## *Similarities and Differences*

World-systems are intersocietal networks of regularized and systemically important competitive and cooperative interaction. It is often the case that such networks are nested and overlapping because different kinds of interaction have different geographical patterns. When we say that world-systems range from small to global we mean that populations are linked by networks that vary in size and with regard to the spatial extent of interactional consequences. These definitional and conceptual matters are described and defended in Chase-Dunn and Hall (1993). In this paper we will formulate hypotheses about similarities and differences among different types of world-systems based on the project of comparing world-systems. Concepts and hypotheses are still being debated, while case studies of single world-systems are being completed.[1] What will eventually be needed is systematic study of a large number of world-systems. It is toward this eventual end that this paper is focused.

We need to have explicit hypotheses about similarities and differences among world-systems and we need to construct a comparative framework for these. We employ the typology advanced in Chase-Dunn and Hall (1993, pp. 866–71). True cross-world-system research would have access to comparable data on at least ten of each of our ten types of world-systems (see Table 4.1). As world-systems get larger they become fewer. Thus it is not possible to have ten whole capitalist world-economies because there has been only one. This "sample" of world-systems would number about sixty. Hypotheses about similarities and differences and the "typical" parameters of systems can be systematically confronted with evidence once we have such a comparative data set. As it is, we must put forth our generalizations based on the patchy evidence of case studies and the comparison of those state-based systems on which we have some comparable evidence.

This paper suggests several hypotheses about similarities and differences across the different kinds of world-systems specified in our typology. We set up a framework for comparisons and we specify some hypothetical parameters of network size and demographic size. This presumes our conceptual approach to world-system spatial boundaries, in which we distinguish between bulk goods, political/military, and prestige goods interaction networks (see Chase-Dunn and Hall 1993, pp. 858–62).

## Size

Our structural approach to studying world-systems abstracts from population size and territorial scale to compare the structural patterns of very small systems with very large ones. Nevertheless, it is worthwhile to consider the "typical" sizes of different kinds of world-systems and to hypothesize how different interaction networks vary in relative size in different sorts of systems.

It is likely to be the case that the sizes of different kinds of interaction networks vary in their ratios to one another across different kinds of world-systems. Table 4.1 shows rough estimates of "typical" population sizes of types of polities, bulk goods networks, intermarriage networks, and prestige goods networks across our world-system types ranging from small to large. By "typical" we mean to hypothesize a central tendency for each type of world-system while recognizing that there are probably wide variations among different real systems of each type. The numbers in Table 4.1 are hypothetical means for the universe of world-systems of each type. Within each type there is undoubtedly considerable variation, and this is likely to be systematically related to the developmental trajectories of particular systems. Additionally, all systems experience "pulses" of expansion and contraction of population and territorial size.

Furthermore, the relative sizes of different networks may differ depending upon the prior developmental history of each system. For example, those simple chiefdom systems that have never been through a phase of complex chieftainship may differ significantly in terms of the size of their trade networks from those simple chiefdoms that have devolved from former prestige goods-based chiefdoms (e.g., Friedman 1981). Such complications need to be subjected to careful cross-world-system research, but for now the following central tendencies are our best hypotheses.

The hypothesized polity sizes are for the *largest* polities in each system. As world-systems have gotten larger the different interaction networks have converged in terms of both population size and territorial extent, and simpler

TABLE 4.1

*Population Sizes of Polities and Interaction Nets Across Different Types of World-Systems*

| Type of World-System | Polity | Bulk Goods | Intermarriage | Military (PMN) | Prestige Goods |
|---|---|---|---|---|---|
| Nomadic foragers | 50 | 150 | 500 | 1000 | 10,000 |
| Sedentary foragers | 250 | 1000 | 2000 | 5000 | 50,000 |
| Big Man | 500 | 2000 | 2000 | 10,000 | 100,000 |
| Simple chiefdoms | 1000 | 4000 | 4000 | 20,000 | 200,000 |
| Complex chiefdoms | 50,000 | 200,000 | 200,000 | 500,000 | 1 million |
| Primary states | 100,000 | 400,000 | 400,000 | 1 million | 2 million |
| Primary empires | 200,000 | 800,000 | 800,000 | 2 million | 4 million |
| Secondary empires | 400,000 | 1.6 million | 1.6 million | 3 million | 6 million |
| Commercializing systems | 50 million | 75 million | 20 million | 100 million | 200 million |
| Modern world-system (AD 1750) | 25 million | 150 million | 25 million | 500 million | 700 million |

SOURCES: Biraben (1979), Chandler (1987), Cook (1976), Durand (1977).

systems have been either eliminated or incorporated into larger, more complex, and more hierarchical systems. Table 4.1 is a heuristic suggesting research questions for comparative studies of interaction networks in different kinds of systems.

## Chronograph

Another way of comparing world-systems is to map spatiotemporally the boundaries of different systems as they merged to become the global modern world-system. Here we will adopt the approach developed by David Wilkinson (1987 [chapter 2, this volume], 1991). Wilkinson bounds his "world systems/civilizations" by means of regularized political/military interaction networks. All states and regions that are regularly engaged in either military conflict or alliance with one another are part of the same political/military network (PMN). Using this rule Wilkinson has produced a chronograph (chapter 2, this volume, Figure 2.1). This shows how thirteen political/military networks containing cities and states were engulfed by what we shall call the "Central PMN." The Central PMN was formed in the merger between the Mesopotamian and Egyptian PMNs in about 1500 BC. Wilkinson, coming from a comparative civilizations approach, excludes systems that do not have cities larger than 10,000 members. Thus, although all stateless and cityless world-systems also have PMNs, those without large cities are not included in Wilkinson's chronograph. If they were included, each of the tributary branches of the Central PMN would be composed of several smaller branches that came together at an earlier time.

Wilkinson's chronograph shows when the several separate PMNs became integrated into the Central PMN. Wilkinson (1992b, 1993) has also designated the spatial boundaries of larger "oikumenes," or trade networks, and the points in time at which they merged. These correspond to the prestige goods networks of our multicriteria approach to spatial boundaries.[2] If we were to redraw Wilkinson's chronograph using the boundaries of "oikumenes" it would look quite similar except that the dates along the left margin would shift down because different regions were usually linked by trade earlier than they were linked into the same political/military network. For example, the linkage of the separate Egyptian and Mesopotamian political/military networks into the same oikumene trade network occurred before 2250 BC, whereas their merger into a single political/military interaction network did not occur until 1500 BC.

From our point of view both prestige goods trade and political/military networks are important for understanding the operation of whole world-systems, so we do not choose to call one or the other the "real" world-system. Rather, the whole system from the perspective of any location is the nested set of networks which impinge systemically upon that place. What Wilkinson calls "civilizations" we will call "PMNs." We shall refer to his trade oikumenes as "prestige goods networks" (PGNs). We also want to consider the importance of bulk goods networks—trade networks that include the flows of basic goods such as foods and everyday raw materials. We shall call Wilkinson's Central Civilization the Central PMN, and his "Old Oikumene" we shall call the Central prestige goods network (PGN).

Here we will summarize Wilkinson's (1992b, 1993) boundaries of trade oikumenes in order to paint a picture of the expansion of the Central PGN. As we have already mentioned, the Egyptian and Mesopotamian PMNs were already joined into the single Central prestige goods network in 2250 BC. This merger of prestige goods nets probably occurred as early as 3000 BC (Marfoe 1987). By 2000 BC the Central PGN had grown to include more of northeast Africa, western Asia, and the Aegean (Wilkinson 1992b, p. 59). By 1800 BC the Central PGN included also the PMN centered in the Indus River valley, which Wilkinson (1992b, p. 60) calls "Indic civilization." In 1600 BC the Central PGN included also the cities of the Aegean PMN on Crete (Wilkinson 1992b, pp. 61–62), but the cities of the Indus had disappeared and Wilkinson indicates that this region was no longer in the Central PGN. In 1360 BC the Mesopotamian and Egyptian PMNs had joined to create the Central PMN, and the Central PGN had expanded to include more of the Mediterranean littoral and had moved back into western India despite the fact that there were no large cities there (Wilkinson 1992b,

p. 63) A separate citified Far Eastern PMN had arisen in China. In 1200 BC the Central PGN had shrunk once again in both the east and the west. India was out, as was the western Mediterranean (Wilkinson 1992b, p. 66). This is an instance of the phenomenon of "pulsation" in which world-systems experience waves of territorial expansion followed by either slower expansion or contraction. In 1200 BC there were separate PMNs and PGNs in India and China.

In 1000 BC the Central PGN had only a single PMN because Central PMN had incorporated the Aegean PMN. The boundaries of the Central PGN had moved south to link with the city of Saba at the southern tip of the Arabian peninsula, but the eastern and western boundaries were about the same as they had been in 1200 BC. By 800 BC not much had changed regarding the boundaries of Central PGN according to Wilkinson. By 650 BC the city of Napata in Nubia had emerged, extending the system south and Wilkinson designates Miletus as being in a separate Aegean PMN that was engulfed by the Central PMN shortly thereafter (Wilkinson 1992b, pp. 69–70). By 430 BC the Central PGN and the Central PMN had begun again to spread east and west. Carthage was part of the Central PGN. Though Wilkinson shows some movement east, the Indic PMN was still characterized as having its own separate oikumene. In Mesoamerica we have the emergence of a new and separate system indicated by the city of Cuicuilco (Wilkinson 1992b, p. 71). Wilkinson notes that "this table is the first to have a notable presence of cities which, though surely or most likely capitals of states, had such small states and/or hinterlands to extract from that they must have flourished (demographically) and lived largely by trade: most Greek and Phoenician cities are of this character" (Wilkinson 1992b, pp. 70–71).

By 200 BC the Central PGN trade net incorporated the Indic region while the PMNs of Central and Indic remained separate. Far Eastern was still outside of the Central PGN according to Wilkinson. This was also the situation in AD 100 except that the Central PMN and the Central PGN had moved northwest a bit to incorporate England. Regarding the relationship between the Far Eastern and the Central PGN, Wilkinson (1992b, pp. 75–76) says:

> The Later Han dynasty is weakening at the center, but has recently extended its power in Turkestan and opened an important silk trade with Rome. Accordingly, it is possible . . . that Far Eastern civilization has now been linked into the Old Oikumene via Rayy, Merv and Balkh. But I have delayed acknowledging that link until AD 622, when the growth of connector cities in Central Asia makes the case more persuasive.

We suggest that this is another case of pulsation, similar in form to the expansion and contraction of the Central PGN mentioned earlier. The Silk

Road trade has been shown to have had important consequences for both Han China and Rome (Teggart 1939). The fact that this trade declined with the decline of the major terminus empires is not surprising and the Eurasian PGN once again became two disconnected systems, not to be firmly attached again for another 400 years. By AD 500 Wilkinson contends that the Central PGN had contracted slightly on its western frontier. The British isles had dropped out with the collapse of the Roman Empire.

In AD 622 Wilkinson shows a single Afroeurasian PGN that included North Africa, Latinized Europe, India, Central Asia, India and Ceylon, China, Japan, the northern Philippines, Sinified Southeast Asia, but not the Malay peninsula or Indonesia. Korea was included in the Far Eastern PMN and in the Central PGN. By AD 800 the Central PGN had fallen back a bit in the northwest, but it had moved southwest into savannah Africa, where it joined with the still separate West African PMN. The Central PGN had also expanded southeast to include by trade the still separate Indonesian PMN. On the eastern edge, within the trade net, was a separate Japanese PMN. In AD 900 the Central PGN had about the same boundaries, but the West African PMN had been incorporated into the Central PMN.

In AD 1000 the boundaries of the Central PGN were nearly the same, but the Central PMN had expanded a bit closer to India. In AD 1100 the boundaries of the Central PGN were about the same, but a new citified political/military network, the Mississippian PMN, centered at Cahokia (East St. Louis), had emerged in North America. Wilkinson (1992b, p. 86) is unsure about whether the Mississippian had its own PGN or was a northern extension of the Mexican PGN. In AD 1200 there were no longer sizable cities in West Africa so Wilkinson does not indicate a citified PMN in that region. By AD 1300 the Central PGN had expanded its boundaries further into Africa and the West African PMN had reappeared. Now the Central PMN was even more separated from the Indic PMN than it had been because of the decline of intervening and linking cities (Wilkinson 1993, p. 43). The citified Indonesian PMN had reappeared.

By AD 1400 the boundaries of the Central PGN remained about the same, but Central PMN had moved again back toward India with the emergence of Samarkand. Large cities had disappeared from the East Indies so Wilkinson does not show an Indonesian PMN. A new citified PMN appeared in Peru, and Wilkinson is unsure whether or not it was part of a larger New World PGN or had its own separate trade net (Wilkinson 1993, p. 5). In AD 1500 the Central PGN was still about the same. This was the last point at which the Indic PMN could be seen as separate from the Central PMN. There were still no large cities in the East Indies.

By AD 1600 the Central PGN and the Central PMN had expanded to include the New World Mexican, Peruvian, and Chibchan PMNs. Chibchan was a separate citified PMN that Wilkinson designates as having arisen in

Colombia. The Central PGN now encompassed all the large cities of the world. The Central PMN had incorporated the Indic and West African PMNs. By AD 1700 things were much the same except that "Tokugawa isolationism has taken Japan out of the Old Oikumene and into an oikumene of its own, where it remains . . . until 1900" (Wilkinson 1993, p. 49). Of course Wilkinson's focus on large cities obscures the rapid incorporation of many new areas in which there were no cities. By 1800 things were much the same regarding the cities, but the Old Oikumene and the Central PMN had continued to expand into nonurbanized regions. European explorers and traders incorporated much of Oceania, North America, and central and southern Africa. By 1900 the Japanese PMN was included in the Central PGN. Wilkinson still shows separate Japanese and Far Eastern PMNs as of 1900, but mentions that these were both incorporated into the Central PMN by the time of World War I. He says that by 1900 we have "the (approximate) end of all oikumenes but the Old Oikumene and (approximate) end of all civilizations but Central civilization" (Wilkinson 1993, p. 51). There may still have been a few isolated stateless and cityless regions outside of the modern world-system, but Wilkinson does not consider these.

In summary Wilkinson (1993, p. 56) says:

> A world economy, lacking a coextensive world polity, but containing world polities of smaller area than its own, existed from (at least) the 4th millennium BC (when it linked the world polities of Egyptian and Mesopotamian civilizations) to the 19th century AD (when a world polity became global, and coextensive with the world economy that had theretofore contained it.) Other such "oikumenes," trade-linked but not politico militarily bonded, probably connected Chibchan with Peruvian civilization, and may have linked Mexican with Mississippian and/or Mexican with Peruvian civilization. But it is particularly noteworthy that Central civilization, from c. 1500 BC to c. AD 1900, formed a politically coherent social system smaller than, nested within, expanding in pace with and into the space pioneered by, an economically coherent but politically unlinked oikumene.

This is the big picture regarding the spreading engulfment of the earth by the Central prestige goods network and the Central political/military network. The details need finer-grained research done on a comparative basis. And the whole chronograph needs to consider the incorporation of stateless and cityless regions as well as the links between those regions in which there were cities. These details can be important for understanding the historical developments that occurred in particular regions, but for comprehending the big picture Wilkinson's monumental work is quite sufficient.

## Pulsation

What are the developmental patterns that can be observed in all world-systems? Remember that our universe of world-systems includes those very small-scale systems composed of sedentary foragers as well as the contemporary global political economy. All world-systems pulsate in the sense that the spatial scale of integration, especially by trade, gets larger and then smaller again. During the enlarging phase trade networks grow in territorial size and become more dense in terms of the frequency of transactions. During the declining phase, trade falls off, local areas become less connected, and they reorganize around self-sufficiency. Local identities and the differentiation of identities between local groups and outsiders are emphasized. We saw several examples of pulsation in the overview of the expansion of the Central PGN above. The point here is that *all* world-systems experience these sequences of expansion and contraction, even very small and egalitarian ones. In hierarchical world-systems these horizontal sequences of linkage and delinkage become entwined with processes of the rise and fall of hierarchies. In these, the processes of universal-local identity formation become linked with the rise and fall of hegemonies (Friedman 1994).

In the next section we shall discuss a pattern which is widespread but not universal: the rise and fall of hierarchy and of the sizes of individual polities. That pattern does not occur in very egalitarian world-systems because there are no hierarchies to rise and fall. Of course there are some inequalities even within and between societies of sedentary foragers. But ethnographers have never observed cycles of increasing and decreasing inequality in such very egalitarian societies. The rise and fall patterns begin in earnest in chiefdoms. But pulsation occurs in all systems.

In systems of sedentary foragers trade networks are institutionalized as down-the-line exchanges of gifts among local leaders. Goods move long distances but there are no long-distance traders. In California we saw archaeological evidence for pulsation cycles as the rise of one trade network, its decline, and the rise of a new, larger trade network (Chase-Dunn 1993). Thomas L. Jackson (1992) links the declines to periods of "localization" in prehistoric California. Similar sequences have been noted in Mesolithic Europe (Price 1991).

In the modern world-system we have had the crisis of the 17th century, and periodic waves in international economic integration followed by declines of trade and emphasis on national autarchy. This system also continues to experience spatial expansion and contraction despite the fact that it encompasses the whole globe. Pressures for the exploration and exploitation of the sea beds, the moon, and outer space obviously vary conjointly with economic cycles. We may ask if there are similar relationships between pulsation and cycles of the rise and fall of hierarchy in different kinds of world-systems? We shall return to that question after we have considered the matter of rise and fall.

## Rise and Fall

All hierarchical intersocietal systems go through sequences of centralization and decentralization of economic, political, and social power. Like states, chiefdoms emerge in sets in which chiefly polities interact and compete with one another, and these "interchiefdom systems" exhibit a pattern of rise and fall in which the territorial and population size of the largest polities rises and then declines (Sahlins 1972, pp. 144–48; Mann 1986, ch. 2; Friedman and Rowlands 1978). The dynamics of this sequence in systems composed of chiefdoms, in which power is organized around hierarchical kinship relations, differ in important ways from the dynamics of rise and fall, political centralization and decentralization, that operate in systems composed of true states.[3] Some chiefdoms develop techniques of power which supplement and go beyond the metaphors of hierarchical kinship. Thus single polities become able to exercise control over larger areas and the interaction networks composed of these larger states grow larger and more densely interconnected.

The cycle of the rise and fall of states occurs in all known interstate systems. In some the competition among a set of states within a single core region of a world-system takes the form of the rise and fall of hegemonic core powers, a process which we know well in the modern world-system. In others, and more frequently, the cycle of political centralization/decentralization takes the form of an alternation between interstate systems (in which there are a number of competing states within a core area, called "states systems" by Wilkinson [1991, pp. 116–21]) and world-empires in which a single state succeeds in unifying an entire core area by means of conquest (called universal empires or world states by Wilkinson). Wilkinson (1992b, p. 54) provides us with periodizations of states systems and world states for eleven state-based PMNs.

In addition to the cycles of the rise and fall of polities, there is a long-run trend toward the increasing size of polities and the decreasing number of autonomous polities on earth (Carneiro 1978). Rein Taagepera's (1978a, 1978b, 1979) studies of changes in the territorial size of the largest empires on earth over the past four thousand years demonstrates the cycles of political centralization and decentralization previously discussed. The combination of the long-term trend of increasing size of polities with the medium-term process of political centralization/decentralization is illustrated in Figure 4.1. Taagepera's studies show that the size of the largest

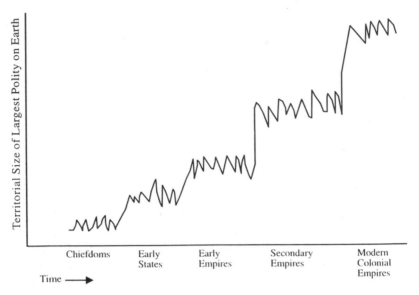

*Figure 4.1.* Cycles and trends of political centralization.

SOURCE: Taagepera (1978).

empire on earth oscillated for long periods and then jumped up in rapid rises corresponding to the wide conquests of semiperipheral marcher states, which created empires across whole core regions. Well-known examples are the Akkadian Empire, the Assyrian Empire, the Alexandrian conquests, and the Roman Empire. Figure 4.1 is a simplified and idealized model based on Taagepera's studies of the territorial size of the largest states and empires on earth and Carneiro's (1978) discussion of the long-term evolutionary trend from many small polities to few large ones.

Of course Figure 4.1 should not be read to imply that each system experiences such a pattern. This is the pattern we get when we plot the largest systems on earth over time on the same graph. Some systems never rise, for example the sedentary foragers of California. Others rise and then decline and never rise again. Friedman's (1981) model of Melanesian systems understands them as former prestige goods chiefdoms that have devolved when trade networks became so dense that hierarchies based on monopolizing imports could no longer be sustained. Even though some individual systems do not exhibit the rise and fall pattern, many experience it repeatedly and also undergo the occasional qualitative leaps in polity size indicated in the graph. These are of interest not only because they change the spatial scale of states and empires, but also because they are associated with the development of new "techniques of power" (Mann 1986) that allow rulers to extract resources over a much broader territory.

It is also the case that the strategies of players at the different size levels in Figure 4.1 are qualitatively different. Thus the strategies appropriate to the creation of a complex chiefdom are quite different from those that will work to create an empire out of separate states or to consolidate hegemony over other core states in the modern world-system. It is also undoubtedly the case that there are qualitatively different strategies that work under different circumstances in *the same world-system types*. Thus Friedman notes that prestige goods systems allow for the creation of complex chiefdoms when long-distance trade is feasible, but that a very different strategy is necessary in regions in which regularized long-distance trade between quite different polities is more costly, and therefore irregular or lacking. So prestige goods chiefdoms emerged in Melanesia and western Polynesia where interarchipelago trade was more feasible, whereas in eastern Polynesia and Hawaii, where long-distance trade was much more difficult, large and hierarchical polities had to rely on the ability of the chiefly class to control access to land and other resources. Blanton, Feinman, Kowalewski, and Peregrine (forthcoming) have analyzed two distinct strategies that interacted in the development of the Mesoamerican world-system. Certainly there are different strategies that are appropriate to the rise of hegemons in the modern world-system. It will not do to simply copy what was done before. But the differences among strategies within similar world-systems (i.e., chiefdom-based systems) are probably smaller than the differences between strategies in completely different types of world-systems.

Andre Gunder Frank and Barry Gills (1993; Gills and Frank 1991) build on the work of Kajsa Ekholm and Jonathan Friedman (1982) to conceptualize and study the sequences of political centralization and decentralization that have occurred in the Central world system over the last 5,000 years. This sequence is well-known to students of political history as the rise and fall of empires. The sequence of political centralization/decentralization is a prime example of a continuity between the modern world-system of the last 500 years and the earlier Central system. Indeed, even chiefdom-based world-systems exhibit a somewhat similar pattern. But these processes also exhibit important differences in different kinds of systems. Both chiefdom systems and state-based systems become centralized through military conquest, but the polities erected by chiefly conquerors must rely on kinship alliances in order to implement regional control, while states make use of specialized nonkin control institutions. This is why state-based empires usually were able to incorporate larger territories and populations than chiefdom-based polities did.

In the modern world-system the pattern of political centralization/decentralization takes the form of the rise and fall of hegemonic core powers. This is analytically similar to the rise and fall of empires, but the differences are important. In the process of empire-formation a "rogue power"—most often a semiperipheral marcher state—conquers the other core states to form what Wilkinson (1987) terms a "universal empire." Well-known examples are the Roman Empire and the Han Empire. This phenomenon corresponds roughly to what Immanuel Wallerstein calls a "world-empire." Wallerstein claims that the modern world-system is politically structured as an interstate system of competing states, while earlier world-systems frequently took the form of world-empires in which the economic division of labor came to be encompassed by a single state.

Rarely did the "universal states" encompass entire world-economies, but they often did conquer an entire adjacent core region. This is the peak of political centralization in such systems. It is convenient to conceptualize centralization and decentralization as two ends of a continuum. Thus, though there have not been true "world-empires" in the sense that a single state comes to encompass an entire world-system, this idea may be understood to point to a relatively high concentration of control over a relatively great proportion of a world-system. The term we prefer, because it is more precise, is "core-wide empire."[4] State-based world-systems prior to the modern one oscillated between core-wide empires and interstate systems. In some regions the decentralization trend went so far as to break up into mini-states. Thus feudalism may be understood as a very decentralized form of a state-based system.

Figure 4.2 illustrates the structural difference between a core-wide empire and a hegemonic core state. This may be understood as simply a difference in the degree of the concentration of political/military power in a single state. It is in this sense that Wallerstein's distinction between world-empires and world-economies points to an important structural difference between the modern system and earlier state-based systems. But this is not only a systematic difference in the degree of peak political concentration. The whole nature of the process of rise and fall is different in the modern world-system. The rise and fall of hegemonies has occurred in a very different way from the rise and fall of empires. Empire formation was a matter of conquering adjacent core states. The rise of modern hegemons did not occur in this way. Modern hegemons did not conquer adjacent core states to extract taxes and tribute. Rather they sought to control international trade, especially oceanic trade, that linked cores with peripheries.

This is why the modern world-system is resistant to empire formation. The most powerful state in the system acts to block empire formation and to preserve the interstate system. Thus the cycle of political centralization/decentralization takes the form of the rise and fall of hegemonic core powers. This important difference is due primarily to the relatively great importance that capitalist accumulation has for the modern system.

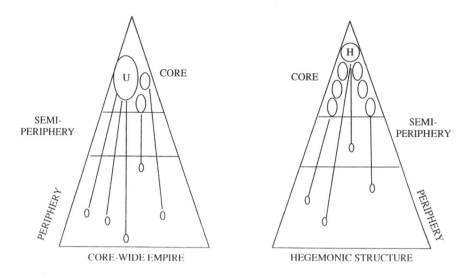

*Figure 4.2.* Core-wide empire (universal state) vs. hegemonic structure.[a]
[a]U = universal state; H = hegemon.

## Settlement Systems

All world-systems have settlement systems in which people locate themselves in space in a certain way and regulate the use of land and natural
resources. Our broadly comparative perspective on world-systems suggests
that we examine the structural similarities and differences of the settlement
systems found in each of our world-system types. As with other differences
in size and scale, we move from the village system of sedentary foragers
to the urbanized world city system of today.[5] Sedentary foragers lived in
rather permanent winter villages, but they traveled to temporary camps
during the summer. The settlement systems of sedentary foragers differ in
terms of their degree of size hierarchy. Some formed clear two-tiered size
hierarchies in which larger villages were regularly separated by smaller
hamlets, while others had no regular distribution of larger and smaller
settlements. In general, polity size and social hierarchy are reflected in the
size hierarchy of the settlement system (e.g., Lightfoot and Feinman 1982;
Nissen 1988, p. 41). But this is not always the case. Some rather densely
populated and hierarchical societies do not concentrate people together in
villages (e.g., ancient Hawaii). Thus it is not always possible to assume a
one-to-one correlation between settlement size hierarchies and political
hierarchies.

## Settlement Size Hierarchies

What is a "city-size hierarchy?" All human settlements interact with other settlements. The size of individual settlements can be studied as they grow or decrease, and the *relative* size of settlements can also be studied. This means looking at the distribution of settlement sizes within a region. Some regions contain settlement systems that are very hierarchical in the sense that there is a single very large settlement that is surrounded by very small settlements. Such settlement systems are called "primate" because there is a single center that is much larger than any other settlement. Geographers have developed theories suggesting that a "normal" settlement size hierarchy will correspond to the *rank-size rule* in which the second largest settlement is half the size of the largest, the third largest is one-third the size of the largest, the fourth largest is one-fourth the size of the largest, and so on. The rank-size rule is also called the "log normal" rule because the distribution of settlement sizes approximates a straight line when the settlement sizes are logarithmically transformed and plotted.

Some settlement systems are "flat" in the sense that the towns or cities or villages of which they are composed are all about the same size. So we can discuss different settlement systems as *primate, rank-size,* or *flat* depending upon the relative size of the settlements of which they are composed. The size hierarchy aspect allows us to compare very different kinds of settlement systems to one another because we are looking at the *relative*, rather than the absolute, sizes of settlements. Thus a system composed of villages can be just as hierarchical as a system composed of great cities if one village is much larger than the other villages.

In order to make such relative comparisons, a statistic called the Standardized Primacy Index (SPI) was developed by Pamela Walters (1985). The SPI takes a value of zero when a settlement size distribution corresponds to the rank-size rule. It takes on negative values when the distribution is less hierarchical (flatter) than the rank-size rule and positive values when the distribution is more hierarchical than the rank-size rule (primacy). Though the measures of urban populations are subject to error, and to greater error as we go further back in time, the SPI is less sensitive to absolute errors because it examines the differences in the population sizes of settlements.

Here we will report the results and conclusions of a research effort that examined the relationship between processes of political centralization/decentralization and changes in the relative population sizes of cities located within several separate political/military networks (Chase-Dunn and Willard 1993). The simplest hypothesis is that city systems will become more hierarchical—that is, the largest cities will be much larger than other cities in the same network—when political/military power is more centralized.

This is based on the idea that political power is an important component of the ability of large cities to gather the resources necessary to sustain large populations. On the other hand, when political power is relatively less centralized within a region, cities should be more equal in size and so the size distribution of cities should be less hierarchical.

The phenomenon of urban primacy—the concentration of population in a very large central city with only much smaller cities in the same region—has been extensively studied in national societies in the modern world-system (Chase-Dunn 1985a, 1985b). It is well known that France has a very primate city-size distribution, as do most peripheral and semiperipheral countries in the modern world-system. Urban primacy is seen as a problem by many contemporary urban and regional planners and they have constructed and tried to implement policies for encouraging the growth of small and middle-sized cities (rather than further increasing the size of the largest city in a country).

The Chase-Dunn and Willard study used data on the populations of cities and the *relative* population sizes of cities within regions defined as networks of political/military interaction. They studied the relationship between changes in the distribution of city sizes, the growth and decline of the largest cities, the rise and decline of centralized polities, and hypothesized long cycles of political/economic expansion and contraction. Gills and Frank (1991) and Frank (1993) have periodized the history of their 5,000-year Eurasian world system into phases of expansion and contraction. Wilkinson (1992a) has examined the relationship between the periodizations proposed by Gills and Frank and changes in the rate of city population growth. He used data from Chandler's compilation of city populations, *Four Thousand Years of Urban Growth* (1987), to study the sizes and number of the largest cities in both political/military interaction networks and larger prestige goods trade networks. Wilkinson found some support for the expansion/contraction periodization proposed by Gills and Frank. The Chase-Dunn and Willard study used the city population data from Chandler in a somewhat different way to examine the Gills-Frank periodizations. And they examined changes in city-size hierarchies of several PMNs over time with Wilkinson's periodization of these into "states systems" and "universal states." This last examines the relationship between settlement size hierarchies and the cycle of political centralization/decentralization previously discussed.

## Power and the City-Size Distribution

Why should a city system have a steeper city-size distribution when there is a greater degree of concentration of power? The simple answer is that large settlements and especially large cities require greater concentrations of resources to support their large populations. This is why population size has itself been suggested as an indicator of power (Taagepera 1978a, p. 111). But these resources may be obtainable locally, and the settlement-size hierarchy may simply correspond to the distribution of ecologically determined resources. For example, in a desert environment populations cluster near oases. It is not the political or economic power of the central settlement over surrounding areas that produces a centralized settlement system, but rather the ecological distribution of necessary or desirable resources. In many systems, however, we have reason to believe that relations of power, domination, and exploitation do affect the distribution of human populations in space. Many large cities are as large as they are because they are able to draw upon far-flung regions for food and raw materials. If a city is able to use political/military power or economic power to acquire resources from surrounding cities it will be able to support a larger population than the dominated cities can, and this should produce a hierarchical city-size distribution.

Of course the effect can also go the other way. Some cities can dominate others *because* they have larger populations. Great population size makes possible the assembly of large armies or navies, and this may be an important factor creating or reinforcing steep city-size distributions.

The Chase-Dunn and Willard research examined the extent to which changes in the degree of population-size hierarchies in city systems correspond or do not correspond with changes in the degree of political centralization. They also examined the hypothesized expansion/stagnation phases proposed by Frank (1993) by observing changes in the size of the urban population. For information about political centralization, Chase-Dunn and Willard used several sources dealing with historical changes in the relationship among states in each PMN.

As stated above, the primary unit of analysis in the Chase-Dunn and Willard study is the political/military interaction network (PMN) as constructed by Wilkinson. Is the PMN the best unit of analysis for studying city systems? We will argue that it is a good unit of analysis, but that it would also be desirable to use PGNs and bulk goods networks and to compare the results with those based on PMNs. For the present, the boundaries of PMNs are well enough specified that we can easily use them for the comparative study of ancient city systems.

The Chase-Dunn and Willard study used Chandler's (1987) data on city population[6] to construct a series of SPI indices showing the steepness of city-size distributions for eight PMNs: Egyptian in 1600 BC, Mesopotamian in 2000 and 1600 BC; Aegean in 1360 BC; Mesoamerican in 200 BC, AD 500, and AD 800; West African in AD 1350, AD 1500, and AD 1550; Indic from 430 BC to AD 1550; Far Eastern from 650 BC to AD

TABLE 4.2

*Standardized Primacy Indices (SPIs) for the Five Largest Cities in Each Political/Military Network (PMN)*

| Year | Egyptian | Mesopo- tamian | Aegean | Mexican | West African | Indic | Far Eastern | Japanese | Central |
|---|---|---|---|---|---|---|---|---|---|
| 2000 BC | | −0.1 | | | | | | | |
| 1600 BC | 0.31 | −0.19 | | | | | | | |
| 1360 BC | | | −2.05 | | | | | | −0.21 |
| 1200 BC | | | | | | | | | −2.2 |
| 650 BC | | | | | | | −0.72 | | −0.21 |
| 430 BC | | | | | | −0.32 | −0.09 | | −0.71 |
| 200 BC | | | | −2.36 | | 0.2 | 0.2 | | −0.4 |
| AD 100 | | | | | | −1.21 | 0.25 | | −0.15 |
| AD 361 | | | | | | −0.22 | −0.52 | | −0.62 |
| AD 500 | | | | 0.102 | | −1.96 | −0.296 | | −0.636 |
| AD 622 | | | | | | −0.82 | 0.02 | | 0.19 |
| AD 800 | | | | −0.873 | | −1.986 | 0.109 | | 0.115 |
| AD 900 | | | | | | −1.702 | 0.175 | | 0.111 |
| AD 1000 | | | | | | −1.793 | 0.033 | | −0.089 |
| AD 1100 | | | | | | −0.595 | 1.667 | | −1.667 |
| AD 1150 | | | | | | −1.474 | −3.906 | | −2.871 |
| AD 1200 | | | | | | −2.052 | −0.677 | | −2.44 |
| AD 1250 | | | | | | −1.705 | −0.231 | | −0.283 |
| AD 1300 | | | | | | −2.584 | −0.461 | | 0.01 |
| AD 1350 | | | | | −2.5 | −1.035 | −0.456 | | −0.074 |
| AD 1400 | | | | | | 0.273 | −0.021 | | −0.295 |
| AD 1450 | | | | | | 0.112 | 0.022 | | −0.13 |
| AD 1500 | | | | | −2.5 | 0.042 | 0.074 | | −0.26 |
| AD 1550 | | | | | −0.103 | 0.186 | 0.052 | | −0.026 |
| AD 1575 | | | | | | | 0.059 | 0.235 | −0.056 |
| AD 1600 | | | | | | | 0.043 | −0.29 | −0.146 |
| AD 1650 | | | | | | | −0.122 | −0.733 | −0.615 |
| AD 1700 | | | | | | | 0.009 | 0.17 | −1.093 |
| AD 1750 | | | | | | | 0.016 | −0.197 | −1.196 |
| AD 1800 | | | | | | | −0.132 | −0.186 | −0.468 |
| AD 1825 | | | | | | | −0.074 | 0.122 | −0.148 |
| AD 1850 | | | | | | | | 0.079 | −0.335 |
| AD 1875 | | | | | | | | | −0.039 |
| AD 1900 | | | | | | | | | −0.222 |
| AD 1914 | | | | | | | | | −0.82 |
| AD 1925 | | | | | | | | | −1.506 |
| AD 1950 | | | | | | | | | −0.503 |
| AD 1970 | | | | | | | | | −0.849 |
| AD 1988 | | | | | | | | | −0.94 |
| Mean | 0.310 | −0.145 | −2.050 | −1.044 | −1.701 | −0.981 | −0.184 | −0.100 | −0.590 |
| SD | 0 | 0.045 | 0 | 1.01 | 1.13 | 0.902 | 0.837 | 0.3 | 0.718 |

1825; Japanese from AD 1575 to 1850 and the Central PMN from 1360 BC to AD 1988 (see Table 4.2). The Central PMN incorporated the other PMNs after the dates at which we cease to calculate their SPIs. Chase-Dunn and Willard produced SPIs for time points at which we have estimated populations for *at least the three largest cities*. They used at least three (but a maximum of five) cities when populations for these were available. The SPI is standardized to correct for changes in the number of cities across time points.

Observe in Table 4.2 that the SPI for the Mesopotamian PMN was –0.1 in 2000 BC. The negative sign means that the Mesopotamian city-size hierarchy was flatter than the rank-size rule. In 1600 BC the Mesopotamian SPI was –0.19 and so the city-size hierarchy had become a bit flatter than it had been in 2000. At the bottom of the table are the average SPIs for each of the PMNs. The grand mean for all the SPIs in the table is –0.820. Thus the average city-size distribution for all the PMNs for which we have data tends to be flatter than the rank-size rule. An earlier study of city-size distributions in modern national societies showed that these SPIs are, on the average, steeper than the rank-size rule (Chase-Dunn 1985b). But modern national societies are parts of a larger intersocietal system, not whole systems unto themselves. An earlier study of the Europe-centered modern world-system as bounded by the Braudel Center scholars (Chase-Dunn 1985a) showed that this larger intersocietal system composed of multiple states has city-size distributions which are usually flatter than the rank-size rule over the period from AD 800 to 1975. Intersocietal systems composed of multiple states are much more likely to have relatively flatter city-size distributions than are single states precisely because political power is more decentralized relative to the relations among cities in these larger systems than it is in single states.

Certainly the way in which we bound the regions within which we study city systems is important for what we find. In principle we want to study cities that are engaging in important interactions with one another. If we include within the same "region" cities that are not connected to one another by such human interactions as trade, warfare, and communications, we are lumping together in our analysis things which were not importantly connected in reality. Thus we could consider the entire earth as a single region since 2000 BC and analyze all the known cities as parts of a single system since then (as seems to be suggested by the approach developed by Gills and Frank [1991]). But this would be a mistake because we know, for example, that Mesoamerican cities were not linked to Old World interaction networks in any important way until the 16th century AD. Lumping them in with the Central world-system before then would be a mistake.

## Comparing the Mean SPIs of Different PMNs

Notice at the bottom of Table 4.2 that the mean SPIs for the different PMNs are quite different from one another. Though the data points are few, it is interesting to note that the Mesopotamian PMN has a flatter city-size distribution than does the Egyptian PMN. This is consistent with what we know about differences between the Egyptian and Mesopotamian political systems. In Egypt a centralized empire formed very early and was relatively stable for a long time, producing a more hierarchical city system. In Mesopotamia a number of city-states emerged and interacted within a larger intercity-state system for a long while before the unification of the Mesopotamian core by the Akkadian conquest. And that early empire was not long-lived. The Mesopotamian city-size hierarchy is flatter than the Egyptian one, and we are tempted to say that this is due to the differences in political structure between the two regions.

The Indic PMN shows an average SPI of –0.981 based on 19 time points. This is flatter than the average for the Central PMN. The Far Eastern PMN has an average SPI of –0.184 based on 27 time points. This is more hierarchical than is the average for the Central PMN. In this case a city system which is more hierarchical corresponds to what many have perceived as a relatively more centralized political system. John Fitzpatrick (1992) has recently emphasized that Chinese development before the Mongol conquest occurred in the context of a competitive interstate system in which geopolitical competition among states often played an important part in shaping outcomes. Fitzpatrick contends that in this respect Chinese development was more similar to that in the European regional system than most of the many contrasters of Chinese empire and European state system would admit. This approach to the Far Eastern PMN is further strengthened by Thomas Barfield's (1989) work on the systemic relations between Chinese and steppe nomad states. While we may agree with Fitzpatrick's overall point, the difference in the average degree of city-size hierarchy between China and the Central PMN indicates that political centralization was greater, on the average, in China.

The Japanese PMN was even more hierarchical on the average than was the Far Eastern, with a mean SPI of –0.100 based on eight time points. This is quite close to the rank-size rule. It might be thought that the relatively hierarchical shape of the Japanese city system is due to the fact that Japan is rather small and small regions are more likely to have hierarchical city-size distributions. Studies of city-size distributions in modern national societies show a negative correlation between the territorial size of a country and the degree of hierarchy of the city-size distribution. Obviously Hong Kong and Singapore, city-states, are extreme cases of urban primacy, but the negative correlation between regional size and urban primacy holds even when such cases are omitted. Does small size account for the relatively more hierarchical average SPI in the Japanese PMN? It might account for some of it, but it cannot account for all of it. Though four of the eight individual SPIs in Japan are more hierarchical than the rank-size rule, the SPI for AD 1650 is –0.733, which is flatter than the average of all the SPIs in Table 4.2. Since the territorial size of the Japanese PMN did not greatly change between 1600 and 1700, the less hierarchical city-size distribution cannot be due to size of the region. If urban hierarchy can be shown to be a reflection of political centralization, the city-size data for Japan will contradict the notion that Japan was a decentralized feudal system between 1575 and 1850.

Though these differences between average SPIs across different PMNs suggest some support for the notion that city-size hierarchies are correlated with regionally centralized political power, the main analysis of the relationship between city-size hierarchies and periods of political centralization/decentralization requires the comparison of SPIs over time within PMNs. Inspection of the standard deviations of the distributions of SPIs for each PMN in the bottom row of Table 4.2 shows that there are big differences over time in all the PMNs for which there are several time points. Chase-Dunn and Willard plotted the changes in SPIs for each PMN for which there were several time points and they compared the changes in the SPIs over time with information about the rise and fall of states and empires.

## Changes in City-Size Hierarchies and Power Concentration

Does the steepness or flatness of city-size distributions vary systematically with changes in the concentration of political and/or economic power? Unfortunately we do not have continuous and comparable measures of the distributions of economic and political power over long periods of time. This is one reason why it would be useful to know whether or not city-size distributions can serve as a proxy for direct measures of the distributions of power. In order to study changes in the distributions of political and economic power Chase-Dunn and Willard relied on historical accounts based on textual evidence. These are imperfect sources that are undoubtedly selective and error-prone in ways that may have led to false inferences. Closer studies of PMNs are needed, especially to improve upon the estimation of changes in the distribution of political power.

These are the conclusions of the study by Chase-Dunn and Willard: *Both political and economic power distributions are reflected in changes in city-size distributions.* In almost every case where a city system significantly changed its degree of flatness or hierarchy Chase-Dunn and Willard found indications of major and corresponding shifts in political power. They found only two cases in which the city-size distribution changed dramatically without an obvious corresponding shift in political power. In the first such case, the Far Eastern city system became much more hierarchical in 430 BC due to the growth of Yenhsiatu in the north. This was the Warring States period well before the rise of the first empire. There was a lot of economic development and urban growth in this period. If Yenhsiatu had been at a hub of transport nets linking the cities of northern China this might have accounted for its rapid rise. But it was not. This is a mystery.

The second case is less mysterious. Wilkinson designates the period between 525 and 316 BC in the Central PMN as one in which a world state was constituted by the Persian and then the Macedonian empires. But the city-size distribution in 430 BC was moderately flat. The Persian Empire was still massive in 430 BC, but important challenging states outside of its domain had developed large cities. Thus the Persian Empire was not a core-wide state in this period. The case of Yenhsiatu may be an exception to the rule or simply one in which some important piece of information is missing. In any case, only two exceptions to the correspondence between the SPI and the concentration of political power would seem to be strong evidence in favor of the above hypothesis.

Another test of the relationship between power and the city-size distributions is provided by using Taagepera's (1978a, 1978b, 1979) data on the territorial size of empires organized by PMNs. Taagepera used maps in atlases to estimate the territorial size of the largest empires on earth from 3000 BC to AD 1975. The first thing to do is to examine the relationship between empire size and city size. If the above hypothesis is correct, large empires should generally have large capital cities, though there may be exceptions. Figure 4.3 plots the population sizes of the largest cities in the Central PMN along with the territorial size of the largest empires. The data on empire sizes are much more complete than the data on city sizes. Figure 4.3 demonstrates that there is no simple correspondence between the two variables.[7] It is possible that this is due to missing data on city populations.

But there is another possibility. It may be that the rise and peaking of the territorial size of empires occurs first and then city size rises after a considerable time lag. This appears to occur in three instances. Empire size rises after 850 BC with the Assyrian conquests and it peaks in 500 BC with the Achaemenids. Then there is another wave due to the Alexandrian conquests. The data on city sizes are sparse in this period, but it looks as if the largest cities came during the trough between the Alexandrian empires and the rise of Rome. The Roman rise is more of a hump than a peak, and Rome was always part of a PMN that contained other large empires. Thus Rome was not a world-empire in the Wallersteinian sense. The city data from Chandler

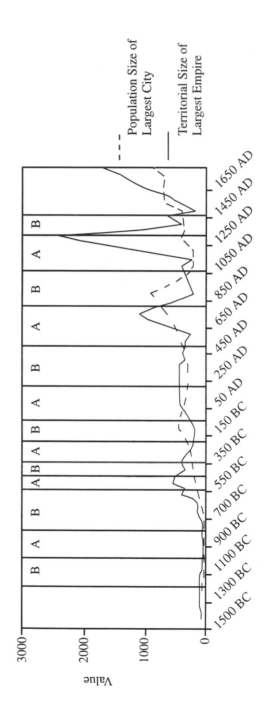

*Figure 4.3.*　City and empire sizes in the Central PMN, 1500 BC to AD 1800. A and B phases according to Frank (1993); Pearson's r = .21.

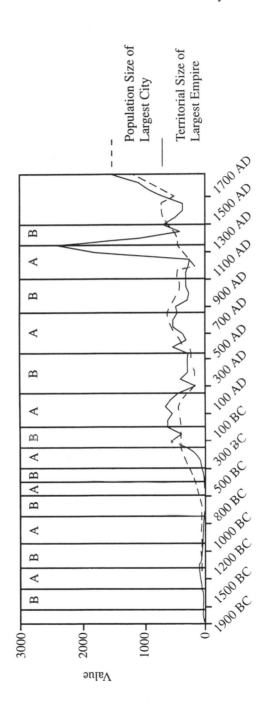

*Figure 4.4.*   City and empire sizes in the Far Eastern PMN, 1900 BC to AD 1850. A and B phases according to Frank (1993); Pearson's r = .33.

are sparse during the Roman Empire. Then the Muslims took empire size to new heights. But it was only after the decline of the large Muslim empires that cities attained their greatest size. The Mongol Empire had little to do with city growth, as is well understood by the Mongol attitude toward cities. So the evidence from the Central PMN, though spotty, indicates that cities and empires do not always grow together. It also suggests that empires grow first, then decline, and then cities grow.

Figure 4.4 examines the same variables for the case of the Far Eastern PMN. Here there is a much more positive relationship between city sizes and empire size, though again the city data are quite spotty early on.[8] The rise and fall of the Han Empire corresponds to a rise and decline in city sizes. From AD 600 to 800 there are a number of large empires, and these correspond to a rise of city sizes. As in the Central PMN, the Mongol Empire corresponds to only a small rise in city sizes, and then both empire size and city size rise rapidly after AD 1600. The evidence from the Far Eastern PMN is much more supportive of a direct relationship between city sizes and empire sizes than are the results for the Central PMN. The hypothesized lag between empires and cities in the Central PMN is not found in the Far Eastern PMN.

A more direct test of the hypothesis of power concentration and city-size hierarchy is the relationship between empire size and the SPI.[9] Correlational analysis finds no relationship between these two indicators for either the Central or the Far Eastern PMN. We have not examined this relationship for possible time lags. It would also be desirable to examine an analogous distributional measure of empire-size hierarchy using data on the second- and third-largest empires in each PMN.

## Conclusion

Further work is needed before we can conclude that the hypothesized relationship between political power concentration and city-size hierarchy is false. One problem with the analysis presented here is that the measures of city populations for earlier time periods are too spread out over time. A data gathering project that supplements the pioneering work of Tertius Chandler (1987) on city populations could provide a much more certain ability to evaluate our hypothesis. There are also holes in Rein Taagepera's (1978a, 1978b, 1979) data set on empire sizes that need to be filled. Taagepera's data concern only the largest empires on earth, and so some empires that were important within regional PMNs are left out. Supplementing these two data sets would not only provide the opportunity of an improved evaluation of the power concentration/city hierarchy hypothesis, but would be a helpful basic step toward the construction of a world history geographical information system.

NOTES

1.  For a review, see Hall and Chase-Dunn (1994).

2.  Wilkinson's (1992b, pp. 55–56) definition of oikumene is as follows: "An 'oikumeme' is here defined as a trading area, a domain internally knit by a network of trade routes, in which there is enough internal trade so that the whole trading area evolves to a significant degree as a system, while trade outside the area, though perhaps important both to the oikumene and to other oikumenes with which it trades, is not sufficiently dense and significant to cause system-level development to encompass these external systems."

3.  We follow Johnson and Earle (1987) in defining true states as polities that are larger than chiefdoms and that have specialized institutions of regional administration and control.

4.  Wilkinson refers to the decentralization phase as constituting a "states system."

5.  An overview of the role of cities in world-system development is presented in Chase-Dunn (1992).

6.  See Wilkinson (1992b) for a comparison between Chandler's city lists and those derived from other sources. The business of estimating the population sizes of cities is fraught with danger, especially when we are limited to archaeological evidence. The estimates get more accurate as we approach the present.

7.  The Pearson r correlation coefficient between Central city and empire sizes is only 0.36 based on 25 time points. This is statistically significant only at the 0.07 level.

8.  The correlation coefficient for Far Eastern city and empire sizes is 0.46 based on 28 time points. This is statistically significant at the 0.014 level.

9.  The Central correlation between the SPI and empire size is 0.15 based on 25 time points. The Far Eastern correlation is –0.02 based on 24 time points.

*References*

Barfield, Thomas J. 1989. *The Perilous Frontier: Nomadic Empires and China*. Oxford: Basil Blackwell.

Biraben, J. R. 1979. "Essai sur l'évolution du nombre des hommes." *Population* 34:13–25.

Blanton, Richard, Gary M. Feinman, Stephen A. Kowalewski, and Peter N. Peregrine. Forthcoming. "A Dual-Processual Theory for the Evolution of Mesoamerican Civilization." *Current Anthropology*.

Carneiro, Robert. 1978. "Political Expansion as an Expression of the Principle of Competitive Exclusion." In *Origins of the State: The Anthropology of Political*

*Evolution,* edited by Ronald Cohen and Elman R. Service. Philadelphia, PA: Institute for the Study of Human Issues.

Chandler, Tertius. 1987. *Four Thousand Years of Urban Growth: An Historical Census.* Lewiston, NY: St. David's University Press.

Chase-Dunn, Christopher. 1985a. "The System of World Cities: AD 800–1975." In *Urbanization in the World-Economy,* edited by Michael Timberlake. New York: Academic Press.

——. 1985b. "The Coming of Urban Primacy in Latin America." *Comparative Urban Research* 11:14–31.

——. 1992. "The Changing Role of Cities in World-Systems." In *Waves, Formations, and Values in the World System,* edited by Volker Bornschier and Peter Lengyel. New Brunswick, NJ: Transaction Publishers.

——. 1993. "Intersocietal Inequalities in Small World-Systems: Northern California." A final project report to the National Science Foundation.

Chase-Dunn, Christopher, and Thomas D. Hall. 1993. "Comparing World-Systems: Concepts and Working Hypotheses." *Social Forces* 71:851–86.

Chase-Dunn, Christopher, and Alice Willard. 1993. "Systems of Cities and World-Systems: Settlement Size Hierarchies and Cycles of Political Centralization, 2000 BC–1988 AD." Paper presented at the annual meetings of the International Studies Association, Acapulco.

Cook, Sherburne F. 1976. *The Population of the California Indians, 1769–1970.* Berkeley: University of California Press.

Durand, John D. 1977. "Historical Estimates of World Population: An Evaluation." *Population and Development Review* 3:253–96.

Ekholm, Kajsa, and Jonathan Friedman. 1982. "'Capital' Imperialism and Exploitation in Ancient World-Systems." *Review* 4:87–109.

Fitzpatrick, John. 1992. "The Middle Kingdom, the Middle Sea, and the Geographical Pivot of History." *Review* 15:477–521.

Frank, Andre Gunder. 1993. "Bronze Age World System Cycles." *Current Anthropology* 34:383–430.

Frank, Andre Gunder, and Barry K. Gills, eds. 1993. *The World System: Five Hundred Years or Five Thousand?* London: Routledge.

Friedman, Jonathan. 1981. "Notes on Structure and History in Oceania." *Folk* 23:275–95.

——. 1994. *Cultural Identity and Global Process.* London: Sage.

Friedman, Jonathan, and Michael Rowlands. 1978. "Notes Towards an Epigenetic Model of the Evolution of 'Civilization.'" In *The Evolution of Social Systems,* edited by Jonathan Friedman and Michael Rowlands. Pittsburgh, PA: University of Pittsburgh Press.

Gills, Barry K., and Andre Gunder Frank. 1991. "5,000 Years of World-System History: The Cumulation of Accumulation." In *Core/Periphery Relations in Precapitalist Worlds,* edited by Christopher Chase-Dunn and Thomas D. Hall. Boulder, CO: Westview Press.

Hall, Thomas D., and Christopher Chase-Dunn. 1994. "Forward into the Past: World-Systems Before 1500." *Sociological Forum* 9:295–306.

Jackson, Thomas L. 1992. "Defining Small-Scale World Systems in California Prehistory." Paper presented at the annual meetings of the Society for American Archaeology, Pittsburgh.

Johnson, Allen W., and Timothy Earle. 1987. *The Evolution of Human Societies.* Stanford, CA: Stanford University Press.

Lightfoot, Kent G., and Gary M. Feinman. 1982. "Social Differentiation and Leadership Development in Early Pithouse Villages in the Mogollon Region of the American Southwest." *American Antiquity* 47:64–86.

Mann, Michael. 1986. *The Sources of Social Power. Volume 1: A History of Power from the Beginning to AD 1760.* Cambridge: Cambridge University Press.

Marfoe, Leon. 1987. "Cedar Forest to Silver Mountain: Social Change and the Development of Long-Distance Trade in Early Near Eastern Societies." In *Centre and Periphery in the Ancient World,* edited by Michael Rowlands, Mogens Trolle Larsen, and Kristian Kristiansen. Cambridge: Cambridge University Press.

Nissen, Hans J. 1988. *The Early History of the Ancient Near East: 9000–2000 BC.* Chicago: University of Chicago Press.

Price, T. Douglas. 1991. "The Mesolithic of Northern Europe." *Annual Review of Anthropology* 20:211–33.

Sahlins, Marshall. 1972. *Stone Age Economics.* Chicago: Aldine.

Taagepera, Rein. 1978a. "Size and Duration of Empires: Systematics of Size." *Social Science Research* 7:108–27.

———. 1978b. "Size and Duration of Empires: Growth-Decline Curves, 3000 to 600 BC." *Social Science Research* 7:180–96.

———. 1979. "Size and Duration of Empires: Growth-Decline Curves, 600 BC to 600 AD." *Social Science History* 3:115–38.

Teggart, Frederick. 1939. *Rome and China: A Study of Correlations in Historical Events.* Berkeley: University of California Press.

Walters, Pamela Barnhouse. 1985. "Systems of Cities and Urban Primacy: Problems of Definition and Measurement." In *Urbanization in the World-Economy,* edited by Michael Timberlake. New York: Academic Press.

Wilkinson, David. 1987. "Central Civilization." *Comparative Civilizations Review* 17:31–59. (Reprinted as chapter 2, this volume.)

———. 1991. "Cores, Peripheries, and Civilizations." In *Core/Periphery Relations in Precapitalist Worlds,* edited by Christopher Chase-Dunn and Thomas D. Hall. Boulder, CO: Westview Press.

———. 1992a. "Decline Phases in Civilizations, Regions, and Oikumenes." Paper presented at the annual meetings of the International Studies Association, Atlanta.

———. 1992b. "Cities, Civilizations, and Oikumenes, I." *Comparative Civilizations Review* 27:51–87.

———. 1993. "Cities, Civilizations, and Oikumenes, II." *Comparative Civilizations Review* 28:41–72.

■ BARRY K. GILLS

*Chapter Five*

# Capital and Power in the Processes of World History

This essay sets out to explain, to extend, and to autocritique the "world system" approach (without a hyphen) developed in recent years by myself and Andre Gunder Frank (Gills and Frank 1990, 1992, 1994; Frank and Gills 1993). I will begin by addressing the issue of what, in my own view, is most distinctive about this approach to the processes of world-historical development, and examine its particular reformulation of historical materialism and structuralism.

## Processes of World Development

My research program focuses on explaining the pattern of relationships between three interlocking processes of world development: (1) the process of capital accumulation at world scale; (2) the historical development of the world economy; and (3) state formation and the development of hegemonic forms of world order. These three processes are linked to the following three historical themes: (1) the historical origins of capital and the continual importance of capital throughout world development; (2) the extension and deepening of commodity relations, for example, production for exchange, exchange systems, trade networks, commodification of labor, the division of labor, and the development of the market, all seen as historical processes; and (3) the process of state formation (including reorganization of class relations and social structure) and the dialectic of world order, and the "rise and fall" of interlinked state structures in relation to rhythms of expansion and contraction in the world economy.

The guiding ideas in this work are that capital is not a modern invention; nor is capital or the process of capital accumulation only of modern political and economic significance; nor is "capitalist production" an invention of the modern West, nor only a modern category; nor did the West create a "capitalist world system" or even the world economy. All of the above are quite ancient institutional features of the world system/economy and have undergone continual "cumulative" development. I call this the "perennial political economy perspective."

## Historical Materialism

The new historical materialism embodied in the world system approach emphasizes the great importance *throughout* Eurasian and world system history of capital accumulation processes. In addition to this, it focuses on the regular production of commodities for international exchange, the inseparability of economic and political systems, and, above all, the world systemic character of this transcontinental trade and its concomitant process of "world accumulation."

It is argued that the production of commodities, commerce, trade, price-setting markets, private enterprise, private capital, capital accumulation, and the international division of labor have all played much more important roles much farther back in world history than has usually been recognized or accepted. It is precisely on this basis that Frank and I make the claim that "capital accumulation" has *always* been a driving force of world development, and not merely of the modern world political economy. This claim is the basis for a new historical materialism, but one which radically departs from the traditional Marxist perspectives on world history.

It is particularly important to clarify the controversial suggestion that "ceaseless accumulation," which according to Wallerstein is *the* differentia specifica of modern capitalism, is in fact a *constant* historical feature of the world system. Though there can be no doubt that the modern industrialization of production played a crucial role in bringing about a qualitative change in the *rate* of ceaseless accumulation, in our view this change is essentially a matter of degree, as opposed to the invention of a new social relation.

Wallerstein concedes that the difference between so-called protocapitalism and full-blown capitalism is a matter of degree, in this case the degree to which the capitalist mode of production (i.e., the capital-wage labor relation) is perceived to be *dominant* in the entire socioeconomic formation (Wallerstein 1991; Frank 1994). Wallerstein's view reflects the general reluctance to acknowledge the systemic importance of capital accumulation in the premodern world economy.

This debate obviously turns on the definition of "ceaseless," since Wallerstein, like Weber, acknowledges both the existence and perhaps even the "prevalence" of capital well before the modern period. Wallerstein's method of erecting a sharp dichotomy between protocapitalist and capitalist economics is, however, quite distinctive from either Polanyi's emphasis on the "great transformation" to the self-regulating market (Polanyi 1944; Polanyi, Arensberg and Pearson, 1957) or Weber's view of unique Western rationality as the watershed of modern capitalism (Weber [1904]1958, [1896–1909]1976, [1927]1981; Blaut 1993). It is not merely academic, however, whether one chooses to take "capital," "market" or "rationality" as the defining characteristic of modern political economy.

In our view, following Marx (up to a point), ceaseless accumulation implies that capital is constantly reinvested in the circuits of production in order to sustain capital accumulation. This ceaselessness is imperative, especially given the facts of competition. The historical evidence suggests to us (Gills and Frank 1990, 1992; Frank and Gills 1993) that capital accumulation of this type has been a feature not only of the modern world, but of much of world system history. Capital accumulation has normally been driven by contextual factors that may be interpreted as imperative and competitive. Likewise, it has long been a process that involved a continual reinvestment in the means of production, and indeed in a whole social and political ensemble of sectors, including infrastructure. This investment process is carried out both by private capital and by the state, in varying combinations that change with political-economic conditions.

I have argued elsewhere (Gills 1993b) that the main problem is the fundamental misconception of the character of premodern economics, particularly of Eurasia, based on the mistaken generalization of the "command economy," or as Perry Anderson (1974) would have it, of the perceived role of coercion, that is, the determination of surplus transfers by the "political instance" rather than by "economics." This bias leads to a systematic underestimation of the role of capital in history. It elevates power to the primary economic category.

Likewise, it is particularly mistaken to generalize the notion of "feudalism," derived as it is from a particular reading of European economic history, to the entire Eurasian world economy (Abu-Lughod 1989; Blaut 1993; Gills and Frank 1994). Moreover, traditional "manorial" views of the medieval European experience confront the argument that cities and commercial life were both more prevalent and more important much earlier than previously acknowledged (Hodges 1989; Lombard 1975). In any event, medieval Europe was only a small part of the actual Eurasian economy of the period, in which the Near East (including Byzantium), India, Central Asia, and China played central commercial roles.

Nor is what Samir Amin (1976) calls the "tributary mode" any real solution to, or refutation of, the above. What Amin calls tribute is merely "taxation" by another name. The fact that all historical states have lived by some form of taxation is hardly a revelation to anyone, but it is not necessarily incompatible with the idea that, more often than not, premodern states coexisted with a vibrant commercial sector in the economy, primarily directed by private merchants and bankers and conducted on international scale. This is also the argument made by Chaudhuri (1991), who says that "even the great territorial empires drawing huge revenues from a productive agriculture could not turn that revenue into disposable state income without the intermediary of merchants and their role as bankers. If these empires were ruled by princes and warriors, they were also *financed* in reality by merchants" (p. 431, emphasis added).

The sheer volume of evidence from each specialist history of the various "parts" of Eurasia corroborates the contention of the centrality of world economic commerce and the role of private (or so-called "merchant") capital within it. Abu-Lughod (1989) has demonstrated this for the Islamic-centered world economy from as early as the 9th century. It seems that what dare not speak its name is the ancient and medieval "capitalist," that is, that the ubiquitous term "merchant" may be a euphemism for the de facto "capitalist" of world history. This reluctance to acknowledge the merchant/banker/manufacturing classes in premodern history as being capitalist classes is simply a product of ideology, not science. The sooner this is corrected the better the analysis will become.

How "capitalist" was the world economy and how early on? It is useful to follow the argument backward in time. I would propose that virtually all Eurasian core economies were already quite "capitalist" at least by the 15th century. However, Braudel says that "capitalist cities" and indeed "capitalism" were already developed in 13th-century Italy. Yet, the cities of the "Islamic world system" in the 13th century were equally (if not more so) such "capitalist" cities. If so, then really the entire Eurasian world economy/system of the 13th century was also perhaps already "capitalist." But Abu-Lughod tells us that the Arabs learned their capitalism from pre-Islamic forms of business contract and credit arrangements, already long extant in the Middle Eastern economy. If that is accepted, and given increasingly strong arguments for the commercial networks of early medieval Europe (Hodges 1989) and Asia (Chaudhuri 1991), then we ought to fundamentally reconsider our view of the medieval economy. We know that China under the Song dynasty was heavily engaged in very extensive commerce at about the same time, as were India and the wider Arab domains. Perhaps the medieval world economy was already quite "capitalist" by the 10th century.

Therefore, the evidence keeps leading us to extend the continuity thesis of the centrality of capital accumulation yet farther back in world-historical development. The ancient economy too, therefore, must also be reconsidered, including the role of markets, credit, and capital within it (e.g., Millett 1990). Rostovtzeff's seminal *The Social and Economic History of the Hellenistic World* (1941) may be interpreted to support the argument that the difference between the (market) economy of the 4th century BC and the modern economy is "quantitative not qualitative." Following Millett, who has reinterpreted the role of credit in the Athenian economy, we may contend that the primitivist approach, which minimizes the role of "credit" (i.e., capital) in the ancient economy, is apparently contradicted by the sheer volume of credit transactions in the ancient sources, and indeed credit (or money capital) was "everywhere" in antiquity.[1]

Indeed, there is evidence of the market/credit economy existing as far back as ancient Assyria, with private capitalists in a single industrial firm organizing production with thousands of wage laborers (Larsen 1967, 1976; Silver 1985; see also Rowlands, Larsen, and Kristiansen 1987). Silver (1985) contradicts Polanyi on ancient markets and argues that in Assyrian trade colonies in Anatolia, for instance, "the evidence on price formation . . . is fully consistent with the operation of market forces of the usual (i.e., price-setting) kind" (p. 74). To Diakonoff's assertion that "no accumulation of capital took place" in the ancient economy, following Silver we may retort that "evidence is abundant of the accumulation of human and material capital, including circulating capital . . . and fixed capital" (p. 107). But even prior to Assyria, what about the Akkadian political economy of the Sargonid and even pre-Sargonid period? Joan Oates (1978, p. 408) argues that new evidence now confirms "the presence of a profit motive already in the mid-3rd millennium BC, . . . a true commodity market," as well as "the importance of entrepreneurial activity together with the interdependence of trade and production."

In 1982, Ekholm and Friedman were the authors of the first explicitly formulated thesis on the continuity of capital accumulation and imperialism in world development. Ekholm and Friedman conclude that "there exists a form of 'capitalism' in the ancient world, that there are 'world economies,' and that many properties of the dynamics of such systems are common to our own world economy" (1993, p. 59). However, they qualify this thesis, arguing that "to say that this ancient 'capital' played a fundamental economic role is not to say that it functioned directly in the production process, but that its accumulation and control were dominant features of those economies" (p. 60).

Like them, I have no intention of suggesting the risible, that is, to contend that all of world history has been the *same* "capitalism," at least not in the same sense as capitalism is conventionally understood after about 1800 and modern industrialization. The point is simply to demolish false dichotomies and allow new thinking on continuity in economic history, especially reinterpreting the role of capital and reexamining its relationship with power.

Once we have acknowledged that private capital has played a continually important role in world economic history, we may proceed to reexamine continuity in the state's role in political economy as well. In the ancient and medieval world economies, as now, states lived partly on "rent" from international commerce; through direct taxation on trade; partly from profits accumulated by their "national" merchants, manufacturers, and money-men; and partly from taxing the national product or income of the general population (including of course agricultural production). Imperialism has provided an additional source of revenue to powerful states throughout history (Ekholm and Friedman 1993), but may also have followed a "capital-imperialism" logic wherein "center-periphery structures are unstable over time; centers expand, contract, and collapse as a regular manifestation of the shift of points of accumulation. These phenomena are . . . more general than modern capitalism" (1993, p. 60). The territorial logic of conquest has also often pursued control of the trade routes and over the sources of raw materials and commodities that were central in the long-distance trade.

The debate over the character of the premodern economy is of course not new at all, and has been conducted for generations between primitivists and modernists, formalists and substantivists. My perspective has more in common with the modernists and formalists, though I do not regard market exchange as being totally exclusive from either "redistributive" or "reciprocal" forms of economic relations. However, our perspective is liberated from the narrow confines of argument based on any individual country by virtue of being concerned with the character of the entire world system/economy.

The rather narrow but well-known debates on the economic character of classical Athens, for instance, miss the larger point. Athens in the 5th or 4th century BC (on analogy with medieval Europe vis-à-vis the whole of Eurasia) was not the whole world economy of the ancient period. Indeed, though Hellas was making rapid economic advances through commercialization in major cities such as Corinth and Athens, it was perhaps still somewhat "peripheral" in character even by the time of the Athenian empire. The real center of economic gravity in the world economy, and the location of the most "advanced" economies of the period, was of course eastward and southeastward of Hellas, as had been the case already for millennia.

In my view, the macroeconomic structures of most of Eurasian history are rather close to what Abu-Lughod (1989) found in the 13th century: a world economy centered around highly commercialized cities linked to each other through systemic exchange networks and economically dominated, or at least "driven," by private merchants (often in control of production and imbricated with private finance as well), albeit coexisting with bureaucratic or imperial state structures. But these states themselves were often a direct reflection of the location and ever-changing direction of this same international commerce. The idea that empires have repeatedly tended to develop in key trading zones was reflected in the notion I have developed earlier that the "Three Corridors" (essentially, the Red Sea, Syria-Mesopotamia, and the "northern" Caucasus routes) were pivotal geopolitical ground in Eurasian political and economic development precisely because they were physically in the midst of the trading crossroads of Eurasia (Gills and Frank 1990). These same routes were, however, in "competition" with each other. The rise and fall of empires, and of major metropoles in Eurasian history, reflect the rivalry among the Three Corridors and concomitant periodic restructuring of the world economy over a period of several millennia, until transoceanic routes supplanted their centrality around the 18th century (i.e., not in the 16th century).

We have argued that the first systemic appearance of the interlinking of city-centered exchange of surplus via international trade began from c. 2700–2500 BC, between Mesopotamian cities, Levantine cities, and Egyptian cities, soon to be (or already) joined by Indus valley cities. This confluence of major centers involved in regular exchange was the foundation for the subsequent development of the Eurasian world economy. Later, Chinese "cities" joined the nexus perhaps as early as 1500 BC, via Central Asia. On this basis, I assume that the cities of Central Asia, especially the Bactrian and Sogdian cities, and Taxila, also came into existence and flourished long before the Persians incorporated them into their empire, followed later by the "Westerner" Alexander. These pivotal Central Asian cities could have flourished on commodities other than silk (e.g., lapis, carnelian, and other precious stones) and therefore did not depend exclusively on the dating of the Chinese silk trade.

Precisely as Abu-Lughod argues for the Eurasian world economy/system of the 13th and 14th centuries (i.e., that the economic system of these interlinked cities does not "fall" so much as the ways in which it is organized change), the Eurasian world economy never truly "falls." Rather, it is continual, and is continually rebuilt or reorganized, especially after each periodic "crisis." It is therefore not the world system which falls, but only temporary configurations *within* the same world economic system, to be inevitably replaced by new configurations on much the same foundation. This is essentially how I arrived at the formulation "the cumulation of accumulation" (Gills and Frank 1990), the title of Frank's and my first joint publication on the new world system perspective.

However, to avoid unfruitful economic reductionism we must be political economists as opposed to being either "economists" or "political scientists." This lesson was reinforced with the discovery of a rhythm of states that seemed to move in tandem with the rhythm of international trade, that is, with the production and exchange of commodities and the transfer of surplus. We posited the existence of a "world system cycle" stretching back some four thousand years from the present (Gills and Frank 1992). Powerful "hegemonic" states or empires seemed to expand simultaneously in tandem with world economic expansion and the increase of international commerce, whereas a period of "decline" was often generalized to many states and empires and coincided with a general world economic crisis of Eurasian scale. Thus, large-scale economic crises, presumably a product of the process of accumulation on a world scale, are inseparable from large-scale political crises. On the more localized scale, each hegemonic or imperial consolidation was normally associated with a period of investment and administrative reforms that produced a "hegemonic prosperity period" followed eventually by an "entropic phase" of gradual economic and political decline leading to crisis (Gills 1987, 1989a, 1989b, 1993b).

Thus we developed the perspective that the modes of production, traditionally the pivotal dimension of characterizing economic transitions, are not so central (Frank 1991; Frank and Gills 1993). Rather, the dynamic of the world system as a whole, including the hegemonic/economic cycle discussed briefly above, is far more important. Transitions are therefore better understood as being the consequence of larger competitive patterns in the world system (including capital accumulation and hegemonic rivalry) than of changes in modes of production *per se*.

Within these larger competitive patterns that periodically act to restructure the world economy, the outcome for each area depends, to a considerable extent, on the role and position that area fills in the world accumulation process. Thus we developed the concept of "superaccumulation" (Gills and Frank 1992) to designate a process of the "centralization of accumulation" lying behind this process of "center-shift." However, this is not simply an economic shift in center(s) of accumulation. Rather, the underlying economic shift in the center(s) of accumulation in the world economy accompanies "simultaneous" political shifts in relative power, and, most of all, such shifts imply profound social change.

I have previously argued on this basis that the concept of the "hegemonic transition" could be an alternative to traditional modes of production analysis, and could become a central concept in the analysis of world-historical development (Gills 1993b). From this perspective, hegemonic transitions have occurred periodically throughout world history and entail not only a shift in the locus of the "centralization" of capital accumulation (i.e., within the framework of the entire world system, among the centers/cores), but also necessarily entail profound changes in social, political, economic, cultural, and ideological aspects of the world system. These phenomena should be analyzed *together*, as aspects of one overall historical process of

change. This point brings us to the second distinctive feature of our world
system theory: its (neo)structuralism.

## Structuralism

World system theory's structuralism rejects the unipolar model of center-
periphery relations, common in most approaches using this concept, in favor
of a multipolar model of center-periphery relations, that is, multiple centers
and multiple peripheries. World system structure does not involve a single core
and a single periphery, but rather an interlinked set of center-periphery
complexes (and also including a "hinterland," as discussed in Gills and Frank
[1990]), joined together in an overall ensemble.

There is, nonetheless, not "equality" between the various centers, but
rather a condition of tension or rivalry; sometimes mediated by collabora-
tion, sometimes deteriorating into open conflict and war. Furthermore,
world systemic multicentricity is hierarchically structured. There is a complex "chain" of "metropole-satellite" relations of extraction and transfer of
surplus throughout the whole world system, a model Frank discussed in his
early work on the world economy, but not concentrating ultimately in only
a single center.

I have previously defined "hegemony" in a way that embodies this notion
of a hierarchical structure of surplus transfer, that is, as a hierarchical
structure of accumulation between classes and states, mediated by force
(Gills 1987, 1989a, 1989b; Gills and Frank 1990, 1992). In this sense, the
center-periphery structure of the world system is simultaneously an economic hierarchy and a political hierarchy, as hegemonic power embodies
both.

It follows that unipolar hegemony at world scale is extremely rare and
perhaps even nonexistent. Rather, the norm is a situation of "interlinked
hegemonies" (Gills and Frank 1992; Gills 1993b). This notion is central to
our understanding of structure in the world system and to our notion of the
centrality of shifts in the locus of capital accumulation as the key process in
hegemonic transitions. The schema of the structure of the world system is
akin to a truncated pyramid, at the "apex" of which there is not one sole
hegemonic center of political power and capital accumulation, but rather
several coexisting and interactive centers. We follow Abu-Lughod in one
further regard: We do not see hegemonic ascent and descent so much as a
process of absolute rise and decline by particular states, but rather as a
situation wherein some nations or groups of nations temporarily gain
relative power vis-à-vis others. On this basis they can set the terms of their
interactions with subordinates as they ascend, but gradually lose this capacity
as they descend (Abu-Lughod 1989).

Thus global or world hegemony is always *shared* hegemony, exercised through a complex network composed of class coalitions, and also alliances and other forms of association between states, including competitive ones. Furthermore, the world system is characterized by a number of coexisting core powers that through both conflictual and cooperative relations become increasingly integrated. Perhaps one might say that the structure of the world system is in this sense somewhat "oligarchic," since it is typically dominated by a restrictive set of wealthy powers at the apex but which have interests that are both mutually supportive and mutually antagonistic.

From our perspective, therefore, hegemonic rivalries are of a complex, multilayered type. Such rivalry is a continual process accompanying the development of the world economy. This world-historical development process favors some at a particular time while discriminating against others, and so on through time. It is of course integral to this structural theory of world development that areas that were once peripheral may ascend to core status, while those once core may descend into the periphery. Our position is further distinguished by the argument (1) that these ascents and declines occur *within* the same world economy/system; (2) that specific historical core/periphery asymmetries are not fixed permanently; and (3) that nevertheless core/periphery hierarchy itself is a structural constant.

## Misperceptions of the "World System" Thesis

Our definition of the world system in "The Cumulation of Accumulation" (Gills and Frank 1990) rests upon the basis of exchange of surplus, but with a degree of regularity and significance that affects the "internal" character of each of the parts of the world system. For Wallerstein (1991) "mere" trade does not makes a "system." We disagree. We define the world system on the basis of regular trade which embodies a transfer of surplus, implies a division of labor, and brings in its train *systemic* political, social, ideological, cultural, and even religious rhythms.

We not only believe that regular and significant trade is a sufficient ground for speaking of a system—or more precisely, of a real "world economy" (without the hyphen)—but also contend that trade integrates social formations into the international division of labor. This takes place because trade and production are not (falsely) separated. The nature of trade directly affects the character of production.

Wallerstein sets very specific criteria for the level of integration in his international division of labor that, for him at least, precludes considering the pre-1500 international division of labor as being in the same formal category. We believe that he has erected a false dichotomy, the aim of which is to preserve the distinctiveness of the modern "capitalist" world-economy axiomatically.

Furthermore, we are not as concerned as some, particularly Wallerstein, with whether this trade is composed primarily of "necessities" or of so-called "preciosities." Rather, we believe that the trade is significant and systemic not because of the specific character of the commodities concerned, but rather because the *transfer of surplus* between zones of the world economy/system that the trade embodies implies effects on the respective production structures.

Our world system approach is based on a *minimalist* definition of what a system is, rather than a maximalist or "totalizing" notion. By minimalist I mean that the key processes of the system are simply the cycles of economic expansion and contraction and the accompanying hegemonic cycle. These system-wide patterns depend on the existence of a world economy, taking the form of extensive regularized trade, that is, transfer of surplus. *This* constitutes a system. In our definition it does not require a higher level of integration than this to constitute a real system. Nor does it imply some overarching iron logic of the system.

Nevertheless, we do *not* argue that there has only been one single world system throughout all of world history. This would be palpable nonsense, given the obviously separate development of pre-Columbian America and Eurasia. Even in Eurasia, it would not be correct to conclude that there has only *ever* been one giant all-encompassing system. There have originally been many streams of regional development, which at some points in their development certainly constituted some kind of separate "system." What we are saying is that one system, judged by the actual historical outcome and not all of the original "fountainheads," gradually came to "incorporate" (if only by "merger") all others—first in Eurasia, and then over the entire globe after "1492." This particular overarching world economy we have called "the world system." It was formed after 1492 by the merger of two preexisting "supersystems," one in Eurasia (incorporating parts of Africa) and one in the Americas (where the Mesoamerican and Andean systems were already in contact).

Perhaps if we simply said that we posit a theory of the development of a very long-standing, indeed "ancient," *world economic system* this would not raise so many eyebrows. The evidence suggests to us that we need a theory (or at least concepts and theses) of the development of the world economy, first on Eurasian scale, even back into ancient history, because such a world economy did in fact exist. It not only existed, but it was very influential in terms of the development of each of the "parts" of the world economic system, which therefore cannot be properly understood if they are taken as separate developments. Not only this, but we argue that essential elements of its perennial political economy operate fairly consistently through history.

This argument cuts against the grain of so much received theory and so many compartmentalized branches of knowledge and so many specialized histories (and historians), that it is still very controversial even when properly understood.

But this position is not economic determinist, precisely because we insist that the "economic" *is* "political." We have, in fact, explicitly rejected what would have been an economistic position, where the economic rhythms simply determine the hegemonic/political rhythms. Rather we have insisted on an inseparable logic of political economic developments from the beginning. For example, in our formulation of hegemony, economic and political power are inseparable, as are economic and political means to the desired ends of hegemonic power and economic wealth.

For those who desire proof of the world system thesis, this large-scale Eurasian world economic system can be demonstrated to have existed precisely on the empirical basis that cycles of the "whole" existed, as we attempted to show in our article "World System Cycles, Crises, and Hegemonial Shifts, 1700 BC to 1700 AD" (Gills and Frank 1992). Second, it can be demonstrated to have existed on the basis of common, or at least sequential, crisis periods empirically supported by data on the rise and decline of urban centers across Eurasia (Wilkinson 1992; Bosworth 1992 [chapter 8, this volume]). Third, it can be demonstrated to have existed from a reading even of the specialist histories of the many parts of Eurasia heavily involved in long-distance and regularized trade over the millennia.

In summary, our world system approach is based on the rejection of three conventional dichotomies: (1) between "premodern" and "modern" economies, or between the supposed "political determination" versus the (modern) "economic determination" of economies; (2) between premodern and modern political cycles: that is, between a premodern "cycle of empires" versus a uniquely modern cycle of (single) hegemons; and (3) between a "precapitalist" world composed of several distinct world-economies and a unitary "capitalist" world system after 1500.

## Extended Theses

This perspective may seem to underestimate the amount of real change in the development of the world economy. However, we do not deny qualitative changes, nor secular trends in world development. Rather, we emphasize the essential continuity of fundamentally embedded patterns of overall systemic dynamics. This requires no strict determinism whereby everything that happens at a "lower" level is simply mechanically "read off" from the world systemic patterns. Indeed, we think that the specific characteristics of each area of the world system at any particular time should be taken into account in order to understand the specific responses each makes to stimuli that come from the systemic rhythm as a whole.

This point leads me to venture to extend our tentative initial theses, and to explore areas for further research. In regard to the complex subject of refining the "calibration" of the overall world systemic cycles across all of the regions, the clearest working hypothesis seems to be that world systemic cycles are probably more "sequential" than "simultaneous," though, of course, there is a causal link in the sequentialization. In this regard, we should clarify the "unevenness" of crisis periods themselves; for example, that even in a general world economic crisis not all core areas are equally affected, nor all peripheral areas either, the same applying to general prosperity periods. Likewise, a general crisis or a general prosperity may in fact be set off initially by events in one center, and then sequentially transmitted to others.

In addition, our project could be enriched by further specification of the existence of other regional "systems" coexisting with the Eurasian world economy/system or separate from it, thus also allowing comparative analyses along the lines proposed by Chase-Dunn and Hall (1991, 1993).

Most importantly, the world system approach must be extended by research into the causality of the cycles, both the economic and the hegemonic, and their mutual relations. As above, this invites research into how local conditions interact with system-level impulses and stimuli. Specifically, there should be further research into how local responses affect ascent and decline in the interlinked hegemonies hierarchy. Furthermore, the role of technology and innovation, especially in "leading sectors," would be a most fruitful addition to our research agenda, and has already become a central aspect of the recent work of Modelski and Thompson (1995).

## An Autocritique of World System Analysis

The new world system theory, while offering a fresh alternative to existing strands of world-system theory (with a hyphen) nevertheless still bears several important similarities to its counterpart, and perhaps has some similar shortcomings. In this autocritique I will first attempt to lay out a series of self-reflective criticisms of the direction and concepts of world system theory as so far constructed. I will then conclude with reflections on a research agenda based on the goal of integrating the history of capital with the history of power.

## Oversystematicity?

As already discussed, the operational definition of the world system rests on the notion of "interpenetrating accumulation" (Gills and Frank 1990), whereby trade performs the systemic function of linking social formations together. Common cyclical rhythms of economic, demographic, and political "rise and demise" are the primary evidence for the existence and spatial extent of the world system (Gills and Frank 1992).

These criteria of defining systemicity may be defensible as a kind of minimalist approach, as previously argued. However, on close inspection, there is still a certain kind of "totalizing notion" lurking within the present formulation of the world system concept. This is perhaps an unavoidable consequence of employing the notion of system itself, but it may be more than that.

This alleged "oversystematicity" of present world system theory rests primarily on its implicit view of the centrality of the common cycles working across the entire system, and, by implication, (over)determining system outcomes in all of the parts of the world system. The question that must now be asked is: To what extent are there world system cycles, as such, and to what extent are there just "sequential events"? Another way of putting this question is to ask how strong the putative linkages actually are between distant zones of the world economy. The real point of this question is to reemphasize the great importance of locating and defining the sources of *causality* in the world system, as opposed to remaining primarily at the level of description.

This problem reproduces a controversy very similar to that generated by structural realism in international relations theory, particularly by the work of Kenneth Waltz (1979; see also Keohane 1986). That is, an attempt at elegant theory construction that emphasizes overarching system level cau sality risks deemphasizing "unit level processes" such that they become either insignificant or are conceptualized as mere epiphenomena of the system itself. Oversystematicity thus implies that system structure (over)determines the behavior of all the constituent elements thereof. It is, therefore, criticized as being reductionist.

In the case of current world system analysis, this tendency to oversystematize the model of causality in the system leads to a similar blurring at the "lower" level, where most historians dwell. Therefore, it is natural that our friend and colleague, William H. McNeill, has already admonished world system theorists to rid themselves once and for all of residual (and Marxist) economic determinism, and to restore the openendedness of historical inquiry.[2] What McNeill means by this admonition is that a historic compromise is badly needed between the world system approach and civilizational or "local" history.

The alternative to a totalizing notion, that is, the idea of a common cyclical causality operating across the whole world system, is a model of "interactive causality," which emphasizes both common and conjunctural rhythms between different local or regional cycles of development. Such a model has been suggested earlier in my own work on synchronization, dissynchronization, and conjuncture (Gills 1989a, 1993b), in which there is no notion of a strictly common overarching systemic causality across the entire world system. In this model, synchronization of basic developmental rhythms between different civilizational/regional ensembles, for instance, is posited to have quite different effects on local outcomes than "dissynchronization" of rhythms. Furthermore, the interaction between different regional rhythms has more dramatic transformational effects at certain important conjunctural moments of intensity or crisis than does routine interaction.

This could be compared to a model that works on the principles of an astrolabe, whereby at certain special conjunctures of different orbital patterns something spectacular may occur, for example, an eclipse of the sun, or the collision of a comet with a planet. The solar system, and indeed the galaxy, is indeed a system, but its parts have their own trajectories and patterns, which together interact to form a larger whole, though there is apparently no overarching central causality, but rather perhaps just "organized chaos," since all may bend to the same elemental laws of physics (with a dose of unpredictable random uncertainty thrown in!).

In the model of interactive causality, historical observation of these interacting regional patterns indicates that important spatial shifts in the locus of power and accumulation between regions is much *more* likely in a situation of *dissynchronization* than in one of synchronized rhythms. For instance, in the particular conjunctural context where region 1 is in a contracting/"B" entropic or decentralization phase, and its interactive partner, region 2, is in an expanding/"A" consolidation or centralization phase, then region 1 (or parts of it) is even more likely to be peripheralized by the expanding region 2. In addition, the depth of decline in region 1 may be intensified by the larger system-scale interaction with region 2, with a variety of rather long-lived consequences for region 1's future development. There are numerous examples in history of dramatic center shifts occurring in dissynchronized conjunctures, for example the British exploitation of the entropic phase of the Mughal Empire, and post-Meiji Restoration Japan's exploitation of the Qing Empire's entropic phase.

## *Economic Determinism?*

World system theory, and indeed most approaches derived from the broad Marxist tradition in historiography, are fairly open to the criticism of being economic determinist perspectives, particularly if they deemphasize the "autonomy" of class relations, or the validity and/or prior existence of the state and the states system (e.g., Skocpol 1977; Zolberg 1981). "Bringing History Back In" should sit alongside "Bringing the State Back In," but neither of these require throwing out the historical materialist baby with the world system bathwater. It all depends on exactly how this "restoration" occurs. Just as Jacob Viner (1948) long ago pointed out in his seminal work on mercantilism, there is no necessary priority of, or mutual exclusivity between, the parallel goals of power and plenty.

The conceptualization of interactive causality between regional rhythms of development, discussed above, does in fact imply genuine acceptance of the causality operating at the local/civilizational level. Therefore, it accepts even a certain amount of realist causality in that state actors are not exogenous to the model. Indeed, state actors, and especially the historical processes of state formation, are central to this model of interactive causality. This approach has elements in common with that of Wilkinson (1993, 1995), Gilpin (1981, 1987), and Modelski and Thompson (1988, 1995), and their insistence on retaining states system dynamics in their respective models of international change. Chase-Dunn and Hall (1991, forthcoming) also emphasize the great importance of state formation processes in their evolutionary and comparative approach to world systems analysis.

Once accepted, this alternative "realist historical materialist" approach alters our general conception of how the world system actually works. In the first instance, it alters our conception of how the world system comes into existence and subsequently expands. Present world system theory is as yet insufficiently specific about the processes of "absorption" versus those of "merger," whereby previously separate or discrete regional systems develop first at least a common set of rhythms, and eventually a high level of systemic integration. The existence of certain common rhythms and eventual high levels of integration are not necessarily in doubt, but they certainly came about through an extraordinarily long historical process, full of "fits and starts." It is precisely this question which is at the heart of the extreme discrepancy between the datings of world system origins and subsequent absorption or merger time points, as posited by Gills and Frank (1990, 1992) using economic criteria, as opposed to the consistently much later dates calculated by Wilkinson (1995), on realist/conflict criteria.

Yet it is consistent with this revisionist realist historical materialist approach to posit the centrality of hegemonic transition, discussed earlier, in the model of large-scale, long-term social change and development (Gills 1993a, 1993b). However, doing so implies a very different agenda of research than the realist method normally suggests. This is because a hegemonic transition encompasses profound social, economic, political, and even cultural and ideological restructuring, and not merely a shift in the distribution of power capabilities. Furthermore, the "neostructuralist" approach (Gills and Palan 1994) calls for problematizing the state rather than merely accepting it as an unchanging and unitary historical actor. This agenda thus reintroduces the notion of dialectical change in the states and the states system(s) themselves, without necessarily rejecting analysis pitched at the state or states system level. States, like classes and nations, are viewed as historical constructs that "come and go" and that are transformed in the general process of world development. Nor are all states categorically similar types simply by virtue of being designated states. Similar concerns are an aspect of the agenda for a more heterodox international political economy (Amin, Gills, Palan, and Taylor 1994). Furthermore, states have existed for millennia, and are not defined only via the most modern forms.

Above all, the ultimate emphasis is placed on the *processes of transformation* themselves (Gills 1993a, 1994a, 1994b; Gills and Palan 1994), conceptualized as consequences of interpenetration between social formations, rather than on conventional realist analysis of position, polarity, and the distribution of capabilities among state actors.

This neostructuralist version of the new historical materialism privileges both domestic and transnational class dynamics in its alternative model of causality, but problematizes the complex interactions between these two supposedly discrete levels of analysis. Internal and external class relations, endogenous and exogenous factors impinging on or determining the character of these class relations, are not automatically dichotomized. On the contrary, it is assumed that they are interactive levels of causality. But they are not, either by subtlety or otherwise, depicted as being the same thing, that is, all being determined by one overarching system-level causality.

Moreover, it is ultimately class-level dynamics, such as the social struggle over concentration versus distribution of social wealth (or social surplus), and the political struggle to control the state as an apparatus of wealth acquisition and distribution, that accounts for, or explains, the cyclical rhythms, both of the parts and of the whole world system, whether in ancient or modern economic conditions.

Following from this position, I have posited a hypothesis on the causes of periodic general crises as being the result of overconcentration of wealth and overextraction of surplus, as well as the deformation of the state from a facilitator of production and distribution to a parasitical and corrupt apparatus of economic exploitation (Gills 1993b). General decline phases tend to reproduce some similar symptoms and effects, whether in the ancient or the modern economy.

## Hegemony?

The direction of this agenda culminates in the general question concerning the relationship between the political framework and the economic world. As previously discussed, when analyzing the hegemonic cycle (Gills 1989b), I posited the working hypothesis that after the consolidation phase of every hegemonic state (hegemony being defined as a hierarchical structure of accumulation between classes/states, mediated by force) (Gills 1987), there invariably follows an "economic prosperity phase" of development. Again, this cycle seems to apply whether we are talking about ancient or modern economies.

This, therefore, leads one to expect that an appropriate political framework is actually a sine qua non of an economic prosperity period. If this is in fact the case, then we should look for the causal explanation of economic decline followed by political decline or fragmentation in some prior class/political dynamic. I suggest that political consolidation usually precedes an economic prosperity phase. However, class dynamics within, and generated by, this same economic dynamism eventually undermine the favorable politico-economic framework. Once a spiral of political and economic disarray sets in, it tends to amplify itself, eventually degenerating into a "general crisis." In this sense, it is not a "chicken and egg" question at all, since the political realm is only ever falsely separated from the economic.

In addition to excessive concentration and extraction, excessive competition (and especially warfare) within the states system is not compatible with sustained economic prosperity, but rather tends to undermine or even destroy it. Interstate rivalry is destabilizing and ultimately "bad for business." Conversely, any workable form of overarching political stability that facilitates an increase in investment (including in infrastructure), production, and trade, whether it be a single state or a group of states collaborating together to these ends, should have a generally stimulating effect on the economy. Therefore, peace is "good for business," just as "distribution" is better than overconcentration. The point of studying world history should be to learn something from it that is useful. War and economic depression are two perennial problems in world history, and lessons can be learned from past patterns that apply to current problems.

In this sense, the liberal inspired and still popular hegemonic stability theory is actually no more than a subset of a far more general historical theory. However, contrary to hegemonic stability theory, it is not necessarily a benign hegemon, as opposed to an imperial-bureaucratic state, nor only a single state/hegemon, that provides the functional prerequisite for economic prosperity and relative peace. On the contrary, this functional prerequisite can be and often was provided by unitary imperial political frameworks, and/or by several powerful states coexisting in the same world economic system. This relationship between power and the economy can be conceptualized via the "interlinking hegemonies" concept, and through the multipolar structural framework. This perspective stands in sharp contrast to the single state hegemonic succession models so prevalent among world system, long cycle, and realist international relations theorists alike.

However, the "normal" (or prevailing) condition of the world economy is not hegemony at all, but rather nonhegemony. From this perspective, none of the countries identified by world system theory or by others as being globally hegemonic were really such. For example, the 19th century is more defined by the Concert of Europe than by putative British hegemony, and is marked at least as much by colonialism, imperialism, national monopoly capital, and protectionism as it was by "free trade" or liberalism. The latter half of the 20th century was more a condominium between the United States, Western Europe, and Japan than a single state's hegemony, which the end of the Cold War has exposed to the light of day.

What is most important to this framework is, therefore, not the element of hierarchy of power capabilities, but the achievement of political cooperation by various means, accompanied by simultaneous growth and the expansion of trade. Often the basic conditions consist of the sheer synchronization of economic and political development phases among several core regions of the world economy, each having already reached a high degree of internal political consolidation and economic development. For example, this type of synchronized hegemonic framework operated at world system scale in the ancient period when the Roman, Parthian, Kushan, and Han empires existed at a high level of consolidation simultaneously in the first century AD.

Therefore, a framework that is both "hegemonic" and essentially "liberal" (in terms of international commerce and trade) should normally be more conducive to and associated with "world" economic prosperity, growth of world trade and production, relative peace, and the progress of the culture of cosmopolitanism. Indeed, such situations have existed before in world history. One such, for example, was the Islamic Asian-centered world economy of the 13th century analyzed so brilliantly by Abu-Lughod (1989).

In addition, I have posited the general working hypothesis that states pursuing a strategy of ascendance in the world system often follow "mercantilist" policies internally and externally, while those states already in a position of advantage in the prevailing status quo tend to defend a more "liberal" or "open" strategy (Gills 1994c). Once again, this is intended to apply broadly to more than just the modern era.

All this being said, it must be added in conclusion that "hegemony" was not the ideal choice among terms to describe a hierarchical structure of accumulation. This was actually improved upon by the development of the concept of "superaccumulation" and its relation to the general notion of the "centralization of accumulation" within the world economy. This can still be usefully distinguished from more politically and militarily defined hegemony, or mere domination. A different rostrum and different chronograms can be developed for the superaccumulator and the dominant/hegemonic power phenomena, and the two can be usefully compared against one another for overlaps. I suspect that the list of candidate superaccumulators in the history of the world economy will have significant overlaps with a list of candidate "forereacher" states/economies as suggested by Wilkinson (1995) and also as against the list of countries with the key "leading sectors" as compiled and analyzed by Modelski and Thompson (1995).

### *Accumulation?*

Marx made the point that all societies could be analyzed on the basis of how surplus was generated, extracted, and distributed or consumed. I believe this was essentially correct and it remains a quite useful tool of comparative analysis. However, what one person means by "surplus" another may see as something else, perhaps merely production or subsistence, and may or may not constitute any sort of "exploitation." These problems of definition are even more compounded, however, by the complexity of the challenge of disentangling the notion of "capital" from those of "accumulation," "capitalist," and, worst of all, from "capitalism."

Though Frank (1994) has advised cutting the Gordian knot in this problem by dispensing with the notion of modes of production altogether, I, like many others, must disagree. However, I certainly accept that the notion of transitions from one all-encompassing mode to another, as a way of organizing the analysis of historical change, should be rejected once and for all. Nevertheless, I would argue that there is still a valuable utility to retaining the analytical category of modes (of accumulation), but to be deployed rather differently from conventional Marxist analyses.

In this respect I argue for following Geoffrey de Ste. Croix's (1981) reformulation of modes of production, defined as the relations through which surplus is extracted from direct producers. No social formation is genuinely characterized by only one mode of surplus extraction, but by several at once. Therefore, one should avoid designating an entire society or historical system on the basis of any single mode. If one feels compelled to do this anyway, then at least it should be on the basis of the one mode, following de Ste. Croix, through which the elite gain the bulk of their surplus at a particular moment in history.

De Ste. Croix's approach is in my view quite compatible with the perspective outlined by Ekholm and Friedman (1993), whereby all or most of the known historical modes of production (accumulation) have existed since about the third millennium BC. This of course includes the capitalist mode, based on the existence of capital, as abstract wealth taking money form, and of wage labor. However, to admit the existence of capital and the capitalist mode even in the archaic stages of the development of the world economy is not to confuse this with designating entire epochs of the past as "capitalist," or even as so-called "protocapitalist" (which Wallerstein and Amin allow). All of this labeling of entire epochs only serves to confuse the issues and detract from the clinical analytical utility of the modes concept. On this I agree with Frank.

The more interesting question is a far more open-ended one. What was the role of capital in world history? And what was the general relationship between capital and power in world-historical development? Capital, the capitalist mode, and capital accumulation have all played a far more important and far more continual role in world-historical development than most other scholars are so far willing to acknowledge. This new research agenda sets out to integrate an analysis of the history of capital with the history of power. To do so requires confronting deeply-embedded conventional wisdom.

The conventional view maintains that prior to the ascendancy of Western capital(ism), only more backward economic, social, and political forms existed, and that Western capital(ism) unified and civilized the world for the first time. This is the mythological idea that progress, the West, and capitalism are all synonymous. This Eurocentric myth of world history precludes a more accurate and historically balanced view of the real role of capital in history, and, by extension, denigrates the role and contribution of all the other peoples of the world to our common historical development. Perhaps this dichotomy was originally erected, some one hundred years or so ago, primarily to defend the idea of Western superiority in world history, as well as to give "scientific" support to the effort to transcend capitalism and achieve socialism.

In so far as the issue of the West's impact on world development is concerned, the conventional demarcation between modern and premodern may have less to do with the development of Western capitalism, and more to do with the quite historically recent development of *European* capital and power (as opposed to Asian capital and Asian power) (Gills and Frank 1994; Frank and Gills 1993; Blaut 1993). However, in our view, this growth of European capital and power occurred in a preexisting world economic system in which capital accumulation and world trade networks were already highly developed, and largely under Asian "hegemony," and in which "capitalist" classes and (usually urban) industrial production already played a leading role (Abu-Lughod 1989; Blaut 1993; Gills and Frank 1994). This is not to say, however, that there was no important capital accumulation in Europe between 1450 and 1750, prior to full-blown European superaccumulation and hegemony in the world system. There was, but its significance is often greatly exaggerated (e.g., Jones 1981; Hall 1985; Mann 1986; Baechler, Hall, and Mann 1988).

The perspective on world history I suggest here attacks not only the idea of the European invention of capitalism, but likewise, as previously mentioned, the much distorted view of world economic history that results from overemphasizing the European "feudal" experience. In reality, outside Europe highly commercialized, urbanized, and industrialized economies flourished throughout the entire medieval period, as well as much earlier. In Europe itself, an urban commercial economy existed before the putative feudal interregnum, and reemerged again once European capital was stimulated by *reintegration* with the Asian-centered world economic system.

The argument also entails an attack on the conventional view of precapitalist power relations, that is, the supposed overwhelming dominance of political extraction of surplus as opposed to economic transfers of value, and the notion that premodern imperial or bureaucratic states always tended to stifle the economy or that they never presided over vibrant commercial economies in the premodern world. On the contrary, great empires often presided over such economies, and private accumulation and the "economic law of value" played an important role not made irrelevant by state reliance on taxation for revenue.

As William H. McNeill commented in the foreword to *The World System* (Frank and Gills 1993), "Marx's vision of the uniqueness of modern capitalism falls to the ground if one affirms, with the editors, that a capital-accumulating core has existed (though not always in the same location) for some five thousand years. This constitutes revisionism expected in liberal discourse but repugnant to dogmatic upholders of Marxist Truth. . . . It may even signify for the history of ideas the confluence of Marxist with more inchoate liberal ideas about world history" (McNeill 1993, pp. viii–ix).

Finally, I would suggest that there may be a general dialectic of world order. (The phrase is borrowed from the project led by Hayward Alker, but deployed differently.) This dialectic is one between the impulses of unity and those of disunity, between integration and disintegration, occurring at the level of the world economy but including the local and regional political and cultural manifestations of this same world dynamic.

The "progress" of humanity can be measured via the periods of unity, that is, through the degree of integration and cooperation achieved on a world scale. World culture, or world civilization, has been a product of the cumulative developments of these large-scale economic, social, and political interactions, taking effect concretely via what McNeill has recently dubbed "communication networks" (in Frank and Gills 1993; McNeill 1995). McNeill is quite right to insist that any inquiry into the development of the world economy/system should include attention to *all* of the things crossing the borders, which I take to include ideas about government, economic institutions, religions, weapons, production technology, science, art styles, and even, of course, diseases.

Nevertheless, it must be recognized that the preferred integrative, more orderly, and normally more economically prosperous and culturally cosmopolitan periods in world history are punctuated by periods characterized by the opposite tendencies. Future world system research should explore both the conditions for such positive progressive periods and those for general world crises. Such general crises are typically characterized by symptoms of large-scale dysfunctions, including economic and organizational retrogression (e.g., so-called Dark Ages), destructive wars or social conflicts, economic depression, trade disruption or contraction, demographic decline, mass migration, plague, and famine, and also by such patterns as either moral decline, an increase in banditry and brigandage, social disorder, crime, and ideological or religious confusion, that is, retreat from unitary doctrines of certainty toward a multiplication of subjectivisms and identities (which some now seek to celebrate as "progressive").

In my suggested general theory of world crisis, general decline occurs not on the basis of mere foibles of diplomacy, nor merely on the basis of the logic of the balance of power. Rather, general crises occur as the result of underlying long-term (cyclical) class dynamics that engender overconcentration of wealth and overextraction of surplus, both by private capital and by states. Economic contraction thus set in motion may have disruptive effects on domestic and international trade. The deterioration of the world economy exacerbates the deterioration of the sociopolitical conditions that prevail within it.

Ultimately, the analysis should capture the overall picture of power relations in the world economy at any particular historical period. An analysis of the synchronization of phases of economic and political development between major states and between regions of the world economy, as well as an analysis of shifts in the locus of the center of gravity of the world economy, are both to be undertaken. The ultimate goal is then to attempt to systematically relate them to one another. Inevitably, this final stage of the construction of the theoretical framework is quite complex, but it is necessary in order to adequately capture the whole dynamic of the relations between capital, power, and world order.

NOTES

1.  Paul Millett (1983, 1990) argues for a political economy approach in which the "primacy of exchange" is central and the economy is "embedded in society." Millett's approach rests on an important criticism of Polanyi's formulation, viz., that Polanyi regarded the forms of exchange (e.g., redistributive, reciprocal, and market) in an evolutionary way, and thus as incompatible with one another (Polanyi et al.

1957). Millett throws doubt on Polanyi's thesis of the "invention" of the market economy in 4th-century Athens by pointing to recent work by anthropologists on the complexity of exchange in "noncapitalist" societies, that is, that the forms of exchange tend to blend together in real societies. Millett reviews the debate between the primitivists (minimizing the role of "credit" and capital in ancient economies) and the modernists (viewing credit, capital, and markets in the ancient economy as being qualitatively similar to the "modern" forms). The modernist position can be found in Boeckh (1817), Glotz (1926), and Davies (1981). The primitivists were headed by Karl Bucher, the modernists by Beloch, Busolt, and Meyer. The debate is summarized by Austin and Vidal-Naquet (1977).

2.   McNeill made these comments at the panel, "Rise and Demise: Comparing World Systems," at the annual meetings of the International Studies Association, Chicago, February 24–27, 1995.

### References

Abu-Lughod, Janet. 1989. *Before European Hegemony: The World System AD 1250–1350*. New York: Oxford University Press.

Amin, Ash, Barry Gills, Ronen Palan, and Peter Taylor. 1994. "Editorial: Forum for Heterodox International Political Economy." *Review of International Political Economy* 1:1–12.

Amin, Samir. 1976. *Unequal Development*. Trans. Brian Pearce. New York: Monthly Review Press.

Anderson, Perry. 1974. *Lineages of the Absolutist State*. London: New Left Books.

Austin, M.M., and P. Vidal-Naquet. 1977. *Economic and Social History of Ancient Greece*. Trans. and rev. M.M. Austin. Berkeley: University of California Press.

Baechler, Jean, John A. Hall, and Michael Mann, eds. 1988. *Europe and the Rise of Capitalism*. Oxford: Basil Blackwell.

Blaut, J. M. 1993. *The Colonizer's Model of the World. Geographical Diffusionism and Eurocentric History*. London: Guilford Press.

Boeckh, A. (1817) 1976. *The Public Economy of Athens*. Salem, NH: Ayer Publishing Co.

Bosworth, Andrew. 1992. "World Cities and World Economic Cycles: A Test of A.G. Frank and B. Gills's 'A' and 'B' Cycles." Paper presented at the Canadian Association of Geographers Conference, Vancouver, Canada, May 21. (Reprinted as chapter 8, this volume.)

Chase-Dunn, Christopher, and Thomas D. Hall, eds. 1991. *Core/Periphery Relations in Precapitalist Worlds*. Boulder, CO: Westview Press.

———. 1993. "Comparing World-Systems: Concepts and Working Hypotheses." *Social Forces* 71:851–86.

———. Forthcoming. *Rise and Demise: Comparing World Systems*. Boulder, CO: Westview Press.

Chaudhuri, K.N. 1991. *Asia Before Europe: Economy and Civilisation of the Indian Ocean from the Rise of Islam to 1750*. Cambridge: Cambridge University Press.

Davies, John Kenyon. 1981. *Wealth and the Power of Wealth in Classical Athens*. New York: Arno Press.

de Ste. Croix, G.E.M. 1981. *The Class Struggle in the Ancient Greek World*. London: Duckworth.

Ekholm, Kasja, and Jonathan Friedman. 1993. "'Capital' Imperialism and Exploitation in Ancient World Systems." In *The World System: Five Hundred Years or Five Thousand?*, edited by Andre Gunder Frank and Barry K. Gills. London: Routledge. (Originally published in *Review* 4:87–109, 1982.)

Frank, Andre Gunder. 1991. "Transitional Ideological Modes: Feudalism, Capitalism, Socialism." *Critique of Anthropology* 11:171–88. (Reprinted in *The World System: Five Hundred Years or Five Thousand?*, edited by Andre Gunder Frank and Barry K. Gills. London: Routledge.)

———. 1994. "The World Economic System in Asia Before European Hegemony." *The Historian* 56:259–76.

Frank, Andre Gunder, and Barry K. Gills, eds. 1993. *The World System: Five Hundred Years or Five Thousand?*, London: Routledge.

———. 1995. "The Five Thousand Year World System in Theory and Practice." Paper presented at the conference World System History: The Social Science of Long Term Change, University of Lund, Sweden, March 25–28.

Gill, Stephen, ed. 1993. *Gramsci, Historical Materialism, and International Relations*. Cambridge: Cambridge University Press.

Gills, Barry K. 1987. "Historical Materialism and International Relations Theory." *Millennium: Journal of International Studies* 16:265–72.

———. 1989a. "Synchronisation, Conjuncture, and Centre Shift in East Asian International History." Paper presented at the annual meetings of the International Studies Association, London, April 1.

———. 1989b. "International Relations Theory and the Processes of World History: Three Approaches." In *The Study of International Relations: The State of the Art*, edited by Hugh C. Dyer and Leon Mangasarian. London: Macmillan.

———. 1993a. "The Hegemonic Transition in East Asia: A Historical Perspective." In *Gramsci, Historical Materialism, and International Relations*, edited by Stephen Gill. Cambridge: Cambridge University Press.

———. 1993b. "Hegemonic Transitions in the World System." In *The World System: Five Hundred Years or Five Thousand?*, edited by Andre Gunder Frank and Barry K. Gills. London: Routledge.

———. 1994a. "The International Origins of South Korea's Export Orientation." In *Transcending the State/Global Divide: A Neostructuralist Agenda in International Relations*, edited by Ronen P. Palan and Barry K. Gills. Boulder and London: Lynne Rienner Publishers.

———. 1994b. "The Internationalisation of South Korea's Political Economy." Paper presented at the International Political Economy Group Conference on East Asian Political Economy, Nottingham, UK, November 18; and at the European Consortium for Political Research, Bordeaux, France, April 27–May 2, 1995.

———. 1994c. "Hegemony and Social Change." *International Studies Review* 38 (Supplement 2):369–71.

———. 1995. "The 'Continuity Thesis' in World Development." In *The Underdevelopment of Development: Essays for Andre Gunder Frank*, edited by Sing Chew and Robert Denemark. Newbury Park, CA: Sage.

Gills, Barry K., and Andre Gunder Frank. 1990. "The Cumulation of Accumulation: Theses and Research Agenda for 5000 Years of World System History." *Dialectical Anthropology* 5:19–42. (Revised version in *Core/Periphery Relations in Precapitalist Worlds*, edited by Christopher Chase-Dunn and Thomas D. Hall. Boulder, CO: Westview Press, 1991.)

———. 1992. "World System Cycles, Crises, and Hegemonial Shifts, 1700 BC to 1700 AD." *Review* 15:621–716.

———. 1994. "The Modern World System under Asian Hegemony: The Silver Standard World Economy, 1450–1750." Department of Politics Discussion Paper, University of Newcastle-upon-Tyne, UK.

Gills, Barry K., and Ronen P. Palan. 1994. "The Neostucturalist Agenda in International Relations." In *Transcending the State/Global Divide: A Neostructuralist Agenda in International Relations*, edited by Ronen P. Palan and Barry K. Gills. Boulder and London: Lynne Rienner Publishers.

Gilpin, Robert. 1981. *War and Change in World Politics*. New York: Cambridge University Press.

———. 1987. *The Political Economy of International Relations*. Princeton, NJ: Princeton University Press.

Glotz, Gustave. 1926. *Ancient Greece at Work: An Economic History of Greece from the Homeric Period to the Roman Conquest*. New York: Alfred A. Knopf.

Hall, John A. 1985. *Powers and Liberties: The Causes and Consequences of the Rise of the West*. Oxford: Basil Blackwell.

Hodges, Richard. 1989. *Dark Age Economics: The Origins of Towns and Trade, AD 600–1000*. London: Duckworth.

Jones, E.L. 1981. *The European Miracle: Environments, Economies, and Geopolitics in the History of Europe and Asia*. Cambridge: Cambridge University Press.

Larsen, Mogens Trolle. 1967. "Old Assyrian Caravan Procedures." Nederlands Historisch-Arekaeologish Institut te Istanbul, 22.

———. 1976. *The Old Assyrian City State and its Colonies*. Copenhagen: Akademisk Forlag.

Lombard, Maurice. 1975. *The Golden Age of Islam*. Amsterdam: North Holland.

Keohane, Robert O. 1986. *Neorealism and its Critics*. New York: Columbia University Press.

Mann, Michael. 1986. *The Sources of Social Power. Volume 1: A History of Power from the Beginning to AD 1760*. Cambridge: Cambridge University Press.

McNeill, William H. 1993. "Foreword." In *The World System: Five Hundred Years or Five Thousand?*, edited by Andre Gunder Frank and Barry K. Gills. London: Routledge.

———. 1995. "Information and Transport Nets in World History." Paper presented at the conference World System History: The Social Science of Long Term Change, University of Lund, Sweden, March 25–28.

Millett, Paul. 1983. "Maritime Loans and the Structure of Credit in Fourth-Century Athens." In *Trade in the Ancient Economy*, edited by Peter Garnsey, Keith Hopkins, and C.R. Whittaker. Berkeley: University of California Press.

———. 1990. "Sale, Credit, and Exchange in Athenian Law and Society." In *Nomos: Essays in Athenian Law, Politics, and Society*, edited by Paul Cartledge, Paul Millett, and Stephen Todd. Cambridge: Cambridge University Press.

Modelski, George, and William R. Thompson. 1988. *Seapower and Global Politics, 1494–1993*. Seattle: University of Washington Press.

———. 1995. *Leading Sectors and World Powers: The Coevolution of Global Politics and Economics*. Columbia: University of South Carolina Press.

Oates, Joan. 1978. "The Balance of Trade in Southwestern Asia in the mid-Third Millennium." *Current Anthropology* 13:480–81.

Overbeek, Henk, ed. 1993. *Restructuring Hegemony in the Global Political Economy*. London: Routledge.

Polanyi, Karl. 1944. *The Great Transformation*. New York: Rinehart.

Polanyi, Karl, Conrad Arensberg, and Harry W. Pearson, eds. 1957. *Trade and Market in the Early Empires*. Glencoe, IL: The Free Press.

Rostovzeff, M.I. 1941. *The Social and Economic History of the Hellenistic World*. 3 vols. Oxford: Clarendon Press.

Rowlands, Michael J., Mogens Trolle Larsen, and Kristian Kristiansen, eds. 1987. *Centre and Periphery in the Ancient World*. Cambridge: Cambridge University Press.

Silver, Morris. 1985. *Economic Structures of the Ancient Near East*. London: Croom-Helm.

Skocpol, Theda. 1977. "Wallerstein's World Capitalist System: A Theoretical and Historical Critique." *American Journal of Sociology* 82:1075–90.

Viner, Jacob. 1948. "Power versus Plenty as Objectives of Foreign Policy in the Seventeenth and Eighteenth Centuries." *World Politics* 1:1–29.

Waltz, Kenneth N. 1979. *Theory of International Politics*. Reading, MA: Addison-Wesley.

Wallerstein, Immanuel. 1991. "World System versus World-Systems: A Critique." *Critique of Anthropology* 11:189–94. (Reprinted in *The World System: Five Hundred Years or Five Thousand?*, edited by Andre Gunder Frank and Barry K. Gills. London: Routledge, 1993.)

Weber, Max. (1904)1958. *The Protestant Ethic and the Spirit of Capitalism*. Trans. Talcott Parsons. New York: Scribner's.

———. (1896–1909) 1976. *The Agrarian Sociology of Ancient Civilizations*. Trans. R.I. Frank. London: New Left Books.

———. (1927) 1981. *General Economic History*. Trans. Frank H. Knight. New Brunswick, NJ: Transaction Books.

Wilkinson, David. 1992. "Decline Phases in Civilizations, Regions, and Oikumenes." Paper presented at the annual meetings of the International Studies Association, Atlanta, April 1–4.

———. 1993. "Civilizations, Cores, World Economies, and Oikumenes." In *The World System: Five Hundred Years or Five Thousand?*, edited by Andre Gunder Frank and Barry K. Gills. London: Routledge.

———. 1995. "Civilizations as World Systems." Paper presented at the conference World System History: The Social Science of Long Term Change, University of Lund, Sweden, March 25–28.

Zolberg, Aristide. 1981. "Origins of the Modern World-System: A Missing Link." *World Politics* 33:254–81.

*Chapter Six*

# The Modern World System Revisited
## *Rereading Braudel and Wallerstein*

The modern history and structure of the world system can and should be (re)interpreted from a world-embracing, more Asian-based perspective than the Eurocentric one proposed by Fernand Braudel (1984) in his *Perspective of the World* and Immanuel Wallerstein (1974, 1980, 1989) in *The Modern World-System*. They contend that their world-economy/system was born in Western Europe shortly before AD 1500 and then expanded from this center to "incorporate" the rest of the world. Yet the "rise of the West" in a supposedly European-centered world-economy and system was part of a much wider and older historical process in a largely Asian-based world economy/system, which had the same essential characteristics that Braudel and Wallerstein attribute to their European-based "world-economy/system." Therefore, the origin of the "rise of the West" in the "modern world-system" must be sought much earlier outside Europe itself. Moreover, this wider world economy/system also continued to thrive in Asia through the 18th century.

Braudel's and Wallerstein's Eurocentric thesis is contradicted time and again by their own ample evidence reviewed below, as well as by the evidence and analysis of others. For instance, Abu-Lughod (1989) described a 13th-century Eurasian world system *Before European Hegemony* and Chaudhuri (1990) analyzed *Asia Before Europe*. Following their lead to reinterpret modern world history from a more Asian perspective has far-reaching implications: theoretical ramifications for our reading of history, cultural connotations that contradict the Eurocentrism of alleged European "exceptionalism," and political or ideological significance, which questions the utility of "capitalism" (or for that matter "feudalism" or "socialism") as a category of scientific analysis and political policy.

We may begin our rereading of Braudel and Wallerstein by asking whether in and since 1500 there were several world-economies, as they claim; or was there only one world economy? The difference a hyphen makes is stressed by Wallerstein (1991, as reprinted in 1993, pp. 294–95):

> Note a detail in word usage. . . . I speak of "world-systems." I use a hyphen; they [Frank and Gills] do not. I use the plural; they do not. . . . For me there have been very many world-systems. . . . My "world-system" is not a system "in the world" or "of the world." It is a system "that is a world." Hence the hyphen, since "world" is not an attribute of the system. Rather the two words together constitute a single concept. Frank and Gills's system is a world system in an attributive sense, in that it has been tending over time to cover the whole world.

Braudel also stresses the difference between *world economy* and *world-economy*. "The *world economy* is an expression applied to the whole world. . . . A *world-economy* only concerns a fragment of the world, an economically autonomous section." Braudel (1984, p. 70) continues: "Immanuel Wallerstein tells us that he arrived at the theory of the world-economy while looking for the largest units of measurement which would still be coherent." Braudel and Wallerstein emphatically deny that there was any such "coherent" world economy before very recent times. Yet time and again in his book, Braudel's own data and analysis of his "world-economies" demonstrate that they were not economically autonomous. Instead, he shows again and again that they were intimately connected and dependent on each other in what should instead be termed a world economy or world system, which included them all. Moreover, apparently this world economy or system also had a coherence of its own, which not incidentally had the very same characteristics as Wallerstein's "modern world-system"—except that it was not European centered and not uniquely "capitalist."

However, Braudel (1984, p. 24) asserts that "there have always been world-economies" and "the world-economy model is certainly a valid one" (p. 69). He analyzes several contemporaneous "world-economies" during the time span covered by his book, which contrary to its title reaches back to the 13th and even the 11th centuries: in Europe, Russia, the Turkish Empire, Islam, India, and China. He is uncertain whether the last three should be considered as three separate world-economies or as the "greatest of world-economies," a "super-world-economy" that also included Southeast Asia and Japan in the Far East. Finally, he considers the creation of a "fourth world-economy" with the arrival of the Europeans in the East.

Yet Braudel and Wallerstein themselves show time and again that all these supposedly autonomous "world-economies/systems" were in fact part of a single world economy and world system. The terms "world economy" and "world system" (without hyphens) should be used to refer to the Afroeurasian "world" economy/system that was already in place and functioning well before AD 1500. Indeed, as I have argued elsewhere, this world economy/system's unitary and continuous development and expansion can be traced over at least the last 5,000 (not 500) years (Frank 1990a, 1991a, 1993b; Frank and Gills 1992, 1993; Gills and Frank 1992). For present purposes, however, we may limit our inquiry to the modern world economy/system and especially to the evidence about its age, extension, and other characteristics adduced by Braudel and Wallerstein themselves.

## World Economy/System Identity and Structure

### *Identifying the System(s)*

Braudel (1984) explicitly denies that there was a single world economy in early modern times. So he reviews a half dozen supposedly autonomous "world-economies." The first world-economy Braudel considers outside the European one is Russia. He regards "the Russian world-economy—a world apart" and "unquestionably a world-economy in itself," which was so "remote and marginal" that "on this point it is impossible to disagree with Immanuel Wallerstein" (p. 441). But why is that not possible, and indeed even necessary? For "Muscovy had never been completely closed to the European world-economy" (p. 441), and "Russia's foreign trade was always manipulated by hidden hands in Peking, Istanbul, Isfahan, Leipzig, Lwow, Lübeck, Amsterdam or London" (p. 462).

> The West took from Russia only raw materials, sending in exchange manufactured articles and currency (which had its importance, it is true), [and] the East bought manufactured goods from Russia, and provided in return dyestuffs . . . luxury goods . . . but also cheap silks and cottons for the popular market (p. 444).

Note how characteristic this role of raw materials supplier is of dependent underdeveloped economies in the world economy and how contemporary this same trade pattern still is in the same region in our own time before, during, and after "socialism"! (Frank 1977, 1980). Yet even then "it was Russia's positive balance [of trade] with the West which injected into the Russian economy the minimal monetary circulation—silver from Europe or China—without which the market activity would scarcely have been conceivable, certainly not at the level it reached in practice" (Braudel 1984, p. 448).

A French consul at Elsinore observed that "considerable sums of money in Spanish pieces of eight pass through here on every English vessel bound for St. Petersburg" (Braudel 1984, p. 463). In Russia also, the exchanges from Europe across Siberia to China "formed a system of interdependence" (1984, p. 458). Moreover, "at the beginning of the sixteenth century, Russia's principal foreign market was Turkey" (1984, p. 442)—which Braudel also classifies as yet another separate world-economy, "reminiscent of Russia" (1984, p. 467).

Braudel terms the Turkish (empire) world-economy "virtually a fortress," but also a "source of wealth" and a "crossroads of trade, providing the Turkish Empire with the lifeblood that made it mighty" (1984, p. 467). How could it be all three simultaneously? The answer is that it was not a fortress, if that implies significant isolation from the rest of the world. Indeed, Constantinople/Istanbul had for a millennium depended on and continued to derive its very life blood from its turntable position in East–West and North–South trade and finance between Asia, Africa, and Europe:

> The list of imported goods is interminable. . . . The catalogue of outgoing products is shorter. . . . A long [contemporary] French report on the Levant trade confirms this impression: "[French] ships carry more goods to Constantinople than to all other ports in the Levant. . . . The surplus funds are transferred to other ports by means of bills of exchange which the French merchants of Smyrna, Aleppo and [Port] Said provide for the Pashas" (1984, p. 471).

Braudel goes on to ask what he calls "the key question" of the place of European trade in the volume of Turkish trade, and he answers that it was little and/or "merely passed quickly through" (1984, p. 471). "The reason was that money, the sinews of western trade, usually only made fleeting appearances in the Turkish Empire": Part went to the Sultan's treasury, part oiled the wheels of top-level trade, and "the rest drained away in massive quantities to the Indian Ocean" (1984, p. 473). In that case, would it not be at least another, if not *the*, key question to ask what intermediary "crossroads" role the Turkish "world-economy" played between Europe (as well as beyond it the Americas) and India and beyond in the world economy? A map of caravan routes, Braudel says, "would show them running from Gibraltar to India and China; and this was the whole movement-in-space which made up the Ottoman economy" (1984, p. 475), which "owed its suppleness and vigour to the tireless convoys which converged from every direction" (1984, p. 476).

That is, far from being a self-contained fortress world-economy, the Ottoman empire drew its own life-blood from being a crossroads between other "world-economies," which also were not independent or autonomous of each other. Of course, the Ottomans tried to maintain as much monopoly power and derive a maximum of rent from their intermediary position and barred others from sharing in it as best they could. Moreover, not content with their intermediary role at home, their merchants "invaded Venice, Ferrara, Ancona, even Pesaro, Naples and the fairs of the Mezzogiorno" in Italy (Braudel 1984, pp. 480–81) and "were soon found all over Europe, in Leipzig fairs, using the credit facilities provided by Amsterdam, and even in Russia or indeed Siberia as we have already seen" (1984, p. 482). None of these commercial relations seem consistent with the thesis of a closed Ottoman fortress world-economy.

Braudel moves on to the Far East, the "greatest of all world-economies," which "taken as a whole, consisted of three gigantic world-economies," Islam, India, and China. "But between the fifteenth and eighteenth centuries, it is perhaps permissible to talk of a *single* world-economy embracing all three" (1984, p. 484). Toward the end of this period, Braudel finds its center of gravity in the East Indies; and he devotes special attention to Malacca—beyond the three above mentioned world-economies!—where he observes that "everything and anything" was to be found in a network of maritime traffic comparable to that of the Mediterranean or the Atlantic coasts of Europe (1984, pp. 486–87).

Also in South Asia, India "had in fact been for centuries subject to a money economy, partly through her links with the Mediterranean world" (Braudel 1984, p. 498). "Cambay (another name for Gujerat) could only survive, it was said, by stretching out its arm to Aden and the other to Malacca" (1984, p. 528). Gold and silver "were also the indispensable mechanisms which made the whole great machine function from its peasant base to the summit of society and the business world" (1984, p. 500). The foundation of Europe's trade with India were the low wages of the "foreign proletariat" there, Braudel suggests, which produced the cheap exports that in turn were the *sine qua non* of the inflow of precious metals to India.

Wallerstein also finds that already by the end of the 14th century

the Indian subcontinent emerged from this crisis as a core production area of cotton textiles in the world economy and became the beneficiary of a huge inflow of bullion as a result of trade surplus. India's trade with West Asia increased exponentially over the next several centuries and tied the economic fates of cities on both sides of the Arabian sea closely together. . . . At the same time, the maritime trade of India to the east, connecting to the China-Malay trade experienced a new resurgence, following Sung China's decision to lift its earlier ban on merchant trade. In the wake of this, Srivijaya declined as an intermediary in Southeast Asia to the benefit of ports on the Malay coast. Trade across the Bay of Bengal witnessed a chronological simultaneity of the rise and decline of the most prominent ports at both ends of the eastern Indian Ocean: Pulicat and Melaka, and . . . Aceh and Masulipatnam (Palat and Wallerstein 1990, p. 26).

Despite these trans-Eurasian connections, Palat and Wallerstein are willing to speak only of an evolving Indian Ocean world-economy. By 1500, this economy combined a set of intersecting trade and production linkages converging on such nodes as Aden and Mocha on the Red Sea; Basra, Gombroon, and Hormuz on the Persian Gulf; Surat and Calicut on the western seaboard of the subcontinent; Pulicat and Hughli on the Coromandl and Bengal coasts; Melaka on the Malay archipelago; and the imperial capitals, such as Delhi and Teheran, connected by caravan trails.

Palat and Wallerstein acknowledge that these centers centralized and dominated transregional trade and that they "lived at the same pace as the outside world, keeping up with the trades and rhythms of the globe" (Palat and Wallerstein 1990, pp. 30–31, quoting Braudel 1984, p. 18) to that effect. Nevertheless, Palat and Wallerstein insist that there were three autonomous historical systems: the Indian Ocean world-economy, one centered around China, and the Mediterranean/European zones which merely converged at intersections. (We may note in passing that these [rather arbitrarily defined?] world-economies and their boundaries are not quite the same as Braudel's "easily described" slow-changing ones!) At these intersections, Palat and Wallerstein also note the "swift collapse of these cities once their fulcral positions were undermined." But they would have it that "their riches accumulated from their intermediary role in the trade between different world-systems" rather than acknowledge the existence of a single world economy. Yet, did not India use its intermediary role in a single world economy to accumulate not only American silver, but perhaps temporarily even to occupy a hegemonic position in competition with other regions that may have permitted India to "superaccumulate" (Gills and Frank 1990a)?

This commercial network spanned Afroeurasia, but not because the Europeans created it. Braudel himself demonstrates that this type of exchange transcends the world-economy boundaries he finds so easy to describe, and that apparently the arterial system of blood flows and creation of uniformities—and also of the disuniformities, which are part of Braudel's ground rules for a world-economy—are not limited to the same but extend through the whole real world economy. Braudel observes that

> prices in Muscovy, in so far as they are known lined up with those of the West in the sixteenth century, probably by the intermediary of American bullion, which here as elsewhere acted as a "transmission belt." Similarly, Ottoman prices followed the European pattern for the same reasons (1984, p. 76).

Indeed, Braudel observes "knock-on effects" as far away as Macao, even beyond the Manilla Galleon route. He also remarks that "historians (Wallerstein included) have tended to underestimate this type of exchange" (1984, p. 76).

Moreover, de facto Braudel also finds—and to his surprise—a global if not a world economy beyond the monetary sphere. "Long-term control of the European world-economy evidently called for the capture of its long-distance trade, and therefore of American and Asian products" (1984, p. 211):

> Who could fail to be surprised that wheat grown at the Cape, in South Africa, was shipped to Amsterdam? . . . Or that sugar from China, Bengal, sometimes Siam and, after 1637, Java, was alternately in demand or out of it in Amsterdam, depending on whether the price could compete in Europe with that of sugar from Brazil or the West Indies? When the market in the mother country was closed, sugar from the warehouses in Batavia was offered for sale in Persia, Surat or Japan. Nothing better demonstrates how Holland in the Golden Age was already living on a world scale, engaged in a process of constant partition and exploitation of the globe. . . . One world-economy (Asia) . . . [and] another (Europe) . . . were constantly acting on one another, like two unequally laden trays on a scale: it only took an extra weight on one side to throw the whole construction out of balance (1984, p. 220).

## *Money Made the World Go Round*

Silver and gold were the life-blood that flowed through the veins of this world economy and made possible both the "international division of labor" and the shifting hegemonies in the world system. Braudel himself recognized as much. He declares himself "astonished," "as a historian of the Mediterranean," to find that the late 18th-century Red Sea trade was still the same "vital channel" in the outflow of Spanish-American silver to India and beyond as in the 16th century. But American silver reached this "world-economy" not only via the Red Sea and the Levant, but also around the South African Cape, and with the Manilla galleons. Moreover, "this influx of precious metal was vital to the movements of the most active sector of the Indian, and no doubt the Chinese economy" (1984, p. 491). India "had in fact been for centuries subject to a money economy, partly through her links with the Mediterranean world" (1984, p. 498). "Cambay (another name for Gujerat) could only survive, it was said, by stretching out its arm to Aden and the other to Malacca" (1984, p. 528). Gold and silver "were also the indispensable mechanisms which made the whole great machine function, from its peasant base to the summit of society and the business world" (1984, p. 500).

The "series of interconnected regional markets dispersed and overlapping around the globe" were really a "world market for silver," which no one disputes, according to Flynn, and in which perhaps as much Spanish American silver as went over the Atlantic also crossed the Pacific to Asia, where it competed with Japanese silver (Flynn 1991, pp. 341, 347, 335). Braudel also recognizes that

> like exchanges elsewhere, trade in the Far East was based on goods, precious metals and credit instruments. . . . European merchants . . . could apply to the moneylenders in Japan or in India (in Surat) . . . and to every local source of precious metals afforded them by the Far East trade. Thus they used Chinese gold, . . . silver from Japanese mines, . . . Japanese gold coins, . . . Japanese copper exports on a massive scale, . . . gold produced in Sumatra and Malacca, . . . [and] the gold and silver coins which the Levant trade continued to pour into Arabia (especially Mocha), Persia and north-west India. . . . [The Dutch East India Company] even made use of the silver which the Acapulco [Manilla] galleon regularly brought to Manilla (1984, p. 217).

By the same token, any temporary scarcity of silver also had negative repercussions in Asia. For instance, it may have helped bring down the Ming dynasty in China. The inflow of silver from Spanish America and Japan until 1630 promoted the monetization of the Chinese economy. The abrupt decline in silver production elsewhere and of its export during the world recession after 1630 caused economic turmoil and bankrupted the Ming government in China, making it an easy prey to the Manchus in 1644 (Shaffer 1989; Atwell 1986). *Not* coincidentally, as Goldstone (1991) argues despite his skepticism about monetary causes, the government fell in Britain at nearly the same time in 1640, and the Ottoman one nearly did.

The argument that capital accumulation and economic development in Europe were furthered by American silver and gold was of course already made by Smith, Marx, and Keynes. Braudel, Wallerstein, and Frank, among others, only elaborated on this role of precious metals—but not enough! For beyond the direct effects these precious metals had in generating accumulation in Western Europe, they also had indirect effects that were perhaps even more important: the conquest of markets in Asia. As James Blaut (1977, 1992) has cogently argued, it was Europe's rape of silver from the Americas that permitted it to buy into the markets of Asia and ultimately to outcompete Asians in their home and other markets. Europeans found and exploited a new source of money that gave them a continual, albeit fluctuating, source of purchasing power with which to outbid Asians for labor and commodities in their own markets. Blaut suggests that already in the 16th century the inflow from the Americas doubled the bullion stock in Afroeurasia. Braudel himself concludes that "in the end, the Europeans had to have recourse to the precious metals, particularly American silver, which was the 'open sesame' of these trades" (1984, p. 217). Of course, Europeans also derived important investible profits from their American plantations, especially from sugar, and brought in slaves to work them from their African slave trade. "From the start, Spanish America had inevitably been a decisive element in world history" (1984, p. 414). "Is not America . . . perhaps the true explanation of Europe's greatness?" (1984, p. 387). Precisely that is also the explanation of Blaut (1977, 1992).

Thus, the Western European competitive advantage in the world economy in general and in the previously more developed Asia in particular was not based on higher economic productivity or even naval military superiority that was limited to a few ports. Still less was it based on any other "exceptionalism" (to which we return in the next section). The European competitive advantage was first and foremost derived from access to American silver. Braudel himself almost recognizes as much in the previously cited passages on the role of gold and silver. He also recognizes, as we will again see below, that this European conquest of Asia took much longer than one (16th) century.

Thus, the evidence is superabundant, also in Braudel and Wallerstein themselves, that the early modern world system had a world economy with a world-embracing division of labor, which was nourished by a lifeblood of precious metals flowing via Europe from west to east around the entire globe.

## Who Incorporated Whom into What System and When?

In Braudel's and Wallerstein's reading of modern world history, a European-centered world economic system spread out to incorporate other world-economies into the modern world-system. Wallerstein's collaborators dedicated a special issue of *Review* (Volume 10, Nos. 5–6, 1987), which he edits, to "Incorporation into the World-Economy: How the World System Expands," and Wallerstein (1989) himself titles a chapter of his *The Modern World-System III*, "The Incorporation of Vast New Zones into the World-Economy: 1750–1850." According to him, it is only then, and more specifically from 1733 to 1817, that the European world-economy "began by incorporating zones which had already been in its external arena since the sixteenth century—most particularly and most importantly, the Indian subcontinent, the Ottoman empire, the Russian empire, and West Africa" (1989, p. 129). "Incorporation" means that at least some significant production in the formerly "external" area is integrated into the division of labor of the capitalist world-economy.

Contrary to this thesis, however, many years ago already Braudel and others like Magalaes-Godinho demonstrated that the wealth, prosperity, and trade of the Asian world-economies relative to the European one—or, as suggested here, of these regions in the single world economy—exceeded those of Europe well into the 18th century or later. Braudel himself argued that the shift of the center of gravity to the Atlantic still required at least two

centuries after Columbus. "The general decadence comes over the Mediterranean in the XVIIth century. In the XVIIth century, we say, not in the
XVIth, as is usually claimed" (Braudel 1953, p. 368). Moreover, the
circum-Asian maritime trade also still did not displace the trans-Asian
caravan trade or the place of Central Asia therein in the 16th century. Indeed,
around 1600 all the silk still moved overland by caravan. Moreover, the
tonnage of spices brought westward and to Europe by caravan through
Central Asia was still twice that brought by ship (Steensgaard 1972, pp.
56–57). Thus, to the end of the 16th century, Central Asia and with it the
Ottomans continued to maintain their place in overland trade against both
the South Asian maritime trade and the West Asian, Mediterranean, and
Atlantic trades. The 17th-century decline was cyclical and common to all of
these regions and routes, including the Americas, during the 17th century
world economic crisis. In the 18th century, trade revived again across
Central Asia, albeit along a more northerly route; and it prospered on the
circum-Asian maritime route. Indeed, Braudel also writes: "But it was only
because the accessible markets of the Far East formed a series of coherent
economies linked together in a fully operational world-economy, that the
merchant capitalism of Europe was able to lay siege to them and to use their
own vitality" (1984, p. 496).

Braudel also notes that the sheer size of the world-economies (or the
super-world-economy) and their trade in the East still exceeded that of the
European world-economy by far. The Director of the British East India
Company, Sir Josiah Child, observed in 1688 that Indian "trade with all the
Eastern nations . . . is ten times as much as ours and all the European nations
put together" (Braudel 1984, p. 494). Indeed, Braudel also cites estimates
of the comparative gross national products constructed by Bairoch for the
West (Western Europe and North America, but also including Russia/USSR
and Japan, which at that time were not part of the European world-economy) and the rest of the world (including Latin America) in the East. In
1750, the first area generated $35 billion (in 1960 U.S. dollars) and the
second one $120 billion. Still in 1860, the respective figures were $115
billion and $165 billion. So in the 18th century, the "Eastern" economy
(including Russia and Japan) was still over five times larger than the
"Western" one whose income was so dependent on Latin American gold
and silver. Per capita incomes ranged between $150 and $300 a year in all
of them (Braudel 1984, p. 534).

So, it may be plausible that Europe "laid siege" to this richer economy in
that poor Europe drew on its new supply of money from the West to conquer
the richer East. (Europe's newly developed military technology was of only
limited use, and then only on coastal localities, until the late 18th or 19th
centuries). However, it is much less plausible to argue, as Braudel, Waller-

stein, and the latter's collaborators would have it, that Europe "incorporated" Asia into its own world-economy.

## Hegemony

A related issue concerns hegemony. Though Braudel does not use this term, the "ground rules" of his world-economies are that each has a dominant capitalist city and a strong aggressive state at its center. However, no particular city maintains its hegemonic position for long, and each is soon replaced by another. While its domination lasts, each hegemonic city acts as a core in its world economy, which is marked by an internal hierarchy of polarized zones with centralization and concentration of wealth, accumulation, and technological development.

For Wallerstein, hegemony is similarly structural but defined by a world-economic core, which has shifted from Iberia, to Amsterdam, to Britain, to the United States. Even according to Wallerstein, each of these periods of hegemony was only temporary, and they were interspersed by periods of rivalry without any hegemonic power. Modelski and Thompson (1988) define hegemony more in terms of political power and find essentially the same instances as Wallerstein. Critics have pointed out that Portugal was not really, and Amsterdam only barely and briefly if at all, hegemonic in the world-economy, especially if political power is taken as one of the criteria. The reference, of course, is to the European world-economy. These writers see most of the world as outside their world-economy and therefore also not subject to the hegemony of its core power before the 18th, or really mid 19th, century.

This exclusion of most of the world (economy) from many, and all of it from some, periods in modern history renders this conception of hegemony rather problematic even for the limited purview of the European world-economy. Braudel's dominant city-states are even more problematic as hegemons. As soon as we look at the world economy as a whole and recognize that the European world-economy was only one part of it, world system-wide hegemony becomes even more doubtful. At best, Britain and the United States each occupied such a position only for brief periods in the mid-19th and mid-20th centuries. Before that, it seems impossible to find a single world economy/system-wide hegemon in modern history—unless and until we go back to the Mongols under Genghis Khan as an only slightly longer-lived candidate in the 13th century!

European hegemonic incursion really only succeeded after about three centuries of trying—indeed after many more if we also count, as we should, the earlier Venetian and Genoan attempts that Braudel reviews. Then between 1750 and 1850, Ottoman, Moghul, and Qing rule was already weakened also for other reasons in West, South, and East Asia, and the world became less multipolar and more unipolar. These and other "world economies" competed with each other and the European one, until the latter won—temporarily!

Therefore, it would seem more prudent to recognize that the world economy/system has been characterized by only temporary and shifting *regional* hegemons in modern times as also in the earlier history of the world system (Gills and Frank 1992). Indeed, from this wider world economic/systemic perspective, any temporary existence of a hegemonic center is much more the exception than the rule (Gills 1993). Rather, various regional "centers" and their rivalry have been the rule both for thousands of years before "the modern world-system" and since it began. Braudel himself claims that

> in the thousand years or so before the fifteenth century, Far Eastern history is simply a monotonous repetition of the same events; one port would rise to prominence on the shores of the Red Sea, only to be replaced in time by one of its identical neighbors. The same thing happened along the coast of the Persian Gulf or in India, or in the islands and peninsulas of the East Indies; and maritime zones too might dominate by turns (1984, p. 485).

This modification of the concept of hegemony has implications for a related problem: accumulation and its concentration. According to Braudel and Wallerstein explicitly, and even Gills and Frank (1991, 1992) implicitly, "hegemony" has not only a structural regional reference, but also a processual one: The hegemon has a privileged core position relative to the peripheries in the process of accumulation. Moreover, for Wallerstein, the system is also defined by its division of labor. One support for the present argument is that, as we have seen above, many parts of the world economy outside the European world-economy demonstrably did participate in such a division of labor. However, it would be more difficult if not impossible to demonstrate that this participation in the world economic division of labor generated a process of accumulation that was concentrated in a single hegemonic core. The above-mentioned continual eastward flow of specie well into the 18th century is suggestive of some hegemonic core accumulation there. If any place was hegemonically "superaccumulating" in this period, it was probably India more than Portugal and Holland, or even Western Europe as a whole (Gills and Frank 1992). Indeed, Braudel and Wallerstein themselves recognize centers of accumulation outside their European world-economy, for example, in Russia and India up to the 18th century. That is one reason why they exclude them from that world-economy despite their participation in a common world-economy-wide division of labor. Would it not be better, then, to accord all parts of the world economy/system their due place and part, without insisting against the evidence that hegemony and accumulation are concentrated in only one core—and only temporarily and briefly at that? Recognizing the same, of course, does not imply that the world economic structure and process generate or even tend toward any kind of equality. Contrary to much contemporary received ideological wisdom, participation—whether privatized or otherwise—in the world economy demonstrably never did and does not now tend to make everybody equal or even richer.

## World System-Wide Cycles as a Bounding Mechanism

Schumpeter (1938) wrote that economic or business cycles are not like tonsils that can be extirpated, but are rather like the heartbeat of the organism itself. There is substantial evidence, also in Braudel and Wallerstein, that the world economy has had a cyclical heartbeat of its own. Even scattered evidence suggests that this cyclical heartbeat has been so common to widely distant—supposedly autonomous—areas of the world as to constitute still another important indication that they were truly part and parcel of a single world economy. George Modelski has suggested that we must first define the system in which we seek to locate the cycles. But operationally it may well be the other way around: Identifying simultaneity of cycles across far-flung areas can offer prima facie evidence of the extension and bounding of the system, as I have argued even for Bronze Age world system cycles (Frank 1993b). Much more evidence to this effect should, and surely could, be brought to light and analyzed for the modern world-system. Unfortunately, only very few historians have troubled to find and present evidence on whether and how cycles coincided across the supposed boundaries of world-economies. Yet that can reveal so much about whether several world-economies really did form a single world economy—which hardly any historians think existed!

On the one hand, Braudel claims that "the world-economy is the greatest possible vibrating surface. . . . It is the world-economy at all events which creates the *uniformity* of prices over a huge area, as an arterial system distributes blood throughout a living organism" (1984, p. 83). Yet, on the other hand, he observes that "the influence of the world-economy centered in Europe must very soon have exceeded even the most ambitious frontiers ever attributed to it" (1984, p. 76), and he muses that "the really curious thing is that the rhythms of the European conjuncture transcend the strict boundaries of their own world-economy" (1984, p. 76).

## Some 18th-Century Short Cycles

Braudel himself offers only a few indications, including some of which he seems unaware, of cyclical simultaneity across the boundaries of his world-economies. Braudel reproduces a graph of the yearly fluctuations of Russian exports and its trade balance between 1742 and 1785. He does not comment other than to observe "two short lived drops in the [trade balance] surplus, in 1772 and 1782, probably as a result of arms purchases" (1984, p. 463). Actually, the graph also shows a third big drop in 1762–63, and all three coincide with a sharp drop on the graph of Russian exports, whatever may have happened to imports of arms or anything else.

"Curiously" however, these three short periods also fall in the same years as three world economic recessions, which Braudel discusses at some length (1984, pp. 267–73) in another chapter devoted to Amsterdam. However, he makes no connection to the same periods in Russia. In still another chapter, Braudel reproduces a graph on Britain's trade balance with her North American colonies between 1745 and 1776. It shows sharp declines in British imports, and lesser ones of exports, in these same years 1760–63 and 1772–73 (alas the graph does not extend into the 1780s). But, again, Braudel does not look for connections either between the two graphs or between either, let alone both of them, and the recessions they reflect. This omission is all the more curious in view of the comments he does make about these recessions. About the first one, he writes that "with the currency shortage, the crisis spread, leaving a trail of bankruptcies; it reached not only Amsterdam but Berlin, Hamburg, Altona, Bremen, Leipzig, Stockholm and hit hard in London" (1984, p. 269). Regarding the next recession, Braudel observes catastrophic harvests in all of Europe in 1771–72 and famine conditions in Norway and Germany. Moreover, he goes further:

> Was this the reason for the violent crisis, aggravated possibly by the conse-
> quences of the disastrous famine which hit India in the same years 1771–72,
> throwing into confusion the workings of the East India Company? No doubt
> these were all factors, but is the real cause not once more the periodic return
> of a credit crisis? . . . Contemporary observers always connected such crises
> to some major bankruptcy (1984, p. 268).

Finally, in the chapter on the North American colonies, Braudel refers to

> the Boston Tea Party when, on 16 December 1774, a number of rebels
> disguised as Indians boarded three ships owned by the [East] India Company
> standing at anchor in Boston harbour, and threw their cargo into the sea. But
> this minor incident marked the beginning of the break between the colonies—
> the future United States—and England (1984, p. 419).

Yet, again, Braudel makes no connection between this event in America and others he analyzes elsewhere in the world for the very *same* years. Why does so experienced a *world* historian, who is also exceptionally sensitive to *conjunctures*, not even seek such connections? Perhaps because he takes his world-economic hyphen too seriously and/or has serious doubts about "how wise [it is] for one historian to try to bring together in a single analysis the scattered fragments of a history still insufficiently explored by research" (1984, p. 468). Wallerstein (1989, pp. 198, 228) briefly refers to a "postwar slump" after the Seven Years War in 1763 and only in passing to "the immediate postwar trade depression" in the 1780s after the war associated with the American Revolution. He makes no mention at all of the intervening recession in the 1770s just before that Revolution.

Yet all of these events and others were connected through a series of world economy/system-wide business cycles within what may be termed a crisis "B" phase of a long Kondratieff cycle, as I argued two decades ago (Frank 1978). Summarizing briefly, the Peace of Paris in 1763 concluding the Seven Years War was already signed under the influence of a recession and long downturn, which began in 1761. From 1764 on, so were the British Sugar, Quartering, Stamp, and Townsend Acts, which caused so much dissatisfaction in the North American colonies that was exceeded only by the prohibition to issue bills of credit and paper money, which aggravated the deflationary conditions and hardship for debtors in the colonies. Yet the Colonists took even these in their stride, particularly during the subsequent cyclical recoveries—until another recession began in 1773. Moreover, the Bengal Famine of 1770–71 had lowered the profitability of the East India Company. It petitioned Parliament for relief and received it in the form of the Tea Act of 1773, which granted the Company the privilege to dump its tea on the American market. The Americans in turn dumped it into Boston Harbor in the "Tea Party" to which Braudel refers. The British reaction through the Quebec and Intolerable Acts of 1774 escalated the economic conflict into political repression as well, which then rallied enough support for "the shot heard around the world" in Lexington and Concord on April 19, 1775 and the Declaration of Independence in 1776.

In Braudel's third period of crisis, he notes changes in both British and Russian balances of trade, which were generated by these recessions (and not just increased Russian arms imports). The same recession, however, also had other more important repercussions in France, where they led to revolution in 1789, and in the new American Confederation. There, the economic bad times of the early 1780s and "the more acute economic downturn of 1785–86 and the [resultant] massive popular political movements, such as Shay's Rebellion in 1786, renewed and increased political support for the federalists" against the Articles of Confederation and for their replacement by the American Constitution in 1787 (Frank 1978, pp.

206–08). For his part, Braudel remarks on the "Batavian" revolution of the mid-1780s in Holland, which "has been insufficiently recognized for what it was, the first revolution on the European mainland, forerunner of the French Revolution" (1984, p. 275).

To return to Braudel's and our point of departure in Russia, it hardly seems that its or any of the other "world-economies" was as "remote" or "autonomous" as he claims. On closer inspection, the three apparently recession-induced declines in Russia's balance of trade were connected to simultaneous and related events in many parts of continental Western Europe, Britain, North America, and faraway India. All of these occurred during three important recessions in what should be termed a world system-wide Kondratieff B phase world economic crisis from 1762 to 1790 (Frank 1978). Other world economy/system-wide short cycles in modern history could surely be identified and analyzed, if only (economic) historians were willing to try.

## *Kondratieff and Longer Cycles*

Braudel also devotes a special section to conjunctures and Kondratieff cycles, as well as to others that are twice as long and more, of which he says "four successive secular cycles can be identified, *as far as Europe is concerned*" (1984, p. 77, emphasis in original). Indeed, his whole exposition and most examples are confined to the "world-economy" centered on Western Europe. The question arises whether this cyclical pattern and the world system it characterized were limited to (Western) Europe, as Wallerstein and Braudel claim, or whether they were far more wide-ranging. We have already noted that Braudel observed how at least the short "rhythms of the European conjuncture transcend the strict boundaries of their own world-economy" (1984, p. 76).

World economy/system-wide, or at least world economy transcending, Kondratieff cycles have recently also been identified elsewhere. Instead of 4 cycles identified by Kondratieff and the 10 identified by Frank (1978) and Goldstein (1988) (the latter also using datings by Braudel and Frank!), Modelski and Thompson (1992) now count 19 such cycles, and Modelski (1993) analyzes 4 of them during about two centuries in China under the Song dynasty after about AD 1000.

Mark Metzler finds Kondratieffs since 1600 in Tokugawa Japan, and demonstrates that *their timing coincided* with those in the European world-economy. One also coincided with the Kondratieff starting in 1762, and particularly with its severe recession of the 1780s, about which we noted "coincidences" above. Moreover *"prices in China were very roughly in sync with prices in Europe. . . . If we take this movement of prices as a gauge, China* could be considered a part of the 'world economy' at this time" (Metzler 1994, p. 39, emphasis in original). Goldstone (1991) also demonstrates widespread and repeated cyclical simultaneity across Eurasia, but his "demographic-structural" analysis leaves little room for international rather than "national" cyclical and other economic processes, and he emphatically rejects any worldwide monetary ones. (See my critique in Frank [1993a].)

Braudel and Wallerstein also seem to recognize other longer cycles. In his review of an earlier period, Braudel notes the decline of the Champagne fairs at the end of the 13th century,

> and these dates also coincide with the series of crises of varying duration and seriousness affecting the whole of Europe at the time, from Florence to London, heralding what was to become, in conjunction with the Black Death, the great recession of the fourteenth century (1984, p. 114).

Wallerstein (1992, p. 587) also emphasizes a period of European-wide cyclical decline from 1250 to 1450, in a pattern "clearly laid out and widely accepted among those writing about the late Middle Ages and early modern times in Europe."

But was this decline limited to Europe? No! The Indian historian K.N. Chaudhuri refers to Braudel's ascription of Cambodian 13th- to 14th-century decline to ecological change and points out that Mesopotamian *irrigated* agriculture was also ruined about the same time; he asks what accounts for the case of "Ceylon and its sudden, catastrophic demise after about AD 1236? First of all, let us note that the Sinhalese collapse was not unique. The period from the 1220s to the 1350s was one of deep crisis for many societies in Asia. . . . That near total demographic catastrophes . . . took place in every region of the Indian Ocean is not in question. . . . Were these events all coincidence?" (Chaudhuri 1990, pp. 246–48).

No, the simultaneity of these catastrophes was no coincidence. Writing about the "13th-century world system," Janet Abu-Lughod (1989) finds first a system-wide expansion and then simultaneous economic and demographic crisis across all of Eurasia from the early 14th century onward. Abu-Lughod analyzes the "13th-century world system" for the period 1250–1350. She describes a series of chain-linked regional subsystems including Europe and West, South, Southeast, East, and Central Asia under Mongol rule, which spread out to include much of the other areas. For her, this multipolar "world system" came and went in little more than a century of "restructuring," later to be replaced by another one centered in Europe. Unfortunately, she says that she is not interested in its origins, and she sees her system as coming to an end in 1350, a century before the supposed birth of Wallerstein's "modern world-system."

Braudel makes a similar argument about Europe and "what I think about crises: they mark the beginning of a process of destructuration: one coherent world system [sic] which has developed at a leisurely pace is going into or completing its decline, while another system is being born amid much hesitation and delay" (1984, p. 85). "Several world-economies have succeeded each other in the geographical expression that is Europe. Or rather the European economy has changed shape several times since the thirteenth century" (1984, p. 70). A more coherent argument, on the contrary, is that the European "destructuration" of Braudel and the "disorganization" and "restructuring" of Abu-Lughod should all be seen as the crisis phases of a long cycle in a single world economy with a continual cyclical development. The expansion noted by Abu-Lughod started much earlier, around 1050, and lasted until about 1250. It was world system-wide and was manifest especially in the commercial and technological development of Song China, but it also included Southeast Asia, India, West Asia, and the Mediterranean (Frank 1990b; Gills and Frank 1992). The whole period between 1250 and 1450 then brought on a world system-wide crisis (Frank 1990b, 1991b, 1993c; Frank and Gills 1993a; Gills and Frank 1992). Abu-Lughod has reconsidered her argument in the light of mine (in Frank and Gills 1993b).

For the same time, even Wallerstein observes an apparently Eurasian-wide longer cycle. The collapse of the Mongols, he says, was a

> crucial non-event. . . . The eleventh-century economic upsurge in the West that we have discussed was matched by a new market articulation in China. . . . Both linked up to a Moslem trading ecumene across the Middle East. China's commercialization reinforced this model [why not system?]. . . . The Mongol link completed the picture.
>
> What disrupted this vast trading *world-system* was the pandemic Black Death, itself quite probably a consequence of that very trading network. It hurt everywhere, but it completely eliminated the Mongol link (1992, pp. 610–11, emphasis added).

So even Wallerstein sees something of a "vast trading world-system" reaching across the Moslem ecumene into China. He even observes in passing that not incidentally Song economic expansion coincided with the 1050–1250 expansion in the European "world-system." We asked above whether this same crucial cyclical pattern may not therefore also extend further back—and forward—in history. The evidence is that it does and that these about two-centuries-long expansions followed by equally long contractions were up and down phases in a world system-wide half-century long cycle (as argued in "World System Cycles, Crises, and Hegemonial Shifts, 1700 BC to 1700 AD" [Gills and Frank 1992]), which may have reached back even to 3000 BC and earlier (as proposed in my "Bronze Age World System Cycles" [Frank 1993b]).

The 17th century AD is another case in point. The "17th-century crisis" has been analyzed many times over—but with a focus on Europe or on the

"European world-system," as in Wallerstein (1974) and Frank (1978). Yet there is evidence, which has not received the attention it merits, that the 17th-century crisis was also world system-wide. Goldstone (1991) analyzed near simultaneous economic and political crises in mid-17th century England, the Ottoman Empire, and Ming China. He attributes them to common demographic changes. However, trade and other economic activity also declined or failed to expand in the 17th century in Inner (Central) Asia and parts of India (Frank 1992). This decline seems also to have been cyclical, for trans-Asian trade recovered and expanded again in the 18th century. As already noted above, the economic declines during the 17th-century crisis therefore did not yet signify any shift of hegemony within the world system, least of all to Europe, which did not achieve it until one or two centuries later. Thus, the earlier and still ongoing Asian-based world economic system raises questions about its origin and about the alleged exceptionalism of the "capitalist modern world-system" that supposedly originated in Europe.

## Theoretical, Cultural, and Political Implications

Thus, our rereading of Braudel and Wallerstein on modern world history has far-reaching implications: It modifies our theory of history and the origin of the modern world system, it challenges the Eurocentric thesis of European "exceptionalism," and it raises questions about the use of the concept and terminology of "capitalism," which is so common from right to left.

### World System Origins

Wallerstein (1974) dates the origin of the modern world-system during the "long 16th century" from 1450 to 1640 in Western Europe. However, Braudel (1984, p. 57) writes that "I do not share Immanuel Wallerstein's fascination with the sixteenth century" as the time the modern world-system emerged in Europe. Braudel is "inclined to see the European world-economy as having taken shape very early on." Indeed he observes "European expansion from the eleventh century" when it was "suddenly covered with towns—more than 3,000 in Germany alone" (pp. 92–93). "This age marked Europe's true Renaissance" (p. 94). Thus, Braudel finds the origins several centuries earlier than Wallerstein, though both see them in (Western) Europe. Yet even Wallerstein (1992) sees something going on long before 1450:

> It is the long swing that was crucial. Thus 1050–1250+ was a time of expansion of Europe (the Crusades; the colonizations in the east and far north, and in Ireland).... The "crisis" or great contractions of 1250–1450+ included the Black Plague (pp. 587–88).
>
> The patterns of expansions and contractions are clearly laid out and widely accepted among those writing about the late Middle Ages and early modern times in Europe (p. 587).

If the long cyclical swing was so "crucial," the implication is—especially by the above-cited Modelski rule or its obverse and contrary to Wallerstein's central thesis about the beginnings in 1450—that there was also systemic continuity back to at least the mid-11th century, as observed by Braudel as well. Moreover, "if today's cycles do in fact have some resemblance to those of the past, that indicates that there is a certain continuity between *ancien régime* and modern economies: rules similar to those governing our present experience may have operated in the past" (1984, p. 73). Indeed, the post-1450 "long 16th century" expansion itself begins to appear as part of a clearly laid-out, long cyclical pattern of expansions and contractions.

Thus, the origin of the world system, and even of the "European world-system" within it, was significantly earlier than the 16th century in which Wallerstein first finds it. As Braudel writes, "the only unresolved question is the date at which this *Weltwirtschaft* really began to exist—and this is well-nigh impossible" (1984, p. 96). In that case also, we must question the supposed *European* origin of the world system. Whenever the system really began to exist, it can hardly have done so in Europe, which remained quite marginal until the modern era, and as we will observe below rather recently at that. Indeed, Abu-Lughod (1989, p. 388) has already argued that "the decline of the East preceded the Rise of the West"—in the same world system, whose origin was elsewhere, outside Europe.

In this regard, an argument similar to ours was already made by Jacques Gernet in his *History of China*:

> What we have acquired the habit of regarding—according to the history of the world that is in fact no more than the history of the West—as the beginning of modern times was only the repercussion of the upsurge of the urban, mercantile civilizations whose realm extended, before the Mongol invasion, from the Mediterranean to the Sea of China. The West gathered up part of this legacy and received from it the leaven which was to make possible its own development. The transmission was favored by the crusades of the twelfth and thirteenth centuries and the expansion of the Mongol empire in the thirteenth and fourteenth centuries. . . . There is nothing surprising about this Western backwardness: the Italian cities . . . were at the terminus of the great commercial routes of Asia. . . . The upsurge of the West, which was only to emerge from its relative isolation thanks to its maritime expansion, occurred

at a time when the two great civilizations of Asia [China and Islam] were threatened (1985, pp. 347–48).

The Braudel and Wallerstein argument about the European origin of the system is not only empirically and theoretically mistaken, but it has very serious Eurocentric overtones or underlying assumptions that are reminiscent of the arguments about European "exceptionalism."

## European Exceptionalism?

A whole library full of books and articles has been devoted to explaining the "rise of the West" in terms of its own supposed "exceptionalism." Interestingly, William McNeill (1963), the dean of world historians who used this title for his pathbreaking book, is among the few Western historians to take exception to this exceptionalism (see McNeill, chapter 13 this volume). Not so E.L. Jones (1981), who revealingly titles his book *The European Miracle*, and many others, like Lynn White Jr. (1962), John A. Hall (1985), or Baechler, Hall, and Mann (1988). They all find the rest of the world deficient or defective in some crucial historical, economic, social, political, ideological, or cultural respect in comparison to the West. Therefore, these authors also revert to an internal explanation of the presumed superiority of the West to explain its ascendance over the rest of the world. For all of them, the rise of Europe was a unique "miracle" and not a product of history and shifts within the world (system). Blaut (1992) derisorally calls this "tunnel history" derived from a tunnel vision, which sees only "exceptional" intra-European causes and consequences and is blind to all extra-European contributions to modern European and world history. Yet, as Blaut points out, in 1492 or 1500 Europe still had no advantages of any kind over Asia or Africa, and there would then have been no reason to anticipate the triumph of Europe or its capitalism two and more centuries later.

As a particularly Eurocentric example, we may choose *The Rise of the Western World: A New Economic History* by the 1993 Nobel laureate in economics Douglass C. North and his coauthor Robert Paul Thomas (1973). The reason is the explicitness of its title, its emphasis on "new," the renown of the authors, and their revision of received theory. Yet under their heading "Theory and Overview: 1. The Issue" and on the very first page, they clearly say that "the development of an efficient economic organization *in Western Europe* accounts for the rise of the West" (p. 1, emphasis added). They then trace this institutional change, and especially the development of property rights, to increased economic scarcity, which was generated in turn by a demographic upturn *in* Western Europe. The rest of the world was not there for them. Moreover, as North and Thomas (p. vii) emphasize in their preface, their economic history is also "consistent with and complementary to standard neoclassical economic theory" and was awarded the Nobel prize.

Marxist economic history seems different in using concepts like "mode of production" and "class struggle," but it is equally Eurocentric. Both of these concepts have generally also been interpreted within a framework of a single "society" or social formation, or at least a single entity, whether that be a state or a civilization. Thus, Marxist economic historians also look for the sources of "the rise of the West" and "the development of capitalism" within Europe and are equally or even more Eurocentric than their "bourgeois" opponents. Examples are the famous debate in the 1950s on "the transition from feudalism to capitalism" among Maurice Dobb, Paul Sweezy, Kohachiro Takahashi, Rodney Hilton, and others (reprinted in Hilton 1976) and the "Brenner debate" on "European feudalism" (Aston and Philpin 1985). De Ste. Croix (1981) on the class struggles in the ancient "Greco-Roman" civilization and Anderson (1974) on "Japanese feudalism," also considered these as particular "societies."

In his excellent critique of Perry Anderson and others, Teshale Tibebu (1990, pp. 83–85, emphasis in original) also argues persuasively that much of their analysis of "feudalism, absolutism, and the bourgeois revolution" and "their obsession with the specificity . . . [and] supposed superiority of Europe" is Western "civilizational arrogance," "ideology dressed up as history" and "*Orientalism painted red*" that is, the "*continuation of Orientalism by other means*. The other means is provided by theoretical Marxism."

Thus, the reverse side of the European exceptionalist coin has been the equally Eurocentric theses about "Orientalism," which have been justly criticized by Edward Said (1978), Martin Bernal (1987), and Samir Amin (1989), writing against Eurocentrism. All of them show how 19th-century European liberalism invented a single "Oriental" grab bag from which to distinguish European "exceptionalism." Marx's "Asiatic mode of production" was no better, and only little better were Weber's studies on other religions that did not share "the Protestant ethic and the spirit of capitalism."

Braudel and Wallerstein at least recognize similarities between Europe and Asia, which, however, undermine their European world-system/economy thesis. For Braudel writes, on the one hand,

> it might also be asked whether Europe was somehow of a different human and *historical* nature from the rest of the world; and thus whether . . . [they] will or will not help us form a clearer judgement of Europe—that is of Europe's success. The conclusions do not in fact all tend in the same directions. For the rest of the world, as we shall see, very often went through economic experiences resembling those of Europe. Sometimes the time-lag was very slight" (1984, p. 387).

On the other hand, and referring to North and West Africa already before the Europeans arrived, "once more we can observe the profound identity of action between Islam's imperialism and that of the West" (1984, p. 434). In Asia, "in the thousand years or so before the fifteenth century, Far Eastern history is simply a monotonous repetition of the same events. . . . For all the changes, however, history followed essentially the same course" (1984, p. 485).

In the same paragraph, Braudel wants to "challenge the traditional image (briefly revived by J.C. van Leur) of Asiatic traders as high-class peddlers." Yet van Leur wrote in a passage about "peddlers" that their afflux could be larger or smaller, and that there could be variations in the state of trade whose volume could increase or decrease, but that

> "international trade", thus, [is] a "world trade". . . . Viewed in the forms advanced here as a hypothesis, the wondrous picture is explained of a trade which went its way from one end of the world to another. . . . Trade, then, can be viewed as an "historical constant." No qualitative transformations can be indicated in the course of history (1955, p. 87).

We might ask then what changed in or after 1500? Not much, is the answer, as Braudel himself demonstrates. For instance, he quotes a contemporary French sea captain writing from the Ganges river in India: "The high quality of merchandise made here . . . attracts and always will attract a great number of traders who send vessels to every part of the Indies from the Red Sea to China. Here one can see the assembly of nations of Europe and Asia . . . reach perfect agreement or perfect disunity, depending on the self-interest which alone is their guide" (1984, p. 511).

Even Wallerstein (1992) now seems to have some doubts about and finds "an uncomfortable blurring of the distinctiveness of the patterns":

> Many of these [previous] historical systems had what we might call proto-capitalist elements. That is, there often was extensive *commodity* production. There existed producers and traders who sought *profit*. There was *investment* of *capital*. There was *wage-labor*. There were *Weltanschauungen* consonant with *capitalism*. But none had quite crossed the threshold of creating a system whose primary driving force was the incessant accumulation of capital (p. 589).
>
> We must now renew the question, why did not capitalism emerge anywhere earlier? It seems unlikely that the answer is an insufficient technological base. . . . It is unlikely that the answer is an absence of an entrepreneurial spirit. The history of the world for at least two thousand years prior to 1500+ shows an enormous set of groups, throughout multiple historical systems, who showed an aptitude and inclination for capitalist enterprise—as producers, as merchants, as financiers. "Proto-capitalism" was so widespread one might consider it to be a constitutive element of all the redistributive/tributary world-empires the world has known. . . . Something was preventing it

[capitalism]. For they did have the money and energy at their disposition, and we have seen in the modern world how powerful these weapons can be (p. 613).

Moreover, Wallerstein also negates the uniqueness of his "modern world-capitalist system" in numerous other passages and ways. But let one example suffice:

> All the empirical work of the past 50 years on these other systems has tended to reveal that they had much more extensive commodification than previously suspected. . . . It is of course a matter of degree" (1992, p. 575).

One of the many implications of the past unexceptionality of Europe or of the West is that "development" today and tomorrow—for example, in East Asia—need and perhaps should not copy Western ways. One's development, like hegemony, is a function—at least in large part—of one's shifting place and changing role in the world economy/system rather than of a particular (Western) way of doing things. Therefore, development can and does also subscribe to the "Sinatra Doctrine" of doing things "my way."

However, this recognition of the unexceptional experience of Europe also casts doubt on the exceptionality of "capitalism" and, therefore, on the usefulness of the "capitalist" label to distinguish one "system" from another.

## Capitalism?

Both Braudel and Wallerstein explicitly address the question whether the European world-system, the other world-economies, and by implication the whole world economy, was or is "capitalist" and whether this term clarifies more than it obscures. However, on this matter Braudel explicitly differs with Wallerstein, and treats the question more satisfactorily—but I believe still not enough so. "This debate is anything but academic" writes Braudel (1984, p. 57). Agreed!—because the answer, and indeed even posing the question, has important ideological/political consequences. They have been the subject of intense debate about the "transition from feudalism to capitalism" (re/edited by Hilton 1976), the "Brenner debate" (edited by Aston and Philpin 1985), about the "European miracle" (Jones 1981; Hall 1985), and others. However, all these debates have been completely Eurocentric, and even Blaut's (1977, 1992) anti-Eurocentric formulation is still limited by his attachment to the idea of transition, indeed a break, between "feudalism" and "capitalism."

However, as Tibebu (1990, p. 50) points out, "feudalism was conceptualized by its enemies . . . long after feudalism itself had ceased to be dominant. . . . The word 'feudal' is almost nothing more than a synonym for the word 'bad.' Perhaps the best analogy is the political use of the word 'fascist.'" Similarly, and by extension to this argument, Tibebu suggests that the fundamental justification among almost all Marxists for the term "bourgeois revolution" is an argument based on an analogy to the long-awaited proletarian revolution. "Just as the transition from capitalism to socialism takes place through proletarian revolution, so in the same way, it is assumed that the transition from feudalism to capitalism must have taken place through a bourgeois revolution" (p. 122). He argues that both revolutions are "imaginary"—so to say, wishful thinking. So are, I submit, both "transitions."

Wallerstein insists that the European-centered "modern world-system" is distinguished by its unique capitalist mode of production. He writes, for instance, that

> despite the temporal contemporaneity of post-1400 expansion of networks of exchange and intensification of relational dependencies in Europe and in the world of the Indian Ocean, the processes of large-scale socio-historical transformation in the two historical systems were fundamentally dissimilar. In one zone, it led to the emergence of the capitalist world-economy. In the other, to an expanded petty commodity production that did not lead to a real subsumption of labor" (Palat and Wallerstein 1990, p. 40; see also Gills and Frank 1992).

Yet, according to Braudel, "capitalism did not wait for the sixteenth century to make its appearance. We may, therefore, agree with the Marx who wrote (though he later went back on this) that European capitalism—indeed he even says capitalist *production*—began in thirteenth-century Italy. . . . I do not share Immanuel Wallerstein's fascination with the sixteenth century" as the time the modern world-capitalist system emerged in Europe (1984, p. 57). As we observed above, Braudel sees the commercialization, expansion, and Renaissance of the European world-economy as occurring since the 11th century. "The merchant cities of the Middle Ages all strained to make profits and were shaped by the strain. . . . Contemporary capitalism has invented nothing" (1984, p. 91).

> By at least the twelfth century . . . everything seems to have been there in embryo . . . bills of exchange, credit, minted coins, banks, forward selling, public finance, loans, capitalism, colonialism—as well as social disturbances, a sophisticated labour force, class struggles, social oppression, political atrocities" (1984, p. 91).

Braudel also challenges the view that capitalism was invented in 12th- or 13th-century Venice (Cox 1959). "Genoa was far more modern than Venice . . . [and] the first in the field, with a uniquely modern approach to capitalism" (1984, p. 118) and might well have taken the lead. "To me

Genoa seems always to have been, in every age, the capitalist city par excellence" (1984, p. 157). Several other Italian cities also had capitalist institutions and/or processes earlier than Venice. In all of them, "money was constantly being invested and reinvested, and "ships were capitalist enterprises virtually from the start" (1984, p. 129). "It is tempting too to give Antwerp the credit for the first steps in industrial capitalism, which was clearly developing here and in other thriving towns of the Low Countries" in the 16th century (1984, p. 156).

But was this past limited to, and "capitalism" invented in, only one world-economy centered in Western Europe, which then exported it to others in Asia? No. For Braudel also observes that

> everywhere from Egypt to Japan, we shall find genuine capitalists, wholesalers, rentiers of trade, and their thousands of auxiliaries, commission agents, brokers, money-changers and bankers. As for the techniques, possibilities or guarantees of exchange, any of these groups of merchants would stand comparisons with its western equivalents (1984, p. 486).

Moreover, neither the Europeans in general nor their Portuguese vanguard brought or added anything of their own, only the money they themselves derived from the conquest of America. The classic Western treatise on Asian trade notes that

> the Portuguese colonial regime, then, did not introduce a single new element into the commerce of southern Asia. . . . Trade did not undergo any increase in quantity worthy of mention in the period. The commercial and economic forms of the Portuguese colonial regime were the same as those of Asian trade and Asian authority. . . . The Portuguese colonial regime, built upon war, coercion, and violence, did not at any point signify a stage of "higher development" economically for Asian trade. The traditional commercial structure continued to exist (van Leur 1955, pp. 117–18).

Whatever their differences, Braudel and van Leur agree, and even Wallerstein is obliged to concede a bit, that there was no dramatic, or even gradual, change in mode/s of production. There was no such noticeable change, not to mention any succession, from other mode/s to a "capitalist" one, and certainly none beginning in the 16th century or in Asia after centuries of European re/incorporation into the Asian "super world-economy."

Braudel himself repeatedly *demonstrates* the same in his history, even as he tries to *say* the opposite with his theory. Therein, Braudel is reminiscent of Marx. Marx also masterfully demonstrated the existence of a real world economy (without a "capitalist" mode of production) in his Volume III, but he did not fit his findings into the mentally constructed "model" or theory of his Volume I. Or more likely, Marx derived his model from "little

England," which was supposed to but did not show the rest of the world the mirror of its future; but the real world he saw in Volume III refused to fit into his English procrustean bed. Similarly, Braudel was also unable to incorporate his Volume III observations from the real world economy into the narrow model "world-economy" bed, or even beds, which he derived from Europe. Or did he derive his model from his student Wallerstein and his macrosocial theory, which led even the master historian Braudel down the theoretical European garden path? Except that the master balked on that de jure theoretical path when he saw Europe's many de facto world economic connections with Russia and Asia and also within the Asian "super world-economy." Finally, the historian Braudel lost his "enthusiasm" on his theoretical garden stroll, turned around, and rejected Wallerstein's proposal of the supposed 16th-century beginning of a European based "capitalist" world-economy.

So these Eurocentric and (anti-)historical categories of "feudalism," "capitalism," and the alleged "transition" between them merit criticism and deserve an alternative world economic perspective. Writing elsewhere to that end under the title "Transitional Ideological Modes: Feudalism, Capitalism, Socialism" (Frank 1991b), I argued that it is time to

> liberate ourselves from the optical illusion of the false identity of "system" and "mode of production." Samir Amin (1991) contends that the system could not have been the same system before 1500 because it did not have the capitalist mode of production, which only developed later. Before 1500, according to Amin and others, modes of production were tributary. My answer is that the system was the same no matter what the mode of production was. The focus on the mode of production blinds us to seeing the more important systemic continuity. Wallerstein makes the same confusion between "mode" and "system." Indeed *the single differentia specifica of Wallerstein's Modern World-Capitalist System is its mode of production*. Wallerstein's identification and also confusion of "system" and "mode" is evident throughout his works and widely recognized by others.
>
> Therefore, also dare to abandon (the sacrosanct belief in) capitalism as a distinct mode of production and separate system. What was the ideological reason for my and Wallerstein's "scientific" construction of a 16th-century transition (from feudalism in Europe) to a modern world capitalist economy and system? It was the belief in a subsequent transition from capitalism to socialism, if not immediately in the world as a whole, at least through "socialism in one country" after another. Traditional Marxists and many others who debated with us, even more so, were intent on preserving faith in the prior but for them more recent transition from one (feudal) mode of production to another (capitalist) one. Their political/ideological reason was that they were intent on the subsequent transition to still another and supposedly different socialist mode of production. That was (and is?) the position of Marxists, traditional and otherwise, like Brenner (1985) and Anderson

(1974). That is still the position of Samir Amin (1989), who, like Wallerstein, now wants to take refuge in "proto-capitalism"—and by extension "proto-socialism."

So is there still a political/ideological reason to hold on to the fond belief in a supposed "transition from feudalism to capitalism," around 1800, or 1500 (i.e., 1492), or whenever—to support the fond belief in a "transition to socialism" in 1917, or 1949, or whenever? Is there any such reason still to continue looking for this earlier transition and its hegemonic development only in Europe, while real hegemony is now shifting (no doubt through the contemporary and near future non-hegemonic interregnum) back towards Asia? NO, there is none (Frank 1991b, as reprinted in Frank and Gills 1993, pp. 213–14).

So we must—or at least should—agree with Chaudhuri (1990, p. 84) when he writes under the title *Asia Before Europe*: "The ceaseless quest of modern historians looking for the 'origins' and roots of capitalism is not much better than the alchemist's search for the philosopher's stone that transforms base metal into gold." Better then to be more "scientific" and, as already argued on other occasions, altogether to abandon the chimera of a unique "capitalist" mode of production, not to mention its supposedly Western European origin (Frank, 1991b; Frank and Gills 1992, 1993b). Instead, as Janet Abu-Lughod (1989, p. 338) insists, "of crucial importance is the fact that the fall of the east precedes the rise of the west." Even that is true only if we date the rise of the West only *after* the closing date of Braudel's book in 1800. Moreover, it signifies that all these "world-economies" in the "West" and "East" were only parts of a single age-old world economy/system, within which this change took place, like all else, only temporarily!

NOTES

This article offers an alternative theoretical perspective that extends the critique of Braudel and Wallerstein presented in Frank (1994). In so doing, the article also represents an extension to modern history of the world system approach to ancient and medieval history on which I have collaborated (e.g., Frank and Gills 1993) with Barry K. Gills, who also made generous comments on drafts for both articles.

*References*

Abu-Lughod, Janet. 1989. *Before European Hegemony: The World System A.D. 1250–1350*. New York: Oxford University Press.
Amin, Samir. 1989. *Eurocentrism*. London: Zed Books.

———. 1991. "The Ancient World-Systems versus the Modern World-System." *Review* 14:349–85. (Reprinted in *The World System: Five Hundred Years or Five Thousand?*, edited by Andre Gunder Frank and Barry K. Gills. London: Routledge, 1993.)

Anderson, Perry. 1974. *Lineages of the Absolutist State*. London: New Left Books.

Aston, T.H., and C.H.E. Philpin, eds. 1985. *The Brenner Debate: Agrarian Class Structure and Economic Development in Pre-Industrial Europe*. Cambridge: Cambridge University Press.

Atwell, William S. 1986. "Some Observations on the 'Seventeenth Century Crisis' in China and Japan." *Journal of Asian Studies* 45:223–44.

Baechler, Jean, John A. Hall, and Michael Mann, eds. 1988. *Europe and the Rise of Capitalism*. Oxford: Blackwell.

Bernal, Martin. 1987. *Black Athena: The Afroasiatic Roots of Classical Civilization*. New Brunswick, NJ: Rutgers University Press.

Blaut, J. 1977. "Where was Capitalism Born?" In *Radical Geography*, edited by R. Peet. Chicago: Maasoufa Press.

———. 1992. "Fourteen Ninety-Two." *Political Geography Quarterly* 11:355–85. (Reprinted in *1492: The Debate on Colonialism, Eurocentrism, and History*, edited by J.M. Blaut, with contributions by A.G. Frank, S. Amin, R.A. Dodgson, R. Palan, and R. Taylor. Trenton, NJ: Africa World Press, 1992.)

Braudel, Fernand. 1953. *El Mediterraneo y el Mundo Mediterraneo en la Epoca de Felipe II*. Vol. I. Mexico: Fondo de Cultura. (English edition *The Mediterranean and the Mediterranean World in the Age of Philip II*. 2 vols. Trans. Sian Reynolds. New York: Harper & Row; original French edition 1949.)

———. 1984. *The Perspective of the World*. Volume III of *Civilization and Capitalism 15th–18th Century*. New York: Harper & Row.

Chaudhuri, K.N. 1990. *Asia Before Europe: Economy and Civilisation of the Indian Ocean from the Rise of Islam to 1750*. Cambridge: Cambridge University Press.

Cox, Oliver C. 1959. *The Foundations of Capitalism*. New York: Monthly Review Press.

de Ste. Croix, G.E.M. 1981. *The Class Struggle in the Ancient Greek World*. London: Duckworth.

Flynn, Dennis O. 1991. "Comparing the Tokugawa Shogunate with Hapsburg Spain: Two Silver-based Empires in a Global Setting." In *The Political Economy of Merchant Empires: State Power and World Trade, 1350–1750*, edited by James Tracy. Cambridge: Cambridge University Press.

Frank, Andre Gunder. 1977. "Long Live Transideological Enterprise! The Socialist Economies in the Capitalist International Division of Labor." *Review* 1:91–140.

———. 1978. *World Accumulation, 1492–1789*. New York: Monthly Review Press.

———. 1980. *Crisis: In the World Economy*. New York: Holmes & Meier.

———. 1990a. "A Theoretical Introduction to 5,000 Years of World System History." *Review* 13:155–248.

———. 1990b. "The Thirteenth Century World System: A Review Essay." *Journal of World History* 1:249–56.

———. 1991a. "A Plea for World System History." *Journal of World History* 2:1–28.

————. 1991b. "Transitional Ideological Modes: Feudalism, Capitalism, Socialism." *Critique of Anthropology* 11:171–88. (Reprinted in *The World System: Five Hundred Years or Five Thousand?*, edited by Andre Gunder Frank and Barry K. Gills. London and New York: Routledge, 1993.)

————. 1992. "Fourteen Ninety-Two." *Political Geography Quarterly* 11:386–93. (Reprinted in *1492: The Debate on Colonialism, Eurocentrism, and History*, edited by J.M. Blaut, with contributions by A.G. Frank, S. Amin, R.A. Dodgson, R. Palan, and R. Taylor. Trenton, NJ: Africa World Press, 1992.)

————. 1993a. "The World Is Round and Wavy: Demographic Cycles and Structural Analysis in the World System. A Review Essay of Jack A. Goldstone's *Revolution and Rebellion in the Early Modern World*." *Contention* 2:107–24.

————. 1993b. "Bronze Age World System Cycles." *Current Anthropology* 34:383–430.

————. 1993c. "1492 and Latin America at the Margin of World History: East-West Hegemonial Shifts, 992–1492–1992." *Comparative Civilizations Review* 28:1–40.

————. 1994. "The World Economic System in Asia Before European Hegemony." *The Historian* 56:259–76.

Frank, Andre Gunder, and Barry K. Gills. 1992. "The Five Thousand Year World System: An Interdisciplinary Introduction." *Humboldt Journal of Social Relations* 18(1):1–79. (Reprinted in *The World System: Five Hundred Years or Five Thousand?*, edited by Andre Gunder Frank and Barry K. Gills. London and New York: Routledge, 1993.)

————. 1993a. "World System Economic Cycles and Hegemonial Shift to Europe, 100 BC to 1500 AD." *Journal of European Economic History* 22:155–83.

————, eds. 1993b. *The World System: Five Hundred Years or Five Thousand?* London and New York: Routledge.

Gernet, Jacques. 1985. *A History of China*. Cambridge: Cambridge University Press.

Gills, Barry K. 1993. "Hegemonic Transitions in the World System: Accumulation and the Making of World Order." In *The World System: Five Hundred Years or Five Thousand?*, edited by Andre Gunder Frank and Barry K. Gills. London and New York: Routledge.

Gills, Barry K., and Andre Gunder Frank. 1990. "The Cumulation of Accumulation: Theses and Research Agenda for 5000 Years of World System History." *Dialectical Anthropology* 15:19–42. (Expanded version in *Core/Periphery Relations in Precapitalist Worlds*, edited by Christopher Chase-Dunn and Thomas D. Hall. Boulder, CO: Westview Press, 1991.)

————. 1991. "5,000 Years of World System History: The Cumulation of Accumulation." In *Core/Periphery Relations in Precapitalist Worlds*, edited by Christopher Chase-Dunn and Thomas D. Hall. Boulder, CO: Westview Press.

————. 1992. "World System Cycles, Crises, and Hegemonial Shifts, 1700 BC to 1700 AD." *Review* 15:621–87. (Reprinted in *The World System: Five Hundred Years or Five Thousand?*, edited by Andre Gunder Frank and Barry K. Gills. London and New York: Routledge, 1993.)

Goldstein, Joshua S. 1988. *Long Cycles: Prosperity and War in the Modern Age*. New Haven, CT: Yale University Press.

Goldstone, Jack A. 1991. *Revolution and Rebellion in the Early Modern World*. Berkeley: University of California Press.

Hall, John A. 1985. *Powers and Liberties: The Causes and Consequences of the Rise of the West*. Oxford: Basil Blackwell.

Hilton, Rodney H., ed. 1976. *The Transition from Feudalism to Capitalism*. London: New Left Books.

Jones, E.L. 1981. *The European Miracle: Environments, Economies, and Geopolitics in the History of Europe and Asia*. Cambridge: Cambridge University Press.

McNeill, William H. 1963. *The Rise of the West*. Chicago: University of Chicago Press.

Metzler, Mark. 1994. "Capitalist Boom, Feudal Bust: Long Waves in Economics and Politics in Pre-Industrial Japan." *Review* 17:57–119.

Modelski, George. 1993. "Sung China and the Rise of the Global Economy." Unpublished manuscript, Department of Political Science, University of Washington, Seattle.

Modelski, George, and William R. Thompson. 1988. *Sea Power in Global Politics, 1494–1993*. London: Macmillan.

———. 1992. "Kondratieff Waves, The Evolving Global Economy, and World Politics: The Problem of Coordination." Paper presented at the N.D. Kondratieff Conference, Moscow, March 17, and at the annual meetings of the International Studies Association, Atlanta, April 1–5.

North, Douglass C., and Robert Paul Thomas. 1973. *The Rise of the Western World: A New Economic History*. Cambridge: Cambridge University Press.

Palat, Ravi A., and Immanuel Wallerstein. 1990. "Of What World System was Pre-1500 'India' a Part?" Paper presented at the International Colloquium on Merchants, Companies, and Trade, Maison des Sciences de l'Homme, Paris, May 30–June 2.

Said, Edward. 1978. *Orientalism*. New York: Pantheon.

Schumpeter, J. A. 1938. *Business Cycles*. New York: McGraw-Hill.

Shaffer, Lynda. 1989. "The Rise of the West: From Gupta India to Renaissance Europe." Unpublished manuscript, History Department, Tufts University.

Steensgaard, Niels. 1972. *Carracks, Caravans, and Companies: The Structural Crisis in the European-Asian Trade in the Early 17th Century*. Copenhagen: Studentlitteratur.

Tibebu, Teshale. 1990. "On the Question of Feudalism, Absolutism, and the Bourgeois Revolution." *Review* 13:49–152.

van Leur, J.C. 1955. *Indonesian Trade and Society: Essays in Asian Social and Economic History*. The Hague and Bandung: W. van Hoeve.

Wallerstein, Immanuel. 1974. *The Modern World-System: Capitalist Agriculture and the Origins of the European World-Economy in the Sixteenth Century*. New York: Academic Press.

———. 1980. *The Modern World-System II: Mercantilism and the Consolidation of the European World-Economy, 1600–1750*. New York: Academic Press.

———. 1989. *The Modern World-System III: The Second Era of Great Expansion of the Capitalist World-Economy, 1730–1840s*. San Diego, CA: Academic Press.

————. 1991. "World System versus World-Systems: A Critique." *Critique of Anthropology* 11:189–94. (Reprinted in *The World System: Five Hundred Years or Five Thousand?*, edited by Andre Gunder Frank and Barry K. Gills. London and New York: Routledge, 1993.)

————. 1992. "The West, Capitalism, and the Modern World-System." *Review* 15:561–620.

White, Lynn Jr. 1962. *Medieval Technology and Social Change*. New York: Oxford University Press.

*Chapter Seven*

# Let's Be Frank About World History

The present debate over the historical length of the world-system is important not only for international relations, world history, and civilizational studies, but also for future analytical frameworks through which collective life will be conceptualized. Since the advent of modern social science the basic unit of analysis has been the societal, whether as social formation, mode of production, nation-state, or simply society. World-system theory, conversely, suggests not only networks on a scale larger than a single society, but also implies that the motor of historical change operates at this distinctly world level. It is the idea that capitalism is a "world" economy, that the most basic political struggles are interstate, and that world culture sets the patterns and cognitive templates that national cultures adopt and press into service. But this movement toward specifying social process at a world level has been slow. While the theoretical laws of motion of social development contained in the older conceptualizations of Marx or Weber are increasingly doubted, there is as yet no successor at the level of general theory. It is to this issue that the debate on the origin/length of world history's systemic tendencies represents an effort at formulating distinctly global theory. This intellectual ferment can be broken down into three identifiable stages, the first of which is largely completed, the second of which we are in the midst of today, and the third of which is yet to come.

## Stage 1: Stretching History Beyond Today's Social Science Models

The first step has been to stretch the idea of historical continuity beyond the scope of existing models of explanation. What is the "social" in life is now seen as wider than just societies or social formations. The new world-historical reality is simply too wide and too long to be captured in sociological models. The documentation of this long continuity of world systemness has been the principal accomplishment of the first generation of world-system scholars. From dependency theory to a modern world-system starting in the 16th century, and then to one starting in the 13th century, and then to one going back 5,000 years, a generation of world-system theorists has pushed and stretched the sense of systemic continuity deeper into the historical past. In a Kuhnian sense, this is something like creating new data that do not fit the old paradigm. For example, the Marxian paradigm has capitalism beginning in the 18th or 19th century with the advent of the factory system, but Wallerstein (1974) argues that it begins further back in the 16th century, and it is not just something in Manchester or England but a global economic reality. Capitalism as such a world-system does not fit the older Marxian paradigm, and its threatened defenders have responded. Robert Brenner (1977) for one classically argues that capitalism is not such a world-system, but is still a national system, still linked to class relations within social formations rather than exchange relations between formations.

Even for those who now believe in "the capitalist world-economy," its distinctly international operating logic is never made very clear. It is mostly a matter of assertion. The equivalent of world class relations or a world mode of production is never formally identified, and what is settled for is a sort of halfway position captured clearly in the idea of the "articulation of modes of production." This means keeping the traditional societal unit, "mode of production," but linking a number of them together in something like a commodity chain to produce, through the economic syntax of aggregated individualism, a capitalist world-economy. The hands that pick cotton in the antebellum American South are, from this point of view, part of a slave mode of production, while the hands that weave cotton into textiles in Britain are part of a capitalist mode of production, with these two modes being "articulated" to comprise a larger world-economy. But why hands that pick and hands that weave are not parts of a single world mode of production is never seriously considered, as the conceptual bricolage of "articulation" is theoretically satisfying.

Wallerstein's (1974) 1970s stretching of world-systemic continuity back to the 16th century, though, lasted for only a decade, and scholars soon became anxious over this arbitrary starting point. World-systemness was stretched back further. Abu-Lughod (1989) took things back to the 13th century. Others pushed further back, with more and more continuity in history and wider and wider webs of connection. Wilkinson (1991) speaks of a Central Civilization; Gills and Frank (1991) speak of 5,000 years of world-system history; and Chase-Dunn and Hall (1991) go all the way back to hunter-gatherers and interband relations to find the primeval origin of intersocietal network ties.

This stretching of history is now somewhat complete, and with every pre-1500 article, book, discussion, and panel, it has become increasingly accepted that systemness starts earlier and earlier. You can stop anywhere you want, or go all the way back. All cases have been made, all positions heard. The question now becomes, How is such long history divided, categorized, and theorized? We are ready for the second stage.

## Stage 2: Challenging Today's Social Science Models

The present social science paradigms, from Marxism to traditional sociology, that are used to break up this newly-stretched web of world history into various phases, transitions, sequences, modes, stages of evolution, and types of social formations, are now themselves starting to break up and dissolve under the weight of the newly-established facticity of world history. With the sense of the world-system now stretched virtually back to human origins, the question turns to dividing up the continuity of such history and identifying the theoretical logic of this world-systemic entity. It is at this point that the older models of social science now confront the new data of a stretched historical continuity that is wider and longer than the propositional grasp of extant models. Again, there is the idea of the Kuhnian paradigm crisis, to which there has been a number of responses, including denial of the new realities, stretching the old paradigms to fit the new world history, and letting go of the old models altogether. Let's consider each.

### Option 1: Denial

One option is to cling to past models and deny the validity of the new stretched historical reality. Robert Brenner, again, is a prime example of the denial response, as he does not accept the idea of his societal structure (capitalism) being stretched to a world level (capitalist world-economy). Things are still societal in their essence, and to the extent that there are international realities they are always a by-product of societal processes. Class struggle *within* social formations precedes and makes possible unequal exchange relations *between* social formations, argue the societal traditionalists. The notion that a focus on the global formation makes such internal/external ideas moot is not persuasive, as capitalism is a system of relations between classes, which are societal, not global, divisions. The new stretched history may, though, be chopped up into national class struggles, but the core-periphery division of labor exists only as a by-product of these more primal societal divisions.

## Option 2: Stretching Old Theory to Fit the New Stretched History

The second solution has been the most popular among world-system scholars. Consider two examples taken from the present division between those who believe (a) that the systemness of world history begins with European colonialism, or (b) that world-system history goes back to the earliest of times.

### Stretching the Logic of Capitalism

Wallerstein represents the essence of stretching past theory over the newly stretched historical record of the world-system. Rather than seeing a world-system as a new emergent reality, he sees it as "capitalism," but now "world" rather than "societal" capitalism. Although attacked by traditionalists like Brenner for daring to say that the societal model of capitalism should be a world model, Brenner and Wallerstein are, from the point of view of global theory, quite traditional. Actually, Brenner is downright reactionary, refusing to allow any meaning for the theory of capitalism beyond that of the social formation, while Wallerstein is more liberal in at least stretching the conceptual entity "capitalism" to incorporate the new facts of world history since the 16th century. The logic of system origin is also borrowed from the old model, as the crisis of feudalism purportedly gives rise to the modern world-system. The world-system's future is also tied to the purported feudalism-to-capitalism-to-socialism transition, as Wallerstein speaks of how the world is in the midst of the transition to socialism, although the evidence offered is a societal transformation, the emergence of the Soviet Union in 1917. Some of the old societal mechanisms are harder to transfer to the new reality, so instead of identifying something like class relations on a world scale, Wallerstein goes with the more Smithian version of capitalism and speaks of a world division of labor with unequal exchange.

Wallerstein, then, understands the interrelatedness of history as going back to the 16th century, when he thinks the modern world-system began. He cannot, though, let go of the conceptual apparatus of the 19th century, and to make that theory fit his new stretched history he has simply stretched the idea of capitalism until it encompasses his world-system. Reservations by others that such societal logic cannot be directly mapped onto world realities have basically fallen on deaf ears.

Stretching The Theory of Social Evolution

Once the idea of a world-system with its stretched history began, the process could not be stopped at the 16th century. Chase-Dunn and Hall have pushed system origins back to the earliest forms of human organization, and then, like Wallerstein before them, have faced the question of what to make of this new historical record. They, also, have stretched inherited models instead of proposing a new framework. Going past the 16th century means that simply stretching the idea of capitalism is inadequate, so they have followed Amin (1980) and stretched the theory of social evolution over the record of world history and spoken of a succession of world-system modes of production from kin-based, to tributary, to capitalist, which is nothing more than the old hunter-gatherer, settled agricultural, and capitalist stages of social development.[1] Again, there is nothing wrong with these stages for societal development, but when the unit of analysis is a world-system then something about intersocietal networks, core-periphery divisions of labor, something, anything, involving more than the properties of social formations is required. None, though, has been offered.

## Option 3: Letting Go of the Old Models Altogether

Deny, stretch, or let go. Those are the options. Modernization theorists, traditional Marxists, and those still attached to societal-level processes, like Brenner, have denied; Wallerstein, Amin, Chase-Dunn and Hall, have all stretched; and now we come to Frank and Gills, who let go, which is the next step toward purely world-systemic models and away from traditional sociological ones. If history is the continuous web that everyone now agrees it is, and, further, if it has constituted a system, then this new global reality is larger and longer than the 19th-century social science models that are predicated upon societal, rather than world-historic, units of analysis. Put another way: The new data to be explained, world-systemic and throughout most of history, are simply too wide and too long for the propositional reach of conventional social science, including Marxism.

Frank seems to paraphrase the old admonition, "If you can't say anything nice, don't say anything at all," by arguing, in effect, "If you can't categorize world history in a new way, don't categorize it at all." Does this mean that thousands of years of history are without an identifiable logic, laws of motion, or a motor of development? No, not at all. But it does mean that seeing the new reality through old conceptual lenses does not move us forward toward an appropriate theory of world-historical development.[2] Frank lets go, and argues that world history is not made up of transitions between feudalism and capitalism and socialism, or of stages of development in the old 19th-century sense. When he says everything is the same over the centuries and nothing has changed there is an uproar by the stretchers, who want to make the world-system an instance of the structures and processes that reflect more of the historical experience of Europe than the reality of world history. It is the Frankian point about there being no feudalism in Latin America; feudalism was a European phenomenon, and haciendas are not a reproduction of European societal evolution but a product of the development of underdevelopment. The same logic now holds for the world-system as a whole. Slicing up world history into societal categories is inappropriate, for the world-system is not a societal entity and has not gone through societal stages of development. Letting go of these distinctions from the past is the next step toward clearing the world-historical board of previous conceptual distinctions, thereby allowing the world-system to be theorized a new way. Otherwise we either deny anything is new, or stretch, patch on, adapt, adjust, and add corollaries to the 19th-century societal models and processes in an effort to make sense of this newly-recognized world-historical system.

When Frank argues that nothing has changed—that the world after 1750 (Marx) or 1500 (Wallerstein and Amin) isn't capitalist, or that the world-system does not begin in the 13th century (Abu-Lughod), or that there is no sequence of societal stages of development that has been stretched worldwide—he is not arguing for nihilism or antitheorism, but simply saying that a new conceptualization is needed. Stretching past theory is not enough, even if it seems roughly to fit. What is needed is new theory, new conceptualizations to fit the new reality of this world-historical systematicity. Everyone has agreed on the new longer history of human organization, but not everyone can let go of the analytical frameworks with which to grasp, slice, decipher, deconstruct, or generate the new wider and longer world-historical system.

Obviously, to say what world history is not does not establish what it is. That final stage, the emergence of a distinctly global model of structure and process for world history, has yet to be reached and may be the task of the next generation of world-system theorists, just as the historical role of the first generation seems to have been to stretch history backward to make the case for a wider and longer unit of collective existence beyond that of the 19th century's "society." There is some agreement on this entity, "world-system," with its precise length and width still to be determined. Its logic, though, is nowhere near being identified, and how this system operates remains to be theorized. Frank, then, may represent the final formulation of this generation of world-system theorists: yes, a world-system; yes, for 5,000 years of historical continuity; but no, not capitalism, feudalism, tributary modes, or transitions. It has to be a new mode, a world mode, and not just stretched capitalism.

# Stage 3: Building a New Model of World-Historical Development

Frank does not have the new model; no one does. But he has begun to open some new avenues of thinking about how the world might work that may point toward a new model of world-historical development. Some of these are briefly outlined in Frank's paper in this volume. I would like to highlight a few.[3]

## Post-Wallersteinian World-System Theory

First, and most generally, Frank is beginning "post-world-system theory." What Frank did to modernization theory he is now doing to world-system theory. It is an amazing feat, hardly realized by many world-system practitioners. From saying developing countries did not get that way through their own internal development but as being part of a larger system of world economic relations, Frank has now placed that Europe-based world-system in a still larger world-historical context, saying that the development of the Wallersteinian/Braudelian world-system is conditioned by, is part of, develops in accord with, its global position within a still larger world-historical system that has had Asia as its center for a long period of time. Frank is now nesting the world-system school's very processes, their set of seemingly ultimate, final, macro dynamics into an even larger set of dynamics that will turn the Wallersteinian world-system into a dependent variable for Frank's Asia-centered world history independent variable.

## No Eurocentric Origin for the World-System

A corollary of the first point is the contention that the world-system does not bubble up out of the feudal West because of an endogenous "Eurocrisis" of feudalism and then go on to incorporate the rest of the world, but is part of the larger world web from the very start. The point is more than Abu-Lughod's "decline of the East before the rise of the West," which still implies some separateness of East and West. Frank has always pushed for ever wider frames of explanation, identifying encompassing structures which explain the dynamics of the social processes within their grasp. Underdevelopment used to be seen as endogenous, but with Frank it became a condition produced by the larger web of metropole-satellite relations. Similarly, the Wallersteinian world-system was once seen as endogenously arising out of the crisis of European feudalism, but now the Wallersteinian modern world-system's endogenous origin is questioned. Just as the understanding of underdevelopment required nesting it within the larger European world-economy, now the understanding of the European world-economy requires nesting it within the larger dynamics of an Asia-centered world-historical process. The analogy is not perfect, but to understand the revolution now going on within world-systems theory itself, underdevelopment is analogous to the whole Wallersteinian world-system since that system is but a zone within a larger, more encompassing, more determinative, Asia-centered world-historical system.

In the history of social thought, then, we have moved to ever wider and more encompassing structures that we believe frame human life. Resituating the earlier Wallersteinian conception of a "Euro-origin" for the world-system into its location within a larger Asia-centered world-historical process is a continuation of ever-widening theoretical frameworks. Levels of analysis are made continually larger, having gone from the individual-to-individual relations of 17th- and 18th-century utilitarianism/classical economics; to the 19th-century group-to-group, class-to-class relations of sociology; to the 20th-century "Eurocore" world-system theory; and now to East-West relations as subunits in an even more macro world-historical set of relations as proposed by Frank.

## Euroconquest of the Americas From Weakness, not Strength

Given the historical hegemony of Asia in world history and Europe's historical semiperipheral status, the "Euroconquest" of the Americas can now be seen as an act stemming from weakness, not strength. Europe could not conquer Asia militarily or economically, and so went west to the Americas and with plundered silver entered into Asian trade routes. It was not production or technique that facilitated early European participation in the Asia-dominated world system, but silver from the Americas, as only later did European productive advantage appear. Such a view represents a change in intellectual psychology, a decentering of the "Eurobias" involved in interpretations of world-historical development. The picture now is one of Europe looking through the window of overland trade routes that brought in the riches of the East as a semiperiphery, looking in at, and trying to get in on, the wealth of the East.

## Humanocentric, not Eurocentric, World-History

The Asian hegemony idea also prompts very macro materialist versions of human history—the most people, production, and wealth over most of the world's history are in the East. This makes the rise of the West a short interlude of perhaps a few hundred years from AD 1750/1850 to 2000, as productive advantage is again returning to Asia. So, a new model of world centers and peripheries: up to 1750/1850 an Asia-dominated world-system, then until 2000 a Euro-North American-dominated system, and then from the year 2000 onward the action swings back to where it has been most of the time—Asia. Speak of decentering. The rise of the West is now a hegemonic blip in world history.

## *Marx and Weber as Eurocentric Ideologists*

Turning Eurocentrism into vanity or false belief is one thing, claiming it is an ideology of "Eurohegemony" is another, but with the final ascendence of Western hegemony in 1750/1850 comes Western social theory proposing, as scientific fact, the autogeneration of the West and the endogenous superiority of everything from religion—the Protestant Ethic and the Spirit of Capitalism—to material technique, organizational structure, and class relations. Marx fits the "Euroideology" model; in theorizing that capitalism rises out of "Eurofeudalism" he gives no acknowledgement of relations between the semiperipheral West and the Asian core as having anything to do with producing the West's upward mobility in world production after 1750/1850. Marx has always been the most radical of thinkers, but from this perspective Marxism is a form of "Euroapologetics" providing a ration-ale for "Euroexceptionalism."[4] The point is whether religion-based (Weber) or modes of production-based (Marx) social science models do not acknow-ledge intercivilizational relations as part of the dynamic of change and development, and the implication is clear: Social science needs to be rethought so that East-West structural dynamics are the centerpiece of theoretical explanation rather than the autogeneration myth that the West rose on its own and went out to conquer, by idea, weapon, and productive innovation, the rest of the world. That is "Eurovanity"; and not just as delusion, but as self-serving ideology.

## *The Renaissance as the End of the Silk Road*

A smaller point, yet provocative, is the idea that the Italian Renaissance had its wealth and presence less because of the Italian city-state system, or the Hapsburg world, but as the termination of the silk road from Asia. This overland route terminating in Italy transformed Renaissance Italian cities into something like port cites for the silk road. Was the Italian Renaissance the creation of Europe or the end point of Asia? Another question that needs to be asked and answered.

## A Final Thought

Putting Asia back into world history seems overdue and a necessary rewrite of world history. It is interesting, though, in terms of the role of the material base affecting forms of consciousness, that we in the West have come to this conclusion now, at the end of the 20th century, when material advantage is moving across the Pacific. I think it is no accident that we are rethinking the role of Asia during a period of the very rise of Asia as the post-American hegemonic center of world production.[5] From a larger point of view hegemonic advantage may be coming full circle, from Asia to Asia, with a Euro-American interlude of a few centuries. It may also be the case that the hoped-for advance in social theory by the next generation of world-system scholars will come from Asia, as the material centrality of Asia will correspond to an Asian hegemony in world thought. Western biases might be such that, while we are capable of identifying the reality of what I have called here the stretched history of a world-systemic presence, theorizing the dynamics of this entity is beyond Western grasp. We can deny, stretch past models, or see the world-system tabula rasa, à la Frank, but we seem incapable of conceptualizing world history in terms other than our Marxian/Weberian perspectives. The passing of Western advantage in world production may also be the passing of Western advantage in social theory, leaving the theorization of the world-system to what will be the new hegemonic center of world intellectual life—Asia.

### NOTES

1.   The tripartite division of evolutionary stages into three is found in Samir Amin (1980). The same scheme was later used by Eric Wolf (1982).

2.   Frank does, though, list some descriptive attributes—there have always been hegemonies and rivalries, centralization/decentralization, and processes of accumulation. But this is rudimentary description, leaving the door open to identifying new laws of motion for world history.

3.   I realize that some of these ideas may have origins in other people's work, which Frank always notes and cites. The importance of Asia and the non-Eurocentrism of world history are ideas that have been discussed elsewhere, and I in no way mean to claim that they are unique to, or only mentioned by, Frank. For two other discussions of similar ideas, see Marshall C.S. Hodgson (1993) and J.M. Blaut (1993).

4.   Blaut (1993) similarly argues that endogenous European rise is a myth, and he links this rise to the conquest of the Americas. This, though, arises for Blaut from the geographical proximity of Europe and America—as opposed to Asia and America—which does not root the European rise in the social dynamics of the larger

world-historic process. That is, if Europe is a semiperipheral zone in the larger world-historical order, then transformations of that order are tied to the rise of the West, not to mere proximity to the Americas that can be looted for silver.

5.  For evidence on the rise of Asia in world production, see Albert Bergesen, Roberto Fernandez, and Chintamani Sahoo (1987). And for a discussion of the rise of Asian culture and archetypes in world consciousness, see Bergesen (1992).

## References

Abu-Lughod, Janet L. 1989. *Before European Hegemony: The World System AD 1250–1350*. New York: Oxford University Press.

Amin, Samir. 1980. *Class and Nation, Historically and in the Current Crisis*. New York: Monthly Review Press.

Bergesen, Albert. 1992. "Godzilla, Durkheim, and the World-System." *Humboldt Journal of Social Relations* 18:195–216.

Bergesen, Albert, Roberto Fernandez, and Chintamani Sahoo. 1987. "America and the Changing Structure of Hegemonic Production." In *America's Changing Role in the World-System*, edited by Terry Boswell and Albert Bergesen. New York: Praeger.

Blaut, J.M. 1993. *The Colonizer's Model of the World: Geographical Diffusionism and Eurocentric History*. New York: Guilford Press.

Brenner, Robert. 1977. "The Origins of Capitalist Development: A Critique of neo-Smithian Marxism." *New Left Review* 104:25–92.

Chase-Dunn, Christopher, and Thomas D. Hall. 1991. "Conceptualizing Core/Periphery Hierarchies for Comparative Study." In *Core/Periphery Relations in Precapitalist Worlds*, edited by Christopher Chase-Dunn and Thomas D. Hall. Boulder, CO: Westview Press.

Gills, Barry K., and Andre Gunder Frank. 1991. "5,000 Years of World System History: The Cumulation of Accumulation." In *Core/Periphery Relations in Precapitalist Worlds*, edited by Christopher Chase-Dunn and Thomas D. Hall. Boulder, CO: Westview Press.

Hodgson, Marshall C.S. 1993. *Rethinking World History*. Cambridge: Cambridge University Press.

Wallerstein, Immanuel. 1974. *The Modern World-System: Capitalist Agriculture and the Origins of the European World-Economy in the Sixteenth Century*. New York: Academic Press.

Wilkinson, David. 1991. "Cores, Peripheries, and Civilizations." In *Core/Periphery Relations in Precapitalist Worlds*, edited by Christopher Chase-Dunn and Thomas D. Hall. Boulder, CO: Westview Press.

Wolf, Eric R. 1982. *Europe and the People Without History*. Berkeley: University of California Press.

■ ANDREW BOSWORTH

*Chapter Eight*

# World Cities and World Economic Cycles

## Introduction

Do economic cycles exist? Are there long fluctuations in the world's economic system? If so, how far back in time are they evident? Most economists acknowledge the existence of seasonal and yearly cycles but there is less agreement over long-term ones such as the 40- to 60-year Kondratieff cycles, and much less over economic cycles of 500 years. Thankfully, a growing body of scholarly work is providing a basis for exploring long-term cycles in greater depth.

In "A Theoretical Introduction to 5,000 Years of World System History," Andre Gunder Frank concludes that "our present world system extends back long before 1500 AD to 2500 BC and probably earlier" (1990, p. 157). Several years later, Barry Gills and Andre Gunder Frank made a bold effort to identify long-term cycles in the world system in "World System Cycles, Crises, and Hegemonial Shifts" (1992), where they subjected the last 5,000 years to an analysis of economic cycles and political hegemony. In it, Gills and Frank present a periodization revolving around "A" phase expansions and "B" phase contractions, each averaging some 250 years in length. Together, these 250–year phases form 500–year cycles.

According to Gills and Frank, an "A" phase is a period of "simultaneously consolidating hegemonies" and is marked by high levels of infrastructural investment, exchange, and expansion of the world economy as a whole. Conversely, a "B" phase is a time of decline, characterized by "economic and political contraction" and reduced economic growth. More crucially, these A and B phases condition one another to generate a cyclic alternation or "world-historical rhythm." However, Gills and Frank recognize that this is a general observation since some regions and states get out-of-phase, or out-of-sync, with the rest of the world. Hence, they emphasize the exploratory nature of their effort, acknowledging questions regarding the "exact timing" of the phases (1992, pp. 6–7).

Is there empirical evidence for the existence of the A-and-B-phase cycle? If so, does the evidence shed light on the exact timing of periods? Fortunately, reliable population estimates exist for the world's largest cities from 2250 BC to the present, providing a tool for testing the accuracy of Gills and Frank's periodization. As will be shown, there is indeed a significant consistency between their periods on the one hand and demographic data on the other. First, however, it is vital to establish a link between cities and economies. How might cities serve as units of measurement? Can cities be used as windows into the past? What is the justification for this test?

## Theoretical Underpinning

This study holds that cities are appropriate barometers of long-term processes and trends. As building-blocks of civilization, and as the only forms of large-scale human organization to endure for 5,000 years, cities have been vital sites for fundamental economic, political, social, and cultural transformations. This is particularly true for "world cities," which are those cities significantly enmeshed in world economic, political, social, and cultural networks. Such a network, this study asserts, constitutes a "world-city system" that forms the skeletal structure of the world system itself.

Christopher Chase-Dunn (1989) recognizes that cities are integral to the world system (which he defines as an intersocietal and transsocietal network of material exchange), and that cities are particularly integral to the core/periphery structure. He contends, for example, that "the level of urban primacy in the world city system varies cyclically and corresponds generally with changes in the distribution of military power and economic comparative advantage among core powers" (p. 259). Chase-Dunn observes that a shifting "nested hierarchy" of a world-city system reveals dimensions of world economic and political competition.

This argument can be taken further. For a 5,000–year span, cities become the most reliable barometers of long-term economic and political developments. By contrast, empires are now dinosaurs, and nation-states, the spring-chickens of history, are modern representations of sovereignty whose borders, for much of the world, are awkward and arbitrary. Indeed, that nation-states are such recent constructions causes Jane Jacobs to question their use as "salient entities" for understanding economies: "The failure of national governments and blocs of nations to do their bidding suggests some sort of essential irrelevance" (1984, p. 31). And unlike empires or nation-states, cities exist in the tangible world of weight, mass, and density, even in terms of human biomass. This allows for a meaningful fit between cities and empirical data.

Estimates of urban populations provide a relatively unbroken stream of data for hundreds, even thousands, of years, unlike data on trade flows, real wages, yields per hectare, commodity prices, coal production, inflation, or military power—none of which can be used for more than two centuries with any reliability. Therefore, to picture what the structure of the world system looked like thousands of years ago, even if it remains an approximation, cities emerge as the sole units of measurement.

There are compelling reasons for viewing cities as economic mechanisms of paramount importance. Jane Jacobs, in *The Economy of Cities* (1969) and *Cities and the Wealth of Nations* (1984), argues that cities are "primary economic organs" stimulated by intercity trade. For her, cities and economies move synergistically: as urban populations grow, so do markets, each enlarging the magnitude of the other. Jacobs conceives of cities as inherently outward-looking and connected to a wider urban network of economic exchange. It is from this network, she argues, that cities and their economies receive their strongest stimulus for growth.

Additionally, Peter Hall, in *The World Cities* (1984), adds that some large cities outgrow local and regional functions to become true "world cities." Generally, he observes, the larger the city the more connected it becomes to a world system of economic exchange—a connectedness increasing with technological progress. And in *Before European Hegemony* (1989), Janet Abu-Lughod makes the same point: "But over and above these regional subsystems there is an overarching world system that works through world cities whose transactions are increasingly with one another" (p. 32).

Clearly, world cities can be seen as deeply embedded in the world system. Usually, such cities are large, but smaller and medium-size cities, such as Hong Kong, are often prominent within the world city system. Every large city, and certainly the world's 25 largest cities, can be called "world cities" whose connections form the basic *architectonics*, or structural order, of the world system. As world cities "rise" and "fall," and as regional city systems evolve and decay, so, too, does the world city system undergo transformation.

Cities, however, do not serve as precise *thermometers* measuring levels or degrees. Instead, they serve as reliable *barometers* of economic activity, measuring pressures, movements, and directions of change. A surge of urban population growth, for example, is suggestive of economic growth and expansion—at least, perhaps, until the mid-20th century. The reverse is also true, as David Wilkinson argues: "Where there is a decline in the number and/or size of the largest cities supported by an area . . . at an interval of a hundred years or more, there is inferred a decline in economic production and hence in its capacity to support urban concentrations" (1992, p. 2). World cities, therefore, become useful measures for testing Gills and Frank's 500–year cycles of economic expansion and contraction.

## Methods

This paper's empirical foundation rests on Tertius Chandler's massive data-gathering enterprise, *Four Thousand Years of Urban Growth* (1987). Chandler has painstakingly assembled numerical data for populations of the world's largest cities beginning at 2250 BC and then proceeding at intervals that vary from 150 to 200 years until AD 1000, after which he provides data every 50 years, even every 25 years after 1800. Before 430 BC, there are often fewer than 20 cities listed, but after 430 BC there are at least 50 listed. To arrive at his estimates, Chandler collected data from a wide variety of sources: official censuses, libraries and archives, church records, and even travel diaries. He obtained his estimates by means of "puzzle construction and solution," which entailed finding a figure like the number of families, houses, or parishes and then using a relevant multiplier. If the number of adult males is known, for example, then a multiplier of four or five can be used to ascertain the total population.

Chandler's estimates become increasingly reliable over the centuries as sources become more immediate and varied. After AD 1000, it is difficult to question his figures, but even for the earliest evidence there is notable congruence between Chandler's data and Colin McEvedy's figures in *The Atlas of Ancient History* (1967). David Wilkinson has based much recent scholarship on Chandler's data, helping to fulfill Chandler's stated purpose of providing "educated estimates" of populations and making them viable for the practical aims of sociological and historical interpretation.

It is possible to quibble with Chandler over the population of this or that city, or over the omission of a particular city from the roster. Beyond question, however, is the broad historical and geographic sweep of the census, beginning in Mesopotamia and Egypt, proceeding through successive phases of the growth of India, China, the Mediterranean, and the Middle East, through the late-18th-century demographic surge of industrial Europe and, finally, culminating in the global population explosion. As a result, generalized conclusions emerging from the data are quite defensible. For this study, the world's 25 largest cities form a workable set, small enough to concentrate on the most important cities but large enough to capture regional and system-level population trends. More potential for argument arises over classifying cities into one category or another. Janet Abu-Lughod, for example, groups cities into trading "circuits" while David Wilkinson groups them into economically-linked "oikumenes" and politically-linked "civilizations," although each scholar notes that boundaries are fuzzy. Indeed, it is possible to view the galaxy of world cities as being multidimensional: economic, political, social, and cultural.

Cities form an economic system if there is a pattern of regular and sustained trade among them. Cities of the Silk Roads and Spice Routes are examples of such economic systems. Cities form a political system if they are bound together by friendly or hostile diplomatic and military relationships, such as cities of the Roman Empire or Europe and its colonies. Cities form a social system, such as cities of the Islamic world or of the North Atlantic, if they share a similar language base, religion, or world view—the infrastructure of community building. Finally, all cities can be said to form one cultural system defined by a turn away from the relative balance of Neolithic life and toward, instead, a sustained synergism between population and technology.

Most of the classification of cities in this study proceeds along social lines. With the obvious exception of a cultural classification, social systems are the most enduring. Economic trade, after all, is subject to blockages. Political empires and nations come and go. Language and religion, however, usually change at glacial pace. Moreover, a social classification is geographically grounded, corresponding to distinct regions whose economies and polities have a certain cohesion and shared historical roots. Hence, for the Bronze Age and much of the Iron Age, cities are classified into Egyptian, Mesopotamian, Levantine, Aegean/Mediterranean, Hittite (Asia Minor), Indian, and Chinese. The rise of universal religions and codes of ethics fuses together some of these regions between 500 BC and AD 700. Confucianism, Hinduism, Christianity, and Islam generated enduring social systems in regions that scholars widely regard as forming distinct, even rival, macrosocieties: China, India, the Middle East, and the Mediterranean (later European-Atlantic).

Keeping in mind this classification scheme, it is possible to use Chandler's data in three basic ways. First, for the earliest cities especially (when estimates are rough and the sizes small), the *number of cities* appearing in any given region becomes significant. Increases in the number of cities on the roster (of, say, Egypt as opposed to Mesopotamia) can suggest relative economic growth and decreases relative decline. Second, *degrees of urban population growth and decline* are telling indicators of a region's overall standing in the world. This is a measure with both an absolute component and, more commonly used here, a relative component, one which is based on a region's share of population living within the set of the world's 25 largest cities. And third, *urban hierarchies* at both regional and world levels are useful measures of economic movement. Urban hierarchy is a numerical ratio produced by dividing the largest city of a set by the smallest. If Detroit, for example, has one million residents and Akron 200,000, then the ratio for this Midwestern set would be 5:1. Increases of this ratio reflect explosive city growth associated with an economic take-off as commercial or industrial activity concentrates in one or several cities. In the 1950s and 1960s, for example, Detroit's population swelled as the auto industry shifted into high gear, raising the region's ratio of urban hierarchy. But as the industry floundered so did Detroit, which lost 15 percent of its two million people in the 1980s.

In sum, the number of cities, their rates of growth, and their hierarchic distribution can each be used as economic barometers. It is now possible to test Gills and Frank's periodization using the methods described above. The test follows their own chronology and identifies major consistencies and inconsistencies between their A and B phases and Chandler's census estimates.

## The Test

### *Ancient and Bronze Age Periods: 3000–1000 BC*

Tertius Chandler's Bronze Age data consist of a few cities in Mesopotamia and Egypt, and these are assigned ranges rather than fixed numerical estimates (above or below 30,000 people, for example). The rough estimates are due in part to a low level of human population. Around 2000 BC, world population amounted to only 25 million, and in Mesopotamia and Egypt there were probably not more than one million in each valley (McEvedy 1967). Indeed, because these numbers are so minute, they bear directly on an important question regarding the Bronze Age. Were Mesopotamia and Egypt isolated valleys, and relatively autonomous, or were they involved in sophisticated and sustained exchange networks? Perhaps, as Gills and Frank argue, we can in fact trace the origins of the world system "back to the interlinking hegemons in the confluence of Mesopotamia and Egypt in the 3rd millennium," but such an observation should be tempered by noting the low voltage of these linkages, or, more precisely, of these *proto*linkages.

Gills and Frank begin their periodization as follows:

- A1: Phase 2000–1800/1700 BC
- B1: Phase 1700–1400 BC
- A2: Phase 1600/1500–1400/1200 BC
- B2: Phase 1200–1000 BC

The paucity of data makes a detailed analysis difficult for the Bronze Age. Nevertheless, it is interesting to compare the phases with Table 8.1, which lists the number of regional cities as they appear and disappear on Chandler's

TABLE 8.1

*Number of Cities Appearing on Chandler's Census, by Region*

| Year BC | Mesopotamia | Egypt | Levant | Mediter- ranean | Asia Minor | India | China |
|---|---|---|---|---|---|---|---|
| 2250 | 4 | 3 | 1 | 0 | 0 | 0 | 0 |
| 2000 | 6 | 3 | 0 | 0 | 0 | 0 | 0 |
| 1800 | 3 | 5 | 0 | 0 | 0 | 1 | 0 |
| 1600 | 3 | 3 | 1 | 2 | 1 | 0 | 0 |
| 1360 | 5 | 4 | 1 | 3 | 2 | 0 | 1 |
| 1200 | 5 | 3 | 0 | 2 | 1 | 1 | 2 |
| 1000 | 4 | 4 | 1 | 0 | 0 | 1 | 3 |
| 800 | 4 | 3 | 2 | 0 | 0 | 1 | 5 |
| 650 | 5 | 2 | 1 | 1 | 0 | 2 | 6 |

SOURCE: Adapted from Chandler (1987).

census from 2250 to 650 BC, through much of the Bronze Age and well into the Iron Age. (Several cities remain "unclear" if they are difficult to classify, like Washshukani atop the Fertile Crescent or Kerma in Sudan.)

Table 8.1 shows that the world's urban center of gravity was located in the Middle East, oscillating between Mesopotamia and Egypt: Mesopotamia around 2000 BC, Egypt around 1800, and then gradually back to Mesopotamia. The data do not bear on the first A phase, but a B phase 1700 to 1400 BC is consistent with a general decline for both river systems. Egypt dropped from five large cities to three and Mesopotamia maintained only three. This was a time, after all, of barbarian invasions: the Kassites among others in Mesopotamia, the Hyksos in Egypt, and the Aryans in India, where Mohenjo-daro disappears from Chandler's list, probably sacked.

Gills and Frank's next A phase was originally dated 1400 to 1200 BC, but they now argue that it might have begun earlier. Clearly, by 1400 BC there is evidence of generalized economic expansion. The sea powers of Knossos and Mycenaea reach their peaks during these centuries, having woven a web of maritime connections that linked Greece, Asia Minor, Egypt, the Mediterranean islands, and possibly even Iberia (where Chandler includes Cordoba and Setubal) and Britain. At the other end of Eurasia, this A phase witnesses the first Chinese city on Chandler's census: Ao, among the first of the Shang cities on the Yellow River.

Finally, Chandler's data support a B phase decline from 1200 to 1000 BC in that the growth of cities stagnates. In 1200 BC there are ten cities near or over 25,000 people, but two centuries later there are only nine, and total urban populations do not increase until after 1000 BC. Aegean and Hittite cities vanish from Chandler's census. Indeed, William McNeill

(1963) points to this period as one of renewed barbarian onslaught, a time when the barbarians mastered iron working and descended on cities with new weapons and chariots.

## The Iron Age

### A3: A Phase 1000–800 BC

For Gills and Frank, this period is distinguished by Phoenician and Assyrian expansion. The Phoenician cities of Sidon and Tyre do not appear on Chandler's census, perhaps because the Phoenician urban model was one of smaller, politically autonomous ports, but Phoenician colonization around the Mediterranean shows its effects centuries later when Carthage and other Mediterranean cities become large. Assyria does figure prominently during this A phase. Gills and Frank mention a shift of power from the southern to northern ends of Mesopotamia to Assyria, which is perceptible. In 1000 BC, only Nineveh appears on Chandler's census, north of Babylon, but by 800 BC Calah and Van reflect this northwestern shift. More important, Nineveh, the seat of Assyrian power and then the world's largest city, peaks between 800 and 650 BC (perhaps suggesting that the A phase can be extended another century).

### B3: B Phase 800–550 BC

Of all the Iron Age phases this is the most problematic, and Gills and Frank recognize the difficulty of finding opening and closing dates. They suspect that this B phase is largely a western phenomenon, and Chandler's census supports this view. Egyptian cities, for example, wane after 800 BC, and there is little growth around the Mediterranean until after 400 BC, when eventually Rome and Carthage rise to power. Mesopotamia and Persia, however, do retain a fair number of large cities. In short, a western decline is perceptible but not dramatic.

In defiance of this B phase, Chinese cities roughly double in size, with China gaining a larger share of people living in the world's largest cities. And in India, a second city appears on Chandler's census by 650 BC. The region begins a period of Iron Age expansion culminating in a population cycle that peaked around 200 BC, just as the Mauryan dynasty unified much of the subcontinent. As a result of these eastern developments (and of persistent growth in Mesopotamia and Persia), this B phase is the most challenged by the data.

## The Axial Age

### A4: A Phase 600/500–450/400 BC

The best indicator that this period is in fact one of general economic expansion is that the world's urban population nearly doubled, the only time it did so during the 1st millennium BC. As a result, regional populations were able to exert a pull of attraction on the rest of the world. Now prominent on Chandler's census are what can be called "link cities," that is, cities serving as trade hinges among regions, such as Marib (in South Arabia), Anuradhapura (in Ceylon), and, by 200 BC, Balkh and Taxila, Central Asian caravan cities. During these centuries, there is growing evidence of an embryonic city system stretching across both Central Asia and around the Indian Ocean (Silk Roads and Spice Routes, respectively), which would become fully defined by the end of the 1st millennium BC, when Rome and Han China emerged as powers at opposite ends of the known world.

Frank is quite right in arguing that "the key area of logistical interlinkage in the world economy/system shifted from Syria and the Levant to Central Eurasia" (1993, p. 401). Perhaps, however, it would be more exact to say that the area of logistical interlinkage was in the process of shifting during these centuries, but had not yet shifted. After all, Central Asian cities remain small until the time of Alexander the Great (around 300 BC), and, moreover, Chinese expeditions do not meet the eastern ends of the Persian roads until the 1st century BC, finally opening up a regular channel for trade.

Last, China, rather than Central Asia, seems to be the primary locus of this A phase. Chinese cities begin as a footnote in Chandler's data, but by 430 BC China has seven of the world's 25 largest cities (Loyang, Hsueh, Soochow, Lintzu, Lucheng, Fenghsiang, and Yenhsiatu, the last the world's second largest at 180,000). Indeed, by 430 BC China has a third more of the world population living in the 25 largest cities than does the entire Mesopotamian/Persian region.

### B4: B Phase 450–350 BC

Unfortunately, Chandler's data overshoot this time frame, going from 430 to 200 BC. Still, it is possible to identify one significant event bearing on this phase. Gills and Frank argue that this is a time of declining Athenian power (a decline hastened by Macedonia and then by Rome). Athens' population, in fact, falls by half from 155,000 in 430 BC to some 75,000 by 200 BC. Simultaneously, Rome's more than quadruples, rising from 35,000 to 150,000, and Carthage's triples from 50,000 to 150,000. These developments, which precede the rise of a unified Mediterranean economic and political structure, effectively shift the region's center of gravity from the Aegean to the western Mediterranean.

### A5: A Phase 350–250/200 BC

This A phase hinges on Alexander the Great's conquest of the Persian empire. As Gills and Frank argue "Alexander's political project died with him in 323 BC. . . . Nonetheless, much of the infrastructural investment was maintained and strengthened, and economic expansion appears to have continued" (1992, p. 18). In 200 BC, cities associated with Alexander's project are indeed prominent: Seleucia with 200,000 people; Antioch with 120,000; Corinth, Rayy, and Balkh, in Central Asia, with 75,000 apiece; and, of course, the city of Alexander himself, Alexandria in Egypt, at 300,000, then the third largest city in the world.

Gills and Frank also point to hegemonic consolidation in China by the Quin dynasty and in India by the Mauryas, as well as to increased trade between these two regions. These Eastern events again deserve top billing. In 200 BC, China has the world's largest city for the first time, Changan at 400,000, and India has the second largest, Patna at 350,000. Also in 200 BC, China and India have the largest shares of population in the 25 largest cities. By AD 100, however, India loses this demographic momentum while China does not.

### B5: B Phase 250/200–100/50 BC

Chandler's tables do not cover this period, jumping from 200 BC to AD 100. Between these two dates, however, there are indeed signs of decline in some regions. Egypt, Mesopotamia, Persia, and India all witness a decrease in their shares of population living in the 25 largest cities, as opposed to the Mediterranean and China. However, Gills and Frank note that China and Rome experience economic expansion during this B phase, making it a problematic one: "That would convert this B phase into a still shorter and more localized phenomenon, hardly worthy of the name" (1992, p. 32).

### A6: A Phase 100 BC–AD 200

By most historical accounts, the first millennium AD opens up with a bang. Gills and Frank also note that it is a time of economic and political growth, one that witnessed the rise of Han China, Kushan India, Parthian Iran, Axium East Africa, and Imperial Rome, thus forming a chain of interlinking hegemonies stretching from one end of Eurasia to the other.

Chandler's data do reveal AD 100 to be the high-water mark of urban population growth during the Axial Age, toward the end of this A phase.

World population in the 25 largest cities peaks in AD 100 with nearly four million people. Particularly prominent are Mediterranean cities, which together contain the largest proportion of people living in the 25 largest cities. By AD 100, in fact, Rome becomes the world's largest city, and 5 of the world's 10 largest cities are under Roman rule. China, too, has an AD 100 peak, with Loyang the world's second largest city and China's share of population living in the world's 25 largest cities not exceeded until after AD 600. For India and the Middle East, however, similarly impressive indicators of urban growth are absent.

Unfortunately, AD 100 is Chandler's only snapshot of this A phase. By 361, Rome indeed declines in size and power as the region's center of gravity shifts back to the eastern Mediterranean, to Constantinople, which replaces Rome as the world's largest city.

### B6: B Phase AD 200/250–500

Gills and Frank state that during this B phase, "the Han and Roman, as well as the intermediary Kushan and Parthian hegemonic structures, simultaneously disintegrated" (1992, p. 22). Moreover, they stress that this is a system-wide period of economic and political decline. Indeed, the total number of people living in the world's 25 largest cities falls between AD 100 and 361—the only time it did so in the last 3,000 years except during the time of the Black Death in the 14th century.

Gills and Frank assert that economic decline is most severe in China. Chandler's figures bear this out. China suffers the steepest relative decline measured by urban populations within the set of the world's 25 largest cities, with its relative share more than halved. This date of 361, therefore, although it is the only one provided by Chandler, provides a good picture of this period, coming as it does at the midpoint of the B phase. Clearly, according to Chandler's data, this is a time not just of slower growth but of actual decline.

## *The Medieval and Early Modern Periods, AD 500–1500*

### A7: A Phase AD 500–750/800

This period witnesses three staggered bursts of urban (and total) population growth—the first, in India, between 500 and 622; the second, in China, between 622 and 800; and the third, and the strongest, in the Middle East, between 622 and 900, a surge marked by the rise of Islam and a high level of economic and social integration across a swath of North Africa, Arabia, the Middle East, and Central Asia. Gills and Frank note that during this A phase most of Eurasia is becoming "again inter-linked and synchro-nized" (1992, p. 26). This interlinkage is logically stronger and more pronounced than that of Rome and Han China, building as it does on their history and incorporating substantially larger populations.

The A phase is first apparent in Gupta India, with cities flourishing in the Ganges basin and along the southern coast and Ceylon. After 622, however, Indian growth slows relative to China, where, under the Tang dynasty, Changan and Loyang once again become anchor cities for the Silk Roads. China's relative share of world urban population swells so that by 800 it is on a par with the entire Middle Eastern region. After 800, however, China's share declines, while that of the Middle East continues to rise until after 900.

In other words, there is room for extending Gills and Frank's endpoint of 800, perhaps by a century. Clearly, between 800 and 1000 there is the climax of what Colin McEvedy calls the "medieval cycle" of world popula-tion growth (coming after the "primary" cycle of the ancient world but before the "modernization" cycle of recent centuries). This medieval cycle is not as dramatic as the primary or modernization cycles, but it does signify a substantial quantitative—and hence qualitative—change in the world system. In sum, this first A phase is compatible with Chandler's data, which suggest that urban growth, staggered among regions, takes hold across Eurasia.

### B7: B Phase AD 750/800–1000/1050

Considering Middle Eastern urban growth, the starting point of 750 or 800 seems early. That generalized decline eventually sets in is more certain. In fact, the world's total population in the 25 largest cities falls between 900 and 1000 by nearly a fourth, and this level is maintained until about 1100. Much of the decline is evident in China, where Changan and Loyang, once among the largest cities in the world, vanish from the list of the 25 largest cities. Decline is also evident in the Middle East, where Baghdad, a city of one million around 900, has a mere 125,000 residents a century later. (Its successor, Cairo, was yet to emerge as one of the world's most important cities.) Expectedly, therefore, Chinese and Middle Eastern populations in the world's 25 largest cities decline between 900 and 1000—while Indian and southern European ones grow only modestly.

### A8: A Phase AD 1000/1050–1250/1300

Because the last A and B phases were about a century out-of-sync with Chandler's data, the misfit continues in this A phase. If this A phase were to begin around 1100 and continue to 1300, then a 200-year period of

218 ANDREW BOSWORTH

growth might still qualify as an A phase. Chandler's data reveal that after 1100 the world's urban population rises, nudged upwards by bursts of growth in India and then, more powerfully, by China and East Asia. The Japanese cities of Kyoto and Kamakura, and the Southeast Asian ones of Angkor and Pagan, now regularly appear among the 25 largest cities. Indeed, Gills and Frank's identification of China as foremost among the regions of expansion dovetails with Chandler's data. Chinese urban populations do in fact increase rapidly, and Hangchow remains the world's largest city for two centuries during the Sung period, a time noted for increased maritime trade.

When does this A phase end? East Asian urban growth appears strong until about 1300, when Indian growth also tapers off. In Europe, a minor period of urban growth is evident from 1100 to 1200, but thereafter urban populations stagnate until the 17th century. The Middle East, finally, appears to be left out of this A phase as its share of population living in the 25 largest cities continues to decline after 1100. In fact, the Middle East never regains the relative demographic and economic prominence it had when Baghdad reigned supreme.

## B8: B Phase AD 1250/1300–1450

There is a lack of scholarly consensus regarding this period, which was characterized by Mongol conquests. What was the effect of the Mongol Empire on the world economy? Was this a time of economic growth or decline?

Janet Abu-Lughod (1989, p. 58) identifies this period as one of heightened trade and integration: "The expanding phase came early in the 13th century, with maximum consolidation by the early 14th century." Abu-Lughod argues that the Mongols facilitated world trade but, in the face of internal weaknesses and finally the Black Death, that the Mongol Empire contracted: "This contraction initiated an exponential cycle of decline" (p. 183). For Abu-Lughod, therefore, cycles of economic and political expansion and contraction are synchronized—at least in this case.

By contrast, Gills and Frank argue that despite Mongol political consolidation "an economic downturn of severe proportions affected most of the continent during Mongol tenure" (1992, p. 33). Indeed, the authors question Abu-Lughod's characterization of 1250 to 1350 as a generalized "up" phase, adding that "the hegemony of the Mongols differs from the more usual case of hegemonic expansion during a period of economic upswing" (p. 33).

Leaving aside the complex relationship between economic expansion and political hegemony, how do Chandler's census estimates bear on the economic argument? First, the world's population in the 25 largest cities gradually increases during these centuries—faster than the previous two centuries (1000–1200) but slower than the next two (1400–1600), which does not suggest much. Second, decline appears most evident in the Middle East, but there are regions of the world that begin to witness the growth of large cities, namely Europe, where Paris, Venice, Genoa, Milan, and Prague rank among the cities breaking into the world's 25 largest. Third, continental Silk Road cities—those lying at the core of the Mongol Empire—are in steady decline after 900 when, at that time, the two largest cities in the world were Silk Road anchor cities (Baghdad and Changan) and four Silk Road cities ranked among the 25 largest (Rayy, Nishapur, Bokhara, and Samarkand). By the time of the Mongol conquests, around 1250, the two largest cities in the world were Spice Route anchor cities (Hangchow and Cairo), and only one Silk Road city made the roster of the 25 largest (Sarai, the only substantial imprint the Mongols made on the world city system, a city atop the Caspian Sea and classified as "Golden Horde" by Chandler). Sarai grows in the 13th century to become the ninth-largest city in the world, but, simultaneously, more impressive urban growth occurs along coastal China (where cities fell to the Mongols for a time) and around the Mediterranean, especially in Italy.

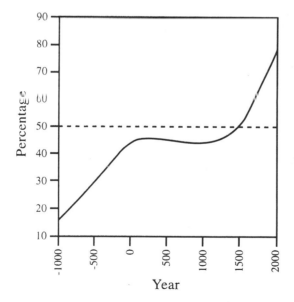

*Figure 8.1.* Maritime shift of the world city system, 1000 BC–AD 2000.[a]
SOURCES: Chandler (1987) and McEvedy and Jones (1978).
[a]The figure demonstrates that a significant percentage of the world's largest 25 cities have become oceanic ports.

Ironically, while this period is noted for the Mongol world empire, it is characterized by the steady disappearance of large, landlocked cities from Chandler's roster and their replacement by ports such as Canton and Venice—thus continuing a millennium-long shift towards a more maritime world city system, as demonstrated by Figure 8.1. Perhaps what made possible the seizure of the Silk Road city system in the first place by such a peripheral power as the Mongols attests to the marginalization of the Silk Roads, supplanted as they were by a system of China Sea and Indian Ocean ports—the Spice Routes. From this perspective, the Mongol Empire represented a futile attempt to revive the dying Silk Roads, to hold back the tides of history.

In sum, Chandler's data for this B phase reveal a diminished importance of the Silk Roads, suggesting that the period is not just one of decline but of reconfiguration along maritime lines.

### The Modern World System Period

Among several pressing questions about the modern period is that concerning the nature of the post-1500 world system, or, indeed, the nature of modernity itself. Gills and Frank (1992, p. 35) criticize an argument found in the work of Immanuel Wallerstein (1974), among others, that there is a sharp break between the medieval and modern worlds and that 1500 represents the beginning of a fundamentally different "modern world-capitalist system": "For us, and alas still few others, still more important is the fundamental continuity with the past within the same world system and its still continuing cycles of accumulation and hegemony." This debate over whether the post-1500 system is the same as or different from the pre-1500 one opens up a host of questions that cannot be resolved by using Chandler's data.

Suffice it to say, however, that demographic evidence reveals both continuity and discontinuity in the world system. On the one hand, Gills and Frank are correct to identify continuity in the world system. The cycles of world urban hierarchy, for example, represent a process with deep roots in the past. Figure 8.2 suggests that the 1500 turning point does not alter the course of this wavelike pattern, thereby lending support to Gills and Frank's argument. On the other hand, this argument risks downplaying just how different the world becomes after 1500. If qualitative and quantitative changes are inexorably bound together, then the "population explosion" of modern times constitutes a fundamental and seismic rupture with the past. From the beginning of civilization to 1500 (or actually to about 1700) the world's population required thousands of years to double itself, but recent doubling has been compressed to only 100 or even 50 years. As Figure 8.3

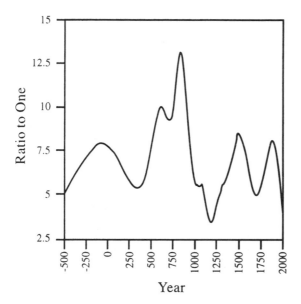

*Figure 8.2.* World urban hierarchy, 500 BC–AD 2000.[a]
SOURCE: Chandler (1987).
[a]The figure displays the ratio of the size difference between the world's largest and 25th-largest cities. Increases of this ratio, which are produced by the pulling ahead of lead cities (Rome, Baghdad, Peking, and London), can be associated with periods of general economic and political expansion, and decreases of the ratio can be associated with periods of contraction.

demonstrates, total world population has grown to 5.5 billion today, and it is expected to increase to between 10 and 12 billion by 2050. Figure 8.3 includes both urban and rural population estimates, but the urban component outpaces the rural, with the level of urbanization having increased from about 15 to 50 percent of the total population.

Another question surrounding the modern age concerns the timing of the rise of the "West." Gills and Frank argue that the early modern period is one of "multipolarity" and that, at least until the early 19th century, "the preponderance of hegemonial transformation did not lie exclusively in the West" (1992, p. 36). This statement echoes Janet Abu-Lughod. In *Before European Hegemony*, she finds the 13th-century world system to be characterized by a "relative balance of multiple centers" (1989, p. 371). William McNeill also notes the strength of a modern East Asia and how, from 1700 to as late as 1850, the world's fourfold civilizational balance "totters" before giving way to a "Western explosion" (1963, p. 728).

Chandler's data reinforce this view. As Figure 8.4 demonstrates, the relative urban hierarchy for East Asia (measuring the growth of its largest

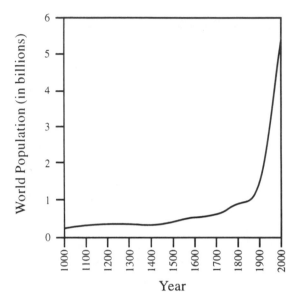

*Figure 8.3.*  World population growth, AD 1000–2000.[a]

SOURCE: McEvedy and Jones (1978).

[a]The figure suggests that the population explosion of recent centuries marks a sharp departure from earlier patterns of growth and decline, thus signaling a fundamental rupture between the medieval and modern world.

cities within the set of the 25 largest cities) is high until about 1650, after which it proceeds along with the ratio of a European/Atlantic city system. This "tottering" lasts more than a century. By 1850, there is a belated "rise of the West." Also by 1850, London displaces Peking as the world's largest city, and New York and Philadelphia become the first modern North American cities to make the roster of the world's 25 largest cities.

Gills and Frank do not furnish specific dates for modern A and B phases, but rather "provisionally accept" the broad periodization of Immanuel Wallerstein and others: economic expansion during "the long 16th century"; the "17th-century crisis"; the 18th century's "commercial revolution"; and, thereafter, the ups and downs of the 40- to 60-year Kondratieff waves. Assigning precise dates for these eras is difficult since various scholars use various turning points. Bearing this in mind, there could be a 1450–1620/'40 "up" phase; a 1620/'40–1750 "down" phase; a 1750–1850 "up" phase (which some scholars take as late as 1915); and, additionally, post-1800 Kondratieff waves of shorter duration.

Figure 8.5 highlights Figure 8.2 to provide more detail on the world's changing urban hierarchy ratio. This measure serves as a barometer of

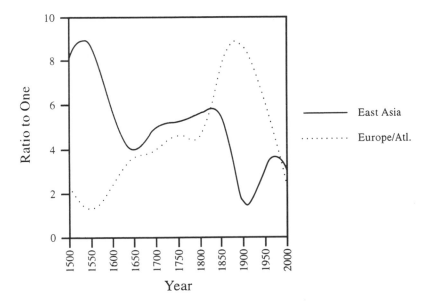

*Figure 8.4.* Relative urban hierarchy, East Asian and European/Atlantic cities, AD 1500–2000.[a]
SOURCES: Adapted from Chandler (1987) and United Nations (1990) estimates.
[a]The figure measures the relative ratios of urban hierarchy for East Asian and European/Atlantic cities within a set of the world's 25 largest cities. The figure reinforces the claim that East Asia remained a dynamic economic region until well into the modern period; that there was a belated "Rise of the West;" and that East Asian economic and demographic growth began to outpace European/Atlantic growth after 1975.

system-wide cycles of economic expansion and contraction. Even allowing for a 50-year margin of error—or, put another way, a 50-year time-lag between urban growth and economic expansion—this measure is still useful, and it yields several conclusions. First, a 1450–1620/'40 "up" phase coincides with one complete wave of hierarchy, including both upward and downward slopes. The crest comes around 1500–1550, straddling the midpoint of the phase. Second, a 1620/'40–1750 "down" phase lies in a depression between the two modern waves of urban hierarchy. For most of the period the ratio is in decline, but it begins to ascend after 1700. The trough of this depression comes around 1700, near the midpoint of the phase. Third, a 1750–1850 "up" phase rides an ascending slope of urban hierarchy for its entirety. The ratio increases until about 1900, when it falls to reach a predicted low point at the year 2000. Scholarly periodizations extending the "up" phase to about 1915 appear to be in closer synchronization with ratios of world urban hierarchy.

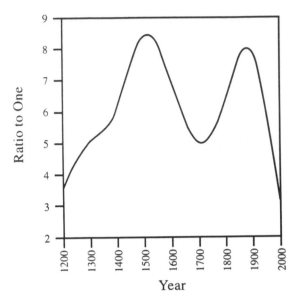

*Figure 8.5.*   World urban hierarchy, AD 1200–2000.[a]
SOURCE: Chandler (1987).
[a]The figure, which zooms in on Figure 8.2, displays changes in the ratio of urban hierarchy for the set of the world's 25 largest cities. These changes are compatible with scholarly periodizations of modern economic history.

There is indeed a rough fit between general economic periodizations and changing ratios of world urban hierarchy, and this correlation suggests that long-term economic cycles continue to operate in the modern period. In recent centuries, however, the 250-year phase and 500-year cycle appear to be compressed into 150-year phase and 300-year cycles, which might or might not warrant the "A" and "B" phase labels. Nevertheless, it is uncanny that this urban hierarchy curve exhibits wavelike patterns of such harmony in the first place.

It seems hasty of Gills and Frank to sound the death knell for longer-term cycles after 1800 and embrace instead shorter Kondratieff waves (if that is in fact their position). The two phenomena—Kondratieff waves and A and B phases—are not necessarily incompatible, since the former might be nested within the latter. George Modelski and William R. Thompson (1995) argue that Kondratieff-type waves (K-waves) are not only evident outside Europe but that these regular pulses of economic activity in leading industries can be traced back to at least AD 930, to Sung China, where there emerged, relative to the rest of the world, an urbanized, unified market of continental proportions. It seems likely, therefore, that economic cycles of varying duration might coexist, especially as regional economic upswings occur during times of more generalized world decline, as they often did before AD 1000. (Perhaps the shorter K-waves might be more adequately measured by examining demographic data within a set of purely regional cities.)

While long-term economic cycles have indeed framed the modern world system, it is another question whether world urban hierarchy—which depends on measuring the largest city in the world—can serve as an economic indicator in the contemporary world. It is unlikely that the largest and fastest-growing cities in the world—"megacities" such as Mexico City, São Paulo, and Jakarta—will, within the usual 50- to 100-year time frame, attain world economic and political prominence. On the other hand, few observers would have thought so of London or Paris in 1700, or New York in 1850, crowded and miserable as they were. Although hard to imagine, technological advances in energy, transportation, and communication could conceivably allow these megacities to become economic powerhouses. Furthermore, it also remains to be seen how cities, as centralized hubs of activity, will fare in a "postmodern" world if technological *access* rather than geographic *proximity* becomes paramount. Will cities be transformed by cyberspace and other innovations? Questions such as this one suggest that while cities have served as the most reliable barometers of past cycles and trends, they are by no means crystal balls for divining the future.

## Summary and Conclusions

Chandler's census sometimes casts doubt on the exact timing of A and B turning points, but the data do not run against the grain of the cycles. Indeed, B3 is the only phase questioned by the data, and Chandler's census generally confirms the operation of Gills and Frank's long waves of economic expansion and contraction.

In "Decline Phases in Civilizations, Regions, and Oikumenes" (1992), David Wilkinson puts Gills and Frank's proposal to empirical test. Wilkinson specifically tested the B phases: "The decline data were consistent with treating phases B1, B2, B6, B7 and B8 as Old Oikumene decline phases, were ambiguous with respect to B4 and B5, and did not reflect B3" (p. 30). Wilkinson's study and this one differed in assumptions and methods but reached similar conclusions.

Finally, for the modern period, the data do not confirm A and B phases as such, but Gills and Frank do not periodize recent centuries in this manner. Still, ratios of regional and world urban hierarchy appear to exhibit rhythmic 300-year cycles of approximately 150-year phases. Moreover, the timing of

TABLE 8.2
*Level of Support for A and B Phases*

| A and B Phases | | Level of Support in Chandler's Data |
|---|---|---|
| A1: | 2000–1800/1700 BC | inconclusive/insufficient data |
| B1: | 1700–1400 BC | mild |
| A2: | 1600/1500–1400/1200 BC | moderate |
| B2: | 1200–1000 BC | moderate |
| A3: | 1000–800 BC | strong |
| B3: | 800–550 BC | contradictory |
| A4: | 600/550–450/400 BC | strong |
| B4: | 450–350 BC | mild |
| A5: | 350–250/200 BC | strong |
| B5: | 250/200–100/50 BC | mild/inconclusive |
| A6: | AD 100–200 | strong |
| B6: | AD 200/250–500 | strong |
| A7: | AD 500/600–750/800 | strong |
| B7: | AD 750/800–1000/1050 | strong |
| A8: | AD 1000/1050–1250/1300 | strong |
| B8: | AD 1250/1300–1450 | moderate |

these phases is highly compatible with scholarly designations of general growth and decline in modern centuries.

Cyclical, pendulum-like periods of expansion and contraction are indeed evident in urban population data. But this does not preclude the possibility that the world system is also characterized by cumulative trends and evolutionary processes. Indeed, what makes a demographic approach to the world system so appealing is that it provides a quantitative tool for examining cycles and trends while opening up other avenues of inquiry.

*References*

Abu-Lughod, Janet. 1989. *Before European Hegemony*. Oxford: Oxford University Press.

Chandler, Tertius. 1987. *Four Thousand Years of Urban Growth*. Lewiston, NY: St. David's University Press.

Chase-Dunn, Christopher. 1989. *Global Formation: Structures of the World-Economy*. Oxford: Basil Blackwell.

Frank, Andre Gunder. 1990. "A Theoretical Introduction to 5,000 Years of World System History." *Review* 13:155–248.

———. 1993. "Bronze Age World System Cycles." *Current Anthropology* 34:383–430.

Gills, Barry K., and Andre Gunder Frank. 1992. "World System Cycles, Crises, and Hegemonial Shifts, 1700 BC to 1700 AD." *Review* 15:621–87.

Hall, Peter. 1984. *The World Cities*. New York: St. Martin's Press.

Jacobs, Jane. 1969. *The Economy of Cities*. New York: Random House.

———. 1984. *Cities and the Wealth of Nations*. New York: Random House.

McEvedy, Colin. 1967. *The Penguin Atlas of Ancient History*. London: Penguin Books.

McNeill, William H. 1963. *The Rise of the West*. Chicago: University of Chicago Press.

Modelski, George, and William R. Thompson. 1995. *Leading Sectors and World Powers: The Coevolution of Global Politics and Economics*. Columbia: University of South Carolina Press.

United Nations. 1990. *Statistical Yearbook*. New York: United Nations.

Wallerstein, Immanuel. 1974. *The Modern World-System*. New York: Academic Press.

Wilkinson, David. 1992. "Decline Phases in Civilizations, Regions, and Oikumenes." Paper presented at the annual meetings of the International Studies Association, Atlanta.

STEPHEN K. SANDERSON ■
THOMAS D. HALL

PART III

---

# Civilizations and World Systems
## *Dialogue and Interplay*

Civilizational analysis and world-system theory are today perhaps the two most significant general approaches to understanding the patterns of very long-term historical change. What are their basic similarities and differences? What are the basic issues that divide them? Is one a superior approach? Can they both be used effectively in combination? Is some sort of theoretical synthesis of the two possible?

In a short essay that originally launched the debate between civilizationists and world-system theorists, Matthew Melko (1994), himself a civilizationist, registered four major complaints about world-system theory. It was much too materialistic, he thought, emphasizing economic relationships at the expense of cultural ones, and thus it needed to give significantly greater attention to the role of ideational forces in social life. In addition, Melko thought it gave too much attention to large-scale intersocietal interactions, and thus neglected the endogenous characteristics of civilizational wholes. He also regretted the evolutionary character of most world-system analysis; historical change, he argued, was much too complex to be captured by simple evolutionary models of linear change. Finally, Melko seemed to think that world-system theory eliminated the possibility of comparative analysis. Some of Melko's points seem valid, yet his critique may also exaggerate the differences between the two perspectives, and a substantial rapprochement may well be possible. Indeed, Melko himself seems to recognize this, as will shortly become apparent.

With the notable exceptions of Quigley and Wilkinson, civilizationists focus primarily on the cultural or ideational dimensions of social life as opposed to the more material or economic side. This is undoubtedly one of the most significant differences between the two approaches. However, it is something of a cliché—and a tired and incorrect one at that—that world-system analysis is strictly materialistic or economic. There has been increasing attention to culture and its role in world-system processes (see Bergesen [1992] for a list of citations). This attention goes beyond culture as epiphenomenon and examines it as an important component of world-system processes.

Alice Willard's (1993) recent article on West African trade and religion highlights the role of Islam in facilitating trade across the Sahara, noting world-systemic pressure driving the trade. Here there are interesting parallels with Jerry Bentley's (1993) discussion of religion in all sorts of exchanges in 1st- and 2nd-millennium Eurasia. Economic and ideational forces often tend to move together, and the patterns of world-system exchanges, especially of luxury goods, often facilitate, and are facilitated by, the spread of new ideologies, most often in the form of religion.

Indeed, both Wallerstein (1992) and, especially, Albert Bergesen (1992) have pointed out that if hegemony in the modern world-system is in the process of shifting from the United States to Japan, this will be the first time (for the modern world-system) that a hegemonic shift coincides with a civilizational shift. Bergesen argues that Godzilla and transformers (the toys and the cartoon characters) are a beachhead of the Japanese cultural invasion of America. Whether Japan is actually becoming hegemonic, and, if so, whether Godzilla is the pointman of the cultural invasion, is not the point. The point is, if such a shift is taking place it is unprecedented in the modern world-system.

What, then, of the charges that world-system theory overemphasizes exogenous or external factors at the expense of internal ones, and that world-system theory eschews comparative analysis? World-system theory has tended to give pride of place to external factors, but this is not always the case, and some world-system theorists see such factors as interacting in important ways with a range of internal forces (e.g., Hall 1986, 1989). Many world-system analysts study the interplay, feedback, or dialectic between the internal structure of the components of a system and their position in the system. While each of the structural positions—core, periphery, semiperiphery—has a "typical social structure" (at least in the modern world-system), the unique features of the social structure of any component of the system significantly shape its potential for change in position in that system. It is the interplay of these two processes that is the focus of much modern world-system research.

Now enter the question of the existence of earlier world-systems and their roles, if any, in the emergence of the modern world-system. It would seem that the only way this question can be addressed empirically is by studying earlier world-systems. It is here that the division between the continuationists and the transformationists becomes singularly salient. If, in fact, there have been many different types of world-systems, the transformation from one type to another is an important problem, and one that can only be addressed comparatively. This also applies to the continuationist camp, but there it is less clear why this is so. Precapitalist world-system analysis, or at least one major strand of it is, then, thoroughly comparative in its focus.

Both camps also face a fundamental problem: How does interaction between world-systems take place? This is especially problematic in a tight definition of a world-system as "self-contained." If world-systems are in regular contact and if they exchange anything (material or ideational), they are no longer self-contained. Chase-Dunn and Hall (1993 [chapter 4, this volume]) address this problem by conceptualizing the boundaries of world-systems as theoretically and empirically problematic. They see three levels of interaction: bulk goods, military/political interaction, and luxury goods. Each level is successively larger, with the smaller ones nested within the larger ones. Interaction within each level is at least partially independent of interactions within the other levels.

Recently Chase-Dunn and Hall (1995) added a fourth level of interaction, which they call the information level. In their view this fourth level is sometimes larger than the bulk goods level, but not always. Like the other levels of interaction, the information level has some autonomy from the others. Willard's (1993) analysis of West Africa also draws attention to the information level of interaction in the form of ideology. Modelski and Thompson (1995) also discuss the role of a cultural network in world-system evolution. Work on this topic is just beginning.

A closely related problem for both camps is how one world-system absorbs or incorporates another. Hall's (1986, 1989) work shows that incorporation even at the very fringes of the modern world-system in its weakest form (Spanish colonization of what is now New Mexico) is an extremely complex process which has been seriously understudied and undertheorized by world-system analysts. Indeed, one of Hall's own research questions focuses on the generality of the specific processes of incorporation which occurred in what is now the American Southwest. This is an issue that can only be studied by a multifaceted comparative strategy: comparing processes of incorporation among areas of the Spanish empire, between different European empires, and among world-systems.

Despite these differences and gaps, it seems to us that the comparative logic is the same for world-system analysts and civilizationists. These two approaches differ primarily in what they see as similar and what they see as different among the world-systems/civilizations they compare. Civilizations and world-systems are not the same thing, but they seem to be close cousins. Both concepts share a frustrating vagueness of definition which seems, at least in part, to be due to a fuzziness of the actual boundaries of each, especially at the information or cultural level. What is different are the criteria each uses to bound systems.

Then there is that frightful "e-word," evolution. Most world-system analysts, like archaeologists and many anthropologists, find it a friendly and useful term. Melko and other civilizationists seem to find it to be something of a grand bugaboo (Wilkinson and, especially, Quigley are notable exceptions). It is important to note here that the concept of evolution as used in world-system approaches refers to patterns in the processes of social change that led from a situation some 10,000 years ago of as many as 100,000 more or less autonomous societies to the present state of an emerging global society or civilization. The term explicitly does not imply a teleological or a rigidly unilinear process, but rather refers to multistranded, complex, and historically contingent processes (Sanderson 1990). A major goal of the world-system approaches is to describe and understand those processes.

But enough of countercritiques of Melko. More important to the aims of this book is the issue of how the two approaches overlap and how a symbiotic relationship between them might be built. One extremely important contribution that can be made by civilizationists to the agenda of world-system theorists has to do with the knowledge of historical detail possessed by the former. Most world-system theorists are not historians. They are social scientists of one type or another (sociologists, anthropologists, archaeologists, political scientists, sometimes economists), and their training has seldom given them the factual knowledge they need to make sense out of world history in their own terms. An open and continuous dialogue between world-system theorists and civilizationists can help provide the former with much of the basic factual knowledge on which they need to draw. Moreover, as we will see below, the dialogue can provide civilizationists with conceptual insights that might prove surprisingly useful in their work. World-system analysts offer a variety of ways to study intersocietal interaction systematically. Much more is involved than simply knowing that civilizations exchanged things and ideas. What were the things and ideas exchanged? How important were they in the respective civilizations/world-systems? How were they produced? How was production changed by the demand for external exchange? Why did the exchange begin? What sustained it? Why did it end? And so on.

The contribution of world-system analysts, and this is what we read in William H. McNeill's autocritique (1990 [chapter 13, this volume]), is that the system itself, no matter how inchoate or ramshackle, provides the fundamental context within which these questions must be answered. It is only by giving attention to the formation and transformation of such systems that we can begin to grasp how we got from some 100,000 small, autonomous bands around 10,000 years ago to our modern global village. The puzzle is sufficiently complex, enticing, and important to warrant a wide variety of attempts to solve it. World-system analysts are not seeking hegemony in the comparative study of civilizations, but rather a theoretical complementarity.

It cannot have escaped attention that there are some close parallels in the bounding of both civilizations and world-systems (Melko and Scott 1987; Chase-Dunn and Hall 1993). Both approaches are often talking about the same fundamental entity but using different boundary criteria: culture versus the combination of trade in bulk goods, trade in luxury goods, and political alliances and war. Both approaches clearly recognize that the bounding of the relevant entities under discussion is problematic. The recent discussions of the information or cultural boundary by world-system analysts suggest that the two approaches may yet achieve a synthesis, or at least a *modus vivendi*. This is closely linked with a second issue: the relevant unit of analysis, or the fundamental entity being discussed. A major contribution of the world-system approach is the focus on the system itself as the fundamental locus of social change. Here, too, there seems to be a close parallel with civilizationists, in that they also attribute significance to a unit of social organization larger than individual states.

Even Melko himself sees that there are good opportunities for a symbiotic relationship between civilizationists and world-system theorists. We shall let this long quotation from his article that touched off the debate and dialogue serve to make our point about the possibility and importance of symbiosis (Melko 1994, pp. 11–12):

> William McNeill (1990) perceives that his book, *The Rise of the West* (1963), suffered from too much emphasis on separate civilizations, and not enough on their cosmopolitan interactions. He does not think he should have ignored civilizations, but that he needed a better balance between the entities and their interactions.

It seems reasonable to suppose, therefore, that world-systems and civilizational research could be mutually supportive. The civilizationists can remind the world-systems theorists of the kinds of concerns I have been expressing here. Be careful that by modernization you don't mean Westernization. Keep in mind the culture and values of other civilizations; don't be a civilizational boor. Try to look at the world from the perspective of other civilizations. Keep open to the possibility that the trends toward merger and communication you have noted in the 20th century can be reversed in the 21st as civilizations reassert themselves, as they have before. Keep in mind that the world-systems approach is an approach, and one that happens to be particularly congenial to historians and social scientists of the 20th century.

Civilizationists can be reminded by world-systemists that civilizations are not Spenglerian autonomes impervious to outside influences; that there are periods when external influences become of considerable importance, when one civilization challenges another or several others; that such interactions take place continually throughout history and need to be given consideration along with comparisons between civilizations; that economic interactions are important and always influence other kinds of development.

Each approach has its validity, and can serve as a useful corrective to the other. From this perspective, civilizationists could see systems theorists, not as viruses, but as salutary breezes. And if a civilizationist wanders into a meeting of systems theorists, he could be perceived, not as an outmoded nuisance, but as a preserver of perspective.

\*     \*     \*

Four articles make up this section. The first, by Immanuel Wallerstein, is unlike the others in that it does not seek to establish a dialogue between precapitalist world-system theorists and civilizationists, and for a very simple reason: Wallerstein is highly critical of both perspectives. Wallerstein is concerned with three temptations, what he calls the nomothetic temptation, the idiographic temptation, and the temptation to reify. To the extent that students of human society and history fall victim to any of these temptations, he believes, their analyses run aground. Chase-Dunn and Hall, he feels, fall victim to the nomothetic temptation, wanting to generalize historically the world-system concept as far as they can. Wallerstein is skeptical of such an attempt, wondering just how much a concept developed for one particular historical situation can be reworked in order to be applied to other situations. Concepts come in packages, he says, and thus his concept of "core/periphery" was closely linked to, among others, the notion of "endless accumulation of capital." Thus, does not a certain sort of incoherence and conceptual violence occur when we attempt to use the concept of "core/periphery" in situations where there is no "endless accumulation of capital?" Andre Gunder Frank's form of precapitalist world-systems analysis, Wallerstein argues, falls victim to the opposite, or idiographic, temptation. For Frank, there is a single world-system that has existed for some 5,000 years, and the modern world-system that is usually dated from about AD 1500 is only a continuation of the development of that system. In Wallerstein's thinking it is always possible to show that a particular system is part of some larger system; however, once we do this where do we stop? And how fruitful is it, he wonders, to make such connections, many of which must be extremely tenuous indeed. The final temptation, that of reification, is the one to which civilizationists have succumbed. They take something like "China" and see it as having a single indivisible history and virtually a life of its own over thousands of years. But there is danger in this, Wallerstein charges, for China since 1945 may be more similar in several respects to Brazil since 1945 than the former is to earlier Chinese dynasties. If this is so, then what sense does it make to consider China a single historical entity with its own cultural essence? Wallerstein thus ends up being skeptical of civilizational analysis just as he is skeptical of the precapitalist world-system analyses of Frank and Gills and of Chase-Dunn and Hall.

David Wilkinson, although usually known as a civilizationist, feels at home in both the civilizationist and world-systems camps. He sees the two camps as doing very similar things and as having complementary emphases. Civilizationists are more interested in the cultural aspects of society, world-systemists in the political and, especially, the economic aspects; civilizationists may be more inclined to explore the earlier epochs of social evolution, world-systemists the later epochs. Wilkinson lays out his own unique perspective in a crisp 10-point summary, and then proceeds to make clear how he stands with respect to Toynbee, Quigley, Spengler, Melko, Hord, Sorokin, Huntington, Chase-Dunn and Hall, and Frank and Gills. He concludes by saying that the entities studied by civilizationists and world-systemists are largely the same, and that their theories should be synthesized.

Stephen Sanderson's article answers the charge made by Melko (1994) and Roger Wescott (1994) that world-system theory is materialistically and evolutionarily biased by insisting that civilizationists have a strong idealist bias and something of an antievolutionary orientation. He argues that they need to pay much more attention to politics and economics, and they need to recognize that patterns of cyclical change may coexist with patterns of long-term social evolution. He then goes on to suggest a new concept, that of "expanding world commercialization," as one that provides something of a bridge between the two perspectives. By expanding world commercialization he means a long-term evolutionary process in which trade networks have become both more extensive and more intensive throughout the agrarian era between about 3000 BC and AD 1500. This idea was derived from the work of Frank and Gills. World commercialization retains the economic focus of world-systems analysis, but it also gives us a feel for what Wescott (1994) has called the "sensuous texture" of the life of civilizations.

The paper by Victor Roudometof and Roland Robertson is long and their agenda is complex, and thus the reader would profit from more than one reading. The authors are concerned about a number of things, but perhaps their major concern centers around the materialism-idealism debate. They see world-systems analysis, in both its classical Wallersteinian and more recent precapitalist forms, as too materialistic. In the whole Wallerstein-Frank debate, they say, cultural factors are not taken seriously. Roudometof and Robertson want to make such factors a much more important part of historical sociological analysis, but at the same time, they insist, not privilege them. They see in the work of Michael Mann (1986) an appropriate model, one of overlapping and intersecting networks of economic, political, and cultural-ideological power. They also strongly endorse the work of Norbert Elias ([1939]1994) on "the civilizing process." They see this as an alternative form of civilizational analysis that transcends the materialism-idealism debate and that also avoids the kind of reification with which Wallerstein is concerned. This ultimately leads them to the concept of *globalization*, a notion that has been developed by Robertson in earlier publications (e.g., Robertson 1992). They spell out the dimensions of this concept and take care to point out some distortions and misunderstandings of the term. Globalization, for them, is a process involving growing contacts between and among different power networks. It does not imply cultural homogenization and is not an evolutionary process. In the end, however, although they formally eschew cultural-ideological reductionism, Roudometof and Robertson seem to have more concern for this dimension of human affairs than for all of the others, and this makes their work closer to the traditional civilizationists than to the world-systems theorists.

## References

Bentley, Jerry H. 1993. *Old World Encounters: Cross-Cultural Contacts and Exchanges in Pre-Modern Times*. Oxford: Oxford University Press.

Bergesen, Albert. 1992. "Godzilla, Durkheim, and the World-System." *Humboldt Journal of Social Relations* 18(1):195–216.

Chase-Dunn, Christopher, and Thomas D. Hall. 1993. "Comparing World-Systems: Concepts and Working Hypotheses." *Social Forces* 71:851–86.

———. 1995. "Rethinking the Evolution of World-Systems: Another Round." Paper presented at the conference World System History: The Social Science of Long Term Change, University of Lund, Sweden, March 25–28.

Elias, Norbert. (1939)1994. *The Civilizing Process: The History of Manners and State Formation and Civilization*. Trans. Edmund Jephcott. Oxford: Blackwell.

Hall, Thomas D. 1986. "Incorporation in the World-System: Toward a Critique." *American Sociological Review* 51:390–402.

———. 1989. *Social Change in the Southwest, 1350–1880*. Lawrence: University Press of Kansas.

McNeill, William H. 1963. *The Rise of the West: A History of the Human Community*. Chicago: University of Chicago Press.

———. 1990. *"The Rise of the West* after Twenty-Five Years." *Journal of World History* 1(1):1–21. (Reprinted as chapter 13, this volume.)

Mann, Michael. 1986. *The Sources of Social Power. Volume 1: A History of Power from the Beginning to AD 1760*. Cambridge: Cambridge University Press.

Melko, Matthew. 1994. "World-Systems Theory: A Faustian Delusion? I." *Comparative Civilizations Review* 30:8–12.

Melko, Matthew, and Leighton R. Scott, eds. 1987. *The Boundaries of Civilizations in Space and Time*. Lanham, MD: University Press of America.

Modelski, George, and William R. Thompson. 1995. *Leading Sectors and World Powers: The Coevolution of Global Politics and Economics*. Columbia: University of South Carolina Press.

Robertson, Roland. 1992. *Globalization: Social Theory and Global Culture*. Newbury Park, CA: Sage Publications.

Sanderson, Stephen K. 1990. *Social Evolutionism: A Critical History*. Oxford: Blackwell.

Wallerstein, Immanuel. 1992. "Geopolitical Strategies of the United States in a Post-American World." *Humboldt Journal of Social Relations* 18(1):217–23.

Wescott, Roger Williams. 1994. "Civil Systems: A Review of the World-System Theories of Andre Gunder Frank and of Christopher Chase-Dunn and Thomas D. Hall." *Comparative Civilizations Review* 30:50–58.

Willard, Alice. 1993. "Gold, Islam, and Camels: The Transformative Effects of Trade and Ideology." *Comparative Civilizations Review* 28:80–105.

*Chapter Nine*

# Hold the Tiller Firm
## *On Method and the Unit of Analysis*

Historical/social analysis is like sailing a boat in rough waters. The dangers come from all sides. It requires not merely good judgment, but the ability and the will to hold the tiller firm. When I first started writing *The Modern World-System* in 1970, I thought the issue was primarily substantive, that is, that I was entering into a debate about what is the most useful interpretation of what happened historically. World-systems analysis was for me a set of protests against prevailing modes of interpretation, at first primarily against modernization theory (see Wallerstein 1979). But I soon came to see that, in order to arrive at a useful interpretation of what happened historically, one had to dispose of a useful method. And that has turned out to be not merely an even more controversial matter than the question of the substantive interpretation of historical reality, but a more slippery one as well.

In my venture into worrying about method, I decided that one key issue was the "unit of analysis," which is why one speaks of "world-systems analysis." The assumption is that the appropriate unit of analysis is a world-system, by which I at least originally meant something other than the modern nation-state, something larger than this nation-state, and something that was defined by the boundaries of an effective, ongoing division of labor. Hence I started with spatial or geographic concerns. The basic metaphor of core/periphery is in origin and etymology a spatial metaphor.

But as I proceeded, it seemed to me that space could never be separated analytically from time, and that the unit of which we were talking was therefore one kind of TimeSpace (see Wallerstein 1991), specifically that which I denoted as structural TimeSpace. To give it a language of easy reference, I thought of structural TimeSpace as divided into "historical systems." I liked the term because it caught what I thought of as the essential tension of structural TimeSpace, that it is a system (meaning it has continuing rules of relation/process, and therefore contains cyclical rhythms) but that it is also historical (meaning that it is different at every moment, and therefore contains secular trends). By combining in one concept both cyclical rhythms and secular trends, I was clearly using an organic analogy. An historical system has a life: it is born or generated, it lives or proceeds, it dies or disintegrates. Each of these three moments of the organism can be analyzed and located in TimeSpace.

From its institutional outset, what came to be called in the 19th century the "social sciences" was beset by a *Methodenstreit*. The classical formulation of this methodological debate was posed in terms of two alternative epistemologies. On the one hand, there were those who believed that the object of research was the discerning of general laws of human behavior, true of all time and space. Their avowed model was to imitate the methods of classical physics to the degree possible and thereby replicate its scientific (and social) success. Windelband called this the nomothetic method, and its proponents became dominant in the emerging university "disciplines" of economics, sociology, and political science. On the other hand, there were those who believed that the search for general laws was not merely futile but dangerous, in that it pushed scholars away from what this group saw as their primary task: ascertaining empirical reality, which was always particular, indeed idiosyncratic. What really happened, in the famous phrase of Ranke, could indeed be discerned and, once discerned, empathetically reconstructed. This was called the idiographic method, and its proponents became dominant in history and for the most part in anthropology.

This difference between nomothetic and idiographic, between synchronic and diachronic, between objective and subjective, between structure and agency, has been renewed and rediscussed under many labels and in many avatars. While the organizational linkages of epistemology and specific disciplines largely reflected university realities between, say, 1880 and 1945, it has tended to break down since then, particularly since the 1970s. That is to say, the debate is still there, but the persons on each side are not so easily recognizable by the name of the university department in which they teach.

Of course, this debate was seldom crude. From its subtleties emerged not two but a thousand positions. Nonetheless, the cleavage was profound. Furthermore, there were always schools of thought which specifically refused the terms of the debate, and suggested either that the dilemma was false, or that the correct position was an intermediate one or one proceeding from an *Aufhebung*. This group was always a numerical minority, if a vocal one. I count myself among them, and I have called this conducting a "war on two fronts" (Wallerstein 1980).

In the period since 1945, there have been a growing number of scholars who became unhappy with Establishment social science (including of course history) on the grounds that its methodological imperatives (whether they were nomothetists or idiographers) had pushed them de facto into the study of the infinitely small in time and space, and that thereby the problems, the realities of large-scale, long-term social change had become eliminated from the purview of scholarship. There was a call for intellectual renewal and for new (actually revived) foci of analysis. This call had many names: dependency theory, civilizational analysis, world history, world-systems analysis, historical sociology, long-run economics, international political economy, and still others. The list is long. Let me call this the family of dissidents, in the sense that they all were dissenting from the views that had dominated, still largely dominate, the universities.

The seas are rough in two senses. Historical/social reality is enormously complex. Indeed, it represents the most complex of all realities. And we know so little still. But the seas are rough in another sense. The study of historical/social reality is a highly sensitive subject, which has immense consequences for the existing structures of power in our existing world-system. Hence, the analyses are closely surveyed, pressured, and kept in check. The Establishment views are not only wrong; they are powerfully protected by extraintellectual means. If we are to proceed in such rough seas, we must hold the tiller firm, and in particular we must not fall prey to the temptations of the world, which are primarily three: to become nomothetic, to become idiographic, to reify. I see very many persons in the family of dissidents paying insufficient attention to these dangers. I discuss each in turn.

## The Nomothetic Temptation

Since all explanation is ultimately in terms of a covering law, however implicit and even if specifically denied, it is tempting to wish to make the covering laws we use as general and as simple as possible. But, of course, there is a price to be paid for generalizing our laws. The more general, the more different things they explain, but the fewer aspects they explain about each thing. It depends on what we want to have explained. For most things, if we use too general a law, the explanation is vacuous, and if we use too narrow a generalization, the explanation is specious. So there is a pragmatic judgment to be made, in terms of payoff. We need to do constant, if not always explicit, cost-benefit analyses.

In world-systems analysis, Christopher Chase-Dunn and others have put to themselves a very simple, obvious proposition. If our unit of analysis is a world-system, and if there are several kinds of world-systems (not an enormous number, but more than one), would it not be useful to compare the three or four or five kinds of world-systems with each other, to discern their similarities and differences, and therefore to arrive at more general explanations of the functioning of world-systems? This is a nomothetic temptation. Chase-Dunn has put his case this way:

> The world-systems perspective has expanded the temporal and spatial scope of theorizing about social change. Our understanding of modernity has been radically transformed by the study of the Europe-centered world-system over the past 500 years. But the analysis of a single system encounters methodological and theoretical limitations. If we would fathom fundamental change we need to comprehend the causes of those structural constants which are usually taken for granted in the modern world-system. These structural "constants" exhibit variation when we broaden the scope of comparison to include very different kinds of world-systems. Are interstate systems of core/periphery hierarchies inevitable features of all organizational wholes? Do all world-systems share a similar underlying developmental logic, or do systemic logics undergo fundamental transformations? These questions can only be scientifically addressed by a comparative perspective which employs the corpus of evidence produced by historians, ethnographers, and archaeologists regarding human activities over *very* long periods of time—much longer than the five hundred year span of the modern world-system (1992, p. 313).

Hence, Chase-Dunn is ready to compare the "world-system" of Cahokia within the middle Mississippian tradition with Mesopotamia and with the modern capitalist world-system. To do this, he adds that "concepts developed for the analysis of the modern system be applied with care; some of them need to be redefined in order to avoid projecting contemporary reality on the past."

This may work, but I remain skeptical. One of the major reasons I remain skeptical is that I wonder if one can take a set of concepts developed for the analysis of one historical system, consider the concepts one by one, redefine each in some more general form (of which consequently the form in the modern world-system becomes but one variant), and then recombine them for the analysis of Cahokia or Mesopotamia. This presumes a certain independence of the concepts from each other which, it seems to me, is doubtful. To be specific, the concept "core/periphery" is not analytically dissociable from the concept "class conflict" or the concept "interstate system" or the concept "endless accumulation of capital." That is to say, the set of concepts developed for a fruitful analysis of the modern world-system is a set. Dissociated, redefined (in the sense of giving different values to each), and reassembled, they may have the coherence of an awkwardly patched pottery bowl.

There are no doubt similarities one can find between Cahokia, as an example of a stateless, classless (?) structure; Mesopotamia, as an example of a world-empire (if that is what it was); and the modern world-system, as an example of a capitalist world-economy. But are these similarities and therefore the differences analytically interesting for problems we wish to solve? There might be some, but looking at these problems does not seem to be the line the "comparative study of world-systems" has been following. The work up to now has emphasized the comparison of the rules governing the system, which I would call looking at the ongoing lives of the systems. Here, I think we are comparing apples and oranges, and I do not think we will get much further than saying they are both fruit and not vegetables.

What might possibly be a fruitful line of enquiry is to compare both the geneses and the terminal crises of systems, to see if there are any patterns, which could then (a) give us some insight into "world history," if by that we mean the synchronic unfolding of human social existence, and (b) illuminate how system bifurcations (*vide* Prigogine) work in historical systems, which in turn might help us with (c) the practical question of how best to navigate the current bifurcation (or systemic demise, or transformation from one historical system to one or more other such systems).

I have said that where we draw the line in our work in this no-mothetic/idiographic divide (or intrinsic tension) is a pragmatic matter, and I have suggested reasons to believe that the "comparative study of world-systems" is not where I would place my bets in terms of useful interpretations. But of course I may be wrong. I would feel more comfortable about this line of work if its practitioners were more cautious about the nomothetic temptation.

## The Idiographic Temptation

In the same article previously cited, Chase-Dunn criticizes two extremes on a continuum, what he calls the "lumpers" and the "splitters." "The extreme lumpers are those who see only one global system far back in time. . . . Extreme splitters are those who focus only on local processes to the exclusion of more distant connections" (1992, p. 317). He comes out sensibly for an in-between position. But the way he puts it, the story is not quite clear. One of his extremes is temporal (too much time), and the other is spatial (too local). Of course, both are in reality spatio-temporal. Most important of all, the two "extremes" are in fact only one: they are both forms of the idiographic temptation. To say that everything is one single thing, or to say that every "unit" is local, that is, different from all the other units, are both ways to avoid structural explanation. In one case, there can be no variation and therefore no alternative structures; in the other, there is nothing but variation, and no two things can be lumped together as structures.

We readily recognize in localism a familiar particularizing face, the standard undergirding of idiographic analysis. Presumably, the dissidents of whom I spoke above have all been allergic to such self-defeating localism. But one big single story is just another form of the idiographic temptation,

IMMANUEL WALLERSTEIN

and this is the route Andre Gunder Frank has chosen to take in his recent writings about "world system history":

> I now also stress and examine "systemic connections in a single historical process" extending back much earlier than 1500. I now examine these systemic connections in a single historical process over a much wider social and geographical range, including at least the entire Afro-Eurasian ecumene, of which Europe and its world is only a part. Thus the historical and socio-geographical scope of this process is no longer seen as beginning and centered in Europe, which, on the contrary, joined it rather late. I will also question the supposed historical uniqueness and perhaps the social-theoretical relevance of the modern capitalist mode of production (1990, p. 164).

This is not the place to review Frank's version of the evolution of world history. Here we are only raising methodological doubts. Everything that can be denoted as a system can be shown to be "open" at some points of its perimeter. One can always take this opening and insist that the presumed system is really part of some larger system. It will not take long to arrive at the largest of all possible systems, the universe from the beginning of its existence to now. Whether even this supersystem is open is itself a matter of philosophical and scientific debate. And in this sense everything is determined by the big bang, if there was a big bang. But while it is salutary to remember this, it is not very useful to build our analysis on this quicksand, which will very rapidly engulf us. Once again, the question is pragmatic.

Frank says the story does not start in AD 1500, but rather in 3000 BC (or so). Perhaps, but by what logic do we stop at 3000 BC? Why not 10,000 BC? Why not go back to Australopithecus, or to prehominids? Once again, it depends on what question we want to answer. And that depends on your chronosophy (Pomian 1979). If you think the history of the world has been a linear upward curve, then it is very important to pursue Frank's line of argument. It is explicitly aimed at undermining a Eurocentric reading of world progress. Basically, it says that the Europeans, whether circa 1800 or circa 1500, did nothing special. They were a part, a "rather late" part, of the story of humanity's achievements. This is the salutary message Frank bears. And I sympathize with it, except that I do not think that the history of the world has been a linear upward curve. I think, to put it crudely, that the curve essentially went up with the so-called agricultural revolution (despite its social negatives), then essentially went down with the arrival of a capitalist world-system (despite some pluses which have been much exaggerated), and may go up again (but then again may not) with the future demise of the world capitalist system. If this chronosophy is adopted, then it positively impedes clarity of vision to efface the 1500 line. Rather we must exert much more energy than we have up to now on the question of genesis—what it was about the situation of the Europeans that accounts for their taking this major, backward step (see Wallerstein 1992). And we need to spend much time as well on the question of bifurcation, demise and/or transition, which may require a comparative look (along the lines I suggested in my discussion of Chase-Dunn).

It is always easy, as I said, to find generalizations that are plausible (if often not very interesting). It is always possible to insist that every particular situation is different from every other in some way, and that therefore all the generalizations are false. And it is always easy to prove continuity of a single reality, in that there are always some things which do not seem to have changed. In any case, there are no caesuras in history that are vacuums, or unbridgeable chasms. The world goes on, microsecond by microsecond. The hard thing is to find the appropriate balance, and to be certain that it is the most *relevant* balance for the question you wish to answer.

## The Temptation to Reify

Analysts do not manipulate data, though many of them like to think that is what they are doing. Rather, analysts manipulate concepts. Concepts become our friends, even our children. They take on a certain life of their own, and it is tempting to stretch their usage beyond the purpose for which they were created. This is what reification is about. In the context of the study of long-term, large-scale social change, one of the concepts most frequently and lovingly employed is that of civilization. Indeed, most of us have a fairly standard list in mind when we use the word: the West (or Christianity), perhaps Russia (or maybe the whole Orthodox world), Islam (or the Arabo Islamic world), Persia, India, China, perhaps Japan and Korea separate from the Sinic world, and then the ones no longer surviving: Byzantium, Mesopotamia, the Incas, Pharaonic Egypt, Classical Antiquity (or are Rome and Greece separate?), and so forth. Are there African civilizations, or one African civilization? The list is of course open to amendment, but that is beside the point. It is a somewhat limited list, usually 20 or 30 examples at most.

What is a "civilization?" It is hard to say because different analysts use different criteria. For most analysts, it usually involves a linguistic element, a religious (or cosmological) element, a distinctive pattern of "everyday life," a spatial locus (however blurred or shifting) and therefore perhaps an ecological element, and perhaps least convincingly continuous ethnicity and some genetic coherence. This list too could go on. If one looks at the names listed above, the one that appears to have the longest continuous history is, by common accord, China. We talk of a Chinese civilization that presumably goes back to the earliest dynasty and continues to today. What continuity does this imply? We can of course find continuities—not perhaps the same exact language, but mostly [*sic*] related ones; not the same religion(s), but some links between older forms and later ones; not the same patterns of everyday life, but some long-lasting peculiarities; more or less the same geography, provided one is not too fussy about the breadth of the boundaries; a limited case for ethnic and genetic descendence.

As with the case for a single world history, one can make a case for a single Chinese history at about the same level of plausibility, or perhaps at a stronger level. And certainly we can make the case that many/most Chinese today (Chinese thinkers, Chinese politicians) believe in this continuity and act in function of this belief. Suppose, however, that someone were to postulate that China since 1945 or since 1850 is closer overall on a multitude of measures of social relations to Brazil since 1945/1850 than it is to the "China" of the Han dynasty. We could not reject the case out of hand.

Of course, one can avoid the decision by a common sense dismissal of the issue—in some ways the one, in some ways the other. The question does not thereby disappear. For many purposes, we have to decide whether it is more profitable to consider contemporary China and Brazil as two instances of the same phenomenon (say, very large underdeveloped nations within the modern world-system or the capitalist world-economy) or to consider the China of today and Han China as two instances of Chinese civilization, comparing it then (I suppose) with the Brazil of today descended from an uncertain something else of 1500 years ago as two instances of I am not sure what (perhaps Christian civilization).

Would it not be more useful if we didn't reify civilizations? One way to think about China is to think of it as a name linked to a geographical location in which there existed successive historical systems, which had a few features in common, and each of which sustained (for a good deal of the time) myths concerning civilizational continuity. In that case, instead of China, the civilization, we are perhaps talking empirically of five, six, or seven different historical systems (each of which could be grist for the eventual fourfold tables that will derive from the nomothetic temptation). At least, I would not like to close off this way of viewing "Chinese history" by a too-rapid embrace of "civilizational analysis." (Of course, one can see why there would be social pressure against adopting such a perspective on "China" or "the West" or most of the names we use for "civilizations.") China is no doubt the strongest case for a civilizationalist thesis. It becomes harder to demonstrate inherent cultural continuities everywhere else. To be sure, if we narrow our analysis to the scale and scope of a single historical system, then a "geoculture" is part of its "systemness."

I have discussed the civilizational hypothesis under the heading of the temptation to reify. It is of course most frequently a variant of the idiographic temptation but occasionally a variant of the nomothetic temptation. But reification as such is a recurring problem because we deal in concepts, and concepts are inherently ambiguous tools. Civilization is by no means the only concept we reify, but for the purposes of the analysis of long-term, large-scale social change, it is the exemplary one.

## Conclusion

What is there to conclude? I suppose that the scholar should be intellectually monastic, and resist temptations. But product that I am of "American civilization," I urge that the resistance be modulated by pragmatism. I see no other way. The issues are too important that they not be faced, and they are too urgent to be closed off to analysis by failing to fight the war on two—indeed on all—fronts at the same time. Above all, I urge prudence in any haste to shout Eureka!

### *References*

Chase-Dunn, Christopher. 1992. "The Comparative Study of World-Systems." *Review* 15:313–33.

Frank, Andre Gunder. 1990. "A Theoretical Introduction to 5,000 Years of World System History." *Review* 12:155–248.

Pomian, Krzysztof. 1979. "The Secular Evolution of the Concept of Cycles." *Review* 2:563–646.

Wallerstein, Immanuel. 1979. "Modernization: Requiescat in Pace." In *The Capitalist World-Economy*, by Immanuel Wallerstein. Cambridge: Cambridge University Press.

———, 1980. "The Annales School: The War on Two Fronts." *Annals of Scholarship* 1(3):85–91.

———. 1991. "The Invention of TimeSpace Realities: Towards an Understanding of our Historical Systems." In *Unthinking Social Science*, edited by Immanuel Wallerstein. Cambridge: Polity Press.

———. 1992. "The West, Capitalism, and the Modern World-System." *Review* 15:561–619.

■ DAVID WILKINSON

*Chapter Ten*

# Civilizations *Are* World Systems!

The title of this article states my position in the rich and burgeoning civilizationist/world-systems debate about as succinctly as possible. Civilizationists and world-systems analysts should be studying the same entities. This will occur if and when civilizationists accept that the many local civilizations of the past have become the single global civilization of today; and when world-systemists accept that the single, global world system of today is the fusion product of a substantial number of smaller-scale world systems of the past; and when both accept that the plural civilizations of the past, and the plural *urbanized* world systems of the past, were, and that today's singular civilization and singular world system are, identical.

A joint intellectual undertaking could then be pursued, probably with different but complementary emphases. Civilizationists might cluster their efforts more (but not exclusively) toward the earlier, more pluralistic epochs of civilizational evolution, world-systemists toward the later, more monistic. Civilizationists already tend, I think, to interest themselves more in the cultural aspects of a society than in the political, and more in the political than in the economic; world-systemists tend oppositely; neither group need surrender its inclinations, though each would have to take account of the other's propositions.

Few readers will be shocked to learn that my proposals suit my own established predilections; for their benefit I should place my cards face up on the table. In 1966 I was urging my graduate students in international relations to find ways of integrating the work of Spengler and Toynbee with what was then called a systems analysis approach to international relations theory, whose chief representatives then were Morton A. Kaplan (1957) on the deductive, theoretical, normative side, Stanley Hoffmann (1960, 1965) on the historical-sociological side, Richard N. Rosecrance (1963) combining both—all three were my teachers—and George Modelski (1961). This is the kind of assignment which one usually winds up having to carry out oneself. That duly occurred, and in 1967 I found myself producing for my students' benefit, or dismay, a manuscript called "Civilizations and World Politics," whose then incarnation drew on most of the aforementioned, plus Charles McClelland (1958), A.F.K. Organski (1958, esp. chaps. 8, 12, and 17), Martin Wight (1946), Raymond Aron (1966), but most centrally on the civilizationist Carroll Quigley (1961), for the desired theoretical synthesis. It did not work.

It did not work because it vacillated between accepting the assumption of the international-systems analysts that the contemporary globe contained one and only one system, which produced the interesting and important phenomena of balance-of-power, states-system-and-empire, order-and-disorder, peace-and-war, and the assertion of the civilizationists that the contemporary globe contained several distinct civilizations, defined by common cultural forms, for which the above-mentioned phenomena were the results of their *internal* processes.

Examining that manuscript at this distance in time, I am struck by the fact that I had all that I needed to reach the resolution I in fact accomplished much later. On the systems side, Modelski had drawn attention to "homogeneity" (one vs. many parallel "traditions") in a social system as an important variable (1961, pp. 126–30). Aron, following Papaligouras's (1941, p. 174) contention that multiple parallel international legal processes had authoritatively posited mutually contradictory international legal norms, had argued that "the distinction between *homogeneous systems* and *heterogeneous systems*" was fundamental (Aron 1966, pp. 99–100), and had defined as "heterogeneous" those international systems in which states were organized according to different principles and obeyed different values (Aron 1966:94, 98–100, 128). Hoffmann, following Papaligouras's connection between heterogeneity and breakdown, had argued that heterogeneous or "uneven" international systems were also unstable or "revolutionary," because the stakes of conflict therein were unlimited (1965, pp. 92–93). In contrast, Rosecrance, following Ashby's cybernetics, had contended that the degree of "variety" in international systems' disturbance and regulation was an important empirical variable in accounting *both* for breakdown and for stabilization (1963, pp. 220 ff). On the civilizationist side, Toynbee, in his *Reconsiderations*, had defined "society" as the total network of relations between human beings, "societies" as particular networks that are not components of any larger network, "civilization" as a state of society in which a minority of the population is liberated from economic activities, and "civilizations" as that species of the genus society whose members are particular historical exemplifications of the abstract idea "civilization" (1961, pp. 271, 278, 280, 282, 287). I also had Quigley's preliminary criterion of cities (and writing) as the external identifiers of a civilization (1961, pp. 31–32). But I tried to compromise among incompatible world-views by adopting the criteria of all simultaneously. I proposed to examine, as civilizations and world systems: large and coherent social areas with a large and fairly dense population, cities, and writing; which comprised social-transactional network structures with closed boundaries; in which wealth is created, savings accumulated, a nonproducing class supported, and economic inventions created and exploited; and having unity of cultural form. These criteria simplified empirical and comparative study famously, as nothing got past them.

My work along these lines accordingly stagnated, though I watched with interest the extension of Kaplan's model to a smaller scale by my then-colleague Anthony Martin (1970), the new work of Modelski (1972, 1987; Modelski and Thompson 1988) on the evolution of the world system, and the beginning of what was to prove continuous development of the world-systems approach of Immanuel Wallerstein (1974), none of which, however, could quite resolve my difficulties. Martin was examining a regional subsystem, a core, rather than a whole system. Modelski and Thompson brought a very useful reflection on geopolitics, and particularly the changing meaning of naval power in systems of different sizes and hence spatial configurations, without resolving for me the problem of the unit of analysis. Wallerstein (like Modelski) went farther back in search of relevant history than most systems analysts, but not as far as Quigley, whose political economy seemed more persuasive.

After participating in the refoundation of the International Society for the Comparative Study of Civilizations (ISCSC) in the United States (Philadelphia, December 1971), and in response to the dialogic initiative of Matthew Melko, reading Melko's 1969 work *The Nature of Civilizations* and the manuscript works of John Hord (q.v.), and having a 1977 redraft of "Civilizations and World Politics" (which tried to produce a Quigleyan model, but in the process found coherence and closure to be incompatible criteria and ended by proposing that the contemporary world constituted a single incoherent civilization with a core-periphery structure) commented on by both, I was impelled, in Melko's ISCSC "Boundaries" sessions of 1978–1983 (documented in Melko and Scott 1987), to a reaffirmation, a radical simplification, a change of direction, a complete abandonment of the coherence criterion, and new conclusions, as follows.

1. Civilizations *are* world systems.
2. Their relevant criteria are cities and closed transactional networks, not size, writing, a Quigleyan "instrument of expansion," or cultural coherence/homogeneity (Wilkinson 1987b).

3. On applying this criterion to the roster of candidate civilizations, we find that many of the "usual suspects"—Egyptian, Mesopotamian, Far Eastern, Indic, Japanese, Peruvian, Mexican—pass muster. But many others—Western, Islamic, Russian, Greco-Roman, Medieval—are not closed societies; they are parts of a larger, culturally heterogeneous network-entity. This civilization, of which these other putative "civilizations" are then regions or epochs, needs a name. I have called it "Central" Civilization (Wilkinson 1987a [chapter 2, this volume], 1987b).

4. There was a plurality of civilizations/world systems on the globe until the late 19th or early 20th centuries. Now there is only one survivor, Central Civilization, whose network expanded to global scale and absorbed all others (Wilkinson 1987a).

5. Civilizations typically show the alternation between political disunity and political unity posited by Toynbee in his revised "Helleno-Sinic model" (1961, pp. 157, 170–209). However, the unity—the phase of the "universal state" (Toynbee), "universal system" (Kaplan), "world state," "universal empire" (Quigley), or "world-empire" (Wallerstein)—is usually brief and fragile, for reasons having to do with the structure and succession of leadership (Wilkinson 1983, 1988).

6. The chief social bond scaled to the dimensions of the civilization is politico-military-diplomatic. Cultural bonds have smaller scales. Until the growth of Central Civilization to global scale, economic bonds had larger scales, and defined oikumenes, trading areas that were larger than the areas in which states could rule, fight, or ally (Wilkinson 1992, 1993a).

7. Central Civilization is only the most blatantly heterogeneous of civilizations. Other civilizations too are polycultures (Iberall and Wilkinson 1993), though when (e.g., Japan) they have possessed a universal state of long duration it has usually had a homogenizing ideology *and* utopia (cf. Mannheim 1936) and policy.

8. The civilization-formation process was still continuing—that is, cities were appearing on preurban social terrain, not as extensions of or reactions to the political impingements of neighboring cities, but often as reactions to the economic impingements of oikumenes—perhaps as late as the 17th, even the 18th century in Africa (Wilkinson 1993c, 1994b).

9. Central Civilization formed in the first instance in the mid-2nd millennium BC, in consequence of the expansion, collision, and fusion of two preexisting civilizations, Mesopotamian and Egyptian. It grew by expanding against, and engulfing, other civilizations, without ever fully homogenizing them or itself (Wilkinson 1984).

10. The heterogeneities of other civilizations may be the result of the same processes. That is, a trade network extends itself into a preurban social terrain; a city forms, perhaps so that a local political elite can avail itself of the local surplus thereby generated; but a larger expanding civilization, its familiars driven by similar motives, in due course recruits the new city to its polity. The motives to recruit it to its (anyway heterogeneous) culture are weaker, and a diversity of languages (and dialects), religions (and cults and schisms), races

(and physiognomies and ethnicities and families), apparels, and so forth persists. Mesopotamian, Egyptian, Indic, Far Eastern, Mexican, and Peruvian civilizations could fruitfully be examined comparatively, with a view to relating their various heterogeneities to the order and independence of their urbanization processes.

This summary leads naturally to the main topic of this paper: the current debate in our overlapping fields, and the positions of the participants. I shall try to locate myself with respect to each of a large number of participants.

*Toynbee.* I draw very heavily on Toynbee, both in agreement and in opposition, but almost exclusively on his extensively revised model of 1961, from *Reconsiderations*, rather than on the much better-known earlier volumes of *A Study of History*. My definition of a civilization/world system takes off from his rethinking (1961, pp. 278–87). My roster is based on a critique of his list and Quigley's. In an empirical test of his civilizational kinematics (phase transition sequence), original and revised versions, versus those of Spengler (1926–28), Philip Bagby (1958), Melko (1969), and Quigley (1961), my data fit the expectations of his revised theory perfectly; those of his original theory came in next best (Wilkinson 1986, p. 29). He is however seduced by the mythos of cultural coherence—not entirely, no one is, and he provides a useful model of cultural contradiction and conflict—but relates it integrally to breakdown. He is replete with fertile notions, and, I believe, is the most liberal of civilizationists, in the oldest sense of that word; an excellent teacher.

*Quigley.* Carroll Quigley provides a single, powerful, illuminating insight into the dynamics of civilizations, the concept of the instrument of expansion, which I view as a nonpartisan and nonsupersessionist empiricization of the Marxian "mode of production," and as such an improvement, with extensive research and practical implications. Some hint of the latter can be found, on suitable occasions, in the kaleidoscopic consciousness of Quigley's one-time student, William Jefferson Clinton. Where many if not most civilizationists have centrally focused on culture, Quigley focuses centrally on economics, and will probably be easiest for the world-systems tradition to come to grips with. However, after spending some time trying to validate his proposition that growing civilizations are pervaded by a single instrument of expansion, I judged that I had disconfirmed it instead, gave up expecting macrosocieties to display much institutional coherence, and began to consider the structure of their incoherence. In that incoherence, I think that many of Quigley's propositions will be *partially* confirmed, and that the location and limits of their application will be significant.

*Spengler.*  Spengler is the Antaeus of civilizationists, brilliantly, perversely, powerfully wrong in more ways than any two others combined. Spengler's key proposition, to the effect that each civilization develops a single prime symbol, an all-pervasive style, is especially brilliantly wrong (the Gramscian doctrine of cultural "hegemony" being less so, except insofar as it is doctrinaire, an answer instead of a question), and should point us to the study of the *failure* of repeated attempts in that direction, and the resilience of deviant, oppositional, variant, heretical, inverted, oppressed symbols, as thematic of polycultural history. Is this failure correlated with the failure to develop a single prime mode of production, class struggle, durable world state and cosmopolis? I suspect so.

*Melko.*  Melko accepts that today many civilizations coexist, and objects to the idea that the only way we can study contemporary civilization comparatively is to do so by reference to history. That is indeed the logical consequence of my acceptance that today only one civilization exists. Our respective rosters are properly derived from different definitions; we can agree on some phenomena common to the civilizations that appear on both our rosters. However, while he, like Spengler (1926, Table III), sees a feudal state-imperial polity sequence (1969, pp. 101–32), I perceive no holocivilizational feudal phase. Feudalism does indeed appear in semiperipheries, with regard to which I find Rushton Coulborn's arguments (1956, pp. 364–66) about feudalism as "a mode of revival of a society whose polity has gone into extreme disintegration" in marginal regions—religion being the general and core-area recovery modality—quite convincing). As for states systems and empires, I find not a supersession but an alternation, following Toynbee's Helleno-Sinic model, in which, consistent with Robert Wesson's work (1967, 1978), the states-system phase is more robust.

Melko is also doubtful, as is Chase-Dunn, about my admission to civilizational status of very small-scale societies, with only one or two cities—Melko questions my "Chibchan" civilization, Chase-Dunn my "Irish." More recently—since I have responded only by accepting even smaller civilizations into my roster (Wilkinson 1993b, 1994b)—Melko has suggested that I will have to locate still others, for example, in Central Asia. My point (10) above concurs with him. I had not closed my roster of civilizations in 1982 or 1987 (Wilkinson 1980–82, 1987b), and I am not ready to close it now. Current candidates not treated then include several African possibilities, and a second (!) Colombian candidate, Tairona "civilization."

*Hord.*  I view all of John Hord's papers (n.d., 1983, 1991) with great interest. Our definitions of "civilization" are irreducibly different, but I believe that the relatively homogeneous political-cultural entities he studies under that label are genuine, and his understanding of them creative and novel. The persistence *and* the fissility of his constitutional traditions has helped to persuade me that (my) civilizations are characteristically, not just incidentally, polycultures.

*Sorokin.* I have discussed Sorokin more fully elsewhere (1995). In brief: I concur with Sorokin's powerful critique (1950, pp. 113–20, 206–17; 1956, pp. 163–64; 1964, pp. 413–19; 1966, pp. 121–22, 548–49) of civilizationists—Spengler, Nikolai Danilevsky (1920), and especially Toynbee—who observed social groups and thought they observed cultural groups. Sorokin however resolves the difficulty by refusing the analytic concept of "civilization." I resolve it by treating civilizations as social groups and not as cultural groups, each, just as Sorokin complained (1950, p. 213), "a cultural field where a multitude of vast and small cultural systems and congeries—partly mutually harmonious, partly neutral, partly contradictory—coexist."

*Huntington.* Sorokin's comment is worth recalling in another context. Samuel P. Huntington has lately (1993) brought a political scientist's perspective to the study of civilizations. He defines civilizations as cultural groupings and cultural identities, accepts the plurality of contemporary civilizations, presents a largely Toynbeean civilizational roster, and hypothesizes that in the next phase of world politics "the fault lines between civilizations will be the battle lines of the future" (p. 22). His argument is detailed and provocative. I believe Sorokin would rightly contend that Huntington's "major civilizations"—"Western, Confucian, Japanese, Islamic, Hindu, Slavic-Orthodox, Latin American, and possibly African civilization" (p. 25)—are "cultural fields" rather than either systems or potential actors. I would add that they are cultural subfields in the global cultural field of a single civilization, a social and not a cultural entity. I consequently doubt the hypotheses that "conflict between civilizations will supplant ideological and other forms of conflict as the dominant global form of conflict" and that "international relations . . . will increasingly . . . become a game in which non-Western civilizations are actors" (p. 48). More likely, nostalgic ideologies of lost civilizational isolation and cultural status will be used to mobilize support for struggles for power and prestige within a solitary, incoherent civilization in which the ideologues have neither the capacity nor the intention to create a coherent cultural system, let alone a culture capable of functioning as an actor.

Melko has objected to my schema (which describes the general course of macrosocial history as the fusion of many small civilizations into the one contemporary global civilization) on the grounds that it destroys the possibility of a comparative study of civilizations, except so far as that study is also historical. That is indeed its logical consequence. But those who nonetheless wish to examine dialogically Huntington's contention that the next stage in global political conflict will be a conflict of civilizations can still do so perfectly well, but employing the different (and to my mind more precise) locution "conflict of cultures within a single civilization." We can then proceed to use for our historical analogs not the past collisions and fusions between civilizations, but the more frequent, more complex and delicate (and, I suspect, more dialogic and *perhaps* even less violent) interplay of the parts of a single society's polyculture. As a first approximation, on account of the analogy I consider appropriate I am probably a bit more sanguine about the outcome of such a conflict, even while being less sure of its coming rise to prominence, than Huntington.

*Chase-Dunn and Hall versus Frank and Gills.* On the issue of whether there are many different precapitalist world-systems with different modes of production (Chase-Dunn and Hall 1991a, 1991b [chapter 4, this volume]) or a single 5,000-year world system with a single developmental logic (Frank and Gills 1993; Gills [chapter 5, this volume]; Frank [chapter 6, this volume]), I partly split the difference and partly disagree with both. First, I do not use the term "precapitalist" to describe any empirical civilization/world system; while capitalist (and socialist) ideals, ideologies, and utopias are rather recent, their accumulative and distributive practices are very old, possibly *both* contemporaneous with the startup of civilization. Second, I find many different world-systems (like Chase-Dunn and Hall), but of such unequal size, duration, and terminus that one of them (essentially that focused on by Gills and Frank) eventually engulfed the others; this is the political/civilizational structure I call Central Civilization. Third, in consequence of not finding one pervasive Quigleyan "instrument of expansion" in any civilization, I don't use the term "mode of production" in any world-system-level application, except as a hypothesis I do not expect to see confirmed. Each of the civilizations is heterogeneous, polycultural, incoherent with respect to its politico-economic patterning; though at some times in each some new or reinvented form has looked like it would spread throughout and extirpate all others, it is "institutionalized" (in the Quigleyan sense, that is, deflected and corrupted) and reaches a limit well short of that. This pattern of *failure* is as interesting as the variety of forms and their mutual displacement processes, and should keep a generation or so of macrosocial theorists productively employed in verifying, describing, and explaining it.

This said, I find the *projects* of these researchers intriguing and productive, and extremely worthwhile discussing. I suspect that all four of these researchers are more sanguine than I am about the possibility of reducing political to economic phenomena. This vision is appealing because it suggests there may be economic (non-zero-sum) solutions to political (and apparently zero-sum) problems. Without necessarily rejecting the vision, I would treat economies and polities as different though always linked. Critical evidence that this is an empirical, and confirmable, proposition is the difference in historical scale between the political-diplomatic constellations of civilizations and the trade-networks of oikumenes/world-economies until the 19th century. A critical case for future discussion is the relationship between Rome and China, in which China, politico-diplomatically and militarily inaccessible to Rome (and not part of the same civilization/world system), seems inadvertently to have inflicted severe economic damage on it (currency drain, implying location in the same world-economy/ oikumene). This proposition is related to, and strengthened by, F.J. Teggart's contention (1939, pp. 239–41) that Chinese statesmen who consciously chose to make wars on their western frontiers caused, without intending or knowing it, invasions of Rome's eastern frontiers, "conflicts and devastations in regions of which they had never heard," by disrupting silk route (and fur) trade. Rome and China in this period present the classic case of states belonging to the same world-economy, or oikumene, and different civilizations, different world-polities, and—in my meaning—different world systems.

*Chase-Dunn.* Since the 1970s I have held that all civilizations are world systems; but since the 1960s I have accepted that there are some world systems which are not civilizations, that is, very small, nonurban polycultures. Christopher Chase-Dunn is now in the lead on this line of research, which should help to detail the differences between the smallest, cityless, world systems and the next level larger, the one- and two-city protocivilizations, of which I now believe several, probably many, more must have existed (most only briefly, "abortive" in a sense analogous to Toynbee's) than have as yet been found. One appropriate line of comparative-civilizational fieldwork for the future will, with luck, be the search for lost and forgotten cities, carried on with new and superior technical means afforded by aerial and satellite photography, with searches for patterned, centric, and radial disturbances of soil and vegetation, showing the patterns of points and lines that usually represent civilizational geometry. The first fruitful zone for such exploration will I think be the forested areas of Africa south of the Sahara.

On another issue (not yet discussed in print), Chase-Dunn is considerably more skeptical, and I considerably more receptive, to the social-physics or complex-systems-physics ideas of Arthur S. Iberall, which I have found productive of useful hypotheses (as to, for example, why and how the several early-born civilizations initially formed near simultaneously (Iberall and Wilkinson 1986); the relation of polyculturality to civilization (Iberall and

Wilkinson 1993); what might be the order of magnitude of the number of cities and civilizations "missing" from current records and to be searched for (Wilkinson 1994a, 1995).

*Gills and Frank.*   Currently the best short compilation of their contentions, examined at length in Frank and Gills (1993), is Frank's five propositions (p. 2). First, the "existence and development of the present world system stretches back at least 5,000 years": I date its *existence* back 3,500 years, when there was a critical fusion of its *predecessors* or *roots*, which go back at least 5,500 years; in essence we concur. Second, the "same process of capital accumulation has played a, if not the, central role in the world system for several millennia": I say "a, but not the" central role, in this and all other *civilizational* world systems (but *not* in the nonurban world systems Chase-Dunn studies). Third, the "Center-Periphery Structure . . . is also applicable to the world system before 1492": having accepted Quigley's (1961) argument on this point when he made it, I more than agree; the structure is applicable to all civilizations, that is, to all *civilizational* world systems (but not necessarily to nonurban world systems); I have provided a more detailed account (Wilkinson 1991). Fourth, hegemony "and rivalry for the same also mark world system history long before" 1492: I agree as to rivalry, extending my agreement to the other world systems; but there is a lot less hegemony achieved than is believed, and most of the best-known "hegemons" (e.g., 19th-century Britain, the United States after World War II) simply are not. Fifth, the "world system cycle" of A phases and B phases extends back many centuries before 1492: I agree fully, and have confirmed this independently (Wilkinson 1992, 1993a), for other world systems as well.

Aside from differences over the centrality of economics and the frequency and nature of hegemony still to be resolved, I see another topic for argument—within basic agreement—over the balance between statist and marketive capital accumulation. There *may* be periods in which states are the main engines of accumulation, and other periods in which private families are; more likely there are *areas* in each period where one or the other form dominates. But I suspect the prevailing pattern and persistent substratum is the cheek-by-jowl coexistence of very different forms even at the very local spatial scale, with a process change at the house threshold, at the market gate, at the cultic center (see my argument about the classical Athenian economy [Wilkinson 1987, chapter 2, this volume]).

\*     \*     \*

I conclude as I began. The best way to deal with the discussions between civilizationists and world-systems analysts is to aver that the entities we are studying largely are, and ought to be, the same. Our theories ought to be merged. Having attempted to develop such a merger since encountering the civilizationist literature in the 1950s and the international-systems literature in the early 1960s, I can only view the current interaction with great pleasure.

*References*

Aron, Raymond. 1966. *Peace and War*. New York: Doubleday.

Bagby, Philip. 1958. *Culture and History*. London: Longmans, Green.

Chase-Dunn, Christopher, and Thomas D. Hall. 1991a. "Conceptualizing Core/ Periphery Hierarchies for Comparative Study." In *Core/Periphery Relations in Precapitalist Worlds*, edited by Christopher Chase-Dunn and Thomas D. Hall. Boulder, CO: Westview.

———, eds. 1991b. *Core/Periphery Relations in Precapitalist Worlds*. Boulder, CO: Westview.

Coulborn, Rushton. 1956. *Feudalism in History*. Princeton, NJ: Princeton University Press.

Danilevsky, Nikolai. 1920. *Russland und Europa*. Trans. Karl Notzel. Stuttgart: Deutsche verlags-anstalt.

Frank, Andre Gunder. 1993. "Latin America at the Margin of World System History." *Comparative Civilizations Review* 28:1–40.

Frank, Andre Gunder, and Barry K. Gills, eds. 1993. *The World System: Five Hundred Years or Five Thousand?* London: Routledge.

Hoffmann, Stanley H., ed. 1960. *Contemporary Theory in International Relations*. Englewood Cliffs, NJ: Prentice-Hall.

———. 1965. "International Systems and International Law." In *The State of War*, edited by Stanley H. Hoffman. New York: Praeger.

Hord, John K. n.d. "An Investigation into Pattern-Repetition in History." Unpublished manuscript.

———. n.d. "Diffusionism Revisited." Unpublished manuscript.

———. n.d. "The Tie that Binds: Dynamics of Constitutional Development." Unpublished manuscript.

———. 1983. "Times of Order, Times of Chaos." Paper presented at the annual meetings of the International Society for the Comparative Study of Civilizations, Buffalo, New York.

———. 1991. "Civilization: A Definition. Part I: Identifying Individual Civilizations." *Comparative Civilizations Review* 25:28–53.

Huntington, Samuel P. 1993. "The Clash of Civilizations?" *Foreign Affairs* 72:22–49.

Iberall, Arthur S., and David Wilkinson. 1986. "Human Sociogeophysics—Phase II (Continued): Criticality in the Diffusion of Ethnicity Produces Civil Society." *GeoJournal* 11:153–58.

———. 1993. "'Polycultures' and 'Culture-Civilizations.'" *Comparative Civilizations Review* 28:73–79.

Kaplan, Morton A. 1957. *System and Process in International Politics*. New York: Wiley.

McClelland, Charles. 1958. "Systems and History in International Relations: Some Perspectives for Empirical Research and Theory." In *General Systems*, Vol. III. Society for General Systems Research.

Mannheim, Karl. 1936. *Ideology and Utopia*. Trans. Louis Wirth and Edward Shils. New York: Harcourt.

Martin, Anthony D. 1970. "The Unstable Balance: A Systems Analysis of the International Politics of Sixteenth Century Western Europe." Ph.D. dissertation, University of Chicago.

Melko, Matthew. 1969. *The Nature of Civilizations*. Boston: Porter Sargent.

Melko, Matthew, and Leighton R. Scott, eds. 1987. *The Boundaries of Civilizations in Space and Time*. Lanham, MD: University Press of America.

Modelski, George. 1961. "Agraria and Industria." In *The International System*, edited by Klaus Knorr and Sidney Verba. Princeton, NJ: Princeton University Press.

———. 1972. *Principles of World Politics*. New York: Free Press.

———. 1987. *Long Cycles in World Politics*. Seattle: University of Washington Press.

Modelski, George, and William R. Thompson. 1988. *Seapower in Global Politics, 1494–1993*. Seattle: University of Washington Press.

Organski, A.F.K. 1958. *World Politics*. New York: Knopf.

Papaligouras, Panoyis A. 1941. "Théorie de la société internationale." Thesis, University of Geneva.

Quigley, Carroll. 1961. *The Evolution of Civilizations*. New York: Macmillan.

Rosecrance, Richard N. 1963. *Action and Reaction in World Politics*. Boston: Little, Brown.

Sorokin, Pitirim A. 1950. *Social Philosophies in an Age of Crisis*. Boston: Beacon.

———. 1956. *Fads and Foibles in Modern Sociology and Related Sciences*. Chicago: Henry Regnery.

———. 1964. *Sociocultural Causality, Space, and Time*. New York: Russell and Russell.

———. 1966. *Sociological Theories of Today*. New York: Harper & Row.

Spengler, Oswald. 1926–28. *The Decline of the West*. 2 vols. Trans. Charles Francis Atkinson. New York: Knopf.

Teggart, Frederick J. 1939. *Rome and China*. Berkeley: University of California Press.

Toynbee, Arnold J. 1961. *Reconsiderations*. Volume XII of *A Study of History*. New York: Oxford University Press.

Wallerstein, Immanuel. 1974. *The Modern World-System: Capitalist Agriculture and the Origins of the European World-Economy in the Sixteenth Century*. New York: Academic Press.

Wesson, Robert G. 1967. *The Imperial Order*. Berkeley: University of California Press.

———. 1978. *State Systems: International Pluralism, Politics, and Culture*. New York: Free Press.

Wight, Martin. 1946. *Power Politics*. London: Royal Institute of International Affairs.

Wilkinson, David. 1980–82. "A Definition, Roster and Classification of Civilizations." Paper presented at the annual meetings of the International Society for the Comparative Study of Civilizations, revised and re-presented.

———. 1983. "Civilizations, States Systems, and Universal Empires." Paper presented at the annual meetings of the International Society for the Comparative Study of Civilizations.

———. 1984. "Encounters between Civilizations: Coexistence, Fusion, Fission, Collision." Paper presented at the annual meetings of the International Society for the Comparative Study of Civilizations.

———. 1986. "Kinematics of World Systems." *Dialectics and Humanism* 1:21–35.

———. 1987a. "Central Civilization." *Comparative Civilizations Review* 17:31–59. (Reprinted as chapter 2, this volume.)

———. 1987b. "The Connectedness Criterion and Central Civilization." In *The Boundaries of Civilizations in Space and Time*, edited by Matthew Melko and Leighton R. Scott. Lanham, MD: University Press of America.

———. 1988. "Universal Empires: Pathos and Engineering." *Comparative Civilizations Review* 18:22–44.

———. 1991. "Cores, Peripheries, and Civilizations." In *Core/Periphery Relations in Precapitalist Worlds*, edited by Christopher Chase-Dunn and Thomas D. Hall. Boulder, CO: Westview.

———. 1992. "Cities, Civilizations, and Oikumenes: I." *Comparative Civilizations Review* 27:51–87.

———. 1993a. "Cities, Civilizations, and Oikumenes: II." *Comparative Civilizations Review* 28:41–72.

———. 1993b. "Civilizations, Cores, World-Economies, and Oikumenes." In *The World System: Five Hundred Years or Five Thousand?*, edited by Andre Gunder Frank and Barry K. Gills. London: Routledge.

———. 1993c. "Spatio-Temporal Boundaries of African Civilizations Reconsidered: I." *Comparative Civilizations Review* 29:52–90.

———. 1994a. "Putting a Little Zipf into the Study of Civilizations." Paper presented at the annual meetings of the International Society for the Comparative Study of Civilizations, Dublin.

———. 1994b. "Spatio-Temporal Boundaries of African Civilizations Reconsidered: II." *Comparative Civilizations Review* 31:46–105.

———. 1995. "Sorokin vs. Toynbee on Congeries and Civilizations: A Critical Reconstruction." In *Sorokin: A Centennial Assessment*, edited by Joseph Ford, Palmer Talbutt, and Michel Richard. New Brunswick, NJ: Transaction Books.

STEPHEN K. SANDERSON ∎

*Chapter Eleven*

# Expanding World Commercialization
## *The Link Between World-Systems and Civilizations*

From the rise of the first states around 5,000 years ago until the last few hundred years, the dominant form of social organization has been the agrarian state, or what Collins (1990, 1992) has called *agrarian-coercive societies*, Kautsky (1982) *traditional aristocratic empires*, and Marxist-oriented scholars the *tributary mode of production* (Amin 1976; Wolf 1982). Regardless of their various differences, agrarian societies share at least four fundamental characteristics. First, they are characterized by a class division between a small landowning (or at least land-controlling) nobility and a large peasantry. The peasantry is compelled on threat of violence to pay tribute in the form of rent, taxation, labor services, or some combination thereof to the nobility for the latter's economic benefit. This relationship is one of naked exploitation backed by military force. Second, the noble–peasant relationship is the principal economic axis in the society, and it is a relationship of production-for-use rather than production-for-exchange. Production-for-exchange exists to some degree, but it is subordinate in importance, often greatly so, to production-for-use. Indeed, the social actors who dominate production-for-use, the urban merchants, were typically looked down upon by the aristocracy as money-grubbing individuals who dared to dirty their hands with the soil of commerce. Merchants sometimes enjoyed great wealth, but their social status was almost invariably low. Third, despite the class division between nobles and peasants, there is no overt class struggle carried on between these two classes (Kautsky 1982; Giddens 1985). There is, of course, a marked conflict of class *interest*, but this does not manifest itself, other than in the most minimal and sporadic way, in deliberate actions by one class against the other. Finally, agrarian societies are held together not by any sort of ideological consensus or common world-outlook, but by military force (Giddens 1985). Agrarian societies are virtually always highly militarized societies, and such militarization is essential to the aims and ambitions of dominant groups. Military might is devoted to the twin aims of internal repression and external conquest.

Agrarian societies have been most intensively studied by historians, and especially by those historians who think of themselves as "civilizationists," many of whom claim allegiance to the works of Arnold Toynbee (1934–61) and Pitirim Sorokin (1957). Civilizationists can be identified by a number of characteristics, but two stand out. First, they exhibit a tendency to think of the agrarian civilizations in a *mentalist* or *idealist* sense. Civilizations are defined and bounded by their cultural themes or motifs, which include such things as philosophies, art styles, religions, and other abstract systems of thought and feeling. Civilizationists have paid some attention to the political features and dynamics of agrarian societies,[1] but they have given little attention to the economic side and certainly have not given it any prominent role in civilizational dynamics. Second, unlike most historians, civilizationists have searched for patterns or regularities in history, the patterns identified usually being cyclical in nature. Thus we have Toynbee's notion that all civilizations tend to go through a life cycle containing four stages—genesis, growth, breakdown, and disintegration—and Sorokin's famous idea that civilizations exhibit a cyclical alternation between Ideational, Sensate, and Idealistic forms. In contrast to most historians, civilizationists have therefore adopted a nomothetic rather than an idiographic stance. Nevertheless, the cyclical nature of their nomothetic view has seemingly excluded from consideration the type of linear developmental patterns stressed by those other students of agrarian societies (and all other types of societies), namely, social scientists who espouse an evolutionary view of history.

I would like to suggest that civilizationists need to pay more attention to economics and to developmental rather than cyclical patterns. (I am not rejecting the notion that there may be cyclical patterns, but only asserting that there are developmental or evolutionary patterns of profound importance.) In recent years a number of social scientists have begun to study agrarian and other types of preindustrial societies from a very different point of view, one that does in fact emphasize both economics and long-term social development. These are scholars who identify with the world-system perspective originally developed in the 1970s by Immanuel Wallerstein (1974, 1979, 1980, 1989). The success of this perspective in interpreting the nature and dynamics of modern capitalist civilization has led to the notion that it may have more general utility—that there may have been other historical world-systems that can only be properly understood from a holistic point of view rather than by considering the parts of the system in relative isolation. The pioneers of this view have been, *inter alia,* Jane Schneider (1977); Kajsa Ekholm and Jonathan Friedman (1982); Janet Abu-Lughod (1989); Christopher Chase-Dunn and Thomas Hall (1991, 1993, chapter 4, this volume); and Andre Gunder Frank and Barry Gills (Frank 1990, 1991, chapter 6, this volume; Gills, chapter 5, this volume; Gills and Frank 1991, 1992). My initial reaction to the attempt to apply a world-system perspective to precapitalist and preindustrial societies was rather mixed (Sanderson 1991). One of my initial objections concerned the attempt to apply a perspective focusing on relations of economic exchange to societies in which production-for-exchange was clearly subordinated to production-for-use. My argument was that precapitalist societies, agrarian societies included, contained so little production-for-exchange that it would be difficult to apply a world-system perspective to them. Or, to the extent that such a perspective could be applied, it would apply to only a tiny portion of economic action, and thus be of very limited use. However, I had an open mind and continued to read and study the works of the "precapitalist world-systemites," hoping that a payoff would eventually be realized.

I did not have long to wait. I gradually came to accept the view, argued most forcefully by Andre Gunder Frank and Barry Gills, that agrarian civilizations had much more commercialism in them than had generally been recognized, and that in fact there had been a long-term process of the growth of commercialism beginning around 3000 BC. Frank and Gills have referred to this process as one of capital accumulation and have suggested that the rise of modern capitalism after the 16th century was only a quantitative extension of the process, not a qualitative shift from a "feudal" to a "capitalist" economy. I break with them on this particular point—it seems to me a considerable overstatement—but I regard their argument for the gradual growth of commercialism over the last 5,000 years as basically sound. Since I see this process prior to AD 1500 as having occurred within essentially noncapitalist, tributary societies, I prefer to refer to it as one of expanding world commercialization rather than capital accumulation. Before AD 1500 the growth of commercialism occurred within societies in which early forms of capitalism (perhaps best called "protocapitalism") existed, but capitalist relations were not yet dominant in the economy. For me, expanding world commercialization is a historical process of tremendous significance that we are only perhaps now coming to appreciate, and it is the link (or if not *the* link, then at least *a* link) between the concerns of traditional civilizationists and the new precapitalist world-systemites. This is, or at least can be, a common focus for both groups of scholars.

As I see it, the process of expanding world commercialization is one that can be assessed primarily in terms of growth in the size and density of trade networks. Some trade existed prior to the rise of the first civilizations in 3000 BC, but its scale began to increase substantially after that date. Early trade was primarily local or confined to relatively small regions, but in due time it expanded to include much larger regions, and then eventually true long-distance trade emerged to link East with West. It is possible to mark off three major stages in this process (McNeill 1982; Curtin 1984). The first stage begins around 2000 BC and ends around 200 BC. During this phase trade was largely local or, at best, regional in scope. By 200 BC there emerged the first truly long-distance trade with the establishment of a trade axis that ran all the way from China to the Mediterranean. After about AD 1000 there was another big leap forward in which trade networks expanded and deepened, especially in the period between 1250 and 1350.

It is interesting to note that the emergence of a long-distance trade axis after 200 BC corresponds fairly closely to Rein Taagepera's date for a sudden surge in the size of agrarian empires (600 BC). Taagepera (1978, 1990) has studied changes in the size of agrarian empires over approximately the last 5,000 years. He shows that there has been a significant increase in empire size during this time and marks off three phases of empire growth. The first phase begins with the rise of the state itself. Before this time there were no political units with a size greater than 0.1 square megameters (1 square megameter = 386,000 square miles). During the first phase of empire building the single largest agrarian empire seemed to maintain a size of at least 0.15 square megameters and to have at least occasionally attained a size of about 1.3 square megameters. A second phase of empire building was inaugurated around 600 BC. After this time the single largest empire was never smaller than 2.3 square megameters, and the maximum imperial size attained was 24 square megameters. Obviously, then, there was a substantial increase in the size of empires after 600 BC. Taagepera believes that the increase in empire size during the second phase probably resulted from increasing sophistication in the art of power delegation, especially through impersonal bureaucratic roles rather than personal relationships. But it is also likely that the size increase was made possible by important developments in the areas of transportation and communication, as Taagepera himself notes. Empires could not become effectively larger until the means were available for controlling and integrating much larger areas. Expanding world commercialization and the growth of empires are undoubtedly causally related, for as E.L. Jones (1988) has argued, truly long-distance trade networks only became possible with the rise of very large empires. Only empires of that size had developed the technology of communication and transportation needed to facilitate worldwide trade.

Philip Curtin (1984) has described some of the basic characteristics of the worldwide trade network that was in effect between 200 BC and AD 1000 (cf. Chaudhuri 1985). As he notes, during this period trade became regularized between the Red Sea/Persian Gulf region and India, between India and Southeast Asia, and between Southeast Asia and both China and

Japan. In the middle Han period, Chinese merchants traveled to the west through central Asia and established an overland trade route between East Asia and Europe. Chinese trade with India had become extensive by the first century AD, and Chinese goods were being sold widely in the Roman Empire. During Roman times trade between India and the Mediterranean was carried on through three different routes: an overland route through Parthia, the Persian Gulf combined with an overland route, and the Red Sea combined with an overland route to Egypt or some part of the Fertile Crescent region. Maritime trade flourished in the South China Sea and the Bay of Bengal, with Canton being an important port for trade to the south.

William McNeill (1982) has described what he regards as a new and major burst of world commercialization beginning around AD 1000, and centering heavily on China. It was during this time that China had by far its greatest burst of economic activity prior to modern times, one that lags behind only late medieval Europe and Tokugawa Japan in scale and scope. Mark Elvin (1973) has referred to this as an "economic revolution," most of which occurred during the period of the Sung dynasty (AD 960–1275). Elvin sees the Sung economic revolution as involving agriculture, water transport, money and credit, industry, and trade (both domestic and foreign). He argues that improvements in agriculture gave China by the 13th century the most sophisticated agricultural system in the world, and one that provided a foundation for major thrusts in commercial activity. Commercial activity was also greatly aided by improvements in water transport. These improvements involved both the construction of better sailing vessels on the one hand and the building of canals and removal of natural obstacles to navigation in streams and rivers on the other. Industry flourished, especially the production of steel and iron. The economy became much more monetized. There was a much greater volume of money in circulation, and the money economy even penetrated into peasant villages. Foreign trade, especially with Southeast Asia and Japan, flourished. Markets proliferated and became hierarchically organized. At this time China was the world's most economically advanced society, and many observers have suggested that it was on the brink of the world's first industrial revolution. However, beginning sometime in the 14th century China began to decline and stagnate economically and gradually to withdraw from foreign trade. It became increasingly isolated and inward looking, a process that had become fairly complete by the middle of the 15th century. The reasons for this economic downturn are still very imperfectly understood today.

McNeill sees the enormous economic growth in Sung China as part of a larger picture of world commercialization. As he says, "China's rapid evolution towards market-regulated behavior in the centuries on either side of the year 1000 tipped a critical balance in world history" (1982, p. 25). And he elaborates (1982, pp. 50–54):

Though the capitalist spirit was . . . kept firmly under control, the rise of a massive market economy in China during the eleventh century may have sufficed to change the world balance between command and market behavior in a critically significant way. . . . Moreover, the growth of the Chinese economy and society was felt beyond China's borders; and as Chinese technical secrets spread abroad, new possibilities opened in other parts of the Old World, most conspicuously in western Europe. . . .

What seems certain is that the scale of trade through the southern seas grew persistently and systematically from 1000 onwards, despite innumerable temporary setbacks and local disasters. Behavior attuned to the maintenance of such trade became more and more firmly embedded in everyday routines of human life. . . .

What was new in the eleventh century, therefore, was not the principle of market articulation of human effort across long distances, but the scale on which this kind of behavior began to affect human lives. New wealth arising among a hundred million Chinese began to flow out across the seas (and significantly along caravan routes as well) and added new vigor and scope to market-related activity. Scores, hundreds, and perhaps thousands of vessels began to sail from port to port within the Sea of Japan and the South China Sea, the Indonesian Archipelago and the Indian Ocean. . . .

As is well known, a similar upsurge of commercial activity took place in the eleventh century in the Mediterranean, where the principal carriers were Italian merchants sailing from Venice, Genoa, and other ports. They in turn brought most of peninsular Europe into a more and more closely articulated trade net in the course of the next three hundred years. It was a notable achievement, but only a small part of the larger phenomenon, which, I believe, raised market-regulated behavior to a scale and significance for civilized peoples that had never been attained before. . . .

It was precisely in the eleventh century, when China's conversion to cash exchanges went into high gear, that European seamen and traders made the Mediterranean a miniature replica of what was probably happening simultaneously in the southern oceans. . . . These separate sea networks were then combined into one single interacting whole after 1291.

Janet Abu-Lughod (1989) has picked up the story where McNeill left it. She describes in great detail for the period 1250–1350 the structure and operation of a vast worldwide trade network from western Europe to East Asia. This huge network contained eight overlapping subsystems that can be grouped into three larger circuits centering on western Europe, the Middle East, and the Far East. She claims that this world trade network (1989, p. 353)

was substantially more complex in organization, greater in volume, and more sophisticated in execution, than anything the world had previously known. . . .

Sophistication was evident in the technology of shipping and navigation,

TABLE 11.1
*World Urbanization, 2250 BC–AD 1500*

| Year | Number of Largest Cities | Population Range of Largest Cities | Estimated Total Population of Largest Cities | Civilizations Represented |
|---|---|---|---|---|
| 2250 BC | 8 | c. 30,000 | 240,000 | Mesopotamian, Egyptian |
| 1600 BC | 13 | 24,000–100,000 | 459,000 | Mesopotamian, Egyptian, Aegean |
| 1200 BC | 16 | 24,000–50,000 | 499,000 | Central,[a] Aegean, Indic, Far Eastern |
| 650 BC | 20 | 30,000–120,000 | 894,000 | Central, Aegean, Indic, Far Eastern |
| 430 BC | 51 | 30,000–200,000 | 2,877,000 | Central, Indic, Far Eastern |
| AD 100 | 75[b] | 30,000–450,000 | 5,181,000 | Central, Indic, Far Eastern |
| AD 500 | 47 | 40,000–400,000 | 3,892,000 | Central, Indic, Far Eastern |
| AD 800 | 56 | 40,000–700,000 | 5,237,000 | Central, Indic, West African, Far Eastern, Indonesian, Japanese |
| AD 1000 | 70 | 40,000–450,000 | 5,629,000 | Central, Indic, Far Eastern, Indonesian, Japanese |
| AD 1300 | 75[b] | 40,000–432,000 | 6,224,000 | Central, Indic, West African, Far Eastern, Japanese, Indonesian |
| AD 1500 | 75[b] | 45,000–672,000 | 7,454,000 | Central, Indic, West African, Far Eastern, Japanese |

SOURCES: Wilkinson (1992, 1993) and Chandler (1987).
[a]Central civilization is Wilkinson's name for the expanded civilization originally centered on Mesopotamia and Egypt. By 200 BC it had engulfed Europe.
[b]The upper limit on the number of cities set by Chandler (1987)

the social organization of production and marketing, and the institutional arrangements for conducting business, such as partnerships, mechanisms for pooling capital, and techniques for monetization and exchange.

Additional corroboration for the notion of expanding world commercialization throughout the agrarian era comes from research on trends in world urbanization. Using data compiled by Tertius Chandler (1987), David Wilkinson (1992, 1993) has shown that urbanization is a striking trend in world history. Of course, commercialization and urbanization cannot be strictly equated, but it is likely that urbanization is more a function of increasing commercialization than of anything else. Cities may grow and expand to fulfill important political functions, of course, and certainly for various other reasons, but commercialization seems to be the main driving force behind urbanization (Bairoch 1988).

Table 11.1 presents data on world urbanization trends from 2250 BC to AD 1500. It is clear that urbanization has been a striking feature of agrarian social growth over a period of nearly 4,000 years. A particularly large leap in urbanization occurs in the period between 650 and 430 BC. During this period the number of cities of 30,000 or more inhabitants increased from 20 to 51, and the total population represented by these cities increased from 894,000 to 2,877,000, a more than threefold increase. It seems very noteworthy that this period marks the early beginnings of Greco-Roman civilization and is the same period that Taagepera has identified as being associated with a major increase in the size and scope of political empires. There is another major urbanization spurt between 430 BC and AD 100, during which the number of cities of 30,000 or more inhabitants increased from 51 to at least 75, and also during which the total population of these cities expanded from 2,877,000 to 5,181,000, an 80 percent increase. This period is essentially the same period that McNeill and Curtin refer to as involving the emergence of the first truly long-distance trade network between East Asia and the Mediterranean.

It cannot escape attention that world urbanization suffered a setback between AD 100 and 500. There were fewer large cities (those with 30,000–40,000 or more inhabitants), and the total population of these cities fell from 5,181,000 to 3,892,000. This was, of course, the period of the decline and eventual collapse of the Roman Empire. However, world urbanization and commercialization suffered only a minimal and quite temporary setback. By AD 800, the total population of the largest cities (5,237,000) had regained the level achieved in 100. It took longer for the number of large cities to return to the level reached in 100—there were 70 such cities in 1000 and 75 or more cities in 1300—but not that much longer. Moreover, after 1000 the scale of world urbanization was clearly very large and continuing to grow, and, as already noted, the period after 1000 has been seen by McNeill and Curtin as involving another major leap in world trade networks.

What are the implications of recognizing a historical process of expanding world commercialization over the period from 3000 BC to AD 1500? I see at least two. First, this process requires strong qualification of what has long been the standard sociological wisdom on agrarian societies: that they exhibited thousands of years of lethargy and stagnation and had no impetus to fundamental social change. This is a view that dates all the way back to the 18th century. Its proponents have included Max Weber ([1896–1909]1976), Gerhard Lenski (1970), John Kautsky (1982), and Immanuel Wallerstein (1974), among many others. It is not completely erroneous, but it is one-sided and misleading. While agrarian societies have generally lacked any strong evolutionary impetus—any tendency toward fundamental structural transformation into a new form of society—it is clear that agrarian societies in AD 1500 were different—some might even say profoundly different—from what they were like in 3000 BC.

We might put the matter this way. A useful distinction can be drawn between *social growth* and *social evolution*. Social growth occurs when there is a quantitative change in one or more dimensions of a system of social organization. Increases in, say, the size of a population, military might, technological efficiency, or political power may be regarded as social growth so long as they do not lead a society into a structurally new mode of organization. This is essentially a distinction between *quantitative* change (social growth) and *qualitative* change (social evolution), or between something *new* rather than something *greater*. The crucial question is, of course, Was there much social evolution during the so-called agrarian era? The answer is no, there was not. But there was considerable social growth. In addition to expanding world commercialization this included two correlative forms of social growth: growth in the size of political empires and in the concentration of political power (Taagepera 1978, 1990; Mann 1986), and technological advance (Lenski 1970; Mann 1986). However, I believe that the growth of commercialism was the most important form of social growth during the long agrarian epoch.

The second implication of acknowledging a process of expanding world commercialization is perhaps even more important. Assuming that the movement out of the stage of agrarian society was going to be a movement into a specifically capitalist system of social and economic life—and historically, of course, this is the way things have worked out—it needs to be stressed that the emergence of capitalism could not be some sort of sudden leap forward to be achieved in a few dozen or even a few hundred years. It was an economic transformation that required a long period of time because of what might be called the "threshold effect." Because of capitalism's requirement for extensive markets (both foreign and domestic), and because of the general hostility of agrarian elites to it, it could only emerge slowly, and as such would require a lengthy period of incubation before it could reach a kind of "critical mass" essential to a tipping of the balance of economic power in its favor. In retrospect we know that the time period actually required was approximately 4,500 years from the beginning of the first agrarian states. In another work (Sanderson 1994) I have attempted to develop this implication at some length by way of formulating a new theory of the rise of modern capitalism.

In conclusion, I feel compelled to say that this essay is only a bare beginning toward understanding the worldwide growth of commercialism over the past 5,000 years. This process cries out for understanding in much greater detail, and many important questions remain to be answered. What was the extent to which earlier forms of capitalism were "rationalized" in the Weberian sense? Were ancient merchants profit maximizers? What was the importance of financial arrangements in earlier forms of capitalism? What was the relationship between technological advance and commercial expansion? What role did the state play in ancient capitalism? Now that we have begun to recognize that there was an important long-term process of expanding world commercialization, these questions and many others await civilizationists, world-systemites, and all other inquisitive parties.

NOTES

1.   One civilizationist who has conceived of civilizations primarily in political terms is David Wilkinson. See, especially, his "Central Civilization" (chapter 2, this volume).

*References*

Abu-Lughod, Janet. 1989. *Before European Hegemony: The World System AD 1250–1350*. New York: Oxford University Press.

Amin, Samir. 1976. *Unequal Development: An Essay on the Social Formations of Peripheral Capitalism*. Trans. Brian Pearce. New York: Monthly Review Press.

Bairoch, Paul. 1988. *Cities and Economic Development: From the Dawn of History to the Present*. Trans. Christopher Braider. Chicago: University of Chicago Press.

Chandler, Tertius. 1987. *Four Thousand Years of Urban Growth*. Lewiston, NY: St. David's University Press.

Chase-Dunn, Christopher, and Thomas D. Hall. 1991. "Conceptualizing Core/Periphery Hierarchies for Comparative Study." In *Core/Periphery Relations in Precapitalist Worlds*, edited by Christopher Chase-Dunn and Thomas D. Hall. Boulder, CO: Westview Press.

———. 1993. "Comparing World-Systems: Concepts and Working Hypotheses." *Social Forces* 71:851–86.

Chaudhuri, K.N. 1985. *Trade and Civilisation in the Indian Ocean*. Cambridge: Cambridge University Press.

Collins, Randall. 1990. "Market Dynamics as the Engine of Historical Change." *Sociological Theory* 8:111–35.

———. 1992. "The Geopolitical and Economic World-Systems of Kinship-Based and Agrarian-Coercive Societies." *Review* 15:373–88.

Curtin, Philip D. 1984. *Cross-Cultural Trade in World History*. New York: Cambridge University Press.

Ekholm, Kajsa, and Jonathan Friedman. 1982. "'Capital' Imperialism and Exploitation in Ancient World-Systems." *Review* 4:87–109.

Elvin, Mark. 1973. *The Pattern of the Chinese Past*. Stanford: Stanford University Press.

Frank, Andre Gunder. 1990. "A Theoretical Introduction to 5,000 Years of World System History." *Review* 13:155–248.

———. 1991. "A Plea for World System History." *Journal of World History* 2:1–28.

Giddens, Anthony. 1985. *The Nation-State and Violence*. Berkeley: University of California Press.

Gills, Barry K., and Andre Gunder Frank. 1991. "5,000 Years of World System History: The Cumulation of Accumulation." In *Core/Periphery Relations in Precapitalist Worlds*, edited by Christopher Chase-Dunn and Thomas D. Hall. Boulder, CO: Westview Press.

———. 1992. "World System Cycles, Crises, and Hegemonial Shifts, 1700 BC to 1700 AD." *Review* 15:621–87.

Jones, E.L. 1988. *Growth Recurring: Economic Change in World History*. Oxford: Oxford University Press.

Kautsky, John H. 1982. *The Politics of Aristocratic Empires*. Chapel Hill: University of North Carolina Press.

Lenski, Gerhard. 1970. *Human Societies: A Macro-Level Introduction to Sociology*. New York: McGraw-Hill.

Mann, Michael. 1986. *The Sources of Social Power. Volume 1: A History of Power from the Beginning to AD 1760*. Cambridge: Cambridge University Press.

McNeill, William H. 1982. *The Pursuit of Power: Technology, Armed Force, and Society Since AD 1000*. Chicago: University of Chicago Press.

Sanderson, Stephen K. 1991. "The Evolution of Societies and World-Systems." In *Core/Periphery Relations in Precapitalist Worlds*, edited by Christopher Chase-Dunn and Thomas D. Hall. Boulder, CO: Westview Press.

———. 1994. "The Transition from Feudalism to Capitalism: The Theoretical Significance of the Japanese Case." *Review* 17:15–55.

Schneider, Jane. 1977. "Was There a Pre-capitalist World-System?" *Peasant Studies* 6:20–29.

Sorokin, Pitirim. 1957. *Social and Cultural Dynamics*. Abr. ed. Boston: Porter Sargent.

Taagepera, Rein. 1978. "Size and Duration of Empires: Systematics of Size." *Social Science Research* 7:108–27.

———. 1990. "Patterns of Empire Growth and Decline." Unpublished manuscript, University of California, Irvine.

Toynbee, Arnold. 1934–61. *A Study of History*. 12 volumes. New York: Oxford University Press.

Wallerstein, Immanuel. 1974. *The Modern World-System: Capitalist Agriculture and the Origins of the European World-Economy in the Sixteenth Century*. New York: Academic Press.

———. 1979. *The Capitalist World-Economy*. New York: Cambridge University Press.

———. 1980. *The Modern World-System II: Mercantilism and the Consolidation of the European World-Economy, 1600–1750*. New York: Academic Press.

———. 1989. *The Modern World-System III: The Second Era of Great Expansion of the Capitalist World-Economy, 1730–1840s*. San Diego, CA: Academic Press.

Weber, Max. (1896–1909)1976. *The Agrarian Sociology of Ancient Civilisations*. Trans. R.I. Frank. London: New Left Books.

Wilkinson, David. 1992. "Cities, Civilizations, and Oikumenes: I." *Comparative Civilizations Review* 27:51–87.

———. 1993. "Cities, Civilizations, and Oikumenes: II." *Comparative Civilizations Review* 28:41–72.

Wolf, Eric R. 1982. *Europe and the People Without History*. Berkeley: University of California Press.

VICTOR ROUDOMETOF ■
ROLAND ROBERTSON

*Chapter Twelve*

---

# Globalization, World-System Theory, and the Comparative Study of Civilizations
## *Issues of Theoretical Logic in World-Historical Sociology*

The debate between world-system theorists and civilizationists centers upon the relationship between the concepts of "world-system" and "civilization." Are the two conceptually identical (Wilkinson 1994 [chapter 10, this volume]) or conceptually distinct? Furthermore, is world-system theory likely to subsume civilizational analysis (Melko 1994) and if so, does this prospect involve a real loss or reduction of the domain available to scholarly inquiry?

In this discussion, we will argue that many of the issues raised in the current debate between civilizationists and world-system theorists involve considerations of culture and agency. In the absence of a direct engagement with these issues, this debate suffers from conceptual ambiguity and the *post hoc* treatment of cultural issues. We suggest that adopting a "middle range" analytical frame of reference may serve as a means of theoretical clarification of this ambiguity. We then proceed to interrogate the concepts of "world-system" and "civilization" from within this "middle range" framework, a framework that derives largely from globalization theory (Robertson 1992).

## Background: The "Ghost in the Machine"

The premise for this debate revolves around the conceptual ambiguity of the employment of the notions of "world-system" (with or without the hyphen) and "civilization." Currently, there is no agreement regarding their exact connotation and employment. Whereas Wallerstein (1992) has suggested that only one modern world-system has ever existed, other world system theorists (Frank and Gills 1992, 1993; Chase-Dunn 1992) have suggested that in world history there has been a multiplicity of world-systems. Abu-Lughod (1989) has put forward the thesis that a network of world-economies existed between the 12th and 14th centuries stretching from China to northwestern Europe. Chase-Dunn and Hall (1991a, 1991b) have gone as far back as prehistoric times in their quest for ancient or precapitalist world-systems.

In the most explicit statement of the pre-1500s camp, Frank and Gills (1993) have argued that the modern world-system has been evolving for the last 5,000 years, and that the "rise of the West" does not represent a really significant break with the general pattern of historical evolution. For them, the process of capital accumulation is the motor force of history and the center-periphery structure is characteristic not only of the modern world-system but also of all historical systems in the past.

Wallerstein (1992, 1993, 1994 [chapter 9, this volume]) has reacted to this interpretation by suggesting that the pre-1500 economic networks were world-empires rather than world-economies, while Amin (1993) has suggested that they were characterized by a tributary and not a capitalist mode of production. For Wallerstein (1993, p. 293) "what . . . distinguishes a self-sustaining long-lived capitalist system [is the fact] that the system was based on a structural priority given and sustained for the *ceaseless* accumulation of capital." In this light, a world-system does not represent a territory linked though commercial exchanges (that would be a world system *à la* Gills and Frank) but it stands for a system that is a "world of its own."

For a precise definition of a world-system, however, it is necessary to provide criteria that clearly demarcate its boundaries. Wallerstein uses two criteria for defining world-system boundaries: mode of production and trade in bulk goods.[1] According to Chase-Dunn (1989; Chase-Dunn and Hall 1991a), both criteria are unsatisfactory. The criterion of mode of production requires a totality assumption that each world-system has only one mode of production. For the *longue durée*, this totality assumption calls for the important political, military, and economic interactions between Europe and other empires and regions (e.g., the Ottoman Empire) to be classified as relatively epiphenomenal.[2] With respect to the second criterion, trade in bulk goods, Wallerstein's restriction of commodity exchanges to basic goods unjustifiably excludes trade in luxury goods. Trade in luxury goods is not epiphenomenal because in precapitalist systems these goods served important functions for the legitimation of local ruling classes.

In turn, Wallerstein (1992) has suggested that the emergence of modern capitalism is the result of a historical conjuncture in medieval Europe.[3] This conjuncture involved the simultaneous collapse of important agents in the European and global scene (the European seigniors, the states, the Church, and the Mongol Empire). Whether plausible or not, Wallerstein's interpretation incorporates another factor that is *not* accounted for via a conjunctural explanation: the fact that the accumulation of capital made possible by such a historical conjuncture is *ceaseless*. Frank and Gills (1993, p. 6) write that

> Wallerstein, Amin, and most others argue that there is something unique and uniquely powerful about modern capital, i.e. an imperative to accumulate "ceaselessly" in order to accumulate at all. We contend that this imperative, both in the familiar money form as well as other forms of capital, is not a unique systemic feature of modern "capitalism." Rather the imperative of ceaseless accumulation is a characteristic of competitive pressures throughout world history.

Whether capitalism has evolved throughout world history or whether it is relatively new is a debate that has its foundations in the very definition of the term. For if capitalism has been present throughout world history, then capitalism is made synonymous with the extraction of surplus by the dominant classes, elites, or status groups within a given territory. Wallerstein has solved this problem by suggesting that the propensity of merchants to accumulate capital is a natural quality that is not influenced by cultural models and modes of expression. But, unless one subscribes to classical economic theory, it is difficult to justify a cultural imperative as a natural propensity.

In effect, in order to specify the modern character of the world-system, Wallerstein has incorporated, unwittingly, elements reminiscent of Weber's Protestant Ethic thesis. The *ceaseless* character of capital accumulation creates a residual category (Alexander 1988) in Wallerstein's theoretical scheme. Generally speaking, the presence of such a category reveals that, in order for a credible explanation to be produced, a variable that is not part of the theorist's general theoretical apparatus has to be introduced. In this case, the variable takes the form of a peculiar cultural value (ceaseless accumulation) that is not part of Wallerstein's analytical model, but is utilized, nevertheless, for the production of a credible explanation.

This residual category is a result of Wallerstein's reluctance to incorporate cultural factors as constitutive elements of the definition of the modern world-system. Among the reasons for this reluctance is that a cultural theoretical turn results in the following logical impossibility: no theoretical space is left to clearly articulate a Marxist or neo-Marxist position as distinct from a Weberian one (cf. Burris 1987). Consequently, if the modern world-system is to be defined via cultural as well as economic factors, the eschatological beliefs espoused by neo-Marxists would come into question. In order to avoid such an important contradiction Wallerstein is forced to introduce a cultural factor in the form of a residual category into his historical explanation.

In the dawn of the post-Soviet era, then, the Wallerstein versus Frank debate signifies the dilemmas faced by the neo- or post-Marxist camp. McNeill (1993, p. ix) rightly observes that the Frank-Gills thesis of a "capital-accumulating core [that] has existed . . . for some five thousand years [is] revisionism expected in liberal discourse but repugnant to dogmatic upholders of Marxist Truth." Ironically, in this debate it is Wallerstein, the savior of neo-Marxist eschatology, who has taken the decisive step of defending not only Marx but also Weber from a neo- or post-liberal reinterpretation of world history.

Beyond political implications, Weber's ([1920] 1978) comments on the origin of capitalism have a decisive bearing on the Wallerstein-Frank debate. The following statement indicates that this debate is by no means new. Additionally, it points toward the "missing link" that both sides refuse to acknowledge:

> "Acquisitiveness", or the "pursuit of profit", of monetary gain, of the highest possible monetary gain, has in itself nothing at all to do with capitalism. It is and has been found among waiters, doctors, coachmen, artists, tarts, venal officials, soldiers, brigands, crusaders, frequenters of gambling dens, beggars—one might say "among all sorts and conditions of men," in all ages and in all countries of the world, wherever the objective possibility for it has existed or still exists in any form. Such a naive definition ought to have been given up once and for all at the nursery stage of cultural history. Unabridged avarice has no resemblance whatsoever to capitalism, still less to its "spirit" (p. 333).

In the Wallerstein-Frank debate, then, the cultural orientation of agents has become the object of *theoretical* dispute. Wallerstein suggests that this cultural orientation is present only in the modern era as the result of a historical conjuncture, whereas the "pre-1500" camp suggests that the structural characteristics identified by Wallerstein within the modern world-system are also present in precapitalist world systems. Within the pre-1500 camp, the cultural orientation of agents ceases to be a residual category. Simultaneously, however, the concept of capitalism is overextended to the point of becoming synonymous with human history *per se*.

Instead of turning agents' orientations into a matter of *theoretical* dispute—that is, whether the accumulation of capital is sufficiently different in the modern world-system to suggest a qualitative break with the past—we would suggest that a more fruitful approach is to make agents' orientations the domain of *empirical* inquiry. Such a move also involves the recognition of nonmaterial factors as an important domain of inquiry and not as epiphenomena whose "evolution" can be accounted for by direct reference to material factors.

But how does this debate connect with the contemporary civilizationist camp? To the aid of the pre-1500 camp came the civilizationist David Wilkinson. According to Wilkinson (1987a, 1987b [chapter 2, this volume], 1993), world history is dominated by what he calls Central Civilization. This civilization was created in 1500 BC via the merging of Egyptian and Mesopotamian civilizations, and in due time it absorbed most other civilizations that existed on the planet.

> Central civilization does . . . have a presently dominant culture within its polycultural mix. The dominant culture is . . . theoretic, secular, Promethean, scientific, technological . . . cosmopolitan, bourgeois, capitalist, liberal, democratic, and above all "modern." Being only dominant but not yet all-pervasive, . . . [this] culture . . . continues to expand savagely against savage resistance, as it has done within Central civilization for the past seven or eight centuries, even while Central civilization itself has been expanding to global dimension (Wilkinson 1993, pp. 228–29).

Shadows of neoevolutionary thinking are pervasive throughout this line of interpretation. The "rise of the West" does not represent a fundamentally qualitative break with past civilizations since the "West" is only the latest manifestation of a cosmopolitan civilization that has been evolving over the course of world history. This viewpoint converges with the pre-1500 camp (Frank, Gills, Chase-Dunn).

Indeed, Jonathan Friedman (1992, 1994) has developed a typology of long-term transitions from prestige goods systems to commercial civilization that renders modernity an emergent property of the larger global system. Even more explicitly, Gills and Frank have suggested that their goal is none other than to undermine the claim of "Western" distinctiveness and the explicit Eurocentrism that underlies it. They propose to do so by emphasizing the intercivilizational connectedness between "Europe" and the rest of Eurasia.

Within the civilizationist camp in the broadest sense, there has been a long-term awareness of the issue of situationally and consequentially meaningful intercivilizational encounters or interpenetrations (Nelson 1981). The assumption of a linear historical process, however, remains heretical within this camp. Although no agreement regarding the exact number of civilizations has ever been reached (see Melko and Scott 1987), the term usually denotes a number of sociocultural formations—estimates vary from six or seven to thirty—that are assumed to be relatively independent of each other and whose rise, dominance, and fall constitute the civilizationists' domain of inquiry (Toynbee 1972). Traditionally, the comparative study of civilizations involves comparisons among different "units" that are assumed to have developed relatively independently of each other. Often times cultural cohesion is taken to be an important criterion for the classification of different civilizations. In this light, McNeill (1993) considers that the choice between the concepts of "world-system" and "civilization" as foundations of human experience reflects a choice between "materialist" and "idealist" interpretations of history.

In contrast to this traditional view of civilizationists, Wilkinson has developed a notion of "civilization" that converges with that of a "world system" (without the hyphen). Wilkinson (1987a) has made a decisive break with most civilizationists by employing the criterion of connectedness, instead of cultural coherence, to define civilizations. Furthermore, Wilkinson (1993) correlates "civilizations" (politico-militarily-linked urban networks) with *oikumenes* (economically-linked urban networks). Oikumenes provide the foundations—the "base"—for the formation of "civilizations." For civilizationists the question then is whether civilizations ought to be defined in this manner or whether cultural relationships ought to be taken into consideration.

This brief overview of the theoretical field and the polar views expressed in the debate regarding the convergence of world-systems and civilizations reveals that issues of culture and agency do in fact constitute an important component of the problems to be tackled. There is a marked shift towards socioeconomic interpretations at the same time that disagreements among theorists center on issues that have less to do with economic factors and more to do with the place of culture in their explanatory apparatuses. However, these issues are not addressed explicitly. Typically, they creep into these debates in an unorganized and rhetorical (as opposed to analytic) manner. The result is an array of different viewpoints that seem difficult to reconcile.

Scholarly discourse displays a marked lack of concepts that operate at a "middle level" of analysis, concepts that have an empirical referent in sociohistorical formations. For if no shared definitions exist regarding what a "world system" (with or without the hyphen) or "civilization" is, a debate about their convergence is bound to remain inconclusive. Since there are no "middle range" conceptual tools to serve as a necessary link between the empirical and the theoretical domains, researchers do not have a common basis in which to ground their divergent viewpoints and assess the suitability and viability of their different conceptualizations. A metatheoretical alternative to such a "dialogue of the deaf" is to provide for a "middle range" analytical frame of reference. Our comments are aimed towards making a contribution to the analytical elaboration of such a linkage between socio-logical constructs and the *longue durée* of world history.

## Power Networks and Civilizations

In contrast to the *post hoc* theorization of cultural relationships characteristic of the current debate, we incorporate cultural factors directly into our proposed line of inquiry. However, our program is to enhance the explana-tory and interpretive power of some of the views expressed in this debate and in no way suggests a privileging of cultural as opposed to economic or material aspects, although it does strongly question the crude and, we believe, entirely unrealistic assumption that there is such a "thing" as a "pure" economic or material interest.

Most social scientists accept an analytical, although not necessarily a substantive, differentiation among at least three fields of social life: eco-nomic, political, and cultural.[4] For world-historical sociology, a more explicit and helpful way of conceptualizing these dimensions is to conceive of them as power networks.[5] Mann's (1986, pp. 1–2) image of societies as consisting of overlapping power networks provides a very useful starting point:

> Societies are not unitary. They are not social systems (closed or open); they are not totalities. We can never find a single bounded society in geographical or social space. Because there is no system, no totality, there cannot be "sub-systems," "dimensions," or "levels" of such a totality. Because there is no whole, social relations cannot be reduced "ultimately," "in the last instance," to some systemic property of it—like the "mode of material production," or the "cultural" or "normative system," or the "form of military organization." . . . Because there is no social system, there is no "evolutionary" process within it. . . . There is no one master concept or basic unit of "society." . . . Conceiving of societies as multiple overlapping and intersecting power networks gives us the best available entry to the issue of what is ultimately "primary" or "determining" in societies. . . . [There are] four sources of social power: ideological, economic, military, and political relationships.

It should be pointed out that Mann (1986) treats ideological power as a constitutive element of cultural orientations.[6] Ideological power can offer a *transcendental* vision of authority that unites human beings on the basis of their common qualities. It can also provide for *immanence*, "the strengthen-ing of the internal morale of . . . [a] social group by giving it a sense of ultimate significance and meaning in the cosmos, by reinforcing its norma-tive solidarity, and by giving it common ritual and aesthetic practices" (Mann 1986, p. 519). Clearly, Mann's view of ideological power is akin to what might be called more accurately cultural-ideological power relationships.[7]

This scheme is of special importance because it highlights a traditionally underestimated historical dimension of social life, namely the importance of violence as a means of obtaining power and perpetuating social inequality.[8] Power networks constitute a "middle range" analytical frame because they can be identified through historical research, and measurements can be utilized to determine their shape and reach. Disagreement concerning their specific aspects can be resolved via empirical referents. The macrosociological constructs of "world-system" and "civilization" should be related to these power networks as a means of providing a grounding of theoretical constructs in concepts that can be operationalized.

Let us address first the issue of causal connections among the power networks themselves, and the ways in which the notion of civilization can be related to them. Then, we will address the connections between our "middle range" framework and the concept of the "world-system."

Mann's conceptualization is far from novel. Sociological work that has grown out of different metatheoretical traditions has consistently employed this analytical distinction. It is less the claim of an analytical differentiation that is controversial and more the problems associated with locating causal connections among power networks. Most social theorists and sociologists have not inquired systematically into the impact that changes in one or more of these networks can have on the others. This issue tends to be theorized under the rubric of "materialism" versus "idealism." Both angles in this spectrum transform the aforementioned empirical problem into a "metaphysical" one. Hence, Marx's postulate of historical materialism dictates that changes in the economic network condition changes in the other networks. A number of classical and contemporary social theorists (Weber, Simmel, Durkheim, Parsons) have attempted to revise Marxist materialism by constructing a series of arguments that reverse the linear connection between material and ideal factors. Contemporary sociological discourse has evolved out of this ideological as well as metatheoretical dialogue with the "ghost of Marx." Suffice it to say that ideological commitment to the two polar viewpoints of idealism and materialism is one of the major difficulties in constructing a single paradigm for sociology.[9]

Norbert Elias (1978b, 1982) was one of the few sociologists to have explicitly attempted to develop an approach aiming at the interrogation of this issue at the empirical level. Elias has suggested that under conditions of chronic interstate conflict in medieval and early modern Europe, particular social changes occurred that transformed both institutions and agents within the western European region. The creation of court societies involved the suppression of emotion and the development of self-restraint and internalization of one's emotions. This internalization constituted a practical imperative required for success in the court societies of western Europe. Affective control at the micro level was coupled with processes of pacification within a particular state territory. The formation of modern European states entailed the suppression of the use of violence by agents not authorized by the central government. The institutionalization of "order" entailed societal transformation both at the micro and macro levels. The consequence of these long-term changes was the formation of a modern self, an agent that has internalized affective controls over his or her public persona. Notions of rationality and interest have emerged in the *longue durée* of this sociohistorical process.[10]

The novel character of this approach rests on the connections established between changes in the economic network (European feudalism), political network (interstate conflict), military network (internal pacification via court societies), and changes in the cultural-ideological network (personality development and sociogenetic processes involving detachment from "passions" and the promotion of interest and rationality). The theory of the civilizing process, whatever its weaknesses, explicitly suggests that "civilization" is indeed a process involving the growing detachment of an agent from his or her own passions and the development of perspectivism as a means of relating to oneself and to others.

In contrast to other viewpoints, Elias's theory avoids the reification that Wallerstein (1994, pp. 78–80) finds so characteristic of the civilizationist perspective. "Civilization" refers to a number of features generated under particular sociohistorical processes in a specific territory within a given *longue durée*. The extension of Elias's figurational perspective outside Europe represents, of course, the major challenge faced by figurational sociologists. Although it is by no means certain that identical outcomes will be present everywhere, the logical connections established between external power relations and internal emotional and affective control constitute a novel contribution to the topic.

It is not accidental that Elias (1978b) introduces the topic of civilization via a lengthy discussion of the origins of the term. In the course of the 18th century, the word was employed in the singular to denote western European achievements, and in so doing, as Elias (1978b, p. 3) notes, it expressed the "self-consciousness of the West." As Elias's discussion illustrates, the German concept of *Kultur* and the French and English concepts of civilization owe much to the particular local and international conditions that shaped the English, French, and German national contexts. Hence, the meaning of the term has come to reflect not only the self-awareness of the western European elites as a whole (i.e., the "West"), but it also obtained particular significance in light of specific national contexts.

From 1819 the word civilization was apparently employed in the plural to refer to characteristics common to the collective life of a period or of a group (Braudel 1994). Wallerstein (1991b, p. 235) points out that a civilization "refers to a contemporary claim about the past in terms of its use in the present to justify heritage, separateness, rights." In other words, civilizations can only exist as ideological constructs, entities that serve rhetorical purposes and legitimation projects for specific groups. Wallerstein correctly points to the ideological function of the word in the context of Eurocentric systems of thought, but he concludes from this that the concept itself exists only as an ideological weapon (cf. Robertson 1992).

Braudel in *A History of Civilizations* (1994) takes a different approach. He defines civilizations in an interdisciplinary manner in terms of geography, cultural (i.e., linguistic and religious) zones, urban cultures and the societies and economies that sustain them, and the ways of thought or mentalities that grow in the context created by all the aforementioned variables. For Braudel, the shifting dust of historical time and space is not a reason to conclude, as Wallerstein does, that little practical value exists in speaking of culture or civilization. On the contrary, he relates civilization to his favorite concept of *longue durée*. In this way,

> civilizations can be seen as distinct from the accidents and vicissitudes that mark their development: they reveal their longevity, their permanent features, their structures. . . . A civilization, then is neither a given economy nor a given society, but something which can persist through a series of economies or societies, barely susceptible to gradual change. A civilization can be approached, therefore, only in the long term, taking hold of a constantly unwinding thread—something that a group of people have conserved and passed on as their most precious heritage from generation to generation, throughout and despite the storms and tumults of history. . . . This long-term history . . . has both its advantages and drawbacks. Its advantages are that it forces one to think, to explain matters in unaccustomed terms, and to use historical explanation as a key to one's time. Its drawbacks or dangers are that it can lapse into the facile generalizations of a philosophy of history more imaginary than researched or proved (Braudel 1994, p. 35).

Braudel proceeds to outline his own particular contenders worthy of being called "civilizations" as those social formations where human effort over time and space was able to produce a distinct "way of life," an outcome determined not only by geography and economy but also by the attitudes, mentalities, and religious or metaphysical beliefs of the people involved in this process. If the concept of civilization is to be a viable one (and agreement on this issue is by no means forthcoming), its operationalizations by Braudel and Elias provide useful guidelines toward an approach that does not conceive them as metaphysical entities but as historical formations that constitute meaningful objects of inquiry.

We shall return to the notion of "civilization" as a process after discussing the differences among the world-system theorists within our "middle range" analytical frame of reference.

## Power Networks, The World-System, and Globalization

Wallerstein (1974) has defined the modern world-system as a world-economy (unified economic network) in conjunction with a fragmented political network (international system of states). In this conceptualization, the military network is subordinated to the political and thus does not constitute an autonomous factor. It should be emphasized, however, that military considerations should not be treated in such a facile manner, since coercion and chronic interstate conflict have had an important impact in the long-term making of the European system (Tilly 1992). In this regard, Weber's definition of the modern state as an organization enjoying a monopoly over the legitimate use of violence within a given territory should not be uncritically projected into the past. This monopoly was established in western European societies only after a long period of time and only at the cost of transforming the relationships between the rulers and the ruled. On the micro level, as Foucault (1978) has observed, the superimposition of the king's power onto the body of the criminal was substituted for control over the internal states of the agent.

With respect to the cultural-ideological network, Wallerstein (1974, 1990) has consistently followed the Marxist logic of "base" versus "superstructure." The problems associated with this conceptualization of social relationships have been repeatedly pointed out in the literature and there is no need to restate them here.[11] As our introductory remarks suggest, it is in the context of his consideration of cultural-ideological relationships that Wallerstein has become vulnerable to the pre-1500s school. In the absence of a nonreductionist account of the changes in the cultural-ideological network, Wallerstein cannot convincingly illustrate the novel character of the modern world-system.

In favor of his position is the notion that the post-1500 world is an increasingly global network; however, this assertion is bound to remain a hollow phrase unless a multidimensional approach to this problem is adopted.[12] In other words, the notion of "globality" has to be clarified in order to make explicit the ways in which the "modern world-system" is different from other "world-systems." In question is the fundamental issue that has helped define sociology as a discipline, namely the sociocultural transformations typically subsumed under the rubric of "modernity."

Wallerstein has been instrumental in making the transition from intrasocietal ("society"-centered) explanations to intersocietal (global) explanations. But the method of "political economy" and the utilization of Marxism as a guiding principle has prevented the development of a multidimensional view of this subject matter. Recently, Wallerstein (1991a) has called into question the existence of academic boundaries, thus in fact opening up space for the construction of a multidimensional world-system analysis that is not limited to the political economy approach.[13]

We believe that the concept of globalization can serve this purpose. Our theorization of the concept does not entail a surrender to a number of interpretations of the term. Therefore, before proceeding any further, we are compelled to dispense with a number of misunderstandings regarding its connotations.

Contrary to what is conventionally assumed, the process of globalization is not a recent one. At least in our view, it is *not* a phase of capitalist development (Lash and Urry 1994) that results from the overexpansion of capitalism in the post-World War II period and the proliferation of mass media technology that transforms the modern world system into a "global village." Global economic integration does not by any means entail the convergence of particular types of capitalism and the cultural homogenization implied in such a convergence. On the contrary, culture becomes one of the important facets to be addressed by transnational business.[14] From our viewpoint, globalization is akin to (and perhaps should be referred to more accurately as) *glocalization*, that is, the simultaneous adaptation of cultural items into different locales via the utilization of local practices and traditions.[15] Glocalization represents a direct acknowledgment by the transnational corporate actors of the necessity to cater to local conditions, transforming commercial items so that they become marketable in different regions and cultures. Instead of monolithic standardization, then, local heterogeneity becomes the normative standard.

Consequently, globalization is *not* a trend toward the homogenization of cultural life under the proliferation of capitalist consumer goods and does not necessarily entail the relativization of the nation-state as a meaningful agent in global politics.[16] Globalization does *not* postulate cultural homogeneity, as is often assumed. Rather, in our view, cultural homogeneity *and* heterogeneity are consequences of the globalizing process. Although cultural diffusion can transform a locale, the recurrent "invention of traditions" makes it possible to preserve, create, or recreate cultural heterogeneity at the local level.

Instrumental in the recurrent reconstruction of particularistic formations (national cultures or subcultures) according to increasingly global referents is the process of cross-societal emulation (Westney 1987). Cross-societal emulation involves the purposeful observation and incorporation of elements of societal and cultural organization from other cultures and societies into a particular culture. Cohen (1987) has used the term "selective receptiveness" to refer to the process of incorporation of external cultural patterns into a particular culture, while Robertson (1995a) has employed the term "selective incorporation" to refer to the same process.

Nationalism and modernization are two main sites where this strategic emulation can most readily be observed. Bendix (1978, p. 292) uses the term *reference society* to refer to cases where "intellectual leaders and an educated public react to the values and institutions of another country with ideas and actions that pertain to their own country." Processes of modernization involve the use of reference societies by the elites of "underdeveloped" states; simply put, the experience of England has been used by Japan and Germany as a guide with respect to the *problematique* of modernization. The intensification of mass communication and cross-cultural interaction has greatly accelerated this process during the late 20th century. But this process remains a *historical* one, and it is misleading to restrict the study of cross-communicative interaction to the era of electronic mass communication.

Greenfeld's (1992) study of the development of nationalism in England, Germany, Russia, France, and the United States indicates that emulation and selective incorporation are important considerations for the articulation of local national identities. Greenfeld suggests that the English model of civic nationalism was used as a cultural model by German and Russian elites. Although these elites adopted the notion of national identity, they rejected the English emphasis on the civic component of nationalism, adopting instead an ethnic-based nationalism as their own particular response to modernity. Despite her use of English nationalism as a global normative standard, Greenfeld successfully illustrates the importance of cross-societal emulation for the formation of local identities. Suffice it to say that the preservation of local difference, despite an intense cross-societal and cross-cultural interaction, is not a phenomenon distinctively associated with modernity.

In other words, it is not only nation-states *successfully* undergoing modernization that emulate developments occurring in other reference societies. The development of secularism in the Ottoman Empire reads, to a considerable extent, as a failed attempt to revitalize that particular "society" by incorporating Western notions of liberty, equality, and parliamentarianism.[17] The emergence of nationalism among Ottoman Christians in the late 18th century was directly linked to the use of the French Revolution as a reference point for societal development in southeastern Europe. Rigas Phereos, admittedly the first national revolutionary theorist among Ottoman Christians, explicitly invoked in 1797 the French Revolution as the model according to which the Ottoman Empire was to be reorganized. Following the 1821 Greek revolution, in the correspondence between Thomas Jefferson and the Greek nationalist leader Adamantios Korais the American statesman offered an overview of the constitutional and organizational structure of the United States aimed explicitly at providing a model for the political organization of the Christian rebels (Lazou 1983, Vol. 1).

Of course, southeastern Europe failed to become a federation; instead, the process of Balkanization fragmented that space into a series of small states. Therefore, the processes of cross-societal emulation (or selective incorporation) are by no means a universal recipe for success. The use of global or other societal recipes for local action does not need to lead to a "success." On the contrary, the outcome depends upon the societal models that are selected, the skill in "copying" different practices from different societies, and so on.

These processes of cross-societal emulation and incorporation can be traced further back in time. We need only recall Braudel's ([1949] 1972–73) kaleidoscopic view of the Mediterranean to be reminded that ethnic groups, customs, lifestyles, and peoples can mix with each other and remain adamantly resistant to processes of acculturation and homogenization. Similarly, we would like to point out that globalization is not, nor should it be conceived as, identical with the development or the "globalization" of the modern world-system. Such a perspective would postulate the growth of modernity in the "West" as primarily a matter of internal processes. Modernity then expands to the rest of the world via the processes of colonization, cultural diffusion, and "cultural imperialism."[18] This enterprise is indeed a reflection of Eurocentric views of modernity that postulate a cultural entity (the "West") as an essentially closed system that allows for the examination of its internal development independently of its contacts with other civilizations and cultures across Eurasia. Civilizationists have always been sensitive to this "labeling" problem and its implications. During the post-World War II period, the issue of cross-cultural contacts has gradually become a central concern both for world historians like Stavrianos, McNeill, and Braudel, and for scholars involved in the comparative study of civilizations.[19]

A consequence of this reorientation of scholarly attention to intercivilizational encounters or cross-cultural contacts is to raise the issue of a unified world-system in the manner posed by Frank and Gills (1993). But it does not follow that a "globology" (Bergesen 1980) must collapse all units into one solely because of the existence of cross-cultural connectedness. The present state of research regarding the extent and strength of commercial ties among Eurasian peoples has yet to provide conclusive evidence supporting the assumption that these ties were stronger than regional ties. But even if this were to be the case, the system does not include the rest of the globe outside the major Eurasian land mass that stretches from northern Europe to East Asia. In other words, a commercial oikumene or a Eurasian political-military network (even if its strength is sufficient to serve as an independent variable) are not identical with a world-economy or the international system of states that has developed over the course of the last 400 years.

# World-Systems and Civilizations:
## A Global View

In the broad definition of the term, then, globalization constitutes a process of mutual interaction among different power networks over a long period of time. Globalization theory concerns itself with the multidimensional interrogation of these intercivilizational "encounters" or interactions. Since both the world-system theory of Wallerstein and the world system theory of Frank and Gills are characterized by the political economy approach, globalization theory represents an attempt toward a more holistic understanding of the phenomena in question by incorporating cultural-ideological factors as autonomous or relatively autonomous forces in the making of the modern "global" system.

In particular, since 1500, but perhaps even before that date, we can discern the following changes among the power networks present in the globe: within the economic network the gradual consolidation of one global world-economy; within the political network the gradual formation of an international system of states; and within the military network the gradual internal pacification within states and a concomitant centralization of the legitimate use of the means of violence. These processes eventually led to the subordination of the military to political control, a development that has been relatively recent by world history standards. Finally, within the cultural-ideological field of relations, there has been a continuous and inflationary contact among different networks.

Before we proceed to a more detailed discussion of the cultural-ideological field, let us locate the Wallerstein-Frank debate in the context of globalization. Presently, we still do not have conclusive evidence that would allow us to date the creation of a common political and military network or of a world-economy. How important was the prestige goods trade in terms of its impact on people's lives? Does the existence of a commercial network throughout Eurasia justify the inclusion of the territory in a single system? These are questions that remain unanswered.

Abu-Lughod's (1989) study seems to indicate, however, that relatively concrete zones of economic activity did exist. But should these zones be considered parts of the same unit or as units in contact with each other? There is no conclusive answer as yet. It could be the case that a Eurasian oikumene existed in the pre-1500 world (Wolf 1982) but no "world-system" as such. Collins (1990a) has interpreted the evolution of different social systems from kinship to agrarian-coercive societies (including feudalism and slavery) as determined by the market dynamics of each particular system. For Collins, capitalism operates at the macro level; its "takeoff" may be the consequence of an increase in the volume of intraregional trade that accelerated the market dynamics of superordinate long-distance trade into the dominant force. Collins follows to a considerable extent the rationale proposed by Frank and Gills, but his interpretation allows for the existence of different markets in space and time. Even if particular markets were united through a network of long-distance trade over the Eurasian oikumene, this does not make them identical, nor does it account for their individual features.

Moreover, a multidimensional approach to the comparative study of historical social systems must take into account the extent and shape of cultural-ideological networks. Were these networks identical with the local world-economies? What was their relationship to political and military networks? From a multidimensional view, these are important issues since they provide the raw material for the theorization of connections among power networks.

Let us now turn to the issue of the transformation of cultural-ideological networks within the modern global world-system. A persistent feature of globalization is the continuous and increasing contact among these different networks. The most visible effects of these contacts can be located in the Ottoman Empire, India, Japan, or in the so-called "Third World" during the 20th century where, under conditions of increased cultural contact, local societies were radically transformed and new nations emerged out of the collapse or transformation of older world-empires. Up to the present, these networks remain fragmented. The "logic of the capitalist system" has not been absorbed uniformly across the globe.

This process of contact, change, and compression is accompanied by the simultaneous proliferation of homogeneity and heterogeneity. Within the modern world-system, heterogeneity is a necessary ingredient of globalization (Robertson 1994, 1995b). The unification of the globe into one economic network does not necessitate the unification of the cultural-ideological network. To the extent that the term global culture can be meaningfully applied to a commonality of cultural items, it exists only on the level of consumer goods and shared formal elements (flags, national anthems, and other symbolic items). The meaning of the specific cultural items is redefined and interpreted according to the specific locality. Conflicts among these cultural networks may well show themselves to be the most important conflicts of the next century.

To a considerable extent, within the Western symbolic universe "culture" has served as a particular way of classifying the Other as an inferior version of the "civilized" Westerner or, in the case of Orientalism, as a member of a social community condemned to inferiority by its very nature (Said 1978; McGrane 1989; Friedman 1994). But these Eurocentric views are by no means the exclusive domain of the "Westerners." The 19th-century Russian Panslavist ideology rested on the premise of a civilizational divide between

Germano-Roman Christendom and Graeco-Slavic Orthodoxy. One of Panslavism's most ardent proponents, Michael Pogodin, declared at the beginning of the Crimean War (1853–56) that "one must understand that the West is West, and East is East," and another prominent author and organizer, Ivan Aksakov, wrote that East and West are "not geographic terms but qualitative terms which denote a difference in cultural principles which have become active forces in the history of mankind" (cited in Petrovich 1956, p. 71). Similar claims are made in the late 20th century by Islamic fundamentalists. Additionally, in the aftermath of the collapse of the Soviet Union, the debate between Slavophiles and Westernizers is being revitalized within the Russian federation. Regardless as to whether the domain of culture is viewed as an expression of underlying economic struggles (Wallerstein 1990), or whether cultural factors are viewed independently of economic relationships (Huntington 1993), theorists of the Left and the Right increasingly converge on culture as one of the major fields of conflict for the next century.

This convergence has its roots in the growing significance of culture in world history. For peasant societies where illiteracy was the rule, access to the "world of the pen" was limited. The technological changes and, more importantly, the intellectual mobilization of the post-1800 period has allowed large masses of people to enter the field of politics and become players in the international arena (Bendix 1978). In this turn from the divine rule of kings to popular participation, culture has been transformed from a concept that indicated the "high culture" of court societies and privileged elites to the "popular culture" of the late 20th century.

Instrumental in this transformation were both Enlightenment ideology and ethnic or "folk" nationalism. Modernization (in the sense of projects attempting to advance "backward" or "premodern" societies) and nationalism provided two major avenues through which peasant culture was gradually transformed into modern national culture. Consequently, control over cultural fields, an important aspect of ideological power, became a matter of great importance for all agents across the globe. Within cultural fields, the inclusion of more and more people into "civil society" has raised the issue of boundary preservation for elites and status groups. In Western democracies, symbolic distinction has become an important part of boundary preservation (Bourdieu 1984).

Under conditions of increased cross-cultural contact, symbolic distinction also raises all cultural features, such as religion, language, and ethnicity, into actual or potential realms of inter- and intrasocietal conflict. In this regard, cultural politics operate at two different levels of cultural organization: the national network and the international or global network. National networks are, of course, increasingly located and influenced—through processes of emulation and selective incorporation—by the *global* political culture (cf. Robertson 1995a). To the extent that the notion of "civilization" is connected with changes and outcomes observed primarily within international cultural-ideological networks, we would suggest that the contemporary international cultural-ideological power networks *are* civilizations. We would like to bolster this thesis by way of the following arguments.

First, the term civilization has been historically interpreted to denote cultural configurations as opposed to purely politico-economic units. Consequently, changing the meaning of the term implies abandoning the distinctive feature of this line of inquiry, namely the concern with the "ideal" or ideological aspects of a particular social configuration. In light of the recent revitalization of the sociology of culture and the centrality of culture in international politics, such a tendency restricts avenues of inquiry.

Second, throughout world-history tributary systems have been extremely common. Analytically speaking, these systems do not necessitate the overlapping of political and economic control with a particular cultural-ideological network. Insofar as the tribute is paid, most often local government is allowed to go about its business. Geopolitical considerations make it difficult to exercise close supervision of locales, and hence social life is less restrained than in the world of nation-states. If "civilizations" are defined in terms of political and military relationships alone, the possibility of addressing issues of interconnectedness among politico-economic, military, and cultural-ideological relationships is lost. This may not appear to be too great a loss to those who are not interested in studying the cultural-ideological dimension, but humanists and cultural social scientists around the world will agree with us, we believe, in advocating the significance of this distinction.

Third, the analytical differentiation proposed in this discussion allows for the interrogation of connections among power networks. Since changes in the political, economic, and military networks influence the shape of the cultural-ideological network, it would be erroneous to subsume into one definition the dependent and independent variables. Even worse, such a conceptual conflation turns issues of culture and agency into objects of purely theoretical debate and metaphysical speculation instead of allowing them to be studied as empirical questions.

Last, if we refer to cultural-ideological networks within the modern world-system as "civilizations," civilizational analysis ceases to be dominated by diachronic (i.e., cyclical or evolutionary) models. Instead, it is possible to develop theoretical models that inquire into the comparative study of civilizations in terms of their synchronic interaction. In essence, our suggestions aim to transform the study of cross-cultural connections among networks in the manner proposed by world-system theorists. Instead of studying these networks in isolation, the central issue becomes one of connections and relationships between cultural-ideological networks.

# Conclusion

In this discussion, we have addressed some central aspects of the place of culture and agency in the debate between world-system theory and civilizational analysis. Our inquiry has led us to conclude that issues of culture are greatly involved in the disagreements among different theorists. We have suggested that in the Wallerstein-Frank controversy, the cultural orientations of agents have been turned into an object of purely theoretical dispute between the two camps. Our recommendation has been that, instead of turning an empirical issue into a theoretical one, the proper solution is to interrogate the topic of the cultural orientation of agents on an empirical level. In this light, Wilkinson's advocacy of a Central Civilization is closely connected with attempts to exclude issues of culture from the civilizationists' domain of inquiry.

We have suggested that a more fruitful perspective with regard to this debate is to adopt what we have loosely called a "middle range" analytical framework and to ground the large-scale metatheoretical constructs of "civilization" and "world-system" in terms of variables that can be directly operationalized. Our solution has been to follow Mann's (1986) conceptualization of societies as overlapping power networks. From within this middle range framework, we suggested that a "world-system" is properly conceptualized as the conjunction of a unified economic network with a fragmented political network. Whether this definition leads to considering Eurasia as one "world-system," or whether prior to 1500 there was more than one "world-system" present in this territory, is a matter of empirical inquiry. Inquiry has yet to provide conclusive evidence.

We have pointed out, however, that two other networks are of great significance for the *longue durée*. The military network, although largely subordinate to the political and economic networks in the modern era, cannot be treated as such in the course of world history. Additionally, the role and significance of the cultural-ideological network should be sufficiently illuminated. This cultural turn is necessary if we are to decisively establish the novel character of the modern world. Wallerstein, despite his commitment to the postulate of historical discontinuity between the modern world-system and precapitalist world-systems, has not developed an approach that incorporates culture and agency as autonomous factors in the making of the modern world. It is for this reason, we suggest, that Wallerstein cannot offer a satisfactory rebuttal to the pre-1500 camp.

The concept of globalization can offer a more holistic approach to the study of intercivilizational encounters than the political economy approach of Wallerstein. Globalization involves the growing contacts among different power networks and their transformations as a result of these contacts. Globalization, in our view, does not entail cultural homogenization; on the contrary, cross-societal emulation offers the possibility of local elites selectively incorporating different cultural elements from other societies and constructing, through a combination of local cultural forms and imported elements, new forms of identity in terms of an increasingly globalized *expectation* of identity. The formation of national identities is exemplary of this process.

The growing contacts among different power networks over the last 500 years or more have led to the consolidation of a unified economic network and the creation of a fragmented political network. Military matters have increasingly come under the control of the political network while cultural-ideological networks, although in close and accelerating contact with each other, have not been unified. In this context, we have suggested that there are two types of cultural-ideological networks, the national and the international or civilizational. Within the national networks processes of emulation and selective incorporation are responsible for the constant revitalization of ethnic, religious, and national identities. These processes operate largely in reference to the broader global political culture, which serves as the global depository of available referents for a particular locale.

On the international level, we believe that the broader cultural-ideological networks present in the globe today ought to be referred to as civilizations. We believe that such a designation preserves the historical connotation of the term, but also allows for the explicit interrogation of the cultural dimension by humanists and social scientists. Additionally, we believe that this dimension can be explored by applying the nonevolutionary approach of the world-system theorists, and hence can focus the attention of cultural theorists on issues of cross-cultural interaction. Cultural-ideological networks ought to be investigated in concrete historical and comparative terms, and not according to evolutionary, cyclical, or metaphysical models.

Finally, the theorization of historical processes in terms of contact among different power networks allows for the examination of the key issue of the causal connections among power networks. In this regard, the legacy of the sociology of Norbert Elias can be used for the development of an approach that systematically attempts to discern the impact that changes in one or more power networks have on the others. The goal of such an inquiry is none other than to transform the central issue of the relationship between material and nonmaterial factors from a theoretical one into an empirical one.

NOTES

Victor Roudometof presented an earlier version of this paper at the annual meetings of the North Central Sociological Association, Pittsburgh, April 1995.

1.   The criterion of the "mode of production" implicitly raises the issue of cultural factors as constitutive of modern capitalism. Instead of an economistic interpretation of the term, it is possible to conceive it as signifying, not only "economic" or strictly material factors, but all factors contributing to the creation of a particular "culture" (in the anthropological sense of the word). As Wolf (1982, p. 386) suggests, "to speak of a mode of production . . . draws attention to the ways in which human beings confront their world in order to modify it in their favor, and focuses on the dynamic consequences of that confrontation." From such a viewpoint, agency becomes part of the interpretation and the question of agents' orientations to action becomes a relevant one.

2.   The 16th-century price revolution, which was the outcome of the influx of American bullion into the European system, undermined the fiscal basis of the Ottoman Empire and may be considered as one of the major factors that led to its decline. Between 1489 and 1616 the price of foodstuffs increased by 334.4 percent while the value of currency decreased by 140 percent (Karpat 1972; for a detailed analysis, see Barkan 1975).

3.   Sanderson (1994 [chapter 11, this volume]) has attempted to find a middle ground between the two approaches by suggesting that up to 1500 there was a historical process of expanding world commercialization. This process provided an important quantitative change over time, and thus facilitated the emergence of capitalism. But it did not represent a qualitative change and thus Wallerstein correctly assumes that the "long 16th century" marks the emergence of a new, qualitatively distinct system.

4.   From Bourdieu's (1986) classification of the forms of capital into cultural, social, economic, and symbolic, to Parsons's (1951) specification of the AGIL model, the themes of this fundamental analytical differentiation provide a major metatheoretical classification. Wallerstein (1991a) has questioned the substantive value of these differentiations insofar as they reflect the distinction between the nomothetic and idiographic approaches to the study of history and social life. However, this differentiation is an analytical one; it is not assumed that these spheres of activity have a concrete referent in social life.

5.   Collins (1990b) has pointed to the utility of this conceptualization and its origins not only in the theoretical tradition of sociology but also in the field of social research. Research into social networks began as a method without a theory, and its marriage to the key sociological concept of power can offer new avenues of activity. The grandfather of this approach, although not an influential one in the American context, is none other than Norbert Elias. In *What is Sociology?* (1978a), Elias elaborated his concept of figuration in a manner that foretold later developments in the coupling of network research with sociological theory.

6.   Frank and Gills (1993) properly have reservations regarding Mann's rejection of all totality systems since this involves the rejection of their own 5,000-year world system. They also have reservations regarding the analysis of the historical record in

terms of power only. Although this may be a legitimate reservation, it pertains—at least according to our view—to the sociohistorical work undertaken by Mann and not to his theoretical scheme. Mann's *tour de force* of world history is a brilliant recasting of many Weberian theses regarding the "rise of the West," and it can be legitimately criticized for insufficient attention to the non-"Western" social formations. But these issues do not necessarily pertain to his proposed analytical scheme.

7. Mann (1986) subscribes to the view that culture is one of the causal factors in social life. This view is but one of the proposed ways of relating culture to structure (cf. Morawska and Spohn 1994). However, we find this perspective useful because the status of culture has been influenced by the processes of modernization and as a result it could be argued that culture plays a more important role in modern as opposed to premodern societies. Our solution is to adopt for our purposes a rather conservative orientation to the power of culture in the *longue durée* of world history.

8. Elias (1987) has suggested that sociological inquiry has not paid sufficient attention to specialists in violence and their central role in world history. Giddens (1985) and Mann (1986) have been instrumental in bringing these issues to the attention of mainstream sociology. On a different level, Foucault's (1978) study of the transformation of the penal system under the impact of modernity has also served to highlight the significance and unique character of the "taming of violence" in contemporary societies.

9. Alexander's (1981–84) quest to reunify sociological theory is almost solely confined to the analytical level. The insufficient integration of world-historical sociology into his analytical scheme is an important obstacle in bridging the gap between sociological theory and world-historical sociology (and reflects the fragmentation of the American Sociological Association into different sections that do not necessarily coordinate with each other).

10. See Mennell (1992) for the best overview of Elias's life and legacy available in print. For an excellent discussion of the Elias theory and its significance for the development of the civilizational frame of reference, see Mandalios (1994, pp. 72–152). On the rise of utilitarianism and rationality in connection with Elias's *problematique*, see Dumont (1977, 1983, 1994) and Hirschman (1977). The *ad hoc* sessions of the 1994 World Congress of Sociology represented the first attempt by figurational sociologists to coordinate and advance Elias's research program.

11. See the critiques by Skocpol (1977), Zolberg (1981), Chirot and Hall (1982), and Robertson and Lechner (1985). Probably the most important critique from within the neo-Marxist camp is the one by Brenner (1977, 1989).

12. See Alexander (1981–84) for the classic statement of multidimensionality. The term is not always consistently employed by Alexander. In our present discussion, multidimensionality refers to the attempt to incorporate partial explanations that privilege particular facets of human behavior into a general inclusive scheme that moves beyond the labels of "conflict theory" and "functionalism" (or other relevant -isms).

13. Wallerstein's (1991a) call for a unified historical social science that would replace interdisciplinary distinctions stands in an uneasy relationship with his advocacy of his particular brand of historical social science. Removing disciplinary boundaries is an issue of politics and struggles within the academy. Removing

epistemological presuppositions can be helpful in constructing a unified historical social science. However, agreement with Wallerstein's critique of the model of the division of labor within the social sciences does not imply agreement with his own particular evaluation of social life.

14.   Researchers in international management have recognized the significance of culture for transnational enterprises. In *Understanding Global Cultures* (1994), Martin Gannon uses the concept of a cultural metaphor—an analytical strategy borrowed from literary studies—in order to communicate the different sensitivities of agents in 17 different national cultures. Interestingly enough, the book is authored by an international management professor and not by a literary writer or even an anthropologist.

15.   According to the *Oxford Dictionary of New Words* (1991, p. 134), the term *glocalization* derives from the Japanese notion of *dochakuka*, originally the agricultural principle of adapting farming techniques to local conditions. According to the *Dictionary*, the term became "one of the main marketing buzzwords of the beginning of the nineties." At the level of culture, this notion of glocalization entails the recognition that local and national cultures are constructed through reference to global discursive formations (for a discussion, see Robertson 1995b).

16.   There is no standardized use of the term in sociological discourse. At the 1990 and 1994 World Congresses of Sociology, a number of presentations made reference to globalization as a key process but no clear, let alone shared, definition is currently available. For different perspectives on this topic, see Giddens (1990), Robertson (1992), Roudometof (1994), Friedman (1994), Lash and Urry (1994), and a special issue of *Theory, Culture, and Society* (1990).

17.   On the development of secularism in the Ottoman Empire and the role of Western liberalism in Ottoman projects of modernization, see Berkes (1964), Lewis (1961), and Ramsaur (1970). On Rigas Phereos, see Kitromilides (1990), Vranousis (1957), and Botzaris (1962).

18.   Giddens's (1985, 1990) recent interpretation of modernity suffers from this methodological weakness. For critiques of this point of view, see Robertson (1992) and Roudometof (1994). Similarly, Wallerstein's system can be considered a Eurocentric one since it takes Europe to be a dominant force. Gills and Frank have challenged Wallerstein's thesis on factual grounds alone. But if Wallerstein's thesis is a vulnerable one it is so because it extends Eurocentric analytical categories and systems of thought to non-European peoples. Gills and Frank, however, remain silent on this issue since to raise this problem is to challenge directly the applicability of Marxism for non-Western territories.

19.   On the emergence of world-historical discourse among historians, see the overview by Allardyce (1990) and in particular the works of Stavrianos (1970), Hodgson (1993), Wallerstein (1974), and Braudel (1981–84). Among the civilizationists, Benajmin Nelson has raised the issue of intercivilizational encounters into a central topic (for assessments of Nelson's theoretical orientation, see Holzner [1982, pp. 15–30] and, in general, Walter, Kavolis, Leites, and Nelson [1985]).

*References*

Abu-Lughod, Janet. 1989. *Before European Hegemony: The World System AD 1250–1350*. New York: Oxford University Press.

Alexander, Jeffrey. 1981–84. *Theoretical Logic in Sociology*. 4 vols. Berkeley: University of California Press.

———. 1988. *Twenty Lectures: Sociological Theory Since World War II*. New York: Columbia University Press.

Allardyce, Gilbert. 1990. "Toward World History: American Historians and the Coming of the World History Course." *Journal of World History* 1:23–76.

Amin, Samir. 1993. "The Ancient World-Systems versus the Modern Capitalist World-System." In *The World System: Five Hundred Years or Five Thousand?*, edited by Andre Gunder Frank and Barry K. Gills. London: Routledge.

Barkan, Omer Lutfi. 1975. "The Price Revolution of the Sixteenth Century: A Turning Point in the Economic History of the Near East." *International Journal of Middle Eastern Studies* 6:3–28.

Bendix, Reinhard. 1978. *Kings or People?* Berkeley: University of California Press.

Bergesen, Albert. 1980. "From Utilitarianism to Globology: The Shift from the Individual to the World as the Primordial Unit of Analysis." In *Studies of the Modern World System*, edited by Albert Bergesen. New York: Academic Press.

Berkes, Niyazi. 1964. *The Development of Secularism in Turkey*. Montreal: McGill University Press.

Botzaris, Notis. 1962. *Visions Balkaniques dans la Préparation de la Revolution Greque (1789–1821)*. Geneva: E. Droz.

Bourdieu, Pierre. 1984. *Distinction*. Cambridge, MA: Harvard University Press.

———. 1986. "The Forms of Capital." In *Handbook of Theory and Research for the Sociology of Education*, edited by John G. Richardson. Westport, CT: Greenwood Press.

Braudel, Fernand. (1949) 1972–73. *The Mediterranean and the Mediterranean World in the Age of Philip II*. 2 vols. Trans. Sian Reynolds. New York: Harper & Row.

———. 1981–84. *Capitalism and Civilization 15th–18th Centuries*. 3 vols. New York: Harper & Row.

———. 1994. *A History of Civilizations*. New York: Allen Lane (The Penguin Press).

Brenner, Robert. 1977. "The Origins of Capitalist Development: A Critique of Neo-Smithian Marxism." *New Left Review* 104:25–92.

———. 1989. "Economic Backwardness in Eastern Europe in Light of Developments in the West." In *The Origins of Economic Backwardness in Eastern Europe: Economics and Politics from the Middle Ages Until the Early Twentieth Century*, edited by Daniel Chirot. Berkeley: University of California Press.

Burris, V. 1987. "The Neo-Marxist Synthesis of Marx and Weber on Class." In *The Marx-Weber Debate*, edited by Norbert Wiley. Beverly Hills, CA: Sage.

Chase-Dunn, Christopher. 1989. *Global Formation: Structures of the World-Economy*. Oxford: Basil Blackwell.

———. 1992. "The Comparative Study of World-Systems." *Review* 15:313–33.

Chase-Dunn, Christopher, and Thomas D. Hall. 1991a. "Conceptualizing Core/Periphery Hierarchies for Comparative Study." In *Core/Periphery Relations in*

*Precapitalist Worlds*, edited by Christopher Chase-Dunn and Thomas D. Hall. Boulder, CO: Westview Press.

———, eds. 1991b. *Core/Periphery Relations in Precapitalist Worlds*. Boulder, CO: Westview Press.

Chirot, Daniel, and Thomas D. Hall. 1982. "World-System Theory." *Annual Review of Sociology* 8:81–106.

Cohen, E. 1987. "Thailand, Burma and Laos—An Outline of the Comparative Social Dynamics of Three Theravada Buddhist Societies." In *Patterns of Modernity. Volume II: Beyond the West,* edited by S.N. Eisenstadt. New York: New York University Press.

Collins, Randall. 1990a. "Market Dynamics as the Engine of Historical Change." *Sociological Theory* 8:111–35.

———. 1990b. "Conflict Theory and the Advance of Macro-Historical Sociology." In *Frontiers of Social Theory: The New Syntheses*, edited by George Ritzer. New York: Columbia University Press.

Dumont, Louis. 1977. *From Mandeville to Marx: The Genesis and Triumph of Economic Ideology*. Chicago: University of Chicago Press.

———. 1983. *Essays on Individualism*. Chicago: University of Chicago Press.

———. 1994. *German Ideology: From France to Germany and Back*. Chicago: University of Chicago Press.

Elias, Norbert. 1978a. *What is Sociology?* New York: Columbia University Press.

———. 1978b. *The History of Manners*. Vol. 1 of *The Civilizing Process*. Oxford: Basil Blackwell.

———. 1982. *State Formation and Civilization*. Vol. 2 of *The Civilizing Process*. Oxford: Basil Blackwell.

———. 1987. "The Retreat of Sociologists into the Present." *Theory, Culture, and Society* 4:223–47.

Foucault, Michel. 1978. *Discipline and Punish*. New York; Vintage.

Frank, Andre Gunder. 1993. "Transitional Ideological Modes: Feudalism, Capitalism, Socialism." In *The World System: Five Hundred Years or Five Thousand?*, edited by Andre Gunder Frank and Barry K. Gills. London and New York: Routledge.

Frank, Andre Gunder, and Barry K. Gills. 1992. "World System Cycles, Crises, and Hegemonial Shifts, 1700 BC to 1700 AD." *Review* 15:621–87.

———. 1993. "The 5,000-Year World System: An Interdisciplinary Introduction." In *The World System: Five Hundred Years or Five Thousand?*, edited by Andre Gunder Frank and Barry K. Gills. London and New York: Routledge.

Friedman, Jonathan. 1992. "General Historical and Culturally Specific Properties of Global Systems." *Review* 15:335–72.

———. 1994. *Cultural Identity and Global Process*. London: Sage.

Gannon, Martin J. and Associates. 1994. *Understanding Global Cultures*. London: Sage.

Giddens, Anthony. 1985. *The Nation-State and Violence*. Berkeley: University of California Press.

———. 1990. *The Consequences of Modernity*. Stanford, CA: Stanford University Press.

Greenfeld, Liah. 1992. *Nationalism: Five Roads to Modernity.* Cambridge, MA: Harvard University Press.

Hirschman, Albert O. 1977. *The Passions and the Interests: Political Arguments for Capitalism Before its Triumph.* Princeton, NJ: Princeton University Press.

Hodgson, Marshall. 1993. *Rethinking World History: Essays on Europe, Islam, and World History.* Edited and with an introduction and conclusion by Edmund Burke III. New York: Cambridge University Press.

Holzner, Burkart. 1982. "The Civilization-Analytic Frame of Reference." *Comparative Civilizations Review* 8:15–30.

Huntington, Samuel. 1993. The Clash of Civilizations?" *Foreign Affairs* 72(3):22–49.

Karpat, Kemal H. 1972. *An Inquiry into the Social Foundations of Nationalism in the Ottoman Empire: From Social Estates to Classes, from Millets to Nations.* Princeton, NJ: Center for International Studies, Princeton University Press.

Kitromilides, Paschalis. 1990. *French Revolution and Southeastern Europe.* Athens: Diatton. [In Greek]

Lash, Scott, and John Urry. 1994. *Economies of Signs and Space.* London: Sage.

Lazou, Christos D. 1983. *America and its Role in the 1821 Revolution.* 2 vols. Athens: Papazisi. [In Greek]

Lewis, Bernard. 1961. *The Emergence of Modern Turkey.* London: Oxford University Press.

Mandalios, John. 1994. *Theories of Civilizational Processes: Identity and Cultural Formation.* Ph.D. Thesis, Deakin University, Australia.

Mann, Michael. 1986. *The Sources of Social Power. Volume 1: A History of Power from the Beginning to AD 1760.* Cambridge: Cambridge University Press.

McGrane, Bernard. 1989. *Beyond Anthropology: Society and the Other.* New York: Columbia University Press.

McNeill, William H. 1993. "Foreword." In *The World System: Five Hundred Years or Five Thousand?*, edited by Andre Gunder Frank and Barry K. Gills. London and New York: Routledge.

Melko, Matthew. 1994. "World Systems Theory: A Faustian Delusion? I & II." *Comparative Civilizations Review* 30:8–22.

Melko, Matthew, and Leighton R. Scott, eds. 1987. *The Boundaries of Civilizations in Space and Time.* Lanham, MD: University Press of America.

Mennnell, Stephen. 1992. *Norbert Elias: An Introduction.* Oxford: Basil Blackwell.

Morawska, Ewa, and Willfried Spohn. 1994. "'Cultural Pluralism' in Historical Sociology: Recent Theoretical Directions." In *The Sociology of Culture*, edited by Diana Crane. Oxford: Basil Blackwell.

Nelson, Benjamin. 1981. *On the Roads to Modernity: Conscience, Science, and Civilization.* Atlantic Highlands, NJ: Rowman and Littlefield.

*The Oxford Dictionary of New Words.* 1991. Complied by Sara Tulloch. Oxford: Oxford University Press.

Parsons, Talcott. 1951. *The Social System.* Glencoe, IL: The Free Press.

Petrovich, Michael Boro. 1956. *The Emergence of Russian Panslavism. 1856–1870.* Westport, CT: Greenwood Press.

Ramsaur, Ernest Edmondson Jr. 1970. *The Young Turks: Prelude to the Revolution of 1908.* New York: Russell and Russell.

Robertson, Roland. 1992. *Globalization: Social Theory and Global Culture.* London: Sage.

———. 1994. "Globalization or Glocalization?" *Journal of International Communication* 1:33–52.

———. 1995a. "Theory, Specificity, Change Emulation, Selective Incorporation, and Modernization." In *Change and Modernization: Lessons from Eastern Europe*, edited by Bruno Grancelli. Berlin: Walter de Gruyter.

———. 1995b. "Glocalization: Time-Space and Homogeneity-Heterogeneity." In *Global Modernities*, edited by Mike Featherstone, Scott Lash, and Roland Robertson. London: Sage.

Robertson, Roland, and Frank Lechner. 1985. "Modernization, Globalization, and the Problem of Culture in World Systems Theory." *Theory, Culture, and Society* 2(3):103–18.

Roudometof, Victor. 1994. "Globalization or Modernity?" *Comparative Civilizations Review* 31:18–45.

Said, Edward. 1978. *Orientalism.* New York: Random House.

Sanderson, Stephen K. 1994. "Expanding World Commercialization: The Link Between World-Systems and Civilizations." *Comparative Civilizations Review* 30:91–103. (Reprinted as chapter 11, this volume.)

Skocpol, Theda. 1977. "Wallerstein's World-System: A Theoretical and Historical Critique." *American Journal of Sociology* 87:1075–90.

Stavrianos, Lefteris S. 1970. *The World to 1500: A Global History.* Englewood Cliffs, NJ: Prentice-Hall.

*Theory, Culture, and Society.* 1990. "Special Issue on Nationalism, Globalization, and Modernity." Volume 7. London: Sage.

Tilly, Charles. 1992. *Coercion, Capital, and European States, AD 990–1990.* Oxford: Basil Blackwell.

Toynbee, Arnold. 1972. *A Study of History.* Abr. ed. New York: Oxford University Press.

Vranousis, Leandros. 1957. *Rigas.* Athens: N. Zacharopoulos. [In Greek]

Wallerstein, Immanuel. 1974. *The Modern World-System: Capitalist Agriculture and the Origins of the European World-Economy in the Sixteenth Century.* New York: Academic Press.

———. 1990. "Culture as the Ideological Battleground of the Modern World-System." *Theory, Culture, and Society* 7:31–56.

———. 1991a. *Unthinking Social Science.* London: Polity Press.

———. 1991b. *Geopolitics and Geoculture.* Cambridge: Cambridge University Press.

———. 1992. "The West, Capitalism, and the Modern World-System." *Review* 15:561–619.

———. 1993. "World System versus World-Systems." In *The World System: Five Hundred Years or Five Thousand?*, edited by Andre Gunder Frank and Barry K. Gills. London and New York: Routledge.

———. 1994. "Hold the Tiller Firm: On Method and the Unit of Analysis." *Comparative Civilizations Review* 30:72–80. (Reprinted as chapter 9, this volume.)

Walter, E.V., Vytautas Kavolis, Edmund Leites, and Marie Coleman Nelson, eds. 1985. *Civilizations East and West: A Memorial Volume for Benjamin Nelson*. Atlantic Highlands, NJ: Humanities Press.

Weber, Max. (1920) 1978. "The Origins of Industrial Capitalism in Europe." In *Max Weber: Selections in Translation*, edited by W.G. Runciman. Cambridge: Cambridge University Press.

Westney, D.E. 1987. *Imitation and Innovation: The Transfer of Western Organizational Patterns to Meiji Japan*. Cambridge, MA: Harvard University Press.

Wilkinson, David. 1987a. "The Connectedness Criterion and Central Civilization." In *The Boundaries of Civilizations in Time and Space*, edited by Matthew Melko and Leighton R. Scott. Lanham, MD: University Press of America.

———. 1987b. "Central Civilization." *Comparative Civilizations Review* 17:31–59. (Reprinted as chapter 2, this volume.)

———. 1993. "Civilizations, Cores, World Economies, and Oikumenes." In *The World System: Five Hundred Years or Five Thousand?*, edited by Andre Gunder Frank and Barry K. Gills. London and New York: Routledge.

———. 1994. "Civilizations *are* World Systems!" *Comparative Civilizations Review* 30:59–71. (Reprinted as chapter 10, this volume.)

Wolf, Eric R. 1982. *Europe and the People Without History*. Berkeley: University of California Press.

Zolberg, Aristide. 1981. "Origins of the Modern World-System: A Missing Link." *World Politics* 33:253–81.

PART IV

# Epilogue

In 1963 William H. McNeill published *The Rise of the West* (University of Chicago Press), a world history treatise/textbook that soon became one of the most important synthesizing historical works of recent times. In 1990 McNeill wrote an essay in which he reflected on the strengths and weaknesses of this book from the vantage point of nearly three decades later. That essay fits the major themes of the current book so well that it seemed appropriate to reprint it as an epilogue.

In this autocritique, McNeill still sees much of value in his great work, but the central failing of the book, he believes, is rooted in his implicit assumption of the autonomous character of the major world civilizations. As he notes, although he recognized intercivilizational interaction over thousands of years, such recognition was never translated into a much-needed emphasis on the formation and development of the ecumenical world system in which we all live today. This world system began in the ancient Middle East, but underwent a major developmental spurt after AD 1000. At the center of the system in this time was China, a civilization that McNeill feels he underemphasized most likely as a result of a residual Eurocentrism. But China was the world's most economically advanced civilization in the century before and the first few centuries after the year 1000, and it was closely linked to the West through trade. Although his career has been that of a fairly traditional historian, McNeill's recent thinking fits extremely well with the type of civilizational perspective adumbrated by Wilkinson, and with the views of Gills and Frank and Chase-Dunn and Hall. He is clearly aligned with their basic agendas, and his essay is a delight.

*Chapter Thirteen*

# The Rise of the West After Twenty-Five Years

Historians approach their subject from the moving platform of their own times, with the result that the past changes shape continually. Anyone who lives to reread his own work long afterwards must therefore expect to recognize signs and hallmarks of the inevitable displacement that time brings to historical understanding. This truism was brought home to me by a seminar devoted to my magnum opus, *The Rise of the West: A History of the Human Community* (McNeill 1963), at Williams College, where I was visiting professor in 1988. It was the first time I had read the book in twenty-five years, and the experience of revisiting an old friend—and incubus[1]—was both humbling and elevating.

The book was a sudden, surprising success when it came out in 1963. Lavish praise from Hugh Trevor-Roper in the *New York Times Book Review* and the onset of the Christmas season briefly lifted it to the best-seller list; the book has remained in print ever since. A cheap paperback ($1.25 for 828 pages!) sold out of an initial printing within a year, and cumulative sales of the full-sized book amount by now to more than 75,000.

In retrospect it seems obvious that *The Rise of the West* should be seen as an expression of the postwar imperial mood in the United States. Its scope and conception is a form of intellectual imperialism, for it takes on the world as a whole, and it tries to understand global history on the basis of cultural diffusion developed among American anthropologists in the 1930s. In particular, *The Rise of the West* is built on the notion that the principal factor promoting historically significant social change is contact with strangers possessing new and unfamiliar skills. A corollary of this proposition is that centers of high skill (i.e., civilizations) tend to upset their neighbors by exposing them to attractive novelties. Less-skilled peoples round about are then impelled to try to make those novelties their own so as to attain for themselves the wealth, power, truth, and beauty that civilized skills confer on their possessors. Yet such efforts provoke a painful ambivalence between the drive to imitate and an equally fervent desire to preserve the customs and institutions that distinguish the would-be borrowers from the corruptions and injustices that also inhere in civilized life.

A second corollary of the proposition that contact with strangers is the major motor of social change is that contacts among contemporaneous civilizations ought to be of key concern to a world historian, for such contacts can be expected to alter the assortment and expression of high skills each civilization possesses, and they thereby affect the local skill-diffusion pattern described above. Moreover, whenever one civilization, through some apparent superiority of its skills, becomes able to influence everyone with whom it comes in contact, then the grain of world history begins to run in a single direction, so to speak; and so by observing the reception of new skills and ideas in distant parts a historian can give shape and meaning to the confusion of detail that otherwise makes world history—quite literally—inconceivable.

In the years 1954 to 1963, when the book was being written, the United States was, of course, passing through the apex of its postwar capacity to influence others thanks to its superior skills and wealth. It follows that my vision of the world's past can be dismissed as being no more than a rationalization of American hegemony, retrojecting the situation of post-World War II decades upon the whole of the world's past by claiming that analogous patterns of cultural dominance and diffusion had existed always. (Of course the obvious rebuttal is to point out that the post-World War II era was part and parcel of world history, and conformed to precedent in a way Americans were not aware of at the time.)

No historian can deny that his views of the past reflect experiences of his own time, interacting with a tradition of learning that, in turn, bears all the marks of the times and places in which it grew. But I can at least say this: when I was writing the book I was entirely unaware of the way in which my method of making sense of world history conformed to the temporary world experience of the United States. In retrospect, it seems the warmth with which the book was received in the early 1960s did arise from this congruence in large part. But if so neither I nor the reviewers noticed it at the time. The hand-in-glove fit between my review of the whole of human history and the temporary world role played by the United States therefore operated, if it operated at all, entirely at a subconscious level for all concerned.

In view of the way historiography has moved in the intervening twenty-five years, a second reproach against my way of viewing the past seems even more obvious. *The Rise of the West* tends to march with big battalions, looking at history from the point of view of the winners—that is, of the skilled and privileged managers of society—and shows scant concern for the sufferings of the victims of historical change. This no doubt reflects personal idiosyncracies—family, ethnic, class, and other identities and experiences—that led me to value the fruits of humankind's accumulated capacity to control the natural and social environment and shape it to our wishes. Profiting from such skills, as everyone constantly does, including the poorest populations alive today, we must, I think, admire those who pioneered the enterprise and treat the human adventure on earth as an amazing success story, despite all the suffering entailed. The obvious ideal is a judicious balance in assessing the gains and losses inherent in each new human attainment. I did of course try to strike such a balance, but what seemed like a just balance to me is liable to strike others as a shabby sort of apologetics for those at the top (adult males) who ran things in each of the world's great civilizations.

These general considerations scarcely came up in the Williams seminar. Instead, by struggling through a chapter a week, variations in the quality of different chapters became rather painfully obvious. The low point came with chapter 4, titled "The Rise of Cosmopolitan Civilization in the Middle East, 1700–500 BC." After a brief introduction, this chapter undertakes to describe the military-political changes, administrative systems, social structure, and cultural conservation and advance across the twelve centuries and amongst the dozens of peoples and scores of states concerned. The result is labored and fragmented, more confusing than illuminating, even for a persevering, patient reader.

Chapter 4 made the fundamental mistake of abandoning a chronological for a topical ordering of the material at the wrong place. It lumped together two eras that ought to have been considered seriatim: the bronze age of chariot warriors and aristocratic rule on the one hand, and the iron age of democratized warriors and culture on the other. There is no excuse for this clumsiness. New data have not much altered what is knowable since I wrote. Nor has any sort of contemporary experience since 1963 altered sensibilities toward the emergent cosmopolitanism of the ancient Middle East. It is a plain case of defective organization, cutting against the grain of things and thereby disguising a simpler, truer, and more adequate way of understanding the history in question. Moreover, the notion of successive bronze and iron ages was completely familiar in the existing literature; and in retrospect, I cannot imagine why I did not use that ordering to put the chapter together.

Another deficiency helped to spoil the architectonic of this chapter—a deficiency, which I shall argue, was also apparent in the later parts of the book. For *The Rise of the West* assumes that separate civilizations form real and important human groupings and that their interactions constitute the main theme of world history. But in this chapter I had to deal with the merging together of what had once been separate civilizations into a new

306 WILLIAM H. McNEILL

cosmopolitanism that extended throughout the Middle East without erasing local differences. Those differences were very considerable, for after 2500 BC, a cluster of interstitial and satellite societies, each possessing all the hallmarks of civilization, had arisen on the rain-watered lands around and between the flood-plains of Egypt and Mesopotamia.

As a result, as long as I thought mainly in terms of separate civilizations, the historical stage became excessively crowded. Not surprisingly, the fragmented, choppy character of this chapter arose from an effort to say something about how each culturally distinct people expressed or exemplified each of the themes I had chosen to emphasize. Firmer focus on the cosmopolitan process itself was called for. I needed to think more carefully about the new sorts of activities that were binding the peoples of the Middle East together, and I should have highlighted these more clearly. But that required new assumptions and concepts that I lacked at the time and have only haltingly explored subsequently.

A second, less embarrassing but more important failure occurred in chapter 10, which treats world affairs between AD 1000 and 1500. In this case, new scholarship since 1963 has pointed the way to a firmer and better understanding of what was going on in the Eurasian world, and it is therefore obvious why I missed the centrality of China and Chinese civilization in these centuries. Instead I concentrated on "The Steppe Conquerors and the European Far West," to quote the title of the chapter. My mistake is therefore entirely forgivable. All the same, it is clear in retrospect how emphasis on steppe conquerors and the rise of medieval Europe reflected the bias of my education. For the chapter looks at Eurasia from a naively Western viewpoint. Turks and Mongols come galloping over the horizon from the east—suddenly, and, so to speak, mysteriously, though I did note the system of bureaucratic management that made Genghis Khan's armies so formidable. Nonetheless, I failed to connect the remarkable upsurge of nomad power with the fact that the new bureaucratic methods of military administration that the Mongols employed were a straightforward borrowing from Chinese practice. As a result, I overlooked the ultimate disturber of world balances in the era itself: that is, an efflorescence of Chinese civilization that raised China's culture, wealth, and power to a new level, far outstripping all the rest of the world for a period of four to five centuries.

Moreover, I gave undue attention to Latin Christendom, being eager to search out seeds and portents of Europe's rise to world leadership after 1500. That is legitimate enough, but it would be better located as a preface to the next chapter. The scholarship in the 1950s ought to have allowed me to see that, despite its vigorous new growth, western European civilization remained marginal to the ecumene and should have been given the same emphasis that I gave to the maturation of Japanese civilization in those same centuries. Instead, I treated Turkish and Mongol conquests and the rise of medieval Europe as of coordinate importance for world affairs. I even relegated China to second place among the civilized victims of nomad assault, treating the transformation of the Muslim world first and at greater length, largely because I knew more about it.

In retrospect it is fascinating to see how some of the material for a proper appreciation of Chinese primacy between AD 1000 and 1500 was available to me before 1963. In particular, I used Stefan Balazs's (1931, 1932) articles on the economic transformation of China in Tang times, and I had seen the first volumes of Joseph Needham's (1967) monumental study of *Science and Civilization in China* as well. But until Robert Hartwell (1966) showed the scale of ferrous metallurgy and the sophistication of economic management under the Song, until Yoshinobu Shiba (1970) provided a portrait of the Song commercial economy as a whole, and until Mark Elvin (1973) set forth a bold and speculative interpretation of the entire Chinese past, the meaning of China's transformation about the year AD 1000 quite escaped me.

My excuse is that the historiography available a generation ago still reflected the traditional valuations of China's past, so that a regime unable to control the northernmost provinces of historic China was, by definition, inferior to those ages when China was intact and united under a properly virtuous emperor. Since the Song dynasty (AD 960–1279) never controlled the northern barbarians and lost China's northernmost provinces to them almost from the start, it followed that their era was not one of China's great periods, even though it had long been recognized that art and literature bloomed under the Song as never before. But that did not compensate for political failure; and no one before Jacques Gernet ([1972] 1982) seems to have noticed how the ill-success that attended the Song armies on the steppe frontier arose from the fact that Chinese skills were spreading beyond the country's traditional borders, upsetting previous balances between China and its nomad neighbors and, as Ghengis Khan's career soon showed, throughout most of Eurasia as well.

In view of the way *The Rise of the West* is put together, my failure to understand China's primacy between AD 1000 and 1500 is particularly regrettable inasmuch as the book would have attained an elegant simplicity of structure if I had done so. As matters stand, the middle part of the book, entitled "Eurasian Cultural Balance, 500 BC to 1500 AD," is built around the idea that Mediterranean Hellenism (500 BC–AD 200), India (AD 200–600), and a reintegrated Middle East under the Muslims (AD 600–1000) entered upon successive periods of cultural flowering that assured each of them a period of primacy among the peoples of the old world. To follow that simple structuring of the past with a Chinese far eastern (1000–1500) and a European far western (1500–2000?) efflorescence and era of ecumenical primacy has a tidiness and precision that the facts seem to sustain,[2] but my ignorance (and residual Eurocentrism) hid this from me in 1963.

This, indeed, is the central failure of the book. Of course there are many other passages where scholarship since 1963 makes the text obsolete, but these are almost always matters of detail. An exception is Africa, where the scholarship of the past twenty-five years has revealed a far more complex interplay of peoples and cultures than was accessible when I wrote *The Rise of the West*. Yet sub-Saharan Africa never became the seat of a major civilization, and the continent therefore remained peripheral to the rest of the world, down to and including our own age. Hence while the brief passages touching on African history are now antiquated and inadequate, the defect does not distort the overall picture of the past as much as the failure in chapter 10 to recognize China's era of world leadership.

In general, the assumption that reaction to contacts with strangers was the major motor of historical change still seems good to me, and the choices of what to emphasize, which derived from that assumption, still strike me as sound, with the exception of the failure to give China its due between 1000 and 1500. In that sense, therefore, revisiting *The Rise of the West* was an elevating, even exhilarating, experience. For all its defects, it is still a good book, and deserves to count as an important way station in the development of a more genuinely global historiography.

Yet on another level, it seems to me now that the book is flawed simply because it assumes that discernibly separate civilizations were the autonomous social entities whose interactions defined history on a global scale. Just what the term "civilization" really means is left fuzzy, though I followed V. Gordon Childe (1943) and others in equating civilization with a society in which occupational specialization allowed the emergence of high skills—administrative, military, artisanal, literary, and artistic. That may be adequate to distinguish early civilizations from Neolithic village societies, but it does not say much about geographical and social boundaries in subsequent eras when a multiplicity of civilizations arose, and when at least part-time occupational specialization extended very widely among peoples supplying raw materials to distant civilized consumers, yet who can scarcely be described as civilized in their own right.

This raises the question of who really belongs to a civilization. Newborn infants clearly do not earn membership until they learn their cultural roles. But what about the poor and unskilled, whose roles are limited at best? And what about those living at a distance, subjected, perhaps, to a superior force—at least occasionally—but otherwise alien? And how do all the different skills and habits and outlooks of sharers in a civilization fit together into a more or less coherent whole? I fell back on the expression "style of life" in affirming the reality of that cohesion. But this metaphor, borrowed from art history, is only a metaphor and is all but useless in actual practice, since stylistic affinities are not nearly as easy to observe when one is comparing human habits and states of mind as when one is looking at works of art or other material objects.

Perhaps a historian is not required to face these questions explicitly. If one insists on precise definitions of terms, discourse at once degenerates into epistemological debate, and is never likely to emerge from that labyrinth. Suffice it to say, therefore, that civilizations do seem real to me, and have in fact united many millions of human beings across millions of square miles and many centuries in significant ways. But they are not the only actors on a world historical scale; this I failed to emphasize sufficiently in *The Rise of the West*. Let me try to explain more fully my current view.

A shared literary canon, and expectations about human behavior framed by that canon, are probably central to what we mean by a civilization. But it is unheard of for all to have access to such a canon. An upper class, educated to revere a body of literature that sets forth rules about how human beings should behave, is what in practice therefore delimits a civilization. The less privileged share such ideas in varying degrees, and no one fully embodies them—not even the holiest moral athlete. Conventional expectations allow for both individual and group shortcomings, while the lower classes and peripheral members of the society adjust and adapt their own, more local, moral codes and customary practices to make room for the ways of the upper class—deferring and obeying where they must, reserving zones of privacy and difference where they can.

But to keep a civilization together, there must also be a continual circulation of news and nuances of meaning, moving from city to city, region to region, and among diverse social classes and ethnic groups that make up the body social. Continual circulation of such messages is required to maintain sufficient cohesion across space and time to count as a single whole—a single civilization. Clearly there are degrees of cohesion, and shared characteristics shade off as one moves toward the frontier. Drawing precise boundaries on a map is nearly always arbitrary, but cultural slopes do exist, and when they become precipitous, the geographical limit to a given style of life may, indeed, become apparent enough for all practical purposes.

Obviously, modes of transport and communication are crucial for the circulation of messages within an established civilization; as they change, the boundaries and reach of the civilization will alter. This assumes a new dimension when, with the improvement of communication, diverse civilizations begin to impinge on one another more and more often and in increasingly urgent ways, since under these circumstances the autonomy and independence of the separate civilizations begin to shrink, and a new cosmopolitan entity—what Wallerstein (1974, 1980, 1989) calls a world system—may start to take over as the key factor in further historical development. This process is what I handled so clumsily in chapter 4 and omitted almost entirely when treating the millennia of the Christian era until after 1850.

Thus, in addition to the problems in chapter 4, the central methodological weakness of my book is that while it emphasizes interaction across civilizational boundaries, it pays inadequate attention to the emergence of the ecumenical world system within which we live today. Instead of organizing the book solely around the notion of a series of efflorescences, first in one, then in another separate civilization, I should have made room for the ecumenical process. How this might be done remains to be seen. Somehow an appreciation of the autonomy of separate civilizations (and of all the other less massive and less skilled cultures of the earth) across the past two thousand years needs to be combined with the portrait of an emerging world system, connecting greater and greater numbers of persons across civilized boundaries.

To make this a feasible enterprise, one needs a clear and distinct idea of the emergent world system as manifested first in the ancient Middle East and a second time in the modern world, and then one must reflect on how these two systems intersected with the more local civilizational and cultural landscapes they impinged upon. It does not follow that the two world systems were the same. Clearly, insofar as each depended on an expanding network of transport and communications, the technical base differed very markedly. And since each world system somehow arose out of political, military, and economic behavior, it is worth remembering that the institutional heritage of the second and first millennia BC were very different from those of the first and second millennia AD.

If one thinks of the world since about 1870, when instantaneous communications and mechanically powered transport started to manifest their influence on a global basis, it is obvious that the modern world system rests on economic complementarities and exchanges in the first place, and secondarily on institutional arrangements—military-political primarily— and on flows of ideas, skills, and tastes that follow in the wake of changed economic and political behavior. One may, perhaps, assume that a similar primacy for economic exchanges existed also in earlier times all the way back to the earliest beginnings of civilization in ancient Mesopotamia, even though, for a long time, such exchanges were marginal in the sense of being confined to strategic and luxury items. It could scarcely be otherwise, since as long as transport was sporadic and subject to frequent interruptions, people could not safely depend on goods from afar to supply daily needs.

Nonetheless, cities constituted something of an exception to this generalization. All cities, of course, had to import food and often found it hard to find sufficient grain in the immediate hinterland. Long before a market system could be relied on to supply cities from afar, a few great capital cities depended on food coming from relatively great distances in the economically unrequited form of tribute and taxes. Thus, the Chinese canal system was initially used to concentrate food and other commodities to support the court, the imperial army, and the hangers-on who clustered in the capital. Similarly, imperial Rome subsidized its proletarians with tribute grain from Egypt and north Africa; Mecca and Medina, the holy cities of Islam, also depended on grain subsidies from Egypt in the early days of the caliphate, and many other imperial and religious centers flourished and grew great on the strength of taxes and tribute in the form of food supplies coming from distant places.

It is no exaggeration to say that the cultural splendor and military formidability of early civilizations depended on the concentration of food and other commodities at court and temple centers by dint of exercise of direct command. The very notion of separate, autonomous civilizations registers this early division of labor, whereby the many toiled in the fields while a privileged few consumed the yield of rents and taxes and experimented with all the arts of civilization. Yet from the start, this simple polarity between taxpayers and tax consumers was complicated by a few outsiders, exempt from the burden of ordinary rents and taxes, who nonetheless had an important role to play as merchants, that is, as purveyors of desirable rarities that could not be secured by command because they originated beyond the reach of the established authorities.

For those who wanted such goods, one possibility was to send armed expeditions in search of what was unavailable at home. Gilgamesh's visit to the forests of Lebanon offers an early literary example of such an expedition, and Sargon of Akkad's military campaigns (c. 2350 BC) may have been aimed at capturing supplies of metal and other strategically valuable goods that were unavailable in alluvial Mesopotamia. But the direct exercise of force to collect strategic commodities from places lying beyond the reach of everyday administration and tax collection was a good deal less efficient than relying on exchange. In particular, accumulated stocks of luxury goods produced by specialized artisans for civilized temples and courts could be offered to distant potentates who could organize local manpower to dig ore, cut timber, or raise grain needed at the civilized center. In this fashion each early civilization created around itself a periphery of trade partners, whose appetite for goods from civilized workshops was as elastic as was civilized appetite for raw materials and other rarities. Even in very early times, such connections ranged across many hundreds of miles. Regular use of animal caravans and of sailing ships for such long-distance trade dates back at least to the third millennium BC, as does the establishment of special legal status for the merchants who accompanied the goods, and whose travels necessarily carried them across political and cultural boundaries.

As long as each civilization was thus surrounded by a network of suppliers who depended on sailing ships and animal caravans to carry rarities from where they were produced to where they were consumed, the notion of separate, autonomous civilizations provides an adequate model for historical understanding. Techniques and ideas were exchanged along with goods, of course, and from time to time barbarians from the periphery conquered civilized centers, since mistrust between rulers and ruled tended to counteract the superiority of numbers on which civilized peoples could always count.

In the ancient Middle East, the resulting interactions among peoples living in different landscapes, with diverse languages and other outward signs of civilized diversity, led to the emergence of a cosmopolitan world system between 1700 and 500 BC. Unlike the world system of recent centuries, in the ancient Middle East the primacy of command was preserved within ever-widening boundaries of a succession of great empires—Egyptian, Hittite, Assyrian, Babylonian, and Persian. But the tax- and tribute-collecting bureaucracies that sustained these empires worked in symbiosis with caravan and shipping networks that antedated the political empires and whose zones of activity always extended beyond even the most far-flung political frontiers. Thus merchants flourished and sometimes even grew great in the cracks and crannies left by the rent and tax systems, supplying wants, old and new, and making a profit on market sales.

The result could be counted as a territorially enlarged version of the sort of separate civilization from which the evolution started. That is what I did in *The Rise of the West*. Yet that way of thinking overlooks the continued diversity of religions, languages, and moral systems that long survived the rise of new empires, and it minimizes the economic role of markets and of long-distance trade in holding the ancient Middle East together while connecting it with an ever-widening and politically independent periphery. Market relations, insofar as they arose from uncoerced human choices, differed in a simple but important fashion from the older way of concentrating resources by rent and tax collection. People are more likely to work efficiently when they do so willingly. As a result, when they can buy and sell things at their own discretion, and satisfy at least some of their wants by doing so, the result is likely to be a general increase in wealth. This, it seems to me, was beginning to be discovered in the second millennium BC and became normal and expected in the course of the next millennium, at least in the principal theater for this dawning of a commercially based world system, that is, in the increasingly cosmopolitan Middle East.

This is all adumbrated in *The Rise of the West* but not pursued. For example, I used the phrase "the great society" to refer to the way trade and markets entered into symbiosis with taxes and rents in Hammurabi's Mesopotamia; but this idea was not used to organize the history of subsequent centuries, and simply disappeared from the rest of the book. Being too much preoccupied by the notion of civilization, I bungled by not giving the initial emergence of a transcivilizational process the sustained emphasis it deserved.

There is a sense, indeed, in which the rise of civilizations in the Aegean (later Mediterranean) coastlands and in India after 1500 BC were and remained part of the emerging world system centered in the Middle East. Historians have always known that archaic Greeks borrowed wholesale from the more skilled peoples of Asia and Egypt. Something similar occurred also in northern India. All three regions and their peoples remained in close and uninterrupted contact throughout the classical era; and in due course Alexander's armies overthrew the Persians and made Macedonians and Greeks into the rulers of the Middle East. Why, therefore, should the Greeks not be counted as one of the family of nations taking part in a common and increasingly cosmopolitan enterprise? No doubt the traditional answer to this question rests very largely on what happened later, and reflects the historic antagonism between Christendom and Islam, and between Hindu India and Muslim rulers of that land—though in these subsequent ages, commercial and other relations across disputed cultural and religious frontiers always remained lively and tended to increase as time went on.

At any rate, without any real reflection about the choice, I conformed to precedent by organizing the history of western Eurasia in the first millennium BC around three separate and distinct civilizations: Middle Eastern, Indian, and Greek. Yet what happened might just as well have been described as the expansion of the Middle Eastern "great society" to embrace new regions and fresh peoples, with variable cultural characteristics of their own. From this ecumenical point of view, even distant China began to tie into the system after 100 BC, when caravans connecting Syria with China began to travel regularly along the so-called silk road. Moreover, sea voyaging supplemented caravans, linking the Mediterranean world with India, and India with China at about the same time.

This ancient world system met serious setback after only two to three centuries of expansion, owing mainly to the way lethal diseases spread along the new trade routes and provoked catastrophic losses of life, especially in the Roman and Chinese empires. Demographic decay invited or allowed barbarian invasion and the resulting onset of the dark ages of European history. Similar though perhaps less destructive disruption also took place in China after the overthrow of the Han dynasty in AD 220. Long-distance trade across Eurasia thereupon dwindled toward insignificance due to the impoverishment and political insecurity that came to prevail at the two extremities of the ecumene. On the other hand, seafaring in the Indian Ocean and adjacent waters probably underwent no comparable decline, although information is so painfully scant that one cannot be sure.

Despite the dark ages, and the disruption of the earliest world system that ensued, revival soon became apparent, and in much the same way that long-range contacts revived in the Middle East after iron age barbarian invasions had disrupted the incipient cosmopolitanism of the bronze age. Moreover, when revival got underway, the Middle East, was, as before, the center; and it was helped by the fact that the domestication of camels had begun to put improved transport at the disposal of warriors and merchants alike. According to Richard Bulliet (1975) domestication of camels was a long drawn-out process, beginning in southern Arabia, perhaps as early as 3000 BC, but it attained decisive importance for the civilized world only between AD 300 and 500. During those centuries, camels displaced wheeled vehicles for transport purposes in the Middle East, and soon became the principal goods carriers in central Asia, north Africa, and adjacent regions as well.

Camels could cross deserts that were otherwise impenetrable. The geographical and cultural effect was analogous, on land, to the far better known opening of the oceans by European seamen after 1500. Places previously isolated now became accessible to camel caravans, and the reach of civilized trade nets extended accordingly. Arabia together with the oases and deserts of central Asia, the steppelands to their north, and sub-Saharan Africa were the regions most powerfully affected by this upgrading of caravan transport. They were all brought into far more intimate contact with the established centers of civilized life—primarily with the Middle East and with China—than had been possible before. As a result, between about AD 500 and 1000 an intensified ecumenical world system began to nibble away at cultural autonomy—a process registered more sensibly than in any other fashion by the spread of Islam into the newly opened marginal regions of the old world.

Indeed the rise of Islam and the revival of a world system reaching across civilizational and other cultural boundaries went hand in hand, and perhaps should be thought of as two aspects of the same process. Assuredly, in the first Muslim centuries, the community of the faithful subscribing to Muhammad's revelation was only one among a number of other religious communities that coexisted in the Middle East and adjacent regions. Religious and cultural pluralism was in fact institutionalized by the prescriptions of the Koran requiring Muslims to tolerate Christians and Jews. The civilization of the Islamic heartland therefore became a mosaic in which separate religious communities managed their own affairs within remarkably broad limits. Conquest and conversions after AD 1000, that carried Islam into India, southeast Asia, and across most of the Eurasian steppes, as well as into southeast Europe and a large part of sub-Saharan Africa, added far greater variety to this mosaic. Only at the extremes of the civilized world, in China, Japan, and northern and western Europe, did more old-fashioned social and cultural homogeneity prevail.

Persistent cultural pluralism within the realm of Islam was matched by the special restraints on political authority that Islamic law imposed. This meant greater autonomy for trade and market behavior than had been common in pre-Islamic times. Merchant communities were seldom completely self-governing in the Muslim scheme of things; but they were respected and could usually count on protection from Muslim political authorities. After all, Muhammad had been a merchant before he became a prophet; and no higher endorsement of the mercantile mode of life could be imagined.

The next landmark in the history of this rising commercial world system arose out of Chinese borrowings from the Middle East, operating in a different natural environment and making use of a new and more efficient transport system. What the Chinese borrowed from the Middle Easterners was the array of customs, practices, and moral attitudes that sustained local and long-distance trade nets. Buddhism, reaching China along the trade routes of central Asia, served as the main transfer agent, implanting habits of mind and moral rules that accorded well with life as a trader. (Confucianism, by comparison, remained disdainful of commerce, viewing merchants as social parasites, who made a living by buying cheap and selling dear, without adding anything to the goods they handled.)

But what gave special importance to the spread of commercial habits and outlook to China was the fact that a canal network already existed, connecting the valley of the Yellow River with the even more extensive valley of the Yangtze. Barges and canal boats could easily move to and fro on those canals, and with almost complete safety, while carrying comparatively enormous loads. China's canals had been constructed for agricultural and tax collecting purposes across many centuries. Then in AD 605, when the Grand Canal linking the two great river basins was completed, China's network of internal waterways became capable of connecting regions with contrasting and complementary resources. As a result, the scale and importance of trade and commerce could escalate within China far beyond anything possible in the Middle East or elsewhere. Old ceilings on interdependence and regional exchange were broken through. A new range for the market integration of human effort came on stream, whereby ordinary people, even poor villagers, could safely depend on buying and selling to pay their taxes and even to provide themselves with food and other items of everyday consumption.

One must not exaggerate. Not all peasants bought rice so as to be able to specialize on raising silkworms, for example, and most of them still provided most or all of the food they consumed. Nonetheless, when specialization proved capable of paying off in the form of even slight improvement in standard of living, Chinese peasants and townsmen began to specialize on a scale never before approached by civilized society. The result, of course, was improved skills and a great increase in wealth for society as a whole. One register was a near doubling of China's population under the Song dynasty. Another was the fact the Chinese artisanal skills began to surpass those of the rest of the world. Silk, porcelain, gunpowder, and shipbuilding were among the more important examples of Chinese superiority, but there were many others. Busy chaffering in innumerable marketplaces and an enormous flotilla of canal boats kept goods in circulation and allowed surpluses of one region to be exchanged for surpluses produced elsewhere, with a reliability and efficiency that had never been possible before.

The effects of China's commercialization were never confined by political borders. Instead, caravan trade intensified across all of China's land frontiers and greatly magnified sea commerce soon developed as well, taking Chinese goods to the Indian Ocean and across the sea to Japan in far greater quantity than before. The world system, previously centered in the great cities and bazaars of the Middle East, thus acquired a new and far more powerful productive center and, not coincidentally, expanded its reach into remote western Europe and other previously marginal areas like Japan (McNeill 1982).

Medievalists have long recognized the importance for Europe of the rise of towns after about AD 1000 and the role of the spice trade that tied European consumers with producers in islands of the distant Indies. But historians have not yet gotten used to the idea that this was only part of a larger phenomenon—the expansion and intensification of an emergent world system that now embraced almost all of Eurasia and much of Africa as well. Nor have European and Islamic historians yet realized that the rise of medieval European civilization after AD 1000 coincided with an eastward shift of the world system's center from the Middle East to China. That is not surprising. Given the past preoccupation of our medievalists with the national histories of England and France—implicitly retrojecting upon the entire human past the circumstances of the late 19th century, when the French and British empires did cover most of the globe—it requires a real leap of the imagination to recognize China's primacy, Marco Polo to the contrary notwithstanding.

The next great chapter in the rise of the modern world system is, of course, far more familiar, and indeed, the scholar who made the phrase famous, Immanuel Wallerstein, once believed that it only began in about 1500 with the European oceanic discoveries and the rise of capitalism. The discoveries certainly did change the pattern of world trade and world cultural relations, bringing the Americas and innumerable oceanic islands into the vortex of the expanding world system. Within surprisingly few decades, the most active center of innovative activity shifted from China to the Atlantic face of Europe. Before 1500, capitalists achieved remarkable autonomy within the walls of a few Italian and north European city-states; and even after that political framework decayed, some few of the new monarchies and emergent national states that supplanted urban sovereignties in Europe continued to give merchants and bankers almost unhampered scope for expansion of market activity, whereas in China, and also in most of the Muslim world, regimes unsympathetic to private capitalist accumulation prevailed. In the name of good government, Asian rulers effectively checked the rise of large-scale entrepreneurship by confiscatory taxation on the one hand, and by regulation of prices in the interest of consumers on the other. This left large-scale commercial enterprise, and presently also mining and plantation agriculture, more and more to the Europeans. Consequently, the rise of the West to its world hegemony of recent centuries got underway.

Scholarly investigation of what happened in China and why the Ming dynasty chose to abandon overseas ventures after the 1430s remain very slender by comparison with the abundant literature on European exploitation of the new worlds their navigation opened to them. Comparative study of the dynamics of Chinese and European expansion before and after the tip point that came about 1450 to 1500 offers an especially intriguing topic for historical inquiry today, poised as we are on the horizon of the 21st century, when, for all we know, the displacement of the far east by the far west, that took place in the 16th century may be reversed.

It is, nonetheless, worth noting that just as China's rise after AD 1000 had depended on prior borrowings from the Middle East, so Europe's world success after 1500 also depended on prior borrowings from China. And if Japan's post-World War II economic record turns out to be the presage of further triumphs for the Pacific rim, it is no less clear that this success, too, will depend on prior borrowings of European (and American) skills. This looks like one of the clearest patterns in world history. It is also something to be expected inasmuch as no population can overtake and then surpass the rest of the world without using the most efficacious and powerful instruments known anywhere on earth; and by definition such instruments are located at world centers of wealth and power—wherever they may be. Thus any geographical displacement of world leadership must be prefaced by successful borrowing from previously established centers of the highest prevailing skills.

The fluctuating growth of this sort of world system, with shifting centers and a great multiplicity of peoples and cultures caught within it, seems to me now to be a part of world history that largely escaped my attention when writing *The Rise of the West*. Even for the centuries after 1500 I was intent on using the civilizational envelope to organize my remarks; only after 1850 did I suggest that the autonomy of the separate civilizations of Asia had broken down, yielding to a new global cosmopolitanism. But autonomy had been eroding long before 1850, long before 1500, and even long before 1000. The process, I now think, dated back to the very beginning of civilized history, and ought to have been presented as such, alongside the history of separate civilizations and their interactions.

Exactly how a narrative could combine both aspects of the human past is not easy to specify. Only by making the attempt can the possibility be tested, and this ought now to become the agenda for serious world historians. Cultural pluralism and differentiation is a dominating feature of human history; yet beneath and behind that pluralism there is also an important commonality. That commonality found expression in the rise of a world system that transcended political and cultural boundaries because human beings desired to have the results of the operation of that system. In other words, they wanted access to rare and valuable goods that could not be found close at hand, and presently they also desired the enrichment that market exchanges helped to provoke and sustain by rewarding efficient producers. In proportion as more and more individuals spent more and more of their time on activities connected with market exchanges, the world system grew from its initial marginality toward the remarkable centrality it enjoys in our own time. Yet this sort of interchange and interdependence remains entirely compatible with cultural diversity, and, at least so far, also with political pluralism and rivalry. All three belong in a proper history of the world—somehow.

Finally, there is another level of human experience that deserves historians' attention: to wit, our encounters and collisions with all the other organisms that make up the earth's ecosystem. Agriculture is one chapter in that story. So is the shifting incidence of disease. And the recent rise of scientific understanding and the extended control that such understanding sometimes allows is yet a third dimension of this story. As hinted above, disease affected the history of the world system of exchange in the first Christian centuries, and again, more briefly, in the 14th, when the Black Death ravaged China, the Middle East, and Europe. More importantly, civilized diseases regularly acted to break down the cultural morale and independence of peoples newly exposed to their ravages. The disaster that struck native Americans after 1492, when they were suddenly exposed to European and then African diseases, is the most dramatic but by no means the only example of this phenomenon.[3] The spread of crops, of domesticated animals, and of unwanted pests and infestations is another side of ecological history about which historians are as yet quite ill informed.[4] Yet these, too, clearly impinged on economic and political history in much the same way that epidemic diseases did, by allowing some populations to flourish while penalizing or even destroying others.

These dimensions of human history therefore also deserve a place in any really satisfactory account of the past; they, too, ought to be woven into the narrative of the rise and elaboration of separate civilizations and cultures and viewed as ecumenical processes comparable in importance with the rise of a world system of economic complementarity and cultural symbiosis.

Such an agenda for world historians is perhaps daunting. Yet anything less is plainly inadequate to the complexities of the human condition as we now understand it. Nor does it strike me as impossible—however ambitious. Data exist; what is needed is to gather and bring them to order and then construct a clear and elegant discourse with which to present the different facets and interacting flows of human history as we now understand them. Historians always face exactly this task, even when writing about comparatively small numbers of people and limited periods of time. Information is almost always overabundant; intelligibility comes only with selection and ordering, somehow embodied in a flow of words to provoke a portrait of the past in readers' minds. It is an art that historians have always cultivated, and we are now in a position to apply that art to the whole of the human past with a precision, richness, and accuracy beyond anything previously possible, simply because historical scholarship has explored the whole of the globe as never before, while the evolution of historical concepts has arrived at a level of sophistication that makes older efforts at world history, even one as recent as mine, seem fundamentally outmoded and obviously in need of replacement. . . .

NOTES

1. While writing *The Rise of the West* I walked home past an elm tree that had lost a large limb in a storm and was slowly covering its wound with an enormous weal of new growth. I used to wonder whether my book would be done before or after the elm tree healed itself. In fact, I got my manuscript to the printer a year before the tree died of Dutch elm disease, with its self-seal still incomplete, so I was never able to carry the completed book past the healed-over tree.

2. Gunpowder, printing, and the compass, three critical factors in Europe's ascension to world leadership after 1500, were Chinese inventions, and reached the far west during the time when the political unification of northern Eurasia by the Mongols made movement back and forth across the whole continent unusually safe, frequent, and easy. Joseph Needham's *Science and Civilization in China: The Gunpowder Epic* (1967) disposes of lingering notions of Europe's equality with China in developing early gunpowder technologies and traces their westward diffusion with new precision.

3. William H. McNeill's *Plagues and Peoples* (1976) is still the best general survey of the subject. A shorter essay, *The Human Condition: An Ecological and Historical View* (1980), offers a preliminary overview of the intersection of ecology with history as more usually understood.

4. Alfred Crosby's *Ecological Imperialism* (1988) is a truly remarkable effort to overcome that ignorance, but constitutes only a beginning.

## References

Balazs, Stefan. 1931. "Beitrage zur Wirtschaftgeschichte der T'ang Zeit." *Mitteilungen des Seminars fur orientalische Sprachen zu Berlin* 34:21–25.
———. 1932. "Beitrage zur Wirtschaftgeschichte der T'ang Ziet." *Mitteilungen des Seminars fur orientalische Sprachen zu Berlin* 35:27–73.
Bulliet, Richard. 1975. *The Camel and the Wheel.* Cambridge, MA: Harvard University Press.
Childe, V. Gordon. 1943. *What Happened in History.* Harmondsworth, UK: Penguin.
Crosby, Alfred. 1986. *Ecological Imperialism.* Cambridge: Cambridge University Press.
Elvin, Mark. 1973. *The Pattern of the Chinese Past.* Stanford, CA: Stanford University Press.
Gernet, Jacques. (1972) 1982. *A History of Chinese Civilization.* Trans. J.R. Foster. New York: Cambridge University Press. (English translation of *Le Monde Chinois*, Paris.)
Hartwell, Robert. 1966. "Markets, Technology, and Structures of Enterprise in the Development of Eleventh Century Chinese Iron and Steel Industry." *Journal of Economic History* 26:29–58.
McNeill, William H. 1963. *The Rise of the West.* Chicago: University of Chicago Press.
———. 1976. *Plagues and Peoples.* Garden City, NY: Anchor Press.
———. 1980. *The Human Condition: An Ecological and Historical View.* Princeton, NJ: Princeton University Press.
———. 1982. *The Pursuit of Power: Technology, Armed Force, and Society since AD 1000.* Chicago: University of Chicago Press.
Needham, Joseph. 1967. *Science and Civilization in China: The Gunpowder Epic.* Cambridge: Cambridge University Press.
Shiba, Yoshinobu. 1970. *Commerce and Society in Sung China.* Ann Arbor: University of Michigan Press.
Wallerstein, Immanuel. 1974. *The Modern World-System: Capitalist Agriculture and the Origins of the European World-Economy in the Sixteenth Century.* New York: Academic Press.
———. 1980. *The Modern World-System II: Mercantilism and the Consolidation of the European World-Economy, 1600–1750.* New York: Academic Press.
———. 1989. *The Modern World-System III: The Second Era of Great Expansion of the Capitalist World-Economy, 1730–1840s.* San Diego, CA: Academic Press.

# Index

Abu-Lughod, Janet, 139, 144, 179, 180, 182, 208, 218, 266–67, 274, 287
agrarian states/empires, 261–70
agriculture, 28, 39, 91, 116, 139, 179, 199, 244, 265, 318; *see also* agrarian states/empires
Amin, Samir, 102, 139, 184, 190, 204
anthropology, 26, 27, 28, 38, 92, 100–03, 116, 232, 303
archaeology, 26, 92, 100, 101, 116, 232, 242
Aron, Raymond, 249
art, 18–19, 30, 41–42, 76, 88
Axial Age, 214–16

Bagby, Philip, 28, 34–38, 73
battles, 82–86
Bergesen, Albert, 102, 105
Blaut, James, 170–71, 205
Bosworth, Andrew, 105
bourgeois, 96, 184, 187
Braudel, Fernand, 95, 139, 163–90, 201, 282
Bronze Age, 175, 180, 210, 211–13, 305, 314

capital accumulation, 91, 104, 137–38, 140, 143, 152, 154, 155–58, 242, 257, 274, 276
   private, 102, 138, 140, 141
capitalism, 20, 67, 95–99, 137–44, 148–52, 186–90, 195–98, 199, 244, 255–56, 263, 269, 274–76, 284

pre- or proto-, 101–03, 137–44, 155–56, 178–81, 231, 235, 262–63, 291
   *see also* Marxist economic theory, world-system/economy
capitalist, 139, 255
Chandler, Tertius, 105–06, 124, 132, 209–11, 215–20, 267
Chase-Dunn, Christopher, 98, 100, 102, 103, 116, 123, 124, 128, 199, 207, 231, 241–42, 243, 255–57, 274
chiefdom(s), 103, 110, 117–20
China, 20, 42, 182, 213, 214–16, 217–20, 235, 245–46, 256, 265–67, 301, 306–08, 311, 313, 315–17, 319; *see also* civilizations, roster of
city(ies), 47, 54–63, 122–26, 128–32, 208, 266–68, 310
   ancient systems of, 123–26, 209–11
   economies of, 141–44, 206–26
   population of, 110–11, 210, 214–20, 267
   rise and fall of, 105, 111–16, 128–33, 142–44, 207–09, 211–26
   stages of, 105–06
   social hierarchy, 123–26, 128–32, 220–25; *see also* polity(ies)
civilization(s), definition of, 22, 32–34, 38, 86, 245–46, 250–52, 274–79, 308–09
   Central, 22, 46–73, 102, 115, 251, 255, 267
   in dialectical evolution, 79–82, 88–91
   evolution of, 28